SHOTS IN THE DARK

The Story of Rocco Balliro and the Tragic
Events of February 2, 1963

DANIEL ZIMMERMAN

WILDBLUE
PRESS

WildBluePress.com

SHOTS IN THE DARK

*The Story of Rocco Balliro and the Tragic
Events of February 2, 1963*

PHIL,

THANK YOU FOR YOUR INTEREST
IN ROCCO'S STORY. ENJOY!

REGARDS,

DANNY Z

Dedicated to my cherished grandchildren,
Julianna and Anthony.

AUTHOR'S DISCLAIMER

The book you are about to read is a biography of Rocco Anthony Balliro, as told during the course of countless prison interviews and via reams of written correspondence. While Rocco's memory was uncanny and the vast majority of the material he shared was later authenticated, there is always the possibility that some of the tales and dialogue had eroded with the passage of time.

While every effort was made to validate Rocco's account, the author accepts no liability for the content or character descriptions within.

CHAPTER 1

"The Lost"
There he sits in his cell
With nothing left but hope
And then he sees a light beyond
The breaking point of dawn
From somewhere comes a voice of love
To let him know he's not alone
To tell him that he knows the truth
And someday not far away
He'll be free because of you.
(Paula L. Bent, ©1967, Somerville, Mass.)

A sudden gust stirred several lonely leaves, brittle and browned from months of exposure to snow and frost. They tumbled randomly along the edge of the gutter, eventually coming to rest at the base of a rusted chain-link fence which separated adjacent parcels of property. Rugged branches of a huge, leafless oak, witness to more than a hundred such bitter New England winters, groaned under the weight of a thick layer of ice and the pressure of a frigid air mass that had moved in earlier that day.

Heaped waist-high at the leading edge of the sidewalk was a bank of frozen snow, raw evidence of the harsh nor'easter that battered the area several days earlier. It marked the third such punishing storm of the season and the winter of 1963 had yet to reach its midpoint.

On this halcyon night, however, the inky-black skies over Boston were clear. Glinting stars and a suspended half-moon cast a bluish-gray tinge over the snow-covered expanse below.

Standing silent sentry over Centre Street, Roxbury, rows of neatly-trimmed tenement apartment buildings co-mingled with several stately, turn-of-the-century homes. All of the residences were hushed against the post-midnight hour. Most of the occupants had retired early on this particular Friday evening.

That quiet was disturbed by the approach of a motor vehicle, coasting haltingly along the slumbering street. The brake lights burned crimson as the vehicle came to a stop in front of a two-family home. Thick plumes of grayish fog billowed from the tailpipe. The operator cut the headlights. Save for a glimmer of moonlight and scant illumination from several distant streetlamps, the roadway ahead was plunged into darkness.

The apartment interior was entirely devoid of light. The occupants of the automobile attempted to discern any sign of movement from within. There was nothing. The dwelling seemed vacant. Could the darkness be intentional? Were there occupants who preferred not to be seen?

After a moment, the car moved forward, turned right on Cedar Street, and came to a stop adjacent to the snow-shrouded sidewalk. In the distance, lights from the city of Boston shimmered.

Minutes elapsed before silent contemplation shifted to that of sudden, decisive action. The driver killed the motor. Without the engine drone, the streets fell into complete silence. Nothing stirred until three of the four car doors opened and a trio of shadowy figures emerged. The threesome began walking along the ice-strewn pavement, maneuvering between waist-high snowbanks. As they drew nearer to their objective, their pace quickened. Moving swiftly now, foggy plumes of winter's breath escaped from their mouths. The men shielded their eyes as a sudden wind gust rippled along the street, buffeting road debris and loose snow.

Upon reaching the front of the apartment, the men paused at the leading edge of a narrow concrete walkway. The street behind them remained still. For the first time, words were spoken.

"That's the window I broke earlier," said one of the men – the crew's leader – in a low, muffled voice. He gestured toward a small, rectangular segment of cardboard that was taped over a gap in the glass panes encircling the door. His companions responded with a nod.

The spokesman then asked, "Are you guys ready for this?" Again, a simple nod.

Each of the three men reached into their jacket pockets and withdrew guns. Moonlight glinted off the brushed metal barrels.

The trio edged closer to the door. The leader, who had laid claim to the shattered window, reached for the cardboard and yanked it aside. He felt warm air escaping from inside. Extending his arm through the breach, he grasped the deadbolt. As he turned and disengaged the lock, it made a loud clicking noise. Pausing briefly, he listened for any sign of movement in the darkness. There was none.

Standing upright, he lowered his shoulder and threw his full weight into the door while twisting the knob. He stormed into the darkened foyer with his two accomplices trailing a half-step behind. As the men advanced, a guttural shout came forth from the lightless depths within.

"This is the police – drop your guns!"

It was a command that would trigger a torrent of deadly gunfire in the pitch-black apartment.

CHAPTER 2

"A man's sense of self is defined through his ability to achieve results." – John Gray

Through the dense, bluish haze of a smoke-filled room, Rocco Anthony Balliro found the woman who would change his life forever.

He wasn't necessarily looking for her; or anyone else for that matter. Truth be told, until that pivotal moment, when this stunning, raven-haired beauty cast a subtle glance in his direction, Rocco had been content to unwind in the company of nothing more than an ice-cold bottle of beer and a pack of cigarettes.

It was a slow night at the New Yorker lounge. The regular clientele that frequented this watering hole wasn't expected for at least an hour or two.

Located in the midst of Boston's notorious red light district, better known to the locals as the Combat Zone, the New Yorker catered to many of the city's underworld figures. As Rocco later described it, the lounge had two floors and two distinct types of patrons. The street level lounge served run-of-the mill customers who were looking for a quiet drink and soft jazz. It was the exclusive club on the bottom floor, however, that was a haven for some of Boston's prominent organized crime figures. On any given night, according to Rocco, a veritable mafia who's who would fill the trendy hangout.

Nearing midnight, the Combat Zone was just coming to life. A midsummer sun had baked Boston throughout the day, leaving in its wake a sweltering cloak of heat and humidity.

On the oppressive streets, festering alcoholics picked through trashcans. And in sleazy, roach-infested rooms perched above storefronts, prostitutes propped up tired hairdos and caked on layers of makeup, primping for yet another night of indecency.

Miles away, in the outlying suburbs, men slipped from the beds of their wives, mumbling an excuse about a friend in need as they embarked on a night of drink and debauchery in the Zone.

In some of the district's more notorious nightspots, such as Jerome's and the Palace, beer taps flowed unabated. On this July night, a navy warship was anchored in the waters of nearby Boston Harbor, and thirsty sailors paraded along the streets. Lonely and far from home, these enlisted men would readily plunk down a few bucks to buy a drink for a go-go dancer in exchange for a lipstick-stained smile, small talk, and unfulfilled promises.

The Combat Zone grew from a need to fill a void following the demise of nearby Scollay Square, which was razed in the late fifties to make way for a significant urban renewal project.

The redevelopment proposal, the largest of its kind in Boston to that point, also spelled doom for the West End, which housed scores of Italian and Jewish immigrants. The misguided construction venture was spurned by many, including the twenty-thousand people who watched as their homes and in some instances, their livelihoods, were bulldozed.

Historic Scollay Square, located west of the landmark Faneuil Hall Marketplace, gained a foothold as the city's designated red light district during World War II but the surrounding neighborhoods soon languished. For instance, the Old Howard Theatre, once a legitimate venue, began to feature burlesque shows and other risqué offerings to entice the soldiers on leave. Countless barrooms and tattoo parlors sprang up and squalor set in. Boston leaders were forced to take measures.

In the early sixties, the departure of Scollay Square led to the birth of the Combat Zone. Purveyors of illicit products migrated to a nearby area that encompassed several city blocks. Pornographic bookstores and peepshows dotted the landscape. At the epicenter, prostitutes peddled their wares without fear of reprisal from an indifferent Boston police vice squad. This lack of police intervention gave rise to organized crime. Over time, most of the lounges, including the New Yorker, were either owned by wise guys or fell under their control.

Rocco scrutinized his beer bottle. Grasping the neck, he pulled it to his mouth and polished it off. As if she could read his mind, the waitress appeared with a replacement.

"I'll add it to your tab," she said without being asked, setting the bottle on the table.

"Thanks, doll. You're unbelievable." He would have to remember to give the attractive forty-something waitress a decent tip at the end of the night.

"Something else?"

He looked at her with a devilish smirk, running his eyes top to bottom, from her pretty face to her shapely legs. She reminded him of film actress Faye Dunaway, blonde with a slightly upturned nose and plump, inviting lips.

"Young Mr. Balliro, get your mind out of the gutter," she lightheartedly scolded with a girlish giggle.

"There is one thing you can do for me, honey."

"Sure."

"You see that pretty girl sitting at the other side of the club?"

"Which one?"

"She's with Goldberg," Rocco replied, pointing to a table adjacent to the stage.

"Oh, I see her now," she acknowledged. "Adorable."

"Do me a favor," he proposed. "Find out what she's drinking and bring her another from me."

"Now who's unbelievable?"

"Huh? Whadda you mean?"

She shook her head gently and said, "She's out with another guy and you're sending over a drink?"

He grinned and asked, "So you'll do it?"

"Sure," she agreed, shaking her head in a half-hearted display of motherly disapproval. "How could I refuse the fabulous Rocco Balliro?"

She collected his empty and wheeled for the return trip to the bar. Watching her strut away, he marveled at her supple, near-perfect hindquarters, neatly packaged beneath a short, black skirt. If only she were ten years younger – or he, ten years older.

While flirting with the barmaid, Rocco noticed that his brother Joe had come into the room. Standing near the bar, his hand encircling a drink glass, the eldest of the six Balliro brothers was speaking with a man Rocco recognized as Matt Caplan. He was easy to spot amid the growing throng because of his poorly-guised comb-over slick with Brylcreem.

Rocco didn't much like Caplan, describing him as a "Jewish money worm." He ran a lucrative loan-sharking operation from a storefront on Massachusetts Avenue in Roxbury and partnered with Joe Balliro who, in 1961, brought his younger sibling into the fold as a bagman.

Rocco, who'd earned release months earlier from MCI-Walpole following a four-year stint for armed robbery, appreciated the work. He'd been off the street too long. This was a chance to climb back in the game. He couldn't deny that it was far better than sitting in a windowless room, answering phones, and writing up betting slips.

Under Caplan, Rocco was dispatched daily on a route through several Boston communities to collect debts from the regulars. A number of these downtrodden men, gamblers and drug addicts mostly, who'd borrowed varying sums of money, were unable to afford the weekly vig – or interest – on their note. In some instances, Rocco would cover the debt with his own cash to defer delinquency.

"It wasn't like you see in all those gangster movies – at least not with me," he later explained, motioning with his hands as he spoke in his typical animated fashion. "That wasn't my style. We didn't go around breaking someone's bones or bashing in their skulls if they couldn't pay up. If you hurt a guy, he might not be able to get steady work and he'd just fall in deeper. Better to keep him afloat until he could come up with the cash."

Despite Rocco's status as one of the more reliable collectors, he and his brother's partner failed to see eye-to-eye. It was the despicable Caplan, not Joe, who monitored the intake and there wasn't an ounce of trust in the man.

"He actually thought I would steal from my brother Joe," Rocco bitterly recalled. "Every Friday, I'd bring a bag of money to a bank over on Commonwealth Avenue. That lil' worm Caplan would repeatedly check the deposit slip. He suspected I was skimming off the top. Imagine that – he thought I would steal from my own blood."

Rocco thought about joining the two men but then reconsidered. He'd rather avoid a confrontation. Perhaps someday, when his brother Joe no longer held a business interest with him, Rocco would pay Caplan a visit and settle the score.

The barmaid returned with another beer and Rocco acknowledged her with a wink.

"By the way, I delivered that drink for you," she said. "Up close, she's even prettier than I first thought. Dark eyes."

His interest piqued, Rocco looked across the room and saw the girl raise her glass of wine – the drink he'd bought for her – in appreciation. Without pause, he stood from his chair and made his way toward her.

Rocco had taken several steps when a hand grasped his elbow.

"Hey, little brother, where you going in such a hurry?"

He turned to see that it was his fraternal twin Salvatore, who went by Rudy within their tight-knit circle of family and associates. It was short for Rudolph, his middle name, and the name of their dear mother's favorite actor, Rudolph Valentino.

"Little brother, my ass."

"Hey, twenty minutes is twenty minutes," Rudy boasted, smiling widely.

Rocco pivoted, grasped his sibling's broad shoulders, and quipped, "Well, in our case, *big* brother, second to arrive got most of the good looks."

Rudy, usually good-natured, was quick to laugh at the banter. He gestured toward the bar and asked Rocco if he'd been over to see their elder brother, Joe.

"No," he replied. "He's with that greaser, Caplan."

"You really don't like that guy, do you?"

It was more comment than question. They both knew that Rocco wouldn't shed a tear if Caplan was exterminated. But loyalty for Joe left him no choice but to tolerate the louse.

"So, where you heading?" Rudy asked.

"Over there," said Rocco, motioning toward the alluring, dark-haired beauty who was drawing him toward her like a powerful magnet. "The good looking chick sitting next to that two-bit hoodlum Goldberg."

"Very nice," Rudy said with a nod.

"Nothing but the best for me, *big* brother," Rocco agreed. "I'll catch up with you later, okay?"

"Yeah, sure, I'll see you in church if the windows are clean," Rudy jested as he gave his brother a light, affectionate punch to the chest.

Rocco chuckled and shook his head as Rudy ambled to the bar to check in with Joe. Rocco would do the same, but not until Caplan moved on. He did hope to bend Joe's ear about a couple of jobs. And to ask about the construction progress of the Intermission Lounge, a new club that Joe and his brothers Frank and Billy planned to open in a year or so. But that would have to wait. Foremost on his agenda – the girl.

Reaching the far side of the lounge, Rocco noted there were four people crammed at a table made for two. Goldberg and a guy Rocco didn't recognize were sitting with the two girls. The barmaid was dead on. This sweet morsel was very attractive, indeed. As his dear mother Angela might say in her native Italian, "*Bella*, Anthony, *bella*." Rocco hadn't considered what he'd say when he reached the table but the girl handled that quite aptly.

"Thanks for the drink," she said, delicately tapping a slender finger on the rim of the glass. "It was very nice of you."

Flashing his trademark grin, Rocco replied, "No problem – looks like you might need another."

Just as she was about to respond, an intruder severed their connection.

"Hey, Rocco," interrupted Goldberg, who obviously didn't appreciate the unsolicited visit. His forehead glistened with sweat and he clasped his hands together to mask trembling.

"How's it going, Goldberg?" Rocco asked, not really caring how it was going for him.

"Not bad, Rocco, not bad," the man chafed. "We'd ask you to join us but as you can see, we don't have much space at this table."

"Uh huh."

"So what brings you over here?"

As if you didn't already know, Rocco thought. It was evident to Goldberg that the interloper was putting the moves on his date. His doughy face grew blotchy red over the trespass. But he was certainly no match for the likes of Rocco Balliro.

"I'm just saying a quick hello to …"

"Toby," the girl blurted out, without hesitation. "I'm Toby."

"Yeah, Goldberg," Rocco continued, winking at her in thanks for the support. "I'm just saying a quick hello to my new friend Toby."

"Hello, Rocco," she said.

"Hello, Toby."

They both smiled at their improvisation. He could sense something building between them. Toby seemed receptive to his charm and brazen advance and he was smitten.

"Well," Goldberg urged, almost pleading. "Whadda you say the four of us go grab some Chinese food?"

The couple sitting with them had remained silent throughout the exchange. They both nodded in agreement to Goldberg's suggestion. Fearful, they wanted nothing more than to separate themselves from this jousting match.

Rocco, on the other hand, was rather amused. He looked at Toby and wondered if she would consider joining him. As underhanded as it might be, he decided to help her make a choice.

"So, Goldberg," he began, a malicious grin spreading across his face. "How's your wife?"

The question evoked the desired effect. Toby's facial expression was absolutely priceless. She glared at her current companion and leveled a single word, wrapping her pretty lips around it.

"Wife?"

Goldberg was a beaten man. Defeated, he glanced down at his hands which were folded together on his lap, like an obedient parochial school child. He tried again to preserve his hope for a prolonged evening.

"Toby, if you're hungry, I know a good restaurant over in Chinatown," he suggested. "It would be great if you would join me."

What a pathetic scene, watching Goldberg grovel, Rocco thought.

"Well, folks, I'm gonna head back before my beer gets warm," he announced. "Toby, it was nice to meet you."

"Me too," she replied, flashing a brilliant smile that warmed his insides. She was simply too stunning for words.

As he turned to walk away from his stricken competition, Rocco couldn't resist a final salvo.

"Hey, Goldberg," he said in parting, with a sinister grin. "You have yourself a great night."

CHAPTER 3

"If you obey all the rules you miss all the fun." –
Katharine Hepburn

The barmaid poured wine from the decanter until the glass was half full.

"C'mon, honey," Rocco urged. He took a last drag on his cigarette and stubbed it out. "Don't be stingy. Fill 'er up."

She frowned in disapproval but resumed pouring.

"Thank you," Toby said meekly.

As she turned to leave, the barmaid shot Rocco a glance that was part approval and part amazement, acknowledging the fact that he seldom failed to get the girl.

Rocco Anthony Balliro was a six-foot-tall strapping young man who sported a deceptively powerful build featuring sinewy arms that poured from the rolled-up sleeves of a charcoal gray, pullover sweater-shirt.

His good looks were highlighted by piercing brown eyes and wavy, coal black hair framing his prominent forehead. Rocco's sturdy jaw looked as if it could withstand a jab or two in a boxing ring, or more suited to his lifestyle, in the midst of street brawl.

He was slouched on the edge of the chair, leaning forward with his long legs crossed at the ankle. Anchoring a pair of imposing, black engineer boots was dark slacks, professionally tailored. If nothing else, he was well-dressed.

"So, Toby," he began. "What brings you to the New Yorker? Besides Goldberg, that is …"

Rocco instantly regretted the question. He was simply trying to break the ice but instead sounded arrogant and sarcastic.

Toby didn't respond right away. Pausing, she raised her glass for a sip. As she did, Rocco used the opportunity to marvel at her beauty. Of course, she possessed all of the physical attributes that appealed to his senses. But there was something more – something he couldn't quite put his finger on. It was as if he could sense that this woman would play a significant role in his life, even though they'd met only moments before.

It was Toby who broke a prolonged silence.

"I came here looking for you," she purred.

Unsure he heard the comment, Rocco mumbled, "Huh?"

"You asked what brought me to the New Yorker," Toby reminded him. "I came looking for you."

He was taken aback by this beguiling girl. As she spoke, she stared at him with a perfectly staid expression. Smooth as silk. Rocco, meanwhile, gathered that he wasn't concealing his surprise. He stared back tacitly, searching for a response that wouldn't embarrass him.

Turns out, he didn't have to. After a pause, Toby broke out laughing and said, "Gotcha!" The laughter made the corners of her dark eyes crinkle.

"Hmmm," Rocco murmured, shaking his head. He smiled to let her know the ruse ruffled him somewhat. "My friends say I'm a wiseass but I guess I've met my match."

"There's a lot of sarcasm in my family," Toby admitted.

Nodding, he remarked, "We'll get along just fine, then."

Rocco lit a pair of smokes and offered one to his companion. Seeking out the clock, he noted it was just after one in the morning. The New Yorker was in full swing. In darkened corners of the room, deals were brokered by Boston's leading underworld characters. Others were nuzzling up to attractive young women trawling for a boyfriend or husband, or someone else's boyfriend or husband.

Many of the men Rocco associated with kept a wife at home and a trophy girlfriend on the side. For the players, it was all about status.

Rocco turned his attention back to Toby, who was examining the glowing embers of her cigarette.

She was petite, perhaps ninety-five or a hundred pounds, at most. She wore a pale yellow button-down blouse that was tight-fitting and accentuated her curves. The same could be said for her hip-hugging navy blue skirt.

He looked closely into her eyes and saw weariness as if she harbored burdens far exceeding her tender age.

Toby glanced up and caught him staring. She cast a sheepish grin and abruptly said, "I knew he was married, by the way."

"Goldberg?"

"Yes."

"You're kidding."

"A woman can usually tell," she continued. "Besides, he wasn't very good at hiding it."

"How so?"

"He had a fresh tan line where his wedding ring would have been."

Rocco snickered and brayed, "What a moron."

"I have to be truthful," she offered.

"About?" he urged.

"Your friend Goldberg."

"He's not my friend."

"I know," she acknowledged. "That was obvious. But ..."

Toby paused. She seemed to be struggling to find the words to convey a message of some importance.

As she stalled, Rocco further apprised his companion who, he noted, wasn't wearing makeup. There was none of the typical rouge, lipstick, and garish green or blue eye shadow that many girls applied with regularity.

Preferring a natural look, he appreciated that. Certainly, a little enhancement from a jar went a long way for fair-skinned types. But for girls blessed with darker tones, like Toby, makeup would detract from the natural beauty.

Rocco wondered if Toby was of European descent – perhaps even Italian. That would please his mother. Like most women of her lineage, his dear mother often encouraged him to "find a nice Italian girl." It didn't matter that there were plenty of *nice* girls who weren't Italian.

Toby, he later discovered, was Jewish. Not that it mattered. Certainly, there were Jews he detested. Caplan, for instance. But when it came to women, it didn't matter, as long as they had the goods.

She lifted her cigarette and drew a prolonged drag. She looked at Rocco and said, "I have to be honest with you."

He waited as she hesitated again. It seemed that the unbridled confidence she displayed earlier was now replaced with measured restraint.

"Go ahead," he urged, his eyes softening. "I can take it."

Toby cleared her throat and divulged, "Goldberg isn't the only one who's already married."

"You're married?"

"Um ... yeah," she uttered, her voice wavering.

"Damn you, Toby," he angrily spat, turning his head away in disgust.

She froze, her mouth gaping, and stammered, "I'm s-sorry. I guess I s-should have told you sooner."

He gazed at her, his expression angry and dark. It must have been an award-winning performance because Toby began to rise from her chair. Rocco was incapable of keeping up the act for more than a few seconds, however, and broke out in a fit of laughter.

Her angst turning to confusion, she asked, "What's so funny?"

"Married?" he said, still chuckling. "I don't care if you're married. I was just giving you some of your own medicine, honey."

"Oh, is that how it is?"

"I'll use your word," he said. "Gotcha!"

In a standoffish posture, Toby folded her arms across her chest. "You're not very funny, Mr. Balliro," she pouted indignantly. He could see her cheeks flush, even in the low light of the club. "Your sense of humor needs work."

His laughter tapering to a grin, Rocco apologized. "I was just kidding around, really."

He leveled the next obvious question, framing it as a statement. "So, this husband of yours ..."

"Barney Wagner," she furnished. "His friends call him Googsie."

"What do you call him?"

"Asshole," she replied, with a deadpan, straight-faced delivery. She didn't even crack a smile. This girl could really spin it.

"True love, I guess," Rocco said.

"Tough to love someone who's always in jail."

His interest was suddenly piqued. This was a topic he knew something about.

"Jail, huh? Which one?"

"Concord Reformatory."

"Oh yeah? What's he in for?"

"He got arrested for breaking into a pharmacy," she answered. "I think he was stealing drugs. He's been in and out of reform schools since I met him eight years ago, when I was thirteen."

Rocco quickly did the math and said, "So, you're ... um ...twenty-one?"

"Uh huh," she replied, nodding. "Since April."

"You look older."

Toby winced. "I guess I'll take that as a compliment."

"It was," he assured her. "I've met girls your age who act like giggling teenagers. You're much more ... uh ..." He paused, seeking words that wouldn't offend her. Once again, Toby came to his rescue.

"Mature?"

"Yeah," he agreed. "Mature."

"I've heard that before," she said. "Must be the kids."

Rocco took a double take, his eyes widening. "Kids?"

"Two of them," she admitted.

He grabbed his beer and downed the remainder in two swallows, as if he were dowsing a burn from scalding food.

"Surprised?" she asked.

"Uh, no ... not at all," Rocco replied. "I'm not surprised. It's just ... well ... you're so thin."

She giggled over his discomfort. For such a big, tough guy, he seemed lost in how to broach the topic. In a playful, celebrity-like move, Toby flipped her jet black, shoulder-length hair and said, "Why, thank you."

Actually, thin was not an apt description. When Toby had earlier approached from across the lounge, Rocco noted that she stood slightly over five foot tall and possessed curvaceous hips crowned with a narrow waist line.

"So, your kids," he inquired. "Boys? Girls?"

"One of each," Toby replied, pleased with his genuine interest. "Mark is eighteen months and I had my daughter Bernice five months ago."

"I'm sure they're beautiful."

Toby didn't respond. It wasn't necessary. He could read it in her eyes. The connection between them had been established. And he'd just cemented that bond by welcoming her children.

They traded pleasantries for an hour or so, sharing details about their respective pasts. Toby, he found, grew up in a small, cramped house in the West End of Boston, several blocks from Rocco's childhood home on Bartlett Place in the North End. As a teenager in the late fifties, her family moved to Brookline when developers claimed their property as part of the West End redevelopment project. She told him her family now made their home in the quaint North Shore coastal community of Swampscott, Massachusetts.

Toby, he discovered, was the only daughter of Herman and Hilda Zimmerman, a couple who were descendants of Jewish immigrants from Eastern Europe.

Her father Herman was an innocent participant in a cover-up of a late fifties mob execution. Soon after a wayward mafia soldier was assassinated in a North End apartment, the killers unsuccessfully attempted to mop up a large pool of blood, much of which had saturated the carpeting. The crew carved out the blood-soaked rug segment and disposed of it along with the bullet-riddled body. Later, the killers hired Herman, or "Zimmie," as he was better known to customers, to restore the floor. Zimmie was the proprietor of a North End linoleum and carpet business. He was ultimately ordered to testify before a grand jury but, understandably, had nothing of significance to share with the authorities.

Toby was the middle child of three. Her brother Malcolm was three years her senior and David, a late addition, was only eight.

Toby grew radiant when she mentioned Malcolm who, at twenty-four, had already been married and divorced and had a two-year-old son Daniel. She explained that she'd arranged for her high school friend Beverly Greenburg to meet Mal and the rest took care of itself. But their marriage was troublesome and ended in divorce after several years.

Rocco recognized, as they chatted into the night, that Toby seemed to be growing more at ease. She shared sensitive topics. For instance, she disclosed that her mother Hilda was a drinker and when intoxicated, would resort to vile verbal attacks. Sadly, her mother became so incapacitated that, at times, she was unable to deliver care for baby David. Toby said she would arrive home from her days at Brookline High School and instead of delving into homework, would be compelled to change diapers and fix meals while her mother slept off a binge. Toby would ultimately drop out in her junior year and when able, took waitressing jobs. Rocco now understood her weariness.

Toby excused herself to the ladies room and Rocco assured her that a fresh drink would be waiting upon her return.

Rocco strained to pinpoint a familiar face in the lounge. Two of the four Angiulo brothers, Gennaro and Donato, were perched at a nearby table. In the years to come, Gennaro, or Jerry as he was better known, would ascend the ladder to assume control of the Boston crime syndicate, and later, face conviction for murder. At another table, Ilario "Larry Baione" Zannino, who was a high-ranking member of the New England clan, sat chatting with a pair of associates. Rocco's brothers Joe and Rudy were huddling at the bar. And sitting in the company of an attractive woman was the blond haired Joseph "JR" Russo, whose direct affiliation was with New England crime boss Raymond Patriarca.

Like Rocco, Russo had gained release from the notorious maximum security MCI-Walpole the year before, in 1961. Several weeks later, as Rocco recalled, he and Russo were tipping back a few cold ones at a popular Revere Beach hangout, the Surf Club, when they were joined by another man who'd served part of a Walpole stretch with them.

Joe "the Animal" Barboza had wandered into the Surf and without invitation, barged in on their conversation. "Hey, Roc," he crooned, slithering on to the adjacent barstool. "How the hell are ya?"

"Good, Joe," he answered. "Yourself?"

"I'm great, thanks," declared Barboza, as he ordered a beer. He then leaned forward to greet Rocco's companion who was clearly ignoring the uninvited guest. "How you doin', JR?"

Russo hesitated and finally grunted, "Not bad." It was barely audible and clearly hostile. Rocco sensed by the tone that his friend Russo didn't much care for the East Boston man who aspired to become a prize fighter and a gangster or a blend of both. Barboza, undeterred, brushed off the chilly reception and persisted.

"So, Rocco, whadda you say later we head into Boston?"

"Me and you?"

"Yeah."

"For what?"

"I'd like to catch up with your brothers and some of the other guys."

As Rocco prepared to respond, he felt a sharp elbow jam into his ribcage. It was Russo delivering the painful jab. "What the ..." He turned to look at JR, whose face was contorted in a grimace. He shook his head once, out of Barboza's line of vision, indicating that the request should be denied.

Without knowing exactly why he was doing so, Rocco pivoted to face Barboza and said, "Umm, Joe, let's make it another time, okay?"

"Sure, sure, no problem," he said, clearly disappointed. "Another time."

The brief exchange was followed by an uncomfortable quiet that lingered like the gray cigarette fog over the bar. The three men drank their beers without talking.

Barboza splintered the silence, stepping away for a pack of cigarettes. Rocco, meanwhile, capitalized on his absence and questioned Russo. "What gives?" he asked, massaging his ribs where a bruise would soon form.

"You gotta keep him the hell away from the New Yorker."

"Uh huh," acknowledged Rocco, waiting for Russo to elaborate.

"It won't be appreciated if he shows up," he continued. "He's no good, that's all. Just take my advice, okay?"

"Alright, no problem."

"Alright what?" Neither man noticed that Barboza had crept back to the bar, a fresh pack of cigarettes in hand.

"Nothing," said Rocco, covering his tracks. "Not important."

During the early years of his affiliation, Barboza professed allegiance to Rhode Island-based crime boss Patriarca. While he was loyal, there were those in the organization who felt the amateur boxer was a loose cannon. He was known for his explosive disposition and was prone to dangerous outbursts. During a provocation in a Revere nightspot, for instance, the physically powerful Barboza slapped around an unaffiliated man who questioned his unruliness. Highly respected underboss Henry Tameleo took exception to Barboza's aggression toward the civilian. Small in stature, but high in rank, Tameleo insisted that he keep his hands off the man. Witnesses claim that Barboza, who was never made by La Cosa Nostra because of his Portuguese descent, ignored Tameleo and bit off a chunk of the man's ear in another unprovoked attack. Afterward, he claimed that he did, indeed, follow orders. Sarcastically, the Animal insisted that he never touched the victim with his *hands*.

Said to have executed nearly thirty men during his tenure, Barboza earned the FBI label as "the most vicious criminal in New England." He often killed with reckless abandon. One night, he gunned down an innocent bystander who had stopped to buy a pack of cigarettes at a Revere bar. According to FBI informant Vincent Teresa, Barboza was in the midst of carrying out a hit on Ray DiStasio. In an unsettling act of cold-blooded ruthlessness, the gunman cut short the life of witness John O'Neil, father of two, who was simply in the wrong place at the wrong time. The malevolent Barboza reportedly put two bullets in the back of DiStasio's head and casually fired three slugs into O'Neil.

But perhaps the most heinous act took place soon after Barboza's 1966 arrest in the Combat Zone on weapons charges. The Boston Police found a concealed pistol in his vehicle. Word on the street was that the weapon had been planted and the cops had been tipped off by the mob itself. Short of sanctioning Barboza for execution, the organization had instead arranged for his imprisonment. The strategy backfired, however.

Locked up in Walpole again and staring down the barrel of a five year sentence, Barboza defected and turned FBI informant. His decision was further prompted by the murders of two close friends who were raising funds toward his release.

Barboza was soon marked for death. The organization was making loud overtures as a result of their suspicion, dead on as it turned out, that he might flap his gums to the FBI.

Barboza later pointed the finger at Tameleo, Peter Limone, and others in the murder of small-time hoodlum Teddy Deegan. He also provided damning testimony that led to indictments of reputed Boston mob boss Angiulo for involvement in the murder of Rocco DiSiglio, as well as helping to put Patriarca away for his participation in the slaying of Rhode Island bookmaker Willie Marfeo.

Much of what Barboza shared from the witness stand during the summer of 1967 was perjured. But a corrupt FBI not only condoned the killer's lies, they scripted it. Unable to get the goods by conventional means, the agents resorted to cultivating untruths via Barboza to earn convictions.

His vile work done, the turncoat was released and fled Massachusetts for Northern California where he continued his killing ways. After serving a five year stint for a second-degree murder conviction, Barboza was paroled from Folsom prison in late 1975 and moved into a San Francisco apartment under an assumed name. He wasn't there for long, however, before his whereabouts were uncovered by the syndicate. In early 1976, Angiulo was tipped off that Barboza was holed up on the West Coast. An executioner was dispatched.

Angiulo's hired gun was none other than JR Russo, who unloaded four shotgun blasts into the rat's midsection. Blood flowed thick on the San Francisco street as Barboza fell in the gutter, silenced, literally steps from his apartment.

Lost in thought, Rocco didn't immediately notice Toby's return.

They sat in silence for a moment, drinking their respective beverages. The New Yorker was bustling as a jazz band played.

"It's getting kinda' loud in here," Toby abruptly said. "What do you say we go somewhere else?"

"What'd you have in mind?"

"My place?"

She didn't have to ask a second time.

CHAPTER 4

"Our prime purpose in this life is to help others. And if you can't help them, at least don't hurt them." – Dalai Lama

Rocco fished a sawbuck from his wallet and handed it over to the Chinese woman standing behind the counter of the modest Brighton variety store.

"Thank you," she said, serving up an engaging smile as she counted out his change. He'd always had a thing for Orientals, perhaps because most were petite with dark hair – his preference. *Like Toby*, he thought.

He stuffed the money in his pocket and scooped up the overflowing bag of groceries. As he turned to depart, he pleasantly said to the shopkeeper, "Have a great night, ma'am." Of course, the night would be over in a little more than three or four hours. It was fast approaching two in the morning when Rocco exited to a barren and deserted Commonwealth Avenue. Only the idling curbside cab fractured the silence.

Climbing into the taxi, he carefully juggled the groceries. As he slid across the wide, vinyl seat, Rocco was greeted with a smile that made his heartbeat quicken. This woman was too beautiful to describe.

"I can't thank you enough for this," Toby said. Her eyes, deep and serious, began to well up with tears. She'd already told him several times how grateful she was for his generosity. He sensed she was deeply embarrassed about making the request. But as she explained when she asked him to float a few bucks, paying the rent had left her short on cash.

"What? These groceries? It's nothing," he insisted.

Actually, for Rocco, it was *far* from nothing. He really liked this girl and by swallowing her pride and asking for help, even something as simple as furnishing food for a couple of hungry kids, Toby helped fulfill an altruistic need in him to provide.

From what he could gather from their earlier conversation, she was barely scraping by. For the most part, she supported her children via a monthly mother's aid subsidy. The Zimmerman family didn't seem to possess the means to supplement her income and he understood all too well that husband Barney certainly wasn't contributing from behind bars.

As the taxicab sped across Brighton, the occupants rode in silence. Rocco cracked the window but there was little fresh air to speak of on this sultry summer night. Despite the late hour, the heat and humidity that had prevailed during the first week of July was forecasted to linger. There was no relief in sight.

"We're here," said Toby as the cab rolled to a halt in front of her Kelton Street apartment. Rocco paid the driver and stepped out. Toby followed, guiding the bag of groceries to the edge of the seat so he could get his hands around it.

They walked toward the entrance to her building, which was a solid, three-story structure featuring granite blocks mixed with ornate yellow brick. It resembled a parapet on the front of a castle. As they mounted a short flight of concrete stairs, Toby pivoted and directed a question.

"So, Rocco," she timidly began and paused, as a grin spread across her pretty, olive-toned face. "Is Rocco really your name?"

He snickered at the question, wondering why it had taken her so long to ask. "My brothers and most of my buddies call me Rocco," he answered. "But my sisters and mother use Anthony."

"Anthony," she echoed. "Tony. I like Tony. Mind if I call you that?"

Rocco smirked and replied, "You can call me anything you like."

Toby opened the heavy glass door as Rocco trailed a step behind, lugging the bulky grocery bag. They entered a dimly lit foyer, cluttered with a stack of yellowing newspapers and several cardboard boxes overflowing with unclaimed junk mail.

Toby gestured toward a wide L-shaped staircase ahead and said, "Sorry, but my place is on the third floor."

"No problem," he fibbed, adjusting the grocery bag for the trek. "I need the exercise."

As he climbed, Rocco gripped the thick, polished banister, using it to pull himself along. Salty drops streamed down his forehead. Toby apologized a second time.

"This is it," she said. Keying the lock, she pushed open the wooden door and stepped across the threshold. Immediately, Rocco's sweat-soaked face was met by cooler air. Toby, he noted, had placed an electric fan in a window. Grateful, he drew a deep breath.

"Tony," she said, pointing in the direction of a small, tidy kitchen. "Put the groceries over there and make yourself comfortable."

"Okay."

"Want a cold beer?"

"Sure."

Rocco glanced inquisitively along a darkened hallway that branched off the living room. He assumed it led to the bedrooms. He sensed the two of them were alone and wondered about the children.

As if she could read his thoughts, Toby said, "They're staying the night at my parents' up in Swampscott."

"I was looking forward to meeting them."

"They'll be home in the morning," she assured.

Rocco made his way to the living room and flopped on a worn, but comfortably plush coach. Behind him was a trio of windows, one featuring a fan set to maximum. The artificial breeze felt good on the nape of his neck.

He couldn't see her from his vantage point but could hear Toby rustling in the kitchen. The fridge door opened and closed several times. She soon rounded the corner with a beer in hand. Joining him, she handed over the icy bottle.

"Like my place?"

Nodding, Rocco looked around the room. In a tone that was equal parts disdain and embarrassment, Toby explained that the furnishings were hand-me-downs from friends and family and were worse for wear. She wasn't exaggerating. Much of it had seen better days, including the couch beneath them. The cushions were frayed and tattered. There were several small puncture holes and what looked like cigarette burns. A nearby chair was similarly dilapidated. Positioned in front of the couch and chair duo, littered with children's books and magazines, was a battered coffee table. It was apparent that husband Barney hadn't been much of a provider.

Across the room, a rudimentary television sat idle. He noted it was a black and white and not one of the modern color sets introduced several years earlier. Glancing at Toby, he noticed she was fixated on a framed photograph resting on top of the TV. It portrayed a pint-sized boy sitting on a swing. He was blessed with an enchanting smile that shimmered with innocence. His eyes, whimsical and curious, twinkled with the joy that can only result from an afternoon spent in a playground. In the photo, a ray of sunshine beamed down, drawing attention to a thick tuft of jet black hair. Dressed in a Batman logo t-shirt and a pair of shorts that revealed scuffed knees, he was *all* boy.

"It that Mark?" he asked.

She nodded.

"Cute kid."

"Thanks," she said. With a slight giggle, she added, "I'm sure he'd agree."

Toby leaned back and stretched out her slender legs. The three glasses of wine she'd consumed at the New Yorker, in addition to an unknown count of cocktails she drank with Goldberg, were taking effect.

When she'd first joined Rocco in the lounge, he sensed she was tension-filled. She sat upright, stiff and straight, as if she was in the midst of a pressure-packed job interview.

But now, she seemed entirely at ease. Toby didn't seem concerned that she was alone with a man she'd met only hours before. For all she knew, the character sitting on her couch was the vicious madman who'd been terrorizing Boston women for the past several weeks. To that date, July 7, 1962, the sick-minded serial killer who'd become known as the Boston Strangler, had raped and strangled four women in rapid succession, including an eighty-five-year-old. In doing so, the Strangler was making a mockery of the Boston Police Department.

It was obvious that Toby trusted him. He felt it might be an opportune time to open up to her.

Clearing his throat, as if he were preparing to deliver an important speech, Rocco said, "Toby, I should probably come clean."

"Sure," she replied. Her eyes became bright and attentive. Perhaps the wine hadn't dulled her senses as much as he thought.

"You mentioned your husband Bernie was in jail ..."

"Barney," she corrected.

He paused and in response to her interruption, quipped, "I thought you called him Asshole?"

She laughed. Her smile could light up a darkened cave. "That's right," she said. "But you can call him whatever you want. Bernie, Barney, Googsie, or Asshole."

He tried his best to keep a straight face. "Alright, Asshole it is," he agreed. "You mentioned, umm ... Asshole ... was doing time?"

"Uh huh. Concord."

"Well, I've spent a little time locked up myself," Rocco admitted. He paused and searched her face. He thought perhaps she might reject him. Instead, she seemed genuinely interested. It wasn't a total surprise. After all, she had been hanging out in a lounge laden with Mafioso.

"When was that?"

"I did four years in the can, at Walpole," he shared. "I got paroled last summer."

"I've heard that place is tough," Toby said.

"Piece of cake," Rocco lied, but didn't elaborate. He chose not to explain that he was sent up for only eighteen months but because of misdeeds, including drug charges and battery on a corrections officer, he remained behind bars for three times his original sentence.

"What was the charge?" she asked.

"Armed robbery."

He thought Toby might crave more details about the crime and was grateful when she didn't ask. Either she'd bridled her curiosity or perhaps sensed, by his pained expression, that it was a chapter in his life he preferred not to revisit. He was ashamed over the ill-advised hold up that cost four years of his youth and added more anguish to his saintly mother Angela, who spent exhaustive weekends trudging from one prison to another visiting her incarcerated sons.

"Another beer?" Toby asked.

"Sure." He nodded.

Rocco heard the refrigerator door open and close, sandwiched between the telltale sound of glass bottles clinking together. Toby soon appeared with a beer in each hand. She paused for several seconds, gazing at him. He waited, visually drinking in her loveliness.

"Tony," she softly uttered. "Let's drink these in the bedroom."

It occurred to Rocco, as he sat on the edge of Toby's comfortable mattress and disrobed, that the man who should rightfully occupy this bed was, at that moment, likely struggling to get a night's sleep on an unforgiving metal rack covered with a flimsy inch-thick pad in a damp, dank prison cell.

No matter, Rocco thought indifferently, as he slid across the smooth bed sheets and enveloped that man's wife in his arms.

CHAPTER 5

"I've made upwards of a million bucks in the cops-and-robbers business." – Broderick Crawford

He slept fitfully, waking every half hour. Rocco couldn't remember the last time he had so much trouble falling asleep. The illuminated alarm clock on the nightstand read five o'clock. He and Toby had climbed into bed barely two hours before.

Conceding to the insomnia, Rocco got up, careful not to disturb a soundly sleeping Toby. She stirred but did not wake.

He shuffled along the narrow corridor, warily navigating in the darkness. Reaching the kitchen, he opened the fridge. Light spilled out, filling the small room. Instead of another beer, he reached for the bottle of orange juice he'd bought earlier and half filled a glass.

Making his way to the couch, Rocco stopped to flip on the television. He twisted the volume knob to lower it. As the rectangular screen came into focus, he recognized the show as *Highway Patrol*, starring Broderick Crawford. He liked the actor, with his gruff demeanor and gravelly voice. But Rocco knew the cop drama was farfetched. In each segment, Chief Dan Mathews, played by Crawford, teamed up with officers of the California Highway Patrol and never failed to capture – or kill – the criminals they pursued.

Rocco sat heavily and sipped the juice. The fan behind him whirred, drawing air that had finally cooled somewhat. He'd all but given up on trying to find sleep – maybe it would find him if he watched enough television.

As the episode of *Highway Patrol* unfolded, Officer Mathews successfully apprehended a fleeing suspect but not before the criminal shot and killed a uniformed highway patrolman during his getaway attempt.

Narrator Art Gilmore stated the obvious, explaining that "a criminal must have transportation to and from the scene." Gilmore went further to introduce the antagonist as "Steve Stankey, a seasoned criminal who solved his transportation problem with the use of an innocent taxi driver." Rocco was struck by the irony of what he watched and heard coming from the television set, especially when Gilmore said, "The taxi driver was able to give a complete description of the culprit."

Six years earlier, a twenty-year-old Rocco Balliro suffered a similar fate following a brazen armed robbery.

He recalled that his troubles began, as they often did, soon after he met a young girl at a popular Boston nightspot.

It was Sunday, February 10, 1957, and he recalled the crowd in the club was loud and boisterous. Drinks were flowing freely when he was approached by an attractive young lass.

"This seat taken?" she asked, raising her voice above the din.

"It is now," Rocco replied, tapping the surface with his fingertips. Controlling his grin was an impossible task as she slid on to the barstool.

Anna Maria Fairbanks was a pretty little thing – a description befitting most of the girls Rocco found attractive. She was blessed with shoulder-length chestnut brown hair, deep olive skin, and innocent, azure blue eyes. She was also, he soon discovered, a seventeen-year-old runaway trying to escape fatherly abuse back in Hartford, Connecticut. She needed a place to stay and Rocco was happy to oblige. It wasn't long before Anna Maria moved her meager belongings into his cramped Beacon Hill flat.

He enjoyed her company but she was another mouth to feed and proved to be a financial burden. He was burning through money faster than he could scrape it together.

One night in early March, roughly a month after Anna Maria took up residence with him, Rocco was sitting at his kitchen table and unwinding over a few too many beers. He was well on his way to complete intoxication. In front of him, on the kitchen table were empties lined in a tidy row like military sentries, a .45-caliber handgun, and an empty leather wallet.

Rocco rose from the chair and made his way toward the living room where Anna Maria was fast asleep on the couch. An open book was spread across her chest. Through blurry eyes, he noted the title — *Fahrenheit 451*. Earlier that evening, as they ate dinner, Anna Maria had enthusiastically summarized a description of author Ray Bradbury's futuristic society which outlawed books. Firemen were tasked with confiscating hidden caches of books and burning them publicly. The shamed perpetrators were humiliated in full view of scornful neighbors.

"How did the firemen find out about the books?" Rocco asked, as he dug a fork into the delicious meatloaf she'd prepared.

Anna Maria glanced across the table at him and smiled, pleased that he was showing interest.

"They had boxes scattered across the city, like mailboxes," she explained. "Citizens could drop notes reporting people who hid books in their homes."

"Rats!" Rocco sneered. He pantomimed two fingers as a little pair of rodent legs creeping across the table in her direction. "They're everywhere – even in the future!"

She chuckled and urged, "You should read it, really."

"Sure, sure," he responded, humoring her. It sounded like a great story but he just didn't have time for reading, at least not as long as the streets beckoned and there was money to hustle.

As he grabbed his jacket, which was slung over the back of a chair, Anna Maria shifted in her sleep. Her book fell to the floor with a clatter. Rocco stooped to pick it up. He placed it neatly on the coffee table and then made his way back to the kitchen where he slipped on his jacket. He grabbed the .45, ensuring the safety was engaged before stuffing the weapon in his pocket.

Once outside, Rocco found an idling cab on Beacon Street, climbed in, and instructed the driver to take him over to Hanover Street.

"Sure thing, boss," said the cabbie who, oddly enough, was wearing a striped railroad engineer's cap.

Rocco wasn't exactly sure what he intended to do once he reached Boston's North End but one thing was certain – it was far too cold to walk the half dozen blocks through Scollay Square.

There was little traffic on the streets and within minutes, the taxicab reached the Italian enclave where Rocco had grown up.

"Anywhere in particular on Hanover Street, boss?" the driver inquired.

With the back of his sleeve, Rocco brushed aside some of the condensation from the window and immediately recognized where he was.

"Drop me at the corner of Parmenter."

"You got it, boss."

He wondered, for a moment, if every sentence this guy's mouth excreted ended in the word "boss." The question was answered as the cabbie violently whipped the car over to the curb, coming to a hard stop. It triggered a sickening spin in Rocco's alcohol-soaked head.

"Here ya go, boss."

Rocco fought off a wave of nausea and handed the driver a five, most of it tip.

"Gee, thanks, boss."

"Don't mention it, boss," Rocco mimicked sarcastically as he emerged from the cab. The pavement seemed to be moving beneath his feet. It was apparent he'd had far too much to drink.

He studied the downward-sloping Parmenter Street, best known for Polcari's Coffee, located on the corner of Salem Street. Within view of the little neighborhood grocery, which opened for business in 1932, was Bartlett Court and the Balliro family homestead.

Rocco didn't wear a wristwatch but his best guess was that it was somewhere around ten or eleven o'clock. It was reasonably early by his standards but certainly too late to drop in on his parents unannounced. Besides, he really didn't want his dear mother to see him in such a drunken state.

Rocco stood idle, contemplating his next move. The frigid cold was sobering. He considered seeking out another cab to ferry him home when unexpectedly, a door to a nearby café opened and a man stepped out.

Without fully weighing the consequences of his actions, Rocco seized the opportunity. He quickly sized up the man: middle-aged, maybe fifties, slightly built, and most important – alone. The guy was a sitting duck. With catlike quickness, Rocco pounced, yanking the .45 caliber pistol from his pocket as he closed the gap. Pointing the gun, he barked, "Hey, mister, don't move!"

"J-Jesus," the startled man gasped, as he pivoted to face the onrushing gunman. There was a single step leading from the restaurant exit to the sidewalk and he nearly stumbled. Gaining his balance, he clasped his chest, feigning heart troubles. "What do you w-want?"

"Give me your wallet! Now! I don't want to hurt you!"

"Sure … sure."

The robbery victim complied, reaching into an interior pocket of his overcoat and withdrawing a thick billfold. He was trembling and nearly dropped the wallet. "Here, take it …"

"Don't do anything stupid," Rocco warned. Edging closer to the terrified victim, he snatched the wallet. As he did, however, Rocco's face briefly came into view beneath a light suspended above. He'd emerged from the shadows for a split second, no more, and the illumination was very dim. But it was, nonetheless, sufficient enough for his quarry to catch a glimpse.

"Hey, I know you!" the man proclaimed. He was suddenly emboldened. Even though a gun was leveled at his midsection, his tone was no longer fearful. He was infuriated. "Jesus, you're a B–"

"Shaddup – not another word!" Rocco ordered. A torrent of anxiety washed over him like the crest of an ocean wave. It intensified two-fold when the stranger confirmed his fears.

"I know who you are," the holdup victim confirmed, imparting his revelation with a snarl. "You're one of them Balliro boys!"

Rocco didn't hang around long enough to argue the point. He stuffed the stolen wallet in his pocket and turned tail, sprinting south along Hanover Street. The soles of his leather boots slapped on the sidewalk. The sound reverberated off the walls of the century-old urban valley of multi-story brick-front buildings. Behind him, the enraged victim hollered again and again, "I know who you are, Balliro! I know who you are ..."

Rocco picked up the tempo, running harder. He was in pretty good physical shape but hadn't run like this in some time and was feeling the strain. The sharp cold burned hot in his heaving chest as he gulped air. In spite of the chill, beads of sweat broke out on his forehead and his shirt was soon plastered to his skin.

The flight from discovery sobered him. The alcohol-induced fog lifted and he was thinking with clarity.

What on Earth had possessed him to perpetrate an armed robbery in his own backyard? He grew up here. He knew a lot of people. And obviously, a lot of people knew him, as well.

Rocco imagined he could hear his exasperated siblings lashing out at him. "Rocco, what the hell were you thinking?" one of the pissed off Balliro brothers might say. "Jesus! Have you lost your mind? The North End, for Crissake! Your own backyard?"

Worse still, what if the guy he just ripped off was connected to the mob in some way? How the hell would he explain that? Could he stay alive long enough to have the chance?

Within a couple of blocks, Rocco felt assured he had put enough distance between himself and the owner of the wallet. He slowed first to a jog and shortly thereafter, a steady walk. He was thankful that he could no longer hear the shouts of the man. He was further thankful when he spotted an idle taxicab parked on the corner of Hanover and Cross Streets.

Rocco turned to look back along Hanover Street. Was the man giving chase? Did he run back into the café to solicit help? Rocco half expected to see a group of men rampaging toward him, led by his stick up victim.

Opening the rear door, Rocco climbed in. "Beacon Hill," he breathlessly instructed. This driver, who was chewing on a ragged, unlit cigar, was far less verbal than his predecessor. He grunted as he pulled away from the curb and made a sharp right on Cross Street.

Back at his apartment, Rocco was met by an indignant Anna Maria, who stood with her arms defiantly folded across her chest. When she got a closer look at him, however, she softened.

"Tony, are you alright?"

"Yeah, I'm fine," Rocco lied. He wasn't fine.

"Where have you been?" she asked. "I was worried."

"I just ran out to see a sick friend."

Anna Maria frowned and remarked, "Well, you look like death. I'll make coffee."

As she fired the stove, he made his way into the living room where a mirror over the mantle revealed a disheveled character that vaguely resembled Rocco Balliro. She wasn't kidding, he thought, as he ran fingers through his frenzied hair.

His face was flushed red and in dire need of a shave. Rocco's eyes were bloodshot even though he had sobered considerably since committing the stick up.

A lightning bolt of anxiety suddenly ripped through him. The wallet! He reached around to his back pocket to feel for the stolen billfold. It wasn't there. After risking his neck to steal it, it was gone. *The cab! I left it in the damn cab*, he thought. But then he slid his hand across to the opposite pocket.

"Phew ..." He whistled, relieved that he hadn't left it behind in the taxi or dropped it in the gutter. He opened the wallet to reveal the loot inside. Without counting, he estimated the wad of bills to be north of three hundred bucks. As he ran his thumb over the edge of the currency, Rocco returned to the kitchen. He failed to notice that Anna Maria had silently crept up behind him.

"Whatcha got there?"

"Shit!" he exclaimed, startled. The wallet slipped from his grasp, falling to the floor. Some of the cash and photos scattered across the worn linoleum.

"Where'd you get that?"

"Never mind," Rocco replied, as he crouched to gather the contents.

As he fumbled with the wallet, a loud, impatient knock sounded at the door.

"What the hell ..." Rocco groaned.

"Who is it, Tony? Should I get it?"

"Go in the bedroom and stay put," he demanded sternly. He stuffed the wallet in his pocket and withdrew the .45 from the waistband of his pants. A cold sweat was now streaming from every pore in his body. A wave of nausea washed over him.

Again, the incessant knocking, louder this time. Banging, actually. *Rap-rap-rap* on the door. Someone *really* wanted to get into his apartment. Rocco looked at the clock. It was nearing midnight. One of his brothers, perhaps, dropping by for a beer after a night at the club? Or could it be …

"Balliro! We know you're in there! Open the door!"

"Oh Jesus," he uttered. He whipped around and saw Anna Maria standing beneath the archway that separated the living room from the kitchen. He was grateful she failed to heed his instruction.

"Anna," he hissed in a half-whisper. "C'mere. Quick."

"Who is it?" she repeated, her fearful gaze fixated on the gun, her face ashen. For an instant, he felt guilty for dragging her into *his* mess. She was only seventeen after all, and at that moment, looked her age.

"It's the cops!" Rocco snapped. There wasn't time for explanations. It was time to act.

"What do they want?" She looked terrified and tears began to flow. He felt a pang of guilt for putting her in harm's way but under these dire circumstances, with the wolf at the door, he had no choice.

"Here," Rocco said in a low pitch, extending the gun toward her. "Quick. Hide this."

Anna Maria grasped the handle of the hefty weapon, tentatively, as if it were a snake that would clamp its fangs on her.

"Balliro!" shouted the gruff, impatient voice from the hallway. "Open this fuckin' door or we'll do it for you!"

Rocco crossed the room and reached for the deadbolt. Before he gave it a spin, he turned to make sure Anna Maria had left the room. He could hear her rummaging in the bedroom closet. *Good girl*, he thought. She was obviously stashing the pistol beneath a loose floorboard he'd once shown her.

He gave the latch a spin and grasped the knob. As he did, the door sprang open abruptly, nearly slamming into his face. "For Crissake!" Rocco bellowed.

A pair of uniformed Boston cops bullied their way in. They rushed at him, grasped his arms, and shoved him toward a segment of empty wall space between windows that overlooked the street below. Rocco stumbled slightly as they pushed him against the wall, face first, and began to frisk him. They ran their hands up and down each leg and arm. One of the officers wedged a boot between their suspect's feet and forced them apart. He then crouched to recheck Rocco's ankles for a weapon.

"What the hell took you so long?"

Facing the wall, Rocco craned his neck to get a look at the cop who'd asked the question. He was short and stout, middle-aged, and balding. His breath reeked of onions.

"I was in bed," he answered. "Sleeping."

"You always sleep with your shoes on, wiseass?" asked Onion Breath's partner, who was tall, thin, and looked more like an accountant than a cop. Rocco had to stifle a chuckle. This oddball pair of lawmen brought to mind the comic team of Abbott and Costello and their hilarious skits.

"You been drinking, Balliro?"

"Yeah," Rocco admitted, shrugging his shoulders. He had to resist an overwhelming urge to suggest to his captor that he chew a mint or a piece of gum. Anything to kill the rotten stench pouring from his trap. "A coupla beers, here in my apartment. There some kind of law against that?"

The dynamic duo didn't appreciate their captive's sarcasm and got a little rough, forcing his face against the wall again, harder this time. There was an audible sound as skin and bone connected with plaster. Later, a bluish-yellow welt would mark evidence of the man-handling he'd received. Not that it really mattered – who would be so bold as to question the brutality of a Boston cop?

"Where's the gun?"

"Gun?"

"Don't give me that shit," Onion Breath snarled. "The gun you used to stick up that guy in the North End."

"Don't know what you're talking about."

"Oh really?" crooned the cop, as he jammed his chubby fingers into Rocco's back pocket and confiscated the stolen wallet. Opening it to a reveal a driver's license that was not Rocco Balliro's, the patrolman waved it in front of his detainee's face. "Then how the hell would you explain this?"

"Hey, what are you doing to him?"

The cops loosened their viselike grip on Rocco's upper arms as they both pivoted toward the voice behind them. Anna Maria had emerged from the bedroom. Her pretty face was contorted in an angry scowl.

Onion Breath barked, "Who the hell are you?"

She remained silent.

"Honey, I asked you a question," the cop persisted. "Who the hell are you?"

Anna Maria continued to ignore him, looking away from the intruders in disgust. Rocco smirked. He hadn't seen the rebellious side of her and liked it. Of course, he knew if she pushed these clowns too far, she'd be joining Rocco for an unpleasant ride in the cage of a cold steel paddy wagon.

"Tony, are you alright? she asked, her expression softening. "Are they hurting you?"

"Tony? Tony?" Onion Breath mocked. "What gives, Balliro? She doesn't even know your real name."

"Leave her be," Rocco appealed, risking a beating. "This has nothing to do with her."

"We'll see about that," said Onion Breath's partner as he pulled Rocco's arms behind his back, yanked them forcibly upward for added measure, and fastened handcuffs. Anna Maria, to his relief, was spared the agony of shackles but there was little doubt that she would be accompanying him to the station for questioning.

"Alright, folks. Let's move it."

The foursome trudged out of the apartment with Onion Breath leading the way, his grubby hand gripping Anna Maria's slender upper arm. Rocco trailed several paces behind. The cold steel of the cuffs bit deeply into his flesh. It was a familiar sensation. He twisted his wrists in an attempt to ease the pressure but it proved fruitless.

The assemblage shuffled along the narrow corridor. Upon reaching the landing that fed a steeply pitched staircase, an elderly resident cracked opened her apartment door and curiously peered out. She recoiled and slammed the door shut as onion breath scolded, "There's nothing to see here, ma'am. Get back inside."

Anna Maria turned and looked back over her shoulder, a gloomy, fearful expression spreading across her pretty face. She began sobbing. Rocco yearned to put his arm around her and tell her it would be alright. It was obvious that she'd never been arrested.

The entourage reached the bottom of the staircase and stepped outside into the chill. His curiosity piqued as they marched solemnly along the sidewalk, Rocco turned to his captor and began, "Hey, you gotta tell me ..."

"Yeah? What is it, Balliro?"

"How'd you guys find me so quick?"

The cop flipped his head once, gesturing toward a man who was in the company of a plainclothes cop. They were standing adjacent to a taxi which was idling curbside, its exhaust pulsing wispy vapors into the night air. The man with the detective wore a striped engineer's cap that looked awfully familiar.

Then it dawned on him. The cops had obviously canvassed the area cab drivers, asking if any of them had picked up a fare fitting Rocco's description. Armed with that evidence, it was simply a matter of ascertaining the Beacon Street pick up location.

As he followed Anna Maria into the steel confines of a waiting paddy wagon, Rocco's suspicions were confirmed.

"That's him, boss!" trumpeted the cabbie excitedly, pointing out the robbery suspect for the benefit of the Boston Police detective, who sported a smug look and nodded. "That's the guy I drove to the North End."

CHAPTER 6

"There's only two people in life you should lie to ...the
police and your girlfriend." – Jack Nicholson

This particular Sunday evening had started off routinely
enough. He left the apartment he shared with girlfriend Toby
Wagner at around ten o'clock, stepping on to a hushed Kelton
Street. Most of the residents had already retired for the night.
A long strand of automobiles lined the street, silently awaiting
the morning commute.

An oppressive heat wave that had saturated the Boston
area for more than a week finally loosened its grip. In its
place, an invigorating Canadian air mass had moved in to
soothe folks who'd grown weary of swelter and sweat. Of
course, there was surely more sultry weather yet ahead when
July yielded to August. But for now, the public could once
again enjoy, in relative comfort, such simple acts as walking
the family dog, tossing a ball in the park with the kids, or, in
Rocco Anthony Balliro's case, robbing a jewelry store.

Reaching his car in a nearby lot, Rocco keyed the lock,
swung open the wide door, and slid on to the leather bucket
seat.

He didn't start the vehicle right away. Instead, he sat for
a few moments and admired the interior trim. Admittedly,
Rocco obsessed over his car and would seldom pass up an
opportunity to brag about it.

"I bought a 1961 Oldsmobile Starfire," Rocco once
boasted in admiration to a rapt audience of male car enthusiasts
during an outing at a local drinking establishment. "It's a
beautifully-crafted four door hard top with dual exhaust and
electric windows."

Toby was indifferent when it came to his pride and joy. "It's a guy thing," she would say to him.

Several days earlier, seeking relief from the heat, he and Toby had taken the kids out for a ride. There was no better way to cool off in the summer, in his opinion, than taking a long, leisurely drive with the windows rolled down. It was one of his favorite pastimes.

Spinning the tuner dial across the radio chatter as Rocco drove, Toby happened upon one of her favorite songs. She immediately cranked up the pulsating volume and joined Fats Domino in singing his rendition of "Blueberry Hill." Mark, seated in the back seat with his sister, giggled as his off-tune mother tried in vain to belt out the melody.

The wind in the willow played
Love's sweet melody
But all of those vows we made
Were never to be
Though we're apart
You're part of me still
For you were my thrill
On Blueberry Hill.

With thoughts of Toby rippling through his mind, Rocco fired up the Olds, flipped on the headlights, and guided the burly automobile on to Kelton Street. He punched the accelerator, just to hear the familiar eight cylinders sing.

His destination was only several blocks distant and he could have easily walked. But lately, Rocco felt vulnerable on the streets. Not that he had many enemies to speak of. That he was aware of anyway. But having several thousand pounds of forged steel wrapped around him was a welcome safeguard.

Wheeling the Oldsmobile on to Commonwealth Avenue, Rocco made his way into Cleveland Circle, where he parked in front of an array of storefronts. Exiting the car, he walked toward a small coffee shop. Rocco paused in front of the café where he and Toby had enjoyed breakfast on several occasions. As he peered through the thick panes of glass, Rocco spotted his friend, Gianni Saroni, seated at a small table in the shadows.

As Rocco opened the door and entered, a familiar bell jingled to announce his arrival. He noted there were just two occupants in the café besides himself – Saroni and the proprietor. When she heard the bell, Sophie, who was standing behind a long Formica counter, glanced up and greeted him with an inviting smile.

"Hello, Anthony," she sang cheerfully.

"Sophie, you're looking lovely as usual."

She blushed like a woman half her seventy years and replied, "Oh Anthony, I'm sure you say that to all the girls."

"Nope, just special ones," he said with a wink.

She reached up with the flat of a wrinkled hand and fluffed her hair, gray and dignified.

"Where's hubby tonight?"

"Maurice? Oh, I sent him home hours ago," she tersely replied. "That old geezer was falling asleep on the job again!"

Rocco chortled and she joined him in laughter. Sophie was a sweet old lady and had been married to that geezer Maurice for fifty years. Sophie often enjoyed sharing, with anyone who would listen, that 1912 was a significant time in history. "That was the year that Fenway Park first opened and the year the *Titanic* tragically sank," she would recite, as she had so many times before. "But it was also the year that I finally got my hooks in Maurice."

"So you've been together for, um, must be fifty years," Rocco would acknowledge.

"Yes, sir," a beaming Sophie proudly boasted. She must have been a knockout in her day, he thought. "As of last month."

"I'm impressed."

"Me too," she said, giggling. "I'm not quite sure how I did it. He can be such a stubborn old fool at times."

Fifty years, thought Rocco with utter amazement. Five decades. It was such a long time to spend together. At the age of twenty-six himself, it was difficult to get his hands around it. How could a person do any *one* thing for fifty years? It was entirely inconceivable.

"Can I get you a slice of apple pie? she asked. "Just came out of the oven."

"No thanks, honey, gotta try and stay slim."

"Slim!" she chided. "Skinny is more like it. One of these days, Anthony, I'm going to put some meat on those scrawny bones of yours."

"Well, how 'bout we start with a cup of your delicious coffee?"

"Sure," she said. "I'll bring it right over."

Rocco walked past the counter and the row of evenly-spaced stools. In recent weeks, he and Toby had sat here and gorged on heaping platefuls of scrambled eggs, home fries, and strips of sizzling bacon. "None better in all of Brighton," Sophie would boast. He would have to agree.

Rocco reached the table were Saroni patiently waited. Sliding out a chair, he gently lowered his six-foot frame.

Saroni, who Rocco and many others in their circle of friends and associates thought was the spitting image of handsome film and stage actor Warren Beatty, raised his mug and noisily slurped the contents.

"Didn't your mother ever teach you manners?" Rocco admonished.

"Didn't your mother ever teach you not to flirt with old women?" replied Saroni, who was short in stature but tall in attitude.

Rocco grinned. He always enjoyed the banter between them. When it came to sarcastic sparring, there were few who could deliver sharp-tongued barbs like Saroni.

"So what'd you have in mind for tonight?"

"I was thinking we'd do that place over in Jamaica Plain."

"The one on Centre Street?" Saroni asked.

"Yeah."

Their conversation was interrupted by Sophie, who arrived with a freshly brewed pot of coffee. As steam spiraled from the pot, the heady aroma infiltrated the area.

"Would you like me to freshen yours, Anthony?" she asked as she refilled Saroni's cup.

"Sure, thanks."

"Just let me know if you boys change your minds about that apple pie."

"Tell you what, darling," Rocco offered. "Why not box up a slice and I'll bring it home for Toby. I'm sure she'll appreciate a little midnight snack."

"Coming right up," Sophie sang cheerily as she sauntered back to her work area.

When she was out of earshot, Rocco and Gianni resumed their discussion, although there was little to add. More or less, it had been decided that tonight's menu, aside from coffee and apple pie, would feature a visit to a jewelry showroom in a small secluded block of storefronts in Jamaica Plain.

Rocco eased the Oldsmobile along Centre Street, applying pressure to the brake until the sedan slowed to a crawl. The Starfire was built for power and speed and the horses resisted his effort. This vehicle, as he described it, yearned to run. He often fantasized someday taking on the cops in a death-defying high speed chase and had no doubt he would leave them choking in a cloud of dust.

Coasting slowly past the front of the target building, Rocco took another glimpse through rectangular glass display windows that fronted the jewelry store. He'd cased this location twice before. The interior illumination was limited to backlit display cases which held a wide assortment of watches, rings, bracelets, necklaces, and a medley of individual, polished gemstones.

Turning into a driveway that led to the rear of the building, Rocco killed the headlights. A small café, situated at the end of the block of businesses, was dark and evidently unoccupied, as he'd hoped. Thankfully, it seemed that the garish, green-lettered neon sign proclaiming the restaurant as OPEN ALL NIGHT was not entirely accurate.

Rocco nosed the Starfire into a narrow alleyway that paralleled the rear of the building and led to an alternate egress to Centre Street. There was very little light and it took a moment for his eyes to adjust. Once he was able to see with some clarity, Rocco scanned the unmarked, evenly-spaced doors, counting aloud until he reached the delivery entrance for the jewelry business. A lack of signage was a weak deterrent. Alarms, on the other hand, concerned him. But he had determined this store was not equipped.

"That's the one," he said, pointing to the door. Saroni hadn't joined him on the earlier scouting missions.

"Uh huh."

Rocco pulled further ahead and parked the Oldsmobile on the left side of the alley beneath a large tree, obscuring the vehicle from view. He cut the motor, immersing the narrow passage in silence.

One of the decisions the pair had made while at Sophie's café was that Rocco would execute the break in. He would make the grab solo. Gianni, meanwhile, would remain in the car as lookout. The lightweight haul from the jewelry store display cases was a one man job. Considering the late hour and the remote location of the store, they didn't anticipate any trouble. But if something did go awry there was no need for both of them to get collared.

"Alright," said Rocco, drawing a deep breath. Adrenaline began to surge through his body. "Hand me the bar, would ya?"

Saroni leaned forward and grasped a two-foot-long steel pry bar that was wedged on the floorboards. Heedful not to gouge the Starfire's leather seats with the tool's sharp claw, Saroni guided it to his partner. Rocco took hold, opened the door, and stepped out.

"I won't be long."

"Sure," said Saroni, as he reached across and pulled the door quietly closed. Rocco approached the building with catlike stealth and the confidence of a man who'd done this dozens of times before. Reaching the entrance, he noted a simple rectangular placard affixed to the surface which read DELIVERIES. There was nothing to indicate that it was a jewelry store.

As he readied the steel bar, gripping it tightly, Rocco studied the fortified enclosure. Reinforced steel, he thought, as he ran his fingertips along the sturdy framework. The store owner had taken some steps to keep his valuables inside and undesirables outside, it seemed. This one might be more difficult than anticipated.

Rocco crouched lower and dug the business end of the steel bar into a slight gap – little more than a sliver – between the door and frame. He was just about to pop the assembly when he heard a noise nearby.

To his right, he detected what sounded like a door opening. *It's the café*, he thought with mounting dread. The café that, at first glance, looked closed. But now there was someone exiting through the rear door. "What the f ..."

The breath caught in his throat and his heart began to pound. His muscles grew taut with apprehension.

Who could it be? Who was coming out of the café at the worst possible time? Could it be a lingering employee, readying the establishment for the next day?

At first, Rocco was unable to budge. But soon he sprang into action. Grasping the pry bar, he bent it downward so it was flush against the door frame. He prayed that it wouldn't dislodge and clatter to the asphalt. Thankfully, the heavy steel rod remained firmly wedged in place.

As he watched and waited, poised to take flight, Rocco's worst fears were realized. Emerging from the café was a pair of uniformed Boston police officers. The light in the alleyway, while minimal, glinted off their badges. One after another, they stepped into the alley, no more than twenty feet from where Rocco stood. As the two policemen caught sight of him, astonishment spread over faces that were illuminated by light streaming from the café's interior.

Rocco began to tremble. Clenching his teeth firmly together, he turned pallid as the blood drained from his face. An odd thought crossed his mind, rippling along frayed nerves. He figured he might as well have been wearing a sign that read: *Hello, officers, yes, I was trying to burglarize this store.* Somewhere in the depths of his reeling psyche, Rocco could almost hear the distant, but all too familiar metallic clang of a jail cell door slamming shut.

"Hey!" shouted one of the cops, obviously just as stunned as Rocco was over the encounter. "What the hell are you…"

"Officers!" he interrupted, now thinking quick on his feet. "Christ, you scared the crap out of me."

"What the hell is going on here!" shouted a middle-aged, portly officer, who had his palm on the butt of his holstered service revolver.

"I'm sorry, sir, but I had to take a piss," Rocco replied, hoping he sounded convincing. He hazarded a sideways glance at the incriminating pry bar as the cops drew near. In the low light, the steel bar could easily be mistaken for part of the door frame. Of course, if it somehow became dislodged and fell to the pavement, all bets were off. If not, he might just walk away from this robbery-interrupted without so much as a scratch.

"What's your name?" asked the cop's partner, who was easily twenty years the man's junior. "Johnny," Rocco lied, borrowing the first name that came to mind. "Johnny D'Angelo."

"Where you from, Johnny?" asked the cop, continuing his alleyway interrogation. Rocco sized him up. This one was in pretty good shape. Rocco might not be able to outrun him if it came to a foot chase.

"Roxbury. Annunciation Road."

"Oh yeah? How'd you end up in Jamaica Plain?"

He'd anticipated the question long before the muscled-headed cop asked it. In a cool, unwavering tone, Rocco replied, "I was playing cards with friends. After the game, I walked a little ways waiting for a cab to come by. But I had to take a mean piss so I ducked in here."

Nothing was said for a moment as the cops digested what he'd told them. He had to make a decision and soon. At any given moment, this pair of Sherlock Holmes wannabes might just wake up and realize that they'd stumbled upon a burglary in progress. They were, after all, standing at the rear of a jewelry store. They might decide it would be in their best interest to slap the bracelets on him, at least until they figured out what he was *really* up to.

"Here. Take a look at this," said Rocco, as he dug for an item buried in the depths of his pocket.

"Hey!" shouted the senior of the two police officers, instinctively drawing his revolver. "Keep your friggin' hands where I can see them!"

"Easy, officer, easy," Rocco soothed, realizing he'd made the move a tad too quickly. Without being asked to do so, he raised his arms in the air.

He wondered, at that moment, how Saroni was reacting. He'd obviously seen or heard the commotion. He was likely halfway back to Brighton – on foot.

"Officers, I'm not armed," he assured them. "Let me show you."

"Alright, but slowly."

He felt as if he was navigating a high wire without a safety net. One stumble and the next and last sound he might hear was a firing gun.

As instructed, Rocco lowered his left arm while keeping the right pointing skyward. Without making any jerky, unnecessary movements, he slid his hand into the front pocket. He slowly withdrew his hand, palm facing upward. As the cops looked on with suspicion, he unfurled his fingers one at a time, revealing a sizeable wad of rolled up cash.

Even under the dim, diffuse light spilling from the café, Rocco could discern that ever-familiar, hungry expression on the faces of the two cops. Growing up on the streets of Boston's North End, Rocco often heard tale of *offerings* made to law enforcement, from lowly beat cops to the highest ranking police officials. Many were on the dole and corruption was rampant. Not that he blamed them for accepting *gifts* – who could expect them to get by on a police officer's salary, after all?

"Where'd you get all that cash?" questioned the suspicious senior officer.

"I won it gambling," Rocco answered, extending the roll of money enticingly closer to his mark. "I was playing cards and had a coupla good hands."

The hook had been set. Now all Rocco had to do was reel in the catch. But just when he thought the bribe might be accepted, the lead officer turned to his partner who was frowning with disapproval.

"Put your money away, D'Angelo, and come with us," the officer insisted after a pause. He sounded perturbed. Rocco gathered he wasn't pleased with his inability to accept the *donation* thanks to his apparently honest cohort. Had he been alone, this veteran cop would likely have taken the dough.

"Where to, officers?" a disappointed Rocco asked.

The younger of the crime fighting pair, who had little to say to that point, chimed in and said, "We need to make sure you are who you say you are."

"Sure, sure," Rocco acknowledged. "I understand."

He actually didn't understand. Neither had requested an ID which Rocco wasn't carrying anyway. How would they determine if his name was really Johnny D'Angelo?

"There's a callbox in front of this building," the junior of the twosome continued as he strode forward to collect the suspect. "We'll just take a quick stroll and call the precinct. If your story checks out, you'll be on your way in no time."

Perfect, Rocco thought, as he considered his options. Just perfect. A callbox right here at the scene of the caper. How convenient. Could he have made it any easier for this duo? One minute, they're feeding their faces on a midnight meal at the *closed* café – likely complimentary – and the next, they're on the precipice of making an arrest of an ex-convict who'd been partly responsible for reducing the inventories of area jewelry stores for several months.

Rocco trailed the senior police officer. The man's partner fell in step behind him. The trio marched single file in silence toward the end of the alley. Filtered light glowed from streetlamps spaced along nearby Centre Street.

A pit formed in Rocco's gut as they approached his Oldsmobile. If the cops spotted his partner sitting idly in the front seat, it was all over.

Thankfully, there was no sign of Saroni. As he and his entourage filed past the Starfire, Rocco glanced and saw the car was empty. Obviously, his accomplice had bolted. If the shoe was on the other foot, Rocco would likely have hatched a rescue plan, even at his own peril.

But then, Rocco Balliro had always been something of a risk taker. As a youth stirring mischief in the North End, he was usually the first to hurl a stone through a glass pane of a vacant building or snatch a piece of fruit from a peddler's cart and thrill in the chase that inevitably followed. And later, when it came to the real life game of cops and robbers, he usually played it to the maximum. He felt confident in his guile and cunning, and believed he was intellectually superior to the police who often pursued him.

"The cops do what they do for a living," Rocco once explained. "They earn a paycheck whether they catch the bad guys or not. For people like me, though, it's a matter of survival. We can't feed our families from behind bars."

As Rocco and his escorts passed the Olds, neither of the cops cast even a wary glance at the vehicle. They had, however, taken up a position to either side of their suspect instead of front to back.

Perplexed, Rocco wondered about the lack of handcuffs. Not that it upset him, of course. As long as the cuffs remained attached to their belts and not his wrists, the avenue of escape remained open.

There were times, Rocco mulled as he trudged along, that a misguided guardian angel of criminal activity seemed to be looking over his shoulder. This was one of those moments.

As the trio approached the callbox, Rocco again considered his options. He had to make a decision and soon.

"Alright, Mr. ..."

"D'Angelo," Rocco answered without hesitation. It was one of the oldest tricks in the book and he wasn't about to fall for it. The senior cop was attempting to bait him into revealing his true name.

"Uh huh," the flatfoot muttered, obviously disappointed. "D'Angelo. Alright, Mr. D'Angelo, you stay put, ya hear?"

Rocco nodded, fighting off an urge to grin. *What an imbecile*, he thought.

While his partner kept a watchful eye, the senior officer strode to the callbox, opened it, and lifted the receiver to his ear.

Rocco strained to listen. The conversation was muffled. But he was able to make out several chilling words which triggered a physical response. He was suddenly awash in adrenaline when he heard the cop ask, "How close is the wagon?"

Several tense seconds ticked by. The cop continued to speak into the receiver but Rocco assumed it was just a ruse to kill time and keep their suspect off-balance. But that wasn't the case – he was already in flight mode.

The officer standing behind him must have sensed something. He reached out and grasped Rocco's upper arm. He could feel the man's fingers squeeze the flesh of his bicep. Rocco braced for the inevitable. Soon, he would feel cold metal meeting the bare skin of his wrists.

At that pivotal moment, the unmistakable silhouette of a Boston Police Department paddy wagon appeared, rumbling along Centre Street. Rocco surmised that the wagon must have been nearby when the dispatcher received the summons to transport one suspect to the precinct. As soon as he caught sight of the jail-on-wheels and heard the telltale metallic sound of handcuffs being readied, Rocco was off like a shot.

As he bolted along Centre Street in Jamaica Plain, Rocco Anthony Balliro gave in to an overwhelming urge to look over his shoulder, risking a stumble. The darkened street behind him was clear. The cops, it seemed, had fallen off the foot pursuit. To his relief, but not at all surprising, the two officers who initially gave chase were unable to keep pace. Rocco was acutely aware, however, the reprieve would be short lived. In no time at all, the area would likely be crawling with patrol cars. He slowed to a brisk walk and allowed his head to clear before weighing his options.

CHAPTER 7

"A recent police study found that you're much more likely to get shot by a fat cop if you run." – Dennis Miller

An exasperated Gianni Saroni collapsed in a heap on the worn couch. In the aftermath of their botched robbery attempt and Rocco's subsequent arrest, his stress level had reached a fever pitch.

Leaning back into the cushions, Gianni tightly closed his weary, bloodshot eyes. When he opened them again, he saw that Toby was standing over him, her arms folded across her chest.

Standing only five feet tall, she was nonetheless imposing. If looks could harm, he was in trouble. He suddenly regretted making the trip to the apartment. He should have gone to some barroom - any barroom - had a drink or three, and called Toby by phone instead.

"Where's Tony?" she asked, her tone razor edged.

He shook his head and responded, "I'm not sure."

"What happened?" she prodded.

He looked at Toby, seeking her sympathy. He had, after all, just watched his best friend get collared by the cops.

She wasn't buying it. He'd woken her – it was nearing two in the morning – and she looked the part. Her hair was bunched up in rollers and her eyes were puffy.

He had a soft spot for crying women and noted that Toby's eyes were welling up with tears. Gianni rested the flat of his hands, palms down, on his thighs and stared at them. "Toby, I'm sorry," he said without looking up at her. "But he got pinched."

Her voice hitched slightly as she fought back the tears. "Where is he? Where did they take him?"

"Not sure," he replied. "We were in Jamaica Plain so I guess he's in their lock up – maybe JP or West Roxbury. I dunno for sure."

Toby sat down in the tattered chair opposite the couch. "Did you see him get arrested?"

"Uh no," he replied, wondering why that made a difference. Considering that his cohort was on foot, it was highly unlikely that he could have eluded the police for very long. "I didn't see them take him away. The last time I saw Roc … um … Anthony, he was running along Centre Street with a couple cops chasing him. I didn't hang around to watch."

Toby got up and made her way over to the kitchen counter. She removed a cigarette from a pack that rested next to a row of cereal and cookie boxes. As she lit it, Toby held the pack out to Gianni, who shook his head. He probably could have used one to calm his frayed nerves. He watched her take a long drag and noticed, from across the room, that her hand was trembling.

"What were you guys doing?"

"Huh?"

"Doing? What were you doing?"

As he pondered the question, Gianni realized there was no need to beat around the bush. He was aware that Rocco limited discussion about his criminal exploits – for her own protection. But she certainly wasn't ignorant. She knew her boyfriend wasn't running off to an office job when he slipped from the apartment each night.

Matter of factly, he finally said, "A jewelry store, we was robbing a jewelry store."

Toby remained silent and returned to the chair. Gianni took the opportunity to stand and stretch his legs. The joints in his knees and hips protested. As he shuffled across the room, he glanced down at his shoes and noticed they were covered with caked-on mud. He must have picked it up while hiding in the brush as the cops escorted Rocco from the alleyway.

"I'll have that smoke now, if you don't mind," he said as slid one from the pack and struck a match. Gianni nearly dropped the burning match when Toby blurted out, "Do you think Tony will be going back to prison?"

He looked at her incredulously. Thankfully, she remained motionless in the chair, facing forward. He didn't want her to see his expression.

"No," he lied. "No, of course not."

The receding flame reached his fingertips and he shook out the match. The cigarette dangled from his lips, unlit. Just as Gianni prepared to strike another, a knock sounded at the apartment door. *Tap-tap-tap*, with a pause between each. Startled, the cigarette fell from his mouth.

"Jesus ..." he said, in a low tone.

"Who the hell could that be?" whispered Toby as she stood bolt upright. Her face blanched.

Gianni, meanwhile, could feel his pulse in his throat. He frantically looked for another way out, but aside from the windows, which held an improbable fall, there was no other outlet. He was trapped like a rat.

"It must be the cops," he moaned. "They tracked me here somehow. Rocco's car! Yeah, that's it. His car was parked in the alleyway. I circled back after Rocco took off and drove the damn thing back here. Jesus!"

"They have no idea he lives here," Toby said as she made her way across the room. "You're not making sense."

"Wait," he urged in a panic. "Wait a minute."

"Gianni," she began impatiently. "If it's the police, they're coming in whether you want them to or not."

Reaching the door, she slid the security chain along its channel and then flipped the deadbolt. As she did, the individual on the other side turned the knob and the door began to slowly open. The tears she had held back earlier now flowed unabated, streaming down her cheeks in a torrent of relief.

"Oh thank God," Toby cried out as she leaped to embrace the disheveled man standing at the threshold. His clothing was tattered and dirty and he had a few minor facial scratches but was otherwise in one piece and a welcome sight.

"Hey, beautiful," said Rocco, who was sporting a huge, ear to ear grin as he embraced her and winked at his associate. "Hey, Gianni."

Sitting on the end of the couch previously occupied by his accomplice, Rocco drank a beer. He tipped the bottle and poured it down his parched throat. He didn't recall a beer ever tasting so good.

"Honey, slow down," asserted Toby, who was sitting adjacent to him on the sofa. "You'll make yourself sick."

"I know, sorry, but I have a killer thirst," he explained, wiping sudsy residue from the corners of his mouth with his sleeve. The shirt had a significant tear near the elbow. He didn't recall ripping it but figured he must have caught it on a bramble while ducking into someone's yard.

"Let me get you another," she offered.

"I really thought they had you," said Saroni.

Rocco glanced up, shook his head, and said, "C'mon, you gotta give me more credit than that."

Saroni was perched on the chair opposite Rocco. He was puffing away on a cigarette and nervously tapping his fingers on the armrest.

"How the hell did you get away?"

"I'm still pretty fast, I guess," Rocco replied, smirking.

Toby returned with his beer and cuddled next to him. The warmth of her body felt good. He tipped the bottle to his mouth and this time, took a single swig. His thirst was finally waning.

"You didn't run all the way from Jamaica Plain to Brighton, did you?" Saroni asked. "That has to be at least …"

"Five miles," Rocco interrupted, chuckling softly. "And no, I didn't run the whole way."

Perhaps not five miles but pretty close considering the zigzag maneuvers he made while eluding the police dragnet.

As he shared his story with Toby and Gianni, Rocco pivoted slightly. He reached over the high back of the couch, moved the curtain aside and peered at Kelton Street below. It was still pitch dark but in several hours, the sun would begin its rise and transform one of the longest nights in his memory into day. As mentally and physically exhausted as he was, however, his two enthralled companions wouldn't think about letting him escape – at least not like the Boston cops had earlier – without first sharing his harrowing tale.

"Not much to tell, really," he began. "One of the cops called for a wagon and once I saw it coming up the street, I just took off."

Rocco recalled that after he made his initial break from the stunned cops, they indeed gave chase. But after a brief stretch of roadway, they quit the foot pursuit. They clamored for him to stop, threatening to shoot. He considered for a moment that they might just do it to save face. Better to bring down a fleeing burglary suspect than come up empty-handed and be ridiculed.

"What the hell were they doing in the alley?"

"They came out of that café," Rocco answered. "They were feeding their faces, I guess."

"What'd you tell them?"

"That I had to take a piss," he answered with a grin. "On the way home from a card game."

"Original."

"Had to think quick," Rocco said. "I'm gonna have to apologize to Johnny D'Angelo though."

"Yeah? What for?"

Grimacing, he replied, "I used his name."

"You're shittin' me!" Saroni exclaimed, momentarily forgetting about the two babies sleeping in a nearby bedroom.

Toby reminded him. "Shhh," she interjected. Incredibly, they'd somehow slept through the commotion.

Saroni glanced at Toby apologetically and mouthed the word "sorry," then continued, adjusting his voice to a lower tone. "So you told them you were D'Angelo?"

"Yeah," Rocco acknowledged. "I'm sure they've been to his place over in Roxbury by now."

"Jesus, he's gonna blow a gasket."

"I'll make it up to him."

Rocco took another draw on the beer bottle. It was nearly empty and Toby, ever attentive, looked at him as if to ask if he wanted another. He shook his head. He didn't want to get drunk, although he certainly deserved it after the ordeal he'd just been through.

"No cuffs, huh?" said Saroni, stating the obvious. He was referring, of course, to the inexplicable failure of the Boston police officers to secure their detainee while they still had a chance.

"I can't figure that one out," Rocco said, shaking his head. "The cuffs didn't come out until the wagon was heading up the street."

"I'm sure they'll take some heat for that."

"Serves them right, I guess. I'm not bitching though. If they did their job, I'd be going back to the can."

Rocco glanced at Toby, who forced a wan smile. In just a matter of weeks, he'd grown to admire this little stalwart of a woman. She was a pillar of strength. Her children, certainly, and now her live-in boyfriend, were recipients of her unflagging devotion and mental toughness. Rocco often described her as "cool as a cucumber."

But while she imparted external tenacity, Toby also exhibited an element of deep-seated, underlying weariness. And it wasn't just derived from recent strife but rather stemmed from a long-term reckless, devil-may-care existence merged with a contentious relationship with her negligent mother. He understood that their chance meeting at the New Yorker in early July was indicative of her lifestyle. She frequented clubs, drank heavily at times, and while he had yet to witness it for himself, he suspected she dabbled in drugs. But still, he found himself captivated by this pint-sized, twenty-one-year-old mother of two, whose smile could instantly warm him. He had fallen for her.

"So how *did* you get back to Brighton?" asked Saroni, interrupting his wandering thoughts.

"Took a cab," he answered smugly.

"A cab? In that neighborhood? At that hour?"

"I had a little help."

After he gave the cops the slip, Rocco did, indeed, begin to travel toward Brighton. At times, he lightly jogged to cover more ground but for the most part, he simply walked. Each time a patrol car rumbled past, the deceptive fugitive was already concealed behind a tree, hedges, or crouched alongside parked cars. Rocco confessed it was flattering to have so much interest devoted to him.

"I think half the police force was out looking for me," he said, beaming. "You'd think they were chasing the Boston Strangler, for Crissake."

"What happened to your clothes?" Toby asked, pointing at the ripped sleeves.

She had remained taciturn to that point, indicative of her attitude toward the whole messy event. She didn't much care about the crime the duo committed or the ensuing police chase or any of the sordid drama, for that matter. She was only concerned for Rocco's well-being.

"I had to dive into a shrub when a cop car whipped around a corner," he answered, gently rubbing the scratch on his cheek. "I think it was full of thorns."

For the first time since he'd arrived safely home, Rocco noticed that his hands were filthy. He was in serious need of a hot shower.

"So who helped you out?" Saroni persisted.

"There was a young couple sitting on their stoop drinking a couple of beers," Rocco recalled. "I asked if they'd call a cab. The girl ran inside and made the call. I offered them some money but they wouldn't take it. Nice kids."

"You were lucky to find someone outside at that time of night."

"Yeah, guess I was."

Rocco stretched his arms toward the ceiling and yawned. Saroni picked up on the signal and said, "It's late. I should get going. Alright if I use your car?"

"Yeah. Just park it off the street."

"Sure, no problem," Saroni agreed, as he rose from the chair and strode toward the door. As he stepped across the threshold into the hallway, he turned and said, "G'night, Toby." He sounded apologetic.

"G'night," she said as she closed, chained, and bolted the door behind him.

Meanwhile, with a great degree of difficulty, Rocco had urged his aching body upright. When she turned and saw him, she literally ran headlong into his waiting arms. He winced when their bodies impacted. "Tony, I was so worried," she cried.

"There was nothing to worry about," he insisted. Fingers of fatigue were clutching at him and sleep beckoned. A pillow would feel nice against his face.

He draped his arm around her soft, delicate shoulders and gathered her close. Artificially joined at the hip, they stumbled clumsily along the hallway. They resisted an urge to laugh, mindful of the sleeping children.

"Toby?" he whispered softly as they squeezed, side by side, through the narrow opening.

"Yes?"

"Remember the other night, when we were watching that cop show on television?"

"Yeah," she replied. "Umm … *Highway Patrol*, wasn't it?"

"Yeah. What'd I tell ya?"

She knew exactly where he was going with this peculiar line of questioning. Reaching his side of the bed, Toby fluffed his pillow. She smiled and imparted, "You said it wasn't real because on the show, the police always catch the crook."

He grinned at her wordlessly as he slid beneath the soft bedcovers and put his head down to sleep.

CHAPTER 8

"Children are the world's most valuable resource and its
best hope for the future." – John F. Kennedy

Canned audience laughter spilled from the speakers mounted
on the front panel of the brand-new RCA color television. The
console, centered along the main wall in Toby's living room,
was nearly twice the size of its black and white predecessor
and usually had a fantastic picture. But for some reason, on
this mid-November afternoon, the reception was a little too
blurry for Rocco's taste. He got up from the couch, where
he had been sitting with Toby, and shuffled across the floor
toward the offending box.

"It's fine," Toby insisted.

"It's fuzzy," he argued.

He began to reposition the twin rabbit ears jutting from
the top of the box. On the screen, a bespectacled Steve Allen
performed a hilarious skit with funny man Irwin Corwin.

"I'm missing my show," she said with a hint of a childish
whine. Rocco ignored her pleas and bent one of the two wires
toward a window while leaving the other upright, pointing
at the ceiling. The manipulation yielded the desired effect.
Comedian Allen's familiar grin came into sharper clarity.

He looked over his shoulder, giving her the recalcitrant
I told you so look. Toby just glared at him playfully, and
scrunched her face in an expression wordlessly agreeing
that the "Amazing Rocco Balliro" was right yet again. She
waved her hand, indicating that he was still impeding her
view. Stepping aside, he announced, "I'm gonna go make
a sandwich." It was mid-afternoon and he'd yet to have
anything for lunch. "Want one?"

"All set," she replied without taking her eyes off the console. She began giggling like a schoolgirl. On the screen, Professor Corey, a frequent guest on Allen's show, was being guided out of the studio by a pair of stone-faced, burly stage hands. It was all part of the gag, of course, but Toby enjoyed it.

She loved watching television, he found, and more so since the color set had arrived several days earlier. It was one of the first in their building and was delivered by a pair of his associates. *The good life*, Rocco thought with a guilty smirk, *care of hijacked trailer trucks.*

Four months had elapsed since the late July night when he slipped from the clutches of a pair of inept Boston police officers.

Prior to that ill-fated night, Rocco was robbing and stealing with reckless abandon, forcing his way into Boston-area businesses and residences. He'd mastered the "fine art" of breaking and entering in the night, as he described it.

To hear him tell it, one got the impression that Rocco often committed robberies not so much for the income but instead for the sheer thrill of the act. In other words, it wasn't always financial gain that was the driving force behind his criminal enterprise but rather an egotistical rush that spurred him along.

But since the near miss in Jamaica Plain, Rocco had adopted more cautious tactics. He began to set his sights on ventures with prudence. For instance, he sought out standalone or secluded stores as opposed to those adjacent to other businesses where employees – or cops – might be lurking after hours. In addition, Rocco selected the best day of the week and time to execute the theft only after checking out his potential targets with added vigilance.

His recent criminal escapades earned a tidy sum, although the take, after unloading the goods through a well-established network of fences, typically yielded thirty cents on the dollar. Lucrative enough to support himself, but Rocco faced a troubling question that he'd been wrestling with as the warmth of summer months drifted relentlessly toward the deep chill of New England winter. Could he give up the only life he'd known since he was a teenager? Would he be able to forgo his illicit activities in favor of a job? Could he tolerate a mundane existence and the inherent financial shortcomings of a legitimate career?

He'd considered the possibilities after his release from prison and now the thought again crossed his mind. He gazed at Toby, a smile adorning her pretty face. Could he do it for her? And for her two children, Mark and Bernice, whom he'd grown quite attached to since he'd moved in? Could it be that the life he led, monopolized by crime and incarceration, was changing for the better by virtue of the warm, loving embrace of this family he now cherished? Was he suited for the stability of a domesticated existence with his girlfriend Toby and her children?

He shelved the thought for the time being. It wasn't a decision he needed to make right away. Perhaps, for the time being, he would scale back on his activities while he weighed the pros and cons of life as a legitimate working stiff.

Rocco began to make his way to the refrigerator but first, he diverted toward the kid's bedroom. Skimming silently along, he was wary of making any undue noise that might wake the napping babies.

Reaching the bedroom, Rocco peered in. Under subtle daylight seeping from around the shades in the window, he could distinguish the shadowy outlines of the two little figures in their beds, both fast asleep. The subdued giggling from the living room, where Toby delighted in the antics of Steve Allen, hadn't disturbed them.

Bernice, just nine months old, was curled in a fetal position in her crib, tucked beneath a knitted blanket while her brother Mark, who would soon be two, had kicked away the covers and was sprawled across his bed.

Rocco considered the little infant for a moment. Her birth name, he learned, was actually Bernice but for reasons never explained, Toby called her Wendy. When he broached the subject, her response was a terse, "I just like the name, that's all." He decided it was best not to press further. Perhaps, the underlying reason could be that the child was named after her father. Maybe Toby, in some small way, sought to severe the connection between her daughter and her incarcerated husband, whom she'd married two years before, in 1960.

One thing was apparent, however. Toby harbored far more love for son Mark than she did for Bernice. At times, she made little effort to conceal her blatant disdain for this innocent infant. It wasn't that Toby was abusive. Certainly not. She fed and clothed the child as needed. But she performed these motherly duties as just that – a duty, with the clinical precision of a hospital nursery staffer.

Mark, on the other hand, was the treasure of her existence. No pedestal was too high, it seemed. Fair-skinned and slight with a thick crop of impossibly jet black hair, Mark would always bring a smile to her face, even when she was in a blue mood. They were virtually inseparable.

Whenever Toby ran an errand, the cherished Mark was ferried along. To the market, the pharmacy, or other errands – it didn't matter. Mother and son were constant companions.

Toby didn't deny the attachment either. She would share comments that family and friends had made about the boundless love she held for her son.

"Toby, I think you may need surgery to remove Mark from your hip," her sister-in-law Beverly once quipped.

Rocco crept soundlessly toward a window that overlooked the rear of the building. The air in the room was stuffy. As he raised the window an inch or two, it squealed in protest. Behind him, Mark stirred.

Pausing for a moment, Rocco waited for the tiny figure to settle back to sleep and then lifted the window a little more, just enough for cool, refreshing air to flow through the gap.

He made a mental note to leave it open just long enough to exchange the stale air. He didn't want the kids to catch a chill.

Rocco approached the bed that was positioned alongside a wall plastered with photos of assorted superheroes, including Batman and Superman. He observed Mark, who was again sleeping soundly. He gazed down at this pint-sized little man, whom he'd grown quite fond of since joining this ready-made family months before. Even in that brief amount of time, he and Toby had gathered a number of endearing vignettes to savor, some quite comical in the aftermath.

On one recent lazy Sunday, for instance, little Mark went missing. He'd been quietly playing with his toys in the bedroom while Toby and Rocco relaxed at the kitchen table, puffing on cigarettes and trading stories.

Rocco chronicled his elementary school years and touched on his mother's quest to steer the Balliro boys on the right path by enrolling them in the North End's highly regarded Saint Mary's parochial school.

"I was an altar boy," he said, placing his hands together as if to pray and bowing his head forward. "Can you believe it? Me, an altar boy?"

Toby laughed at his mockery and said, "While you were hanging out at church, I was beating up twelve-year-old boys."

He donned an amused expression and said, "You're kidding me?"

"Nope – true," she affirmed. "After we moved to Brookline – I think I was nine or ten – a group of bullies came after my brother Mal. He could put up a pretty good fight but there were four of them."

"What'd you do?"

"I always wore heavy shoes," she answered, gesturing toward her feet. "I took one off and started beating them on the head with it, one after another. They all ran away."

Now it was Rocco's turn to laugh. "I could've used you in *my* gang when I was a kid. You were a tough lil' punk, I guess."

They fell into silence. Toby stabbed out the remnants of her cigarette and declared, "Mark seems awfully quiet in there."

She got up from her chair and headed toward the kid's bedroom. Several seconds passed before Rocco heard her call out to her son. All she had to do was utter his name and he instantly knew something was amiss. It was barely discernible but her tone was wavering. "Mark? Mark, honey?"

Rocco was quickly on the way to see what the trouble was when Toby darted from the room, nearly colliding with him.

"What is it?" he asked, catching her in his arms.

"Mark's not in there."

"What do you mean?"

"Where is he?" Her voice rose in pitch as fear welled up.

Rocco stepped around her and peered into the bedroom. Bernice was asleep in her crib. Mark's bed was empty. On a small circular throw rug in the center of the room, several yellow Tonka trucks sat idle. There was, however, no sign of little Mark.

"Closet," uttered Rocco, as he crossed the room in several loping strides. "He must be in the closet!"

He wrenched open the door and crouched to inspect the narrow rectangular space. "Mark, it's Tony. You in there? Mark?"

He expected – actually hoped – to hear Toby's little boy giggle and shout out, "Boo!" Rocco had recently taught him hide n' seek. Instead, nothing. Not a peep. The boy was nowhere to be found.

Without turning around to look at her, Rocco could sense that Toby was growing increasingly frantic.

"Where is he?" she moaned. Tears were streaming down her face. He stood up from his brief search of the closet and reached out to embrace her.

"We'll find him," he assured her. "Don't worry."

Without further delay, they began to scour the apartment, probing beneath beds and behind furniture. They searched each closet. When Mark didn't turn up, they retraced their steps, checking each likely hiding place repeatedly. The pair wound up in the kitchen and paused for a moment to collect their wits.

In crisis, fond memories of Mark crept into Rocco's thoughts. In his mind's eye, he could hear the tiny tot, his voice all at once shrill and sweet, shouting his name from the top of the staircase. Peering through the living room windows, Mark would often scout for Rocco's return from the day's business. Once he spotted the man making his way along the sidewalk, Toby would allow Mark to go out into the hallway where he would wait for the telltale sound of the lobby door opening and closing. It was his signal that his mother's friend had indeed reached the foyer and would soon be ascending the staircase. "Tony!" he would yell excitedly, hugging the man in a warm greeting. "Tony! You're home!" He knew that *Tony* would soon be roughhousing and playing games with him before they all sat down to dinner.

Toby brought him back to the reality of the moment. Trembling, she lamented, "Oh God, where is he?" She began to sob uncontrollably. As Rocco looked on, she lifted the receiver of the telephone mounted on the kitchen wall. Her intentions were obvious.

"Sweetheart, umm, hold on a minute," he calmly urged. He had to deal with this thoughtfully. He didn't want to seem callous, under the circumstances, but the last thing he needed was a bunch of cops traipsing through their apartment. Certainly, they would investigate the claim of a missing child but later, after Mark was reunited with his grateful mother, the cops would likely inquire about the stockpile of electronics, fur coats, and other luxury items neatly stored in a spare closet.

"I know what you're thinking," Toby said. "But Tony, listen, we need their help."

"Look, honey, I agree," he responded in a soothing tone. "But before we call, let's take one more look around, just to be sure."

Toby nodded reluctantly. She dabbed fresh tears from puffy, bloodshot eyes with a handkerchief he'd given her. Rocco crossed to where she stood, gently pried the receiver from her grip, and returned it to the phone cradle.

He wrapped a comforting arm around her slender shoulders. "C'mon," he coaxed. "I'm sure he's just hiding somewhere."

They resumed the search. While Rocco examined beneath the beds again and revisited the closets, Toby walked from room to room, calling out to her son. "Mark!" she shouted. "Mark, where are you, honey?"

As they rummaged through the kid's bedroom closet for a third time, Bernice awoke and began to fuss in the crib. It wasn't lost on Rocco that Toby literally ignored her whimpering infant daughter. He crossed to the crib and stooped over the side to tend to the baby.

"Tony?"

"One minute."

"Tony, I'm calling the police," she defiantly declared. She wheeled and left the room in a huff. Rocco trailed her, but suddenly stopped short. He thought they'd left no stone unturned but apparently that wasn't the case. The door to the utility closet, he noticed, was slightly ajar. Inside, he could hear the muted sound of the clothes dryer tumbling. Toby had earlier tossed in a load of laundry.

They hadn't bothered to look in this particular closet because there wasn't any interior space to speak of: the washer and dryer took up every inch, wall to wall.

As he listened to the rhythmic thump of the spinning dryer drum, a terrible chill ran up his spine. He shuddered violently. *No*, he thought, *it can't be.*

Toby appeared at the threshold of the hallway and stopped. When Rocco hadn't followed her as anticipated, she hung up the phone a second time and returned to investigate.

"What is it?" she asked. The uneasiness in her voice was obvious.

"Stay there," Rocco demanded, raising his hand. He was fearful of what he might discover. The dryer continued its muffled *thump-thump-thump* drumbeat. His heart was suddenly doing the same in his chest.

"What is it?"

He didn't answer. Instead, he reached tentatively for the knob and ever so slowly pulled the door open. A build up of warmth from the dryer rushed out. He drew a deep breath and swallowed hard. Dread washed over him. Reaching for the pull string attached to a light fixture, he gave it a sharp yank. The closet was suddenly flooded with glaring light. Rocco peered inside at the dryer and an expression of relief overspread his face. "I'll be damned," he said.

Toby was now standing behind him. She was unable to see what he was looking at so she nudged him aside and gazed into the brightly lit utility closet. The vision of her beloved Mark, sleeping soundly atop a laundry basket filled halfway to the brim with recently dried bath towels sparked a fresh torrent of tears.

Later, when they could laugh about the trying incident, Toby gently explained to Mark that he nearly frightened her to death and should never, ever hide from her again. The little peanut uttered in response that he was "sleepy."

Somehow, he found the means to climb atop the appliances and into the straw laundry basket. The warmth of the freshly dried towels and vibration of the dryer had literally rocked him to sleep. And obviously, the noise of the machine had drowned out their calls for him.

Rocco, for his part, breathed a sigh of relief, grateful that his worst fears weren't realized and Mark wasn't inside the spinning dryer. Jesus! The thought turned his stomach.

Additionally, his anguish over the cops poking around the apartment was allayed. A little less dramatic than his flight from the inept officers in Jamaica Plain, certainly, but he'd sidestepped another arrest.

Rocco tenderly brushed a stray lock of hair from Mark's forehead with the flat of hand. He had lost track of time as he stood bedside reminiscing and the room was already growing chilly. He quietly closed the window and meandered back to the living room to rejoin Toby.

"Weren't you making a sandwich?" she asked as he sat down next to her, empty-handed.

"Jesus," he said, slapping his palms on his thighs. "I knew I forgot something. I stopped in to check on the kids and lost my train of thought."

"Is Mark alright?"

Mark, he thought. *She's asking about Mark but no mention of Bernice.*

"He's fine. I was just remembering the time he fell asleep in the laundry basket. Funny, huh?"

"Not really," she replied with a thin smile. "Lemme get that sandwich for you. Wanna beer with it?"

"Sure."

After she got up, Rocco shifted his position and promptly sank deep into a failing cushion. He made a mental note to contact his associates and inquire about a new couch.

CHAPTER 9

"Thieves respect property. They merely wish the property
to become their property that they may more perfectly
respect it." – Gilbert K. Chesterton

Beverly Zimmerman shifted the baby stroller in front of her, moving it slightly forward so she could inch closer to the apartment door. Standing before it, she raised her hand and was poised to knock when it unexpectedly swung open, startling her.

"Jesus!" she exclaimed. "You scared the shit out of me."

Toby didn't say anything and instead glanced down at the little boy seated in the stroller. Quietly contemplating his surroundings, he looked up at his aunt and offered her a big, toothy grin. The toddler was bundled in an oversized winter parka. A knit hat was pulled down to his eyes. Exposed skin was at an absolute minimum.

The answer was obvious but Toby asked, nonetheless. "Is it cold out, Bev?"

"A little." With her fingertips, Beverly attempted to groom her waist-length, jet black hair to some semblance of order. "Windy too."

"Come in," Toby invited. "I'll need a minute to find a pair of mittens for Mark."

"Sure," Bev agreed, maneuvering the stroller across the threshold. She paused just inside the doorway.

"I'll be right back," Toby said. She spun around, strode across the living room, and disappeared into the hallway.

Left to her own devices, Beverly warily glanced across the room at Toby's houseguests, prepared to avert her gaze should any of them take notice of her.

Sitting around a folding table, five men were smoking cigars and playing cards. Certainly no aficionado of poker, Beverly assumed a serious game was underway. Cash and piles of multi-colored chips were stacked in front of each player.

She crinkled her nose to stifle a sneeze as a noxious gust of cigar smoke reached her nostrils.

Scattered across the surface of the flimsy table were scores of beer bottles and a number of ashtrays brimming with stubbed out cigars and cigarettes.

Beverly didn't recognize the men, save for one. It was Toby's boyfriend who caught her attention. Until now, she had not seen him in person. But she knew who he was because Toby had shown her a wallet-sized photo. There was no mistaking the suave, handsome Rocco Balliro.

As she considered him from across the living room, he turned from the card game, tipped his head slightly in a respectful salute, and said, "Hi, Bev."

Stunned by the unanticipated greeting, she failed to say anything. But it didn't matter because by the time she fumbled for a response, he'd already turned his attention back to the card game.

The hairs on the nape of her neck stood up and she fought off an anxious shudder. Her heart began to race. Unconsciously, she gripped the handles of the stroller so tightly that her knuckles turned white. Trying to convince herself there was nothing to worry about, Beverly regretted not waiting for Toby in the hallway.

Seconds dragged agonizingly by. Where the hell was Toby? She wished the girl would hurry. Not a moment too soon, Toby emerged from the bedroom with Mark slung over her hip. *If ever a statue was sculpted of this inseparable mother and son,* Beverly thought, *this would likely be the pose.*

As Toby walked past the card table, Rocco reached out and seized her child's dangling leg, giving it a gentle tug.

She stopped short. Mark, buried in layers of winter clothing, giggled and then broke out in laughter as his captor yanked off one tiny shoe and began to tickle the sole of his foot.

"Stop! the little boy howled. "Stop!"

"Shhhh," Toby hushed. "You'll wake the baby."

"Sorry," Rocco said as he gently twisted Mark's shoe back into place. "Where you going?"

"We're just taking the boys out for a walk," she answered, running a loving hand through the man's thick growth of wavy black hair. "Need anything at the market?"

Without looking up from his cards, one of his companions belched and gruffly mumbled, "More beer."

Rocco glanced at her and nodded.

"Alright," she agreed. "More beer."

"Thanks, honey."

"Please listen for Wendy while I'm gone."

"Sure."

Beverly observed the brief exchange with amusement. She went to great pains not to alter her expression. Under no circumstance could she reveal the underlying discomfort she felt over this dubious relationship. Sure, it was pleasant enough on the surface. Rocco Balliro *seemed* like a nice enough guy. More importantly, what Toby did with her life was her own business, Beverly concluded. And who was she to impart relationship advice after her recent separation from Toby's brother Malcolm? But she and Toby had been very close since meeting in a Brookline High School classroom five years earlier and she cared deeply for her. If she could ask Toby a single question – just one – without being permanently cast from her life, Beverly would simply say, "What's going to happen when your husband gets out of jail?"

She certainly hoped Toby was prepared to cope with the emotional strife looming on the horizon like ominous black storm clouds.

Toby finished her goodbyes and said, "C'mon, Bev, let's go."

Once in the hallway, she retrieved her own stroller from a storage alcove and lowered little Mark to the padded seat. Dressed more for a North Pole expedition than a brief November stroll, Mark teetered slightly and struck a comic pose. Toby leaned and fastened the seatbelt around his tiny waist.

As the women descended the wide staircase side by side, Beverly noted that Toby was wearing a rather expensive suede coat. Draped over her petite shoulders, it was stunning. Bev had always wanted one herself but couldn't afford it.

"Where'd you get that?"

"What?"

"The coat," Beverly asked. She knew right well where the coat came from but she was aching to hear Toby's explanation.

"Anthony gave it to me," she answered matter-of-factly.

"Anthony?"

"Rocco," Toby groaned, with an exasperated sigh. She rolled her eyes impatiently. Beverly realized it was better not to prod further.

The two young women reached the landing and pushed their respective strollers through the dimly lit vestibule, parading past the bank of mailboxes and newspapers littering the floor. Beverly glanced down at the front page of an unclaimed *Boston Herald American*, yellow with age, and noticed a photo on the cover of former Massachusetts Senator John F. Kennedy. He was nearing the midpoint of his first term as president and seemed to be mugging it up for the cameras just weeks after a successful October 1962 campaign to oust the Russians and avert nuclear war during the infamous Cuban Missile Crisis.

At twenty-three and raising a child on her own, Beverly wasn't much into politics. But she liked and respected Kennedy, partly because he was one of Massachusetts' own.

Ahead of her, Toby had pushed through the door and was attempting to prop it open with one free hand while struggling to angle through the narrow breach. Just in time, a neighbor arrived home and graciously held the door.

"Thank you, ma'am," Toby said.

"He's so adorable," the elderly woman gushed. She crouched lower to get a closer look at the little character in the carriage and was met with a warm smile.

"Careful," Toby warned. "He's almost two and already a lady killer."

The woman laughed and reached to stroke little Mark's soft chin. Trailing behind, Beverly strode through the opening and thanked the woman in passing. The duo leaned their respective strollers back on the rear wheels and lowered the boys over the half flight of steps to the street below.

They turned right on Kelton Street and walked toward the business district, roughly a half mile distant. It was heavily overcast, chilly, and raw.

"Feels like snow," Beverly said, snapping a silence that had persisted for a city block.

"Yeah, but I'm looking forward to it," Toby proclaimed. "I think the boys are old enough to enjoy it this year."

"Uh huh."

Beverly decided to venture into conversational no-man's land and said, "Toby, remember that time Barney and Mal sent us to the market with the boys?"

A forlorn expression shrouded Toby's face. The identical three-story apartment buildings on opposite sides of Kelton Street created a manmade valley that artificially channeled the wind.

"How could I forget," her ex-sister-in-law voiced with disdain. "I'm embarrassed to think about it."

Beverly was referring to a mission the two women embarked upon for their respective husbands a year earlier. Hankering for a steak dinner and short on funds, it was suggested to Toby and her sister-in-law that they might *borrow* the main ingredient for that evening's meal.

Admittedly, Beverly was no stranger to crime and punishment. As a youth, she was invited by the Boston Police to spend one sleepless night in a cold, dank cell at the Charles Street Jail following an arrest for shoplifting women's clothing from the Turn Style, Brighton's trendy department store. But a night in the company of hardened criminals wasn't enough to deter her from later entering a local grocery market and along with co-conspirator Toby, slipping assorted cuts of expensive beef beneath the baby carriage mattresses occupied by then one-year-old cousins, Mark and Daniel.

"Well, at least we didn't get caught," she emphasized to Toby, with a hint of self-reproach in her tone. There was no reply. Her silent walking companion seemed preoccupied and didn't have much interest in revisiting their earlier escapades.

She mulled over Toby's comment about her embarrassment over the theft of the meat. *Hypocritical*, thought Beverly. She was, after all, wearing a pricey coat that was likely stolen. Moreover, Bev recalled a recent night when she volunteered to babysit so Toby could catch a break from the kids. As was her nature, Bev used the opportunity to sift through closets. Intermingled with clothing and shoes were cardboard boxes filled with transistor radios, cameras, stereos, and other assorted electronics.

Of course, Beverly didn't have to snoop through closets to recognize that Toby had reaped the benefits of Rocco Balliro's presence. All she had to do was look around the apartment.

There was a brand new color television, which had replaced an aging black and white set. Her living room furnishings, including a plush couch and matching chair, were also brand new.

When Barney was the breadwinner, before they dragged his carcass off to jail, Toby resorted to shoplifting steaks from the market at his behest. But since Rocco Balliro had settled into her life, prosperity took hold and she no longer lacked for anything.

Beverly considered the risks associated with this newfound lifestyle. Toby's closets, after all, were brimming with stolen goods. Her apartment had become a miniature warehouse for assorted plunder. She assumed, correctly, that Rocco Balliro used Toby's place to temporarily store his loot. But what if a nosy neighbor – and there were plenty of them in the building – alerted the authorities to his suspicious activities? Certainly he couldn't possibly be lugging the stolen goods in and out of the apartment without someone taking notice.

And what about the kids? Had Toby considered Mark and Bernice? They, too, were benefactors of Rocco's largesse. Beverly's treasure hunt through Toby's apartment included a peek in the pantry and the fridge, which were both overflowing. Did her ex-sister-in-law understand that she was risking the well-being of her children while carrying on with Rocco Balliro? Was she really counting on a sympathetic judge to return her children after she was arrested for harboring a criminal or possession of *his* stolen goods? Toby had to realize that she could end up behind bars.

Before long, they reached the market. Beverly retrieved a hand basket near the entrance and slipped her arm through the handles. She only needed a few things.

"I'll meet you at the front of the store," Toby said. "I have to pick up the beer for the boys."

Bev leaned over to check on her son. He was sleeping soundly. She adjusted the basket and made her way through the aisles, gathering her items.

The store clerk, a woman with a huge beehive hairdo, rang up her purchase. As Bev transferred the last of the contents to the counter, Toby materialized behind her, precariously balancing a case of Schlitz beer between the handles of Mark's stroller.

"Need a hand?"

"All set," Toby insisted, hoisting the heavy carton to the moving conveyor belt.

Beverly reached into the depths of her purse and counted out exact change for her items. She was more than a little stunned when Toby unsnapped a leather clutch and peeled off a crisp one hundred dollar bill from a wad of cash. Bev resisted an urge to comment about the origin of the money. She knew where it came from.

A pang of jealousy gripped her, slight at first, but intensifying as she observed Toby cramming change into the bulging wallet.

Beverly had struggled financially since she and Toby's brother had split. She managed to scrape by as a coffee shop waitress and supplemental support she received from generous family members. Bev swallowed her pride each time she accepted a helping hand. But to keep a roof over the head of her two year old and food in his mouth, she had little choice.

Bev understood that Toby wasn't flaunting her windfall. The coat. The cash. She wasn't throwing it in her ex-sister-in-law's face. She was simply enjoying a lifestyle that had been elusive until now. Toby had been destitute herself and stooped to borrowing money or went without. But Rocco Balliro changed all that, raining luxuries upon her. Ready cash, it seemed, no longer posed a problem.

The two women eased the strollers along the sidewalk, retracing their steps. Dark clouds threatened and it had grown even colder. There was a distinct possibility that snow would fall on Boston by nightfall, uncommon before Thanksgiving, which loomed a week ahead.

Toby quickened her pace and Beverly followed suit. Both women balanced their grocery purchases atop the strollers – one with a few ingredients for that evening's dinner and the other a case of beer.

Reaching the building, they abandoned the strollers in the lobby and carried the boys and groceries up the stairs.

"This is a killer," Beverly gasped, as she reached the landing.

"I'm used to it," Toby said. "I climb these things a few times a day."

"You should try and get a first floor apartment," her companion suggested.

"I thought of that," she admitted. "But Anthony said we might get a place over in Chelsea."

"Chelsea?"

"Closer to his family," Toby explained.

Reaching her apartment, Toby set both Mark and the case of beer on the floor to free her hands. She inserted the key and turned it with an audible click. She opened the door, but only slightly, as if trying to keep a pet from escaping, and peered in.

Standing behind Toby, Beverly's view of the apartment interior was somewhat obscured but she could see through a narrow seam that the card game had ended and only Rocco Balliro and one other man remained.

She also saw that the table had been cleared of empties and the two men were poring over a tablet of paper positioned between them.

"Bev, I'm sorry," Toby uttered softly. Her face grew serious. "But I can't invite you in right now."

"Oh?"

"Another time, okay?"

"Sure," Beverly said. "Something wrong?"

"Nothing's wrong," Toby replied. Her tone was subdued. "Anthony is talking about, uh, a job, that's all."

"Toby, that's great!"

"Huh?"

"I'm so glad that Rocco – umm, Anthony – is getting a job."

Toby stared at her incredulously and started to say something but instead, shook her head and slipped into her apartment.

CHAPTER 10

"After a good dinner one can forgive anybody, even one's own relations." – Oscar Wilde

"I'm not sure why they asked us to come over," she admitted, speaking through an unlit cigarette dangling from her lips. She placed the smoke on the edge of an ashtray; it would have to wait until she finished feeding Bernice, who was balanced across her lap. Rocco was on the opposite end of the couch, facing her. Mark, meanwhile, sat on the living room floor and was transfixed by the cartoons on the television.

Intrigued, he asked, "What's your best guess?"

She glanced up from her work with the bottle and said, "My best guess is they want to meet you."

"I thought it might be the kids," he countered.

"They can see the kids anytime."

"So …" he said with a pause for effect. "You wanna go?"

"I dunno," she said, shrugging her slender shoulders. She hoisted Bernice and stood up. "I'll think about it."

"It's not a big deal either way," he offered. "Whatever you decide."

He didn't share his thoughts at that moment but Rocco found it peculiar that Toby's parents would so readily welcome him into their home. He was, after all, the man who was nurturing an illicit affair with their only daughter while her husband was incarcerated in the Concord Reformatory. Most parents would be scornful of such an arrangement.

Why weren't they indignant? Why weren't they upset about their daughter's infidelity?

Sure, from what he had learned, Barney Wagner was nothing more than a two-bit loser who'd spent the last several years as a sporadic guest of the Massachusetts correctional system. Nonetheless, he was *still* Toby's husband and the father of her children. Toby's parents had to be somewhat concerned.

Then again, Rocco surmised, perhaps the Zimmermans wanted more for their daughter and understood that he might be a better provider than this Wagner character.

For instance, there was a recent telephone conversation he overheard between Toby and her mom. It didn't fully register with him but as he recalled Toby's comments, it dawned on Rocco that he represented a financial security blanket she'd lacked for some time.

"Yeah, Ma," she spoke softly into the receiver. "He took me to the market yesterday and bought us enough groceries to last a week."

Rocco cherished the comment. It warmed him. He was reminded of the night he first met this special woman and the brief stop they made at a Brighton convenience store to pick up a few necessities for her kids: bread, milk, and a few snacks. It was a fulfilling moment for him.

While hesitant at first, Toby ultimately accepted her parents' invitation. As the holiday drew near, she busied herself with preparations, including a trip to a North End bakery he'd recommended. He pointed her in the right direction, suggesting several popular establishments where she purchased assorted Italian cookies and a few loaves of freshly-baked bread.

Early on Thanksgiving morning, Rocco and Toby packed the kids in the Oldsmobile along with a number of toys and books to keep them occupied during the ride up to Swampscott. They made room on the wide leather rear seat, between Mark and Bernice, to stack the cake boxes stuffed with baked goods.

She suggested they use the trunk but Rocco mumbled an excuse about the lack of space. He didn't elaborate but in the trunk was a duffel bag filled with burglary tools. He preferred she didn't see it. The less Toby was exposed to his business, the less the cops could pry from her if ever she were brought in for questioning.

They drove in silence for much of the thirty-minute trip. A misty rain intensified as Rocco maneuvered the Olds along the streets of downtown Boston. The rhythmic *slap-slap-slap* of the windshield wipers was soothing. Rocco broke the silence and asked, "So, think they'll like me?"

"Huh?" Toby responded.

"Your mother and father - Zimmie," he said. "Do you think they'll like me?"

"What's not to like?"

He turned to look at her and chuckled. "You've got a point there," he said.

Reaching Swampscott and navigating through the tiny community alongside the rocky Atlantic coast, a dozen or so miles northeast of Boston, Rocco was struck by the tranquility. It was a far cry from the bustle of the city.

"Nice town," he stated. "Peaceful."

"Turn left here," she instructed.

Rocco complied. Traffic was light and, as planned, they reached the Zimmerman home by noon.

He pulled up in front of a two-story, wood-framed house. Fronted by a brick staircase, he noted there was a pair of entrances leading to what appeared to be separate apartments. As if she could read his thoughts, Toby apprised him.

"It's a two-family. My parents live on the second floor."

They got out of the car and opened the rear doors. Toby retrieved Mark, who was now awake. Rocco, meanwhile, unbuckled Bernice from the clutches of her child safety seat. Hilda Zimmerman, Rocco noticed, was eagerly waiting at the top of the stairs. When they reached her, she stooped over and smothered a squirming Mark with a grandmotherly hug. She next reached out to collect Bernice and squeezed her firmly. As she cuddled her granddaughter, Hilda frowned at Toby and said, "Aren't you going to introduce your friend?"

"Mom," she said, gesturing toward Rocco, who had stepped back after handing over Bernice. "This is, um, my friend Tony."

"It's nice to finally meet you, Tony," she cordially extended.

Rocco stepped forward and lightly embraced her, careful not to crush the baby she held in her arms. Hilda struck a pose of surprise but certainly didn't seem displeased by the affectionate display.

"The pleasure is all mine, ma'am." He beamed with the sophistication of a polished gentleman. Based upon Toby's expression, he knew he had just scored valuable points.

Hilda guided the group inside and to the living room where a sturdy middle-aged man of medium stature rose gingerly from a chair to greet them. It looked to Rocco as if the man was in some form of pain – perhaps arthritis. Then he remembered that Toby's father was the proprietor of a carpet and linoleum business and apparently spent considerable time working on his hands and knees.

"Dad," Toby said, "this is Tony."

Rocco extended his hand and found it encased in the iron grip of Herman Zimmerman. *Sore knees, maybe, but this guy certainly doesn't lack hand strength*, Rocco thought.

"Good to meet you, sir." *Polite and respectful but not overbearing*, thought Rocco as the men shook hands. He sought to strike a balance and make a good first impression. He wanted to impress but not sound phony.

"Good to meet you, too," Herman said. "How was the trip up from Brighton?"

"Not bad. No traffic."

"Holiday."

Rocco nodded.

Toby joined her mother in the kitchen, leaving Rocco at the mercy of her dad. Thankfully, Herman suggested he take a seat on the couch. He then turned his attention to his two grandchildren.

There was a little tension in the air. It wasn't that Herman made Rocco feel unwelcome. But like any relationship between man and woman, there is often a father waiting for an opportunity to dish out retribution to anyone who could harm his baby girl.

And from the looks of him, the elder Zimmerman had the physical means to mete out such a beating. He wasn't particularly tall but was broad across the shoulders with a strapping, muscular upper body. Rocco surmised that the man, who had dark eyes and a thick head of black hair, could deliver a crushing blow if needed.

Herman Zimmerman had added reason to distrust his guest. Rocco Balliro was, after all, the *boyfriend* of his only daughter. And there was still the matter of her husband, languishing in prison. Rocco hoped there would come a day when it would be prudent to ask for Toby's hand in marriage without experiencing one of Herman's sledgehammer fists up close and personal.

Herman balanced his grandchildren on his lap. While supporting Bernice on one leg, he bounced little Mark up and down on the other, eliciting a boisterous giggle from the pint-sized little man. As Rocco observed, a young boy entered the room.

"You must be David," he jovially said.

"Hi."

"Whatcha got there?"

David, Toby's younger brother, held up a coloring book and a box of crayons for display.

"How old are you?" Rocco asked.

"Eight."

"Eight, huh?"

"Yeah, but I'll be nine in January," the youngster boasted.

"Uh huh. How old do you think I am?"

"Fifty?"

A sarcastic eight year old, thought Rocco. *Like his older sister. Must run in the family. Perfect.*

"Not quite," he corrected, with a chuckle. "I turned twenty-six last month."

Weary of the exchange, David abruptly lost interest. He broke off the brief chat and knelt in front of the coffee table where he began to color in his book.

Toby had once explained that the youngster was a late addition for her mother and father, who were thirty-seven and forty-two, respectively, when the little package arrived in January 1954. He was fourteen years younger than Toby and separated in age from his elder brother Malcolm by seventeen years.

Rocco glanced up from his observation of David's artwork and noticed Herman was staring at him. It seemed as if he might want to resume their conversation but just in time, Toby announced from the kitchen that dinner was ready. Rocco breathed a sigh of relief.

"C'mon, gang," Herman said while raising Bernice to his shoulder. "Time to eat."

Once seated, Rocco assumed that the questioning would start in earnest. Surely Toby's parents harbored curiosity about this mysterious man who was courting their married daughter. Instead, the discussion was rather mundane; boring, in fact.

Herman sat at the head of the table with Hilda to his left and young David next to her. Toby and Rocco faced them, seated along the opposite side of the table. Bernice was snuggled between them, perched in a high chair. Mark sat adjacent to his cousin David atop several phone books fashioned as a booster. One solitary chair positioned at the far end of the table remained unoccupied. Rocco presumed, correctly he later found, that it was reserved for Toby's elder brother Malcolm, who was conspicuously absent. When asked, she explained that he was something of a loner and seldom made an appearance at family gatherings, even the holiday variety.

A large porcelain bowl brimming with mashed potatoes made its way around the dining table, which was covered with white linens, glassware, and silver place settings. Each individual, upon receiving the bowl, scooped out a portion before passing it along. When the potatoes reached Toby, she ladled sparingly onto her plate and then shoveled an ample serving for her companion.

"Nothing like mine," she said, smirking as she doled out the creamy spuds. "No lumps."

"I like your lumps," Rocco murmured under his breath.

She smiled, blushing slightly.

At times, they ate in relative silence. The only sound was the *clink-clink* of forks and knives making contact with china. Rocco reached for a dinner roll and sliced it through the middle. He then began a search of the table surface for butter and finding none, turned to Toby. "I don't see any butter," he said in a low voice so that none of the others could hear.

"Butter on the table is not kosher," she murmured. He returned her comment with a quizzical stare. Only slightly aware of Jewish traditions, he found the rules about food confusing. "I'll explain later," Toby added.

Rocco was truly savoring this pleasant Thanksgiving dinner with the Zimmerman family. He felt at ease and was glad he agreed to join Toby for the trip to her parent's charming North Shore home.

A conversational pause was interrupted by Hilda, who broached a topic that, directed at most individuals, would be routine while getting to know someone. Not so in the case of Rocco Balliro.

"So … Tony," she began. "What do you do for a living?"

In his peripheral line of vision, Rocco could see Toby glaring. He could almost read her mind. "How dare she ask a question like that? She knows what he does!" He envisioned the talk they might share during the ride back to Brighton. "I knew we should never have agreed to come here today," she might say. "I'm sorry I dragged you into this."

But Rocco was prepared and eased into his response with the confidence and surety of a man who'd been questioned by some of the best over the years.

"I work with my brothers," he replied.

When they later discussed it, Toby said she thought he was going to come clean and admit that he and his brothers were, more or less, professional thieves with connections to organized crime factions.

"Really?" Hilda continued. "What business are they in?"

"Nightclubs mostly," he answered. As Hilda looked down at her plate to gather another forkful, Rocco winked at Toby. She breathed a sigh of relief. There would be no confessions on this day.

"Interesting."

"It can be," he added. "There's a lot of competition out there for customers."

"Really?" She seemed genuinely interested.

"Yes, ma'am," he continued. "A good act brings 'em in."

"Act?"

"Music," he elaborated. "For dancing. The busier clubs have the better music bands."

He stopped short of mentioning that many of the clubs in Boston, specifically those in the Combat Zone, featured burlesque and strip shows as well.

While Herman seemed less than fascinated, Hilda continued with her fishing expedition. Rocco didn't mind. He was content that he'd ingratiated himself with his girlfriend's mother. He relished the fact that he seemed to be getting along rather nicely with her.

"So, Anthony, what are your responsibilities?" she pressed.

"You name it," Rocco replied. "Bartend, stock the liquor, sweep the floor, clear tables. Anything they need me to do."

As he mentioned the liquor, Rocco recalled some of the painful stories Toby had shared with him about her mother's excessive drinking. Of course, she seemed perfectly sober on this day. If she'd been drinking, he couldn't tell.

As he and Hilda continued their bland exchange, Rocco slipped his foot to the right, out of view beneath the table, until he made contact with Toby. She responded by rubbing her foot up and down his lower leg. She had grown far more relaxed than earlier when her mother first raised the topic of Rocco's profession.

Earlier, she'd expressed concern about what questions her parents might ask. Her father's linoleum and carpeting business was, after all, located in the North End. The eldest Zimmerman would have to be both deaf and blind not to know what the Balliro family represented and where they stood in the hierarchy of the close-knit neighborhood. But Herman, to that point, seemed almost apathetic and Hilda's interrogation had been surprisingly generic.

"Anthony, I understand you have a large family," Hilda remarked.

"Twelve kids," he said proudly, nodding in agreement. "Six boys and six girls."

"God bless your dear mother."

"Yep, the woman is a saint," he agreed sincerely. He often referred to his mother that way. It a was a well-deserved moniker for a woman who not only raised twelve children of her own, but also lovingly helped out the neighborhood downtrodden with clothing and nourishment, all while putting up with a cantankerous husband.

Rocco thought back to his youth and memories of meals shared at the Balliro dinner table. While his parents had a dozen children, there existed a twenty-one year separation between the first born, Josephine, and the last, Bruno. It was seldom that the entire family gathered around the table at one time. When Rocco was growing up in the forties and fifties, several of his older siblings had already fled the nest and were starting families of their own. Dinnertime, as a result, wasn't as hectic as one might think.

It was, however, hazardous to the health of the last Balliro boy to reach the table following wash-up time. That individual, often Rocco himself, would be relegated to the final remaining chair which was positioned at the end nearest to his father, Rosario. If the mood struck the man or if he had a particularly hard day, the unfortunate son occupying that chair would bear the brunt of his verbal wrath and often, the backside of his powerful hand, only because the boy just happened to be within arm's length.

Lucy Winship, Rocco's older sister, said their father's coarse behavior, because of his own upbringing, was all the man knew. "Our father worked very hard," she wrote in a letter describing the man who hailed from Catania, Sicily, and immigrated to America at the age of twenty. "But he didn't know how to show love and affection to his children. Instead of a hug, it was a slap. Instead of a kiss, it was a whipping with a belt."

Rocco bristled at the thought of his father's abuse. He doubted that a man like Herman Zimmerman would ever raise a hand to his children, although Toby had explained that such opportunities were limited because her brother Malcolm chose to live with their grandmother, who owned a home on the same street in the West End.

Still, thought Rocco, Herman seemed to be gentle and caring despite the gruff exterior and he believed the man to be the polar opposite of his own father.

"Anyone want desert?" announced Hilda, thankfully interrupting his train of thought. The more he reminisced about his father, the more upset Rocco grew. And he didn't want to ruin this special day. It was going far too well.

"Sure," agreed Rocco, rubbing his hands together in anticipation. "I'd love dessert."

"I'll get the cookies," said Toby as she rose from the table. "I've been aching to have one myself."

"Have two," Rocco suggested. "You need to put some meat on those bones."

"See, I told you Toby!" Hilda chided. "I'm not the only one who thinks you're too skinny.

"Tony likes me just the way I am."

She leaned over the high chair occupied by Bernice, who was quietly observing the adult interaction, and mussed Rocco's neatly combed hair. He smoothed it back into place. Out of respect for her parents, he resisted the urge to give Toby a loving pat on her hindquarters as she departed for the kitchen.

"So what do you kids have planned for the weekend?" Hilda asked.

"Not sure," he answered, shrugging his shoulders. "We'll do a little shopping, maybe. I think Toby could use a new coat for winter."

"Well, don't spend too much money," Hilda suggested.

"Oh, I'm sure we can find something on sale," Rocco said with a mischievous grin.

CHAPTER 11

"If two men on the same job agree all the time, then one is useless. If they disagree all the time, both are useless."
– Darryl F. Zanuck

Despite the offhanded suggestion he'd made to Hilda Zimmerman days earlier about shopping for coats, the decision to make off with scores of furs from an upscale women's apparel store was not premeditated. Rather, it was a spontaneous scheme Rocco and his oft partner Gianni Saroni cooked up while downing a couple of beers at a Brighton watering hole. The two men agreed there was no time like the present to make a quick score and line their pockets.

"It was a spur of the moment decision to rob that store," Rocco later confided. "After I was almost captured in Jamaica Plain, I knew I should plan jobs more carefully. But this one seemed too easy to pass up."

Rocco had learned recently through word of mouth of a growing demand in underworld circles for fur coats and women's fine clothing. He knew of just the place to fill that order.

Soon after dark, the ambitious duo drove the short distance to Worth's of Boston, which was actually in neighboring Brookline. The plan was simply to break in and liberate as many furs as they could offload and cram into the trunk of the Olds. Later, after dispensing a few coats to associates, they'd fence the remainder. It promised to be a decent payday.

It was a windswept November night, several days after enjoying a sumptuous Thanksgiving dinner with his girlfriend Toby and her parents in their warm Swampscott home, when

Rocco found himself once again navigating a dark, narrow alleyway.

With partner Saroni riding shotgun, he eased the Oldsmobile Starfire from well-lit Boylston Street to a murky alley that paralleled the rear of the department store.

Once he'd entered the passageway that was primarily utilized by delivery trucks, Rocco snuffed out the headlights. A sliver of a crescent moon overhead, shrouded by wispy clouds, yielded sparse illumination.

In the scant light, Rocco nearly tapped a row of aluminum trash cans with his front bumper. He cut the wheel just in time, avoiding impact. Even the slightest contact could have sent the cans tumbling and most certainly alerted someone nearby.

Saroni exclaimed, "Jesus, that was close!"

Rocco said nothing. He pulled a handkerchief from his coat pocket and dabbed at a thin layer of perspiration on his forehead.

His heart racing from the near miss, Rocco took a deep breath and urged the car forward, eventually coming to a stop adjacent to the delivery entrance for Worth's. He sat back heavily in the bucket seat.

"You alright?" Saroni asked.

"Yeah," he said. "This shit will make you grow old fast."

Rocco turned toward his companion and said, "Alright, let's do this."

The intrepid thieves emerged from the Oldsmobile into the refreshing night chill. A stiff breeze whisked the sweat from Rocco's skin. He began to bounce back.

He gave their surroundings a quick once over. Adjusting to the dimness, Rocco's eyes settled on a solitary flood light mounted on the wall. He was prepared to eliminate lights, if necessary, but this one had already blown out or was inadvertently left off. *How convenient*, he thought. It added more credence to his belief that this would be an easy undertaking.

Saroni was already crouched in front of the delivery door, inspecting the lock assembly. Rocco circled the car, opened the trunk, and retrieved a canvas duffel bag.

"How's it look?" he asked.

"Piece o' cake – we should be able to crack this one with the bar," his experienced accomplice confidently pointed out. Rocco trusted the man's assessment. Saroni was armed with years of experience and had successfully burglarized countless buildings, each featuring its own set of roadblocks.

Rocco lowered the duffel to the ground. The metal on metal clinking within was music to his ears. A few bucks and a few good tools from Sears and Roebuck had turned into thousands in loot over the years. An impressive return on his investment.

Unzipping the bag, he withdrew "old reliable," a heavily-weighted steel pry bar.

He'd sacrificed his favorite steel bar during the memorable flight from the Boston police several months earlier. He wondered if the cops retrieved the burglary tool right away, perhaps to be used as evidence if they ever managed to apprehend their elusive suspect. Or maybe, he pondered, it remained wedged firmly in place for a day or two, unnoticed until jewelry store workers opened the door. He would never know for sure.

Nonetheless, Rocco had several other bars that did the job just as effectively, including the hefty one now balanced in his hand.

Saroni stepped aside to give him room to work. Without hesitation, Rocco slid the teeth of the two foot long metal shaft into the door jamb and went after it. Clutching the end of the bar with both hands, he dug in his heels for leverage and applied steady pressure. At first, the door wouldn't budge. He gave it another try, this time putting his entire body weight behind it. His teeth were clenched with the effort and his biceps protested.

Rocco's diligence soon paid off, however, as the door began to buckle. Grimacing from the strain, he uttered one word at a time between gulps of air. "We're ... almost ... there," he gasped.

Unconsciously, Saroni had meandered closer to the door as his partner toiled to spring it. "Think there's an alarm?" he wondered as he leaned in.

"I don't ... think ... so," said a tenacious Rocco, as beads of sweat appeared on his brow despite the chill of the autumn night. "But ...we'll know ... in a second. I almost have ..."

Before he could finish the comment, the stubborn lock yielded, shredding into glittering shards of metal. Shrapnel flew everywhere. As the lock gave in, the door swung outward uncontrollably, nearly slamming into Saroni's face. He deftly sidestepped a broken nose and teeth.

The pry bar assault not only shattered the lock assembly, it also mutilated the reinforced door frame. Rocco stepped back to admire his handiwork. "Never had any doubt," he said aloud with a devilish smirk. "I knew I could get that bastard open." Saroni nodded in agreement.

After returning the duffel bag to the trunk, Rocco rejoined Saroni, who was peering into the breach and sizing up the interior of Worth's. They couldn't rule out that someone might still be in the store. Perhaps an overnight cleaning crew was on hand. Or maybe a conscientious employee was working late to restock inventory.

Then again, if there was someone inside, they would surely have been alerted by the commotion at the delivery entrance.

The two men stepped through the doorway, with Saroni blazing the trail. Rocco followed and took note of a number of cardboard boxes stacked along the walls. He assumed this was a recent delivery.

Saroni, Rocco noticed, was standing in front of a door with his hand poised on the shiny knob. He grasped firmly, twisted it, and pushed the door open. Once again, he leaned forward to inspect the cavernous store.

"Anything?"

"Nope. All quiet," Saroni reported.

"Lemme take a quick look."

It wasn't that he didn't trust Saroni's appraisal, but before they ventured inside, Rocco just wanted to see for himself.

Grasping the doorframe with both hands for balance, he leaned his upper body across the threshold and surveyed the expanse.

Lined in intervals across Worth's ample floor space were scores of metal display racks brimming with clothing. At first glance, Rocco could only distinguish women's dresses, blouses, and sweaters suspended from hangers. But no coats. Where were they? His stomach began to roil. Had they broken in needlessly? Was the inventory of furs secured elsewhere in the building? A large safe, perhaps? Burglar, yes. But he certainly wasn't a safecracker. His mind raced through the possibilities. Had they wasted their time?

Saroni must have sensed his partner's unease. "What's the matter?"

"I don't see any furs."

"Nothing?"

"Not unless I'm missing something."

"What do you wanna do?"

"I'm going in," a resolute Rocco replied. "I need to get a better look."

"Let's split up," Saroni suggested.

"Sure, good idea."

The two intruders slipped into Worth's, treading lightly across the worn tiled floor. Saroni turned right, moving into the depths of the store. Rocco, meanwhile, began to make his way along a long narrow aisle in the opposite direction.

As he searched for the furs, Rocco's mind began to play tricks on him. Scores of mannequins were scattered across the floor and he swore they were watching him. A chill ran up his spine when, in the murkiness, he could have sworn he saw one of the plastic figures move.

Rocco felt something scurry over his foot – a mouse, perhaps – and then, simultaneously, a hand grasped his shoulder. He nearly jumped out of his skin as he took a half-hearted swing at the unseen character.

"Jesus Christ!" hissed Saroni, who awkwardly stepped backward, nearly stumbling into a clothing rack.

"What gives?" Rocco hissed in a raspy voice. He scolded his partner for sneaking up on him.

"Relax, man," urged Saroni as he, too, put a hand to his chest. "I didn't mean to startle you."

"That's twice tonight I've almost had a friggin' heart attack," Rocco snarled, referring to the near miss with the trash cans. "You're lucky I didn't shoot you."

Standing next to a rack stuffed with clothing, he reached out and guided the silky sleeve of a blouse to wipe dry his sweat-drenched forehead.

"I found them," Saroni said.

"The coats?"

"Yeah," he said, pointing toward the area he had just scouted.

"How many?" Rocco excitedly asked.

"Coupla hundred," Saroni replied, shrugging. "Maybe more."

"Unbelievable."

"They're near the dressing rooms."

"Not for long," Rocco said, rubbing his hands together. "C'mon, let's go."

The two marauders, the loot now within reach, moved quickly. It occurred to Rocco that time was of the essence – they'd been in the store far too long. The potential for discovery grew heightened with each passing minute. If there were a couple hundred coats to move, it would take some time.

Saroni led the way to the mother lode while Rocco followed, noting that there were more of the mannequins standing sentry at this end of the building. He was too focused on the task at hand, however, to consider the eerie phantoms but the embedded vision would later make for a fitful, nightmare-strewn sleep.

Reaching the cache of fur coats, the men dove into their work without pause. Rocco extended his arms straight out, palms facing upward. Saroni pulled coat after coat from the racks and draped them, one by one, over his associate's outstretched arms.

Rocco's carrying capacity was a half dozen furs at a time. Reaching that count, Saroni seized a couple more, tucking them under his arms, and then made for the delivery entrance. Pushing the exterior door slightly open, he peered into the alley. He half-expected to emerge and fall into the hands of a waiting police detachment, guns drawn. Thankfully, all was as they'd left it.

Rocco relished a refreshing breeze that pressed against his face. It relaxed his taut senses. Reaching the Oldsmobile, Saroni quickly began offloading the heavy furs from his partner's straining arms, transferring them into the trunk. In anticipation of making a dozen or more trips, the men pigeonholed the first bundle of coats into the deepest recesses of the compartment.

It took nearly two hours to complete the caper. Rocco's arms grew weary after several forays so the men traded off and Saroni assumed the role as human pack mule.

Thankfully, they were both in pretty good physical condition. A decade earlier, Rocco recalled, he and Saroni did a two year stint together at the Billerica House of Corrections for a jewelry store break in on Summer Street in downtown Boston. While in the joint, to stay fit and trim, they frequently participated in pick-up basketball games.

"He would always want us to be on the same team," Rocco recollected sentimentally. "I would set him up with good feeds and he would ball handle like Bob Cousy to the basket. We always won out in the prison yard. After we got out, we made a lot of money together in our criminal enterprise."

In later years, Saroni told a tale about a caper that he and pal Rocco took part in which nearly cost them their lives.

"We got our hands on some five hundred record albums," Saroni recalled. "We were told they were Frank Sinatra albums and figured they'd fetch a coupla bucks each so we fenced the whole lot to Ralphie Chong."

Ralphie Chong Lamattina, a ruthless soldier in the Angiulo organization, who did hard time for clipping a pair of Barboza associates, among other brutal tasks, bought the albums for a song, so to speak.

Turns out, Saroni explained, he and Rocco were misled to the actual content of the cardboard boxes. They were not Sinatra records as advertised. Rather, the cartons contained Johnny Mathis Christmas albums – virtually worthless – particularly in July.

The no-nonsense Lamattina was enraged and swore to spill the blood of the two boys who duped him. He wasn't going to be made a fool. Rocco and Gianni were summoned to the "Dog House" and forced by Gennaro Angiulo himself to apologize to Lamattina, as well as refund the man's money with interest. As they forked over the cash, the duo felt fortunate. Lamattina could have easily put a couple of slugs in each of their skulls. Instead, he gave them a pass. He understood there was no need to raise the ire of the Balliro brothers.

Before long, Rocco and Gianni had stuffed the trunk of the Oldsmobile to the brim. With more fur coats to be had, they resorted to the spacious rear seat for additional storage.

This was a dangerous move. If they were pulled over for a traffic violation, real or imagined, which was not uncommon at three in the morning as the cops sought drunken drivers, the officers might not seek to inspect the contents of the trunk. But there would certainly be suspicion about what lay beneath the tarp in the back seat.

Rocco understood the risk but, nonetheless, was willing to roll the dice. The more coats they gathered, the better the payoff. Besides, it was a brief drive to the lot behind Toby's building.

Rocco and Saroni resumed the larceny, fetching another twenty furs over two additional trips into the store.

After covering the coats with a canvas, Rocco stood upright and stretched his aching lower back. He ran his hand through his thick hair, matted with sweat after the feat, and glanced at the delivery door of Worth's, which remained ajar.

Saroni noticed him looking. "What is it?" he asked.

"What about the boxes?"

"Boxes?" he asked.

"Yeah," said Rocco. "In that little stock room. I wanna see what's in them."

Saroni shook his head and pointed toward the back seat of the car, which was stacked high with furs. There was simply no space for more loot.

"Okay," he agreed. "But there is one last thing."

Rocco reentered the store as Saroni protested. He made his way back to the remaining furs and snatched one last item. It was a dark seal coat that stood out from the rest. Classy and striking, he reckoned it would make a fine gift.

CHAPTER 12

"It was dangerous to hit the wrong kid in my neighborhood, because a lot of the guys I played with had fathers in the Mafia." – Tim Robbins

Seated at a table adjacent to the front windows of a nondescript Italian restaurant in Brighton's Oak Square, Rocco kept his eyes glued to the sidewalk for the approach of his associate Johnny D'Angelo. When they'd spoken via telephone earlier that afternoon, this long-time friend insisted he knew exactly where the place was. But Johnny was prone to getting lost and Rocco grew uptight. They could not be late for their meeting slated for later that evening – or worse still, not show up for it at all.

Several pedestrians strolled leisurely past the eatery, including an elderly woman, bundled against the late November chill and pushing a grocery-filled cart. Trailing several steps behind was a young couple wrapped in an impossible embrace. Somehow, they managed to walk along without stumbling.

There was no sign of Johnny, however, and Rocco grew more concerned as the minutes ticked by.

Dusk had fallen and by his estimate, they had an hour-and-a-half to inhale a bite to eat, discuss the rudimentary plan they'd earlier pieced together, and then make their way out to Dedham. Under no circumstances did they want to keep their contact waiting. That would be a serious mistake.

He redirected his scrutiny to the interior of the restaurant, which was located a few blocks from the apartment he kept with Toby. There were several other patrons scattered about the room, elderly couples mostly, seated at wooden tables covered with red and white checkered placemats. Mounted on the walls surrounding them were scores of framed paintings depicting scenic Italian vistas.

He and Toby had dined at this establishment a number of times, mostly for the convenience alone. It was close to home, a brief stroll from Kelton Street. But the food, he felt, left something to be desired. Despite quick service and heaping portions, this joint couldn't hold a candle to the North End restaurants they regularly patronized.

If he wasn't pressed for time, Rocco would have much preferred trekking across town for a delicious, *real* Italian meal somewhere in his old stomping grounds. He might enjoy a plate of steaming pasta covered with gravy, a cannoli or two, a freshly-brewed cup of cappuccino, and of course, an after-dinner cigar.

He again glanced through the windows overlooking Market Street and observed several boys, perhaps twelve or thirteen years of age, who had gathered beneath a solitary streetlamp. One lad, in particular, caught his interest. The boy was tall and lanky, and stood leaning against the lamppost with a cigarette dangling from his lips. The sight triggered for Rocco a distant memory of his days as a youth on the streets of the city.

Dressed in a pair of baggy, khaki shorts and a loose fitting, white t-shirt, Anthony – the name Rocco went by as a youth – sat perched on the edge of a granite sidewalk curbstone facing bustling Hanover Street in Boston's Italian-American enclave best known as the North End.

The year was 1948 and Boston, like the rest of the country, was two years into recovery following a costly victory in Europe. Under the leadership of President Harry S. Truman, returning World War II veterans were finding ample work amidst a robust economy fueled by a huge demand for domestic goods.

Locally, Bostonians enjoyed their fair share of prosperity due to plentiful jobs, a building boon, and the introduction of the Master Highway Plan for the Boston Metropolitan Area, which featured the proposed construction of the Central Artery and other infrastructure projects.

The sweltering summer of 1948 was a far cry from the weather conditions endured by Boston residents earlier that year. Record-setting snowfall crippled the city prompting then mayor James Michael Curley to actually suggest flamethrowers as an option to gradually melt the snow before "perhaps disastrous flooding," as he described it, occurred at the end of the season. Curley's plan was shelved.

The mountains of snow that blanketed the city became a rapidly fading memory for most of the city's inhabitants once summer arrived, including young Anthony Balliro, who ran his hand over a thick crop of unkempt jet black hair, pushing it back off his forehead which glistened with sweat beneath a white hot scorching sun. He wiped his sweat-soaked palm on the front of his shirt.

With thumb and forefinger, Anthony plucked the remains of a cigarette from between his lips, squeezing it at the filter. Contemplating the embers, which were steadily advancing toward his fingertips, he figured there was just enough for a last drag.

Squinting against the sunlight, he inhaled deeply on the smoke and then flicked it to the street. He timed the launch so the tire of a passing automobile crushed and extinguished it. "Never miss," said the eleven-year-old Anthony aloud, smirking at his aptitude.

He and his ragtag gang of friends were hanging out on the corner of Prince Street. The boys were bored and hot – a volatile combination.

A heavyset, stout woman in her seventies appeared, dressed entirely in mourning black. Taking a wide, circuitous detour around the boys, she protectively embraced a satchel filled with loaves of freshly-baked bread. The aroma of her goods reached Anthony's nose. He breathed deeply of the scent and considered his mother's home cooking. She was a maestro in front of the oven, churning out spectacularly tasting meals with the barest of ingredients. Pure magic.

As Anthony mulled over a rapidly developing craving for a plateful of his mom's gravy-soaked spaghetti, one of his so-called friends suddenly lunged at the helpless elderly passerby. She shrieked, frightened by the unprovoked attack. He grabbed one of the loaves, which was protruding from the top of the sack, and yanked it out. The woman, her worn, leathery face contorted in a hateful grimace, howled in revolt at the intrusion. She cursed in Italian but the hooligan just laughed, mimicking her. He cradled and rocked the stolen bread in the crook of one arm, as if coddling an infant. Then, he pretended it was a sword and stabbed it in the air, simulating a hotly-contested fencing duel with a make-believe opponent. Dancing in circles, he held the bread out to her as if to return it, but retracted the loaf just as she reached out with a wrinkled hand. He repeated this antic several times, taunting the poor lady to near exhaustion.

Anthony had seen enough.

"Give it back to her," he demanded sternly. His brow was furrowed in reproach as he glared at the young ruffian.

His friend spewed a venomous reply. "Screw you, Balliro!"

"I have no beef with you, Jack," he said. "But if you don't give her the bread, I promise I'll hurt you."

"C'mon," the woman's tormenter asserted, now fearful. He knew he wouldn't stand a ghost of a chance against Anthony Balliro in a fistfight. "It's nothin'. I'm only messin' with her."

"You're messing with an old widow, for Crissake. You ever think she might have a son or a grandson who could come down here and put a bullet between your stupid eyes?"

Stubbornly, Jack extended the loaf of bread to the old woman, who snatched it from his hand. As she stuffed it back in the sack and turned to continue her trek along steamy Hanover Street, she paused briefly to curse at her assailant. "*Figlio di una mignotta!*" she spat.

Jack didn't understand and looked to Anthony, who was smiling. "What was that? What'd she say?"

He wasn't fluent in Italian but, in this instance, was able to decipher the message. "She said you were a bad boy," Anthony lied. "C'mon. Let's get outta' here."

"Bad boy, huh?"

"Yeah," Anthony replied. "Bad boy."

"Well, I guess I am a *bad* boy," Jack boasted, proud of his new title. He traipsed along the sidewalk, puffing out his scrawny ribcage in an awkward display of unfounded bravado.

Anthony didn't have the heart to tell his friend the woman actually said he was a son of a whore.

Deep in thought, Rocco Balliro didn't hear the waitress approach. He also failed to realize that he was subconsciously smiling ear-to-ear as he reminisced about his childhood and particularly, the sway he held over most of his young friends. Even as an eleven-year-old, he had a taste for power and influence. He was a tough kid and could back it up when necessary.

"Something funny, doll?"

He looked up with a start and saw a short, plump woman, about sixty, hovering over him. It was the restaurant's sole waitress, beaming with a warm, friendly smile.

"Uh, no," he answered, feeling somewhat foolish. With that big grin, he must have looked like a crazy man. "Just thinking about when I was kid."

"I can't remember that far back," she said, titling her head back with a raucous chortle that caught the attention of nearby diners. Several glanced up from their meals to see what the commotion was all about. When they spotted Rocco looking back at them, most sheepishly averted their stares. Like his young friend Jack had discovered fifteen years before, these people sensed that he wasn't a man that you wanted upset with you.

By coming to aid of the old woman on that hot summer day in 1948, Rocco proved that he could be kind and compassionate. He would demonstrate that time and again over the course of his life. But when provoked, he wouldn't hesitate to parcel out a serious beating to a deserving foe.

The waitress yanked a small notebook from the front of her apron. She added a pencil that had been stuck in a baseball-sized bun of graying hair knotted at the top of her head. She smiled warmly and said, "So darling, what can I getcha today?"

"Actually," he began, "I was waiting for a friend."

As if on cue, the door to the restaurant swung open and in stepped Johnny D'Angelo.

"I take it back," Rocco voiced to the jovial waitress. "That's him now."

"I'll come back in a few minutes to take your order," she said, her eyes crinkling. "We'll give your friend a chance to get settled."

Johnny made his way across the small room under the watchful eye of the restaurant patrons. If the sparse gathering thought Rocco was an imposing figure, this new arrival, with the slicked-back head of dark, closely-cropped hair, black leather jacket, and biker boots really made them cringe.

"You had me worried," Rocco said to his friend when he reached the table.

"You're like an old woman," Johnny retorted as he peeled off the leather and slung it over the back of his chair. He matched Rocco's height, six foot or so, but boasted a thick, muscular frame.

"We can't be late."

"Yeah, yeah, I know," his friend responded. "You told me. Fifty times."

Rocco paused. Johnny was right. He was badgering and nagging his friend and that wasn't his style. He had to settle down and get his mind back in the game.

"Sorry," he offered.

"No big deal. You're usually not this jumpy. What gives?"

"I don't want to piss off our fence."

"Who is it?" Johnny asked.

Rocco had withheld the name when he and Johnny had spoken earlier. He had called his cohort from a payphone near a busy Brighton bus stop. He wanted to be certain nobody was eavesdropping.

He leaned forward and in a hushed tone began, "It's Henr—"

He broke off mid-syllable. The waitress had returned. Johnny leaned back in his chair and stroked a thin growth of whisker on his chin.

"Have you gentlemen decided?"

Rocco was nervously smoothing out the checkered tablemat. He looked up and said, "I'll have pasta and meatballs, light on the gravy."

She scribbled the order and then looked at Johnny who raised two fingers to indicate he would have the same.

"And a couple of beers," added Rocco, as an afterthought.

"Thanks, guys. It'll be up in a jiffy."

As the waitress headed for the kitchen, Rocco scanned the restaurant once again before he continued. All the diners were absorbed in their meals.

Rocco slid a cigarette from the pack and lit up. He offered one to Johnny who waved it off.

"I'm buying, by the way," Rocco extended.

Johnny's eyes narrowed to slits and he leaned back precariously in his chair. He leveled a caustic look at his friend and insisted, "Damn right, you're buying."

"You're not still sore over that shit, are you?

"What do you think?"

"Christ," Rocco whined. "It was months ago."

"Yeah, and my wife still gives me shit about it," Johnny explained. "She was pissed. The cops nearly broke down my fuckin' door that night. It took me an hour to prove I wasn't the guy they was looking for."

"I had to think quick when they asked for my name."

"You should have said you were Gianni Saroni instead of Johnny D'Angelo."

Rocco nodded. He had to agree. Compared to Johnny's rap sheet, Saroni was relatively clean and the cops might not have checked out his alibi as thoroughly. But in the heat of the moment, under duress behind that Jamaica Plain jewelry store, Rocco sputtered the first name that came to mind. He later joked that he should have been flattered. Johnny failed to see the humor in it.

"How's the wife, by the way?"

"Elaine? She's good," Johnny said. "Much happier since I started bringing home a regular paycheck."

"That's right," Rocco acknowledged with a nod. "Machinist?"

"Yeah. I've been working at the Mason-Neilan Company over in Norwood."

"They looking for help?"

"What? You? A legit job?" D'Angelo remarked with a light chuckle.

"Sure, why not? I could be a machinist. I used some of that stuff in the joint."

"C'mon, Roc," his companion said with a shake of his head. "You could never give up the *life*. You'd be bored stiff."

Johnny had a point there. Rocco craved excitement and variety. Taking chances – that's what he was all about. He seriously doubted he could stand the repetitiveness of factory work or an assembly line. He'd go stir crazy. There was no challenge in the work.

Then again, he hadn't forgotten the thoughts that crept into his mind during those tender moments months earlier when he hovered over a sleeping Mark. If he eventually married Toby and made her children his own, he would seriously consider becoming a wage slave, as unappealing as that might be. He learned a few things during his earlier stint in prison. He'd worked every job available, from cook to carpenter, and picked up a few skills along the way that might someday be valuable.

"Speaking of Saroni ..." Johnny began, but paused as their waitress returned with their beer. D'Angelo waited until she departed before resuming.

"Yeah? What about him?"

"How come he's not making the trip?"

"Dunno," Rocco replied. "He said something about not trusting the Providence guys."

"That so?"

"Yeah. He thought we could fence the coats here in Boston. Said he knew a coupla guys who'd take the whole load."

Johnny paused to raise his beer mug for a swig. He looked at his tablemate and asked, "Why not go with that?"

"I'd already made the deal," Rocco answered, shrugging. "There was no backing out – too risky."

"Uh huh," Johnny mumbled. He understood fully.

"He'll get his cut," Rocco added without being asked.

Johnny changed his mind about the smoke and reached for the pack. Rocco slid the Zippo lighter to him. His partner fired it, took a drag, and blew a wispy blue ring that spun toward the yellowed ceiling.

"So, this guy we're meeting ..."

"Henry Tameleo," Rocco finally revealed, lowering his tone so none of the other customers could overhear. Voices seemed to carry in this place.

"Tameleo?"

"Yeah."

"Patriarca's guy?"

"Yeah."

"Jesus."

"They want the coats," Rocco said, shrugging his broad shoulders nonchalantly in response to his partner's surprise.

"Good thing there's still a few left," Johnny chided.

Rocco chuckled. "You ain't kidding."

Johnny was referring to the dwindling inventory as Rocco, in a required gesture, shared the spoils of his heist by inviting friends and associates to select a coat or two – one for their wife and the other for their girlfriend or mothers. In the organization, one hand washed the other. Rocco Balliro hadn't forgotten the generosity of the men who'd collectively furnished Toby's apartment and provided her with a new color television, amongst other luxuries.

The two men drew on cigarettes and drank their beer in silence for a moment. Rocco thought back to the days immediately following the robbery of Worth's.

On the afternoon of Wednesday, November 28, Saroni gave Rocco a lift over to the Wayside Truck Rental agency in Somerville. There, he leased a medium-sized Chevrolet panel truck under the name of Arthur Piccirilli, who was a friend of the twosome and had provided falsified papers to make it possible. Rocco's license, at the time, remained suspended due to a 1954 conviction for unauthorized use of a motor vehicle and operating negligently. Because of the revocation, he couldn't legitimately rent a truck.

During the trip back to Brighton, each in separate vehicles, the duo made a brief detour to the Model Hardware store on Harvard Avenue to purchase a number of heavy-duty closet rods and mounting brackets. After loading the materials in the truck, the men continued on for Kelton Street and the fur-laden Oldsmobile, which was parked in a secluded lot near Toby's building.

Rocco positioned the rental truck adjacent to his car and was joined by Saroni in fabricating a series of metal racks across the width of the cargo box interior. Using the adjustable rods he'd bought, Rocco anchored the ends of the shafts by screwing support brackets into the walls of the truck. He rendered irreparable damage to the aluminum but wasn't overly concerned. He wouldn't be returning the truck to the agency. Instead, he'd likely ditch it somewhere along Route 1 and later, acting as Piccirilli on the telephone, report it stolen. That would get his helpful associate off the hook with the rental folks.

After nightfall, the hardworking pair began to transfer the plunder from Rocco's car to the truck. Under the cover of darkness, they labored quietly. He had intentionally parked both vehicles in an obscure corner of the lot, out of view of apartment windows and the prying gaze of tenants.

He and Saroni had the foresight to retain the hangers as they conveyed the coats from Worth's to his waiting car. In this way, they were able to suspend the furs from the rods they'd installed. Arranging the fragile goods in this manner would not only prevent damage, it would also provide easy access for Rocco's visitors to inspect the inventory. After they put the finishing touches on their enterprise, the two men called it a night.

Early the next morning, on Thursday, November 29, a steady flow of associates visited the "coat store on wheels," as Rocco later described it. Prior to the arrival of the first customer, he'd scouted out an alternate parking lot further along Kelton Street that was not in plain view. Someone would have to go out of their way to see them. He could now conduct business with lessened fear over meddlesome neighbors.

The transactions were seamless and within a matter of hours, all of his invited guests had come and gone, each departing the truck with a gratis fur coat or two. For the most part, the organization dispatched subordinates to retrieve Rocco's gifts. Better a minion gets pinched for receiving stolen goods than a high-ranking La Cosa Nostra capo or boss. Rocco didn't mind, however. He knew word of his generosity would spread. It was hazardous work, hauling the coats out of Worth's, but he would soon parlay the achievement, boosting his reputation in mob circles.

"So how many coats you got left?" Johnny asked as he downed the remainder of his beer.

"A hundred or so," Rocco answered. "I gave away about thirty."

"How much they paying us to move the rest?"

"Two or three hundred. Each."

It was generally accepted that hauls of stolen goods earned the participants thirty cents on the dollar. In Rocco's case, with the furs, the payout was far less but he didn't care. Neither did his partner.

"Hmmm, not too bad," Johnny said, raising his eyebrows in surprise. "And all we have to do is drive a truckload of coats to Providence?"

"Yeah," Rocco said. "When we leave here, we'll pick up the truck and head to Dedham to meet Tameleo."

"Where's the truck?"

"Near Toby's place."

"So you'll take my car and I'll drive the truck?"

"Uh huh," Rocco acknowledged with a nod.

"Sounds simple enough."

The waitress returned balancing a pair of dinner plates overflowing with piping hot pasta and meatballs along with a second set of beer mugs. Rocco usually preferred his suds from a bottle but he didn't complain. This would do.

"Can I get you boys anything else?"

"I think we're good for now," replied Rocco as he stabbed his fork into the mound of pasta and gave it a twirl.

Johnny, his eyes bulging, gazed at the heaping plate of food. "That's gotta be a pound or two of spaghetti," he wisecracked.

The waitress giggled. Jokingly, she said, "Finish all of it – you don't want to go to bed hungry tonight, do you?"

She had no idea how close that comment was to the truth.

CHAPTER 13

*"I wouldn't be in a legitimate business for all the money
in the world.." – Gennaro Angiulo*

Rocco paid the check and the duo left the restaurant just shy
of seven o'clock, bellies bulging after the meal. They made
their way to the Kelton Street lot where Rocco had stashed
the truck.

"This it?"

"That's it," Rocco replied, handing over the keys.

Johnny unlocked and opened the door. He stepped up into
the cab and adjusted the seat. Meanwhile, Rocco went to the
rear of the truck, removed the sturdy padlock, and raised the
cargo door. He heard Johnny start the motor as he climbed
into the compartment for a last check of their freight. The
truck hadn't been driven since he and Saroni had installed the
metal rods and he wanted to ensure the coats didn't end up on
the soiled floor. One after another, he forcefully yanked the
rods. There was no give. All were securely rooted.

Rocco jumped to the ground and locked the truck. He
walked around to the driver's door and tapped on the window.
Johnny cranked the handle, lowering the glass.

"Can I help you?" he asked sarcastically.

"I'm glad you're so relaxed," Rocco said.

"No sweat."

"Alright, let's get going."

"Ready when you are, boss."

The comment conjured up a painful memory of his North
End hold up debacle which ultimately cost him four years of
freedom and the rat cabbie that ended each of his comments
with the word "boss." Rocco said to Johnny, "Don't call

me boss," but his partner had already rolled up the window against the night chill.

Rocco shook his head, walked over to the Galaxie, and climbed in. Firing the throaty engine, he threw it into gear and fell into behind the truck. While Johnny paused to check for oncoming traffic before easing into the street, Rocco reached down and felt around beneath the driver's seat. His fingertips met with cold steel. The gun was there, exactly where he'd stashed it earlier.

As they pulled out of the lot, Rocco half expected to see Toby walking the stroller, occupied by the children.

A day earlier, she'd questioned him about the truck. His intent wasn't to hide the vehicle from her but rather from gossip-hungry neighbors. But while he and Saroni labored to store the furs, Toby had stumbled upon them while out for some fresh air. She didn't ask at the time but when he checked in for dinner, she broached the subject. Positioned in front of the oven and slowly stirring a simmering pot of beef stew, she didn't look up when she spoke.

"What's the truck for, Tony?"

Her probing caught him off guard. Typically, Toby avoided mention of his business and there had been little, if any, discussion in that regard since he first moved in with her, at least none since his near capture in Jamaica Plain. But it seemed the truck rental had gotten the best of her curiosity.

"I have to make a delivery tomorrow night," he replied after a pause while he mulled over what to say. He decided honestly was the best policy.

When they began their conversation, Rocco had been in the living room. He joined Toby in the kitchen and grabbed a bottle of beer from the fridge.

She briefly stopped stirring the contents of the pot and put down the ladle. Taking the beer from him, she pried the cap off with an opener, and handed it back.

"Where are you going?" she asked.

For the most part, Toby refrained from pointed questions like this. She knew it was frowned upon. "The less you know about what I'm up to," he once explained, "the less the cops will be able to pry out of you." She couldn't protest.

And yet, this time it was different. She seemed more concerned than usual; actually, worried would better describe it. Was it intuition? Did she sense he was in danger?

He pushed the thought aside. There was no way he could postpone the delivery to Providence, for her sake or his. A deal had been struck and the wheels were already in motion. There were people who would be very displeased if he failed to deliver the promised goods.

"Down to Providence," Rocco reluctantly answered.

She pursed her lips as if she'd just eaten something sour. Toby had been to Providence with him a time or two, after they grew tired of the bar scene in the Combat Zone. She confessed she didn't like the place. Her impression was there were far more shady characters in and around Federal Hill, the Providence mob's stronghold, than in Boston's North End. When she made the comment, following a brief visit with his friend Paulie Colicci at a popular Atwells Avenue nightclub, Rocco suggested that it was just her imagination at work. But deep inside, he knew she was right.

"You're not going alone, are you?" Toby questioned.

"Johnny D is helping out."

If nothing else, Rocco knew that would ease her tension. She liked his friend Johnny D'Angelo and trusted that he would do his very best to keep her boyfriend out of hot water.

"Alright," she relented, knowing it was fruitless to try and talk him out of it. "But please be careful."

Rocco stressed, "I'll be okay."

She nodded in response but he could see that she remained unconvinced. He had to do something to take her mind off the topic, to diffuse her apprehension.

"Hey, I have a little surprise for you," he ventured.

"Oh yeah?"

"Stay put," he insisted. "Don't move."

As instructed, Toby obediently remained motionless in the middle of the kitchen as Rocco headed for their bedroom. Reaching the closet, he knelt down and began to break down a stack of a half-dozen cardboard boxes, each containing several brand new transistor radios. At the base of the cache of electronics was one last carton, about the size of a large hat container.

He rose to his feet and returned to Toby, who had not budged from where she stood.

"I picked this one out especially for you," Rocco boasted. He tore off the cardboard cover with a flourish, tossed it aside, and brandished a deep, dark seal fur coat from the depths of the box. He held up the exquisite coat, spreading the sleeves wide.

"It's beautiful," she sang. "What a gorgeous coat."

Of all the furs he and partner Gianni Saroni poached from Worth's store, the seal coat was the finest of the take, bar none. He had meant to keep it concealed until Christmas, a month distant, but felt the gift would ease her angst over his upcoming trip to Providence.

In no time at all, she had donned the luxurious fur and was parading around the apartment like a model on a fashion show runway. It was a sight to behold.

In the 1953 film *Gentlemen Prefer Blondes*, Hollywood starlet Marilyn Monroe sang the lyrics of *Diamonds are a Girl's Best Friend*. But Toby would disagree. It was fur coats, not diamonds, that girls loved more. She danced around the room wearing the deep brown, ankle-length coat. Soft and supple, the fur was accentuated with a wide fluffy collar, two rows of fifty-cent piece-sized buttons, and a wide black belt fed through loops, cinched off at her waist.

"It's too bad we couldn't get a babysitter," she suggested with a frown.

"Why's that?" Rocco asked.

Wrapping the luxurious coat tightly around her slender figure, she replied with a beaming grin, "I'd love to go out and show it off."

"You'll have a chance later," he assured her. "I promise I'll take you out to a fancy restaurant in a day or two. And we'll hit a few clubs afterward."

Prudently, he sidestepped further mention of the Providence deal. There was no more talk of it as they settled on the couch to watch television. Toby, as he recalled, didn't remove the seal fur coat until it was time for bed.

Typically, the drive from Brighton to Dedham would take no more than thirty minutes. Instead, the drive took twice that long. D'Angelo drove the rental truck. Rocco drove the Ford Galaxie. Both stayed well below the speed limit. Driving slowly and methodically, they used turn signals, avoided lane changes unless absolutely necessary and paid close attention to motorists in their vicinity. There was far too much at stake for them to be stopped for a simple traffic violation.

Rocco thought more of Toby's concern as he made his way through West Roxbury, driving past some of Boston's stately homes. *Was she right? Should he worry?*

To take his mind off it, he gave the Galaxie's radio dial a spin, never taking his eyes off the panel truck ahead. He stopped his search when he recognized Tony Bennett's popular romantic song. "I left my heart in San Francisco," Bennett crooned. "High on a hill it calls to me."

Rocco grinned to himself, thinking warm thoughts about the popular West Coast destination captured in Bennett's song. *Now there's a place I wouldn't mind visiting someday,* he mulled. He would take Toby and the kids on a nice train trip – he didn't like to fly – and visit all the well-known sights.

But before he could make travel plans to San Francisco, or anywhere else for that matter, he would first have to wrap up his Providence run. And before that, a brief stop in Dedham to join up with their fence, Henry Tameleo.

It was nearly eight o'clock when the turn signal on the tail of the truck ahead began to rhythmically blink. Seconds later, Johnny turned into the parking lot of the Dedham Plaza, which was brightly lit against the night sky. Trailing closely behind, Rocco entered the expansive lot of the popular plaza, which had opened for business two years earlier in 1960.

Rocco remembered visiting this mall several months earlier with Toby and the kids for an impromptu shopping expedition. While there, he gathered mental notes, sizing up candidates for a later visit. Roman Jewelers, which was nestled midway between F.W. Woolworth's and a Friendly's Restaurant, caught his attention, as he recalled.

As he and Johnny rolled across the gravel surface of the lot, Rocco noticed a glossy black Lincoln Continental Mark V parked in front of Roman Jewelers. *Ironic*, he thought, *that he'd park there.*

They drew closer, one vehicle after the other, a plume of gray dust kicking up beneath their tires. Johnny came to a stop and Rocco pulled into an adjacent spot. He got out and waited for his partner to ensure the truck was secure. The last thing they needed was for someone to steal *their* stolen goods.

"Is that him?" Johnny murmured as he pocketed the keys.

"Yeah," Rocco answered. "That's him."

For the first time since he started this venture, he doubted his decision to fence the coats through Providence. Maybe he should have taken Saroni's advice and used the Boston connection. Too late for that, however, as he glanced across the lot at Tameleo, who patiently stood next to his car.

"Nice wheels," D'Angelo commented.

"He's a big earner for the Man."

The "Man," in this case, was Raymond Patriarca, who ran the New England mob.

"We should ask for more money," D'Angelo suggested with a grin.

The duo strode toward the imposing black Continental. Neither man spoke as they crossed the gap. The only sound was loose gravel beneath their shoes. Tameleo, seeing their approach, took a step toward them. He dropped a half-smoked cigar to the ground and applied the heel of his shoe to extinguish it. The pungent aroma of lingering cigar smoke enveloped the three men as they gathered in a semi-circle.

"Henry," Rocco uttered in greeting, as he reached out to shake the man's hand.

"Rocco, how've ya been?" Tameleo asked with a guarded smile as he buttoned his jacket against the chill prior to accepting the handshake.

"I'm good, thanks."

"And your family? How are your brothers?"

"They're good," Rocco replied.

"They must be getting close to opening their new place by now."

"The Intermission Lounge," Rocco volunteered. "Yeah, next summer."

"That's great," Tameleo said. "I'm looking forward to paying them a visit."

"I'm sure they'll be glad to see you."

Tameleo, sixty-one, was lean and of medium stature with rapidly thinning hair. He had a large, bulbous nose centered between dark, narrow eyes and wore a pair of glasses framed with thick black rims which made him look like an accountant or a bookkeeper. Tameleo, whose birth name was Enrique, was certainly no bean counter. Far from it. He had loyally served mafia kingpin Patriarca as underboss for a decade.

"So, who's your friend?" Tameleo asked, gesturing toward Rocco's closemouthed associate. Before he could be introduced, however, Johnny took the initiative.

"It's great to meet you, Mr. Tameleo," he blurted, stepping forward and extending his hand. "I'm Johnny D'Angelo."

"We're all friends here," the mob boss insisted, grasping D'Angelo's hand in his. "Call me Henry."

"Okay," Johnny agreed as he vigorously shook his hand. "Henry it is."

While the two men exchanged pleasantries, Rocco spotted a Dedham Police patrol car which had turned into the plaza and embarked on a wide swing of the lot.

"We have company," he announced nervously.

"No problem," Tameleo placated. "Probably just making his rounds."

The men made small talk, attempting to look inconspicuous as the cruiser pressed forward, tracing the perimeter of the unpaved lot, a trail of dust streaming behind like a contrail from a soaring jet airplane.

Either he hadn't noticed or didn't care, but the cop wasn't paying much mind to the trio of men chatting in front of Roman Jewelers. *Why were they were loitering in the Dedham Plaza, in front of a jewelry store, in the murky darkness?* he might ask. After a few tense seconds, however, the officer was back on his way, wheeling the black and white on to the asphalt surface of Route 1.

"I think we should be going too," Tameleo remarked, saying aloud what Rocco was thinking. "Follow me, I'll lead the way."

CHAPTER 14

*"The best car safety device is a rear-view mirror with a
cop in it." – Dudley Moore*

The last thing Rocco Anthony Balliro wanted to see in the
rear-view mirror as he drove through the sleepy town of
North Attleboro, Massachusetts, was a police cruiser steadily
gaining on him.

It was wishful thinking on his part, or perhaps it was
just his weary eyes playing cruel tricks on him after a long,
arduous day, but maybe the headlight beams dancing in the
wide, rectangular mirror affixed to his windshield didn't
belong to a patrol car after all, but rather a vehicle that shared
a similar profile. Taxicabs, he surmised, also had beacons
fastened to the roof. "Yeah," he said aloud, trying to convince
himself. "It must be a cab."

It was mid-evening, around nine or so, and inky dark
along the desolate stretch of Route 1 he and his small
entourage had been traveling. It was a strain to see much of
anything except for the road ahead, which was illuminated
by the headlights of the Galaxie. His eyes darted back and
forth from the panel truck lumbering ahead to the rearview
mirror. He soon confirmed his suspicions. As he motored by a
brightly lit automobile dealership, which cast sufficient light
to make the roadway more visible, Rocco further scrutinized
the vehicle behind him. It was, without a doubt, a police
cruiser. It was now trailing by less than a hundred yards and
closing fast.

Did the cops have a bead on him or were they on his
tail by some twist of ill-fated coincidence? Had he, or his
two partners — Johnny D'Angelo, who was driving the

rental truck, or Henry Tameleo, who was leading the pack in his Lincoln — done something to warrant this unwanted attention? His mind raced as he checked off the possibilities. Did the cops somehow know they were transporting stolen goods to Providence? Had they been tipped off, and if so, who was the rat behind it?

Did this have something to do with Tameleo? Someone settling an old score perhaps? Only a few people knew about the coats but word traveled fast. Maybe a Tameleo rival *arranged* for his arrest and Rocco and Johnny were just unsuspecting pawns caught in the midst of gangster retribution.

Rocco kept to the left side of the two-lane road. When he first realized the cops were creeping up behind him, his initial instinct was to cross over to the right. But anything sudden might suggest to his unwelcome company that he was considering a move, such as ditching the car and making a run for it. He resisted the urge. He also stayed glued to the speed limit. Picking up the pace was certainly not an option. Then again, slowing down might draw added suspicion. Nerves taut, Rocco white-knuckled the steering wheel.

It took less than a minute for the black and white to close the remaining gap and settle in behind him. The car lingered just off his bumper, shadowing closely. They had yet to flash the blue beacons affixed to the top of the cruiser, but in a provocative move, the driver angled his vehicle in such a fashion that the headlights shone in the mirror mounted on the driver's side door. It was blinding and angered Rocco.

This cat-and-mouse game went on for roughly a mile. *They're taunting me,* he thought, outraged. *Assholes! Just get it over with and pull me over, for Crissake!* He drew a deep breath and exhaled loudly. He considered his options. There was just one police car and maybe just one cop, although in the darkness, he couldn't tell for sure. Should he skip out?

If he did take off, the cops might just let him go and instead grab the truck, a far slower target. And what about

Tameleo, who was coasting along ahead of D'Angelo? Had he spotted the cops yet? Was he aware of what was surely soon to happen to the three of them? Rocco certainly couldn't speed past the mob underboss.

The burning question was answered as the trio of vehicles rolled up to a signal light that had just changed from green to yellow. Rocco watched as Tameleo, who had agreed to orchestrate the exchange in Providence, slowed for the yellow signal but safely cleared the intersection before the light went red. Both Johnny and Rocco eased to a stop for the traffic light. There was no need to give the cops a reason to stop them if that wasn't already their intention.

Tameleo paused, undoubtedly now aware of the building crisis behind him. All of a sudden, Rocco observed the crimson brake lights on Tameleo's car dim and the big Continental was gone in a torrent of swirling dust and road debris.

Oddly enough, the cops didn't give chase. Instead, they seemed content to patiently wait. But wait for what? Perhaps they'd radioed ahead for assistance. Maybe their brethren were setting up a roadblock further along Route 1 to ensnare their prey in the event a pursuit took place. If that was indeed the case, Tameleo would soon be in the hands of the authorities.

As it turned out, there was no such roadblock. Tameleo skirted the North Attleboro police with ease and soon after, arrived safely back at the 164 Atwells Avenue headquarters of reputed mob boss Raymond Patriarca; minus the truckload of fur coats, of course.

Enrique "The Referee" Tameleo would ultimately fall into the hands of law enforcement some five years later in 1967. But it wasn't for a petty crime such as transporting or receiving stolen property. Instead, Tameleo was indicted for his alleged role in the brutal gangland slaying of Edward

"Teddy" Deegan, a smalltime Malden, Massachusetts, hoodlum.

The details of the Deegan murder vary but according to the charges that were brought against Tameleo and co-defendants Wilfred French, Louis Greco, Ronald Cassesso, Joseph Salvati, and Peter Limone, the men reportedly lured Deegan to his execution on March 12, 1965, under the false pretense that he would be lending a hand with a break in of a Chelsea financial business.

Deegan was gunned down in a dark, dreary alley, viciously shot multiple times in the face.

By most accounts, Deegan signed his own death warrant when he burglarized the home of a North End bookmaker who was friendly with high-ranking mob leadership and therefore, dubbed hands off. Deegan was also said to have killed low-level thug Ricci Sacramoni during a heated argument.

Murder in the strictly governed syndicate required permission. Generally, killings took place only after an approval was granted at the highest levels – in this instance, from Patriarca himself. Deegan was a renegade and it wasn't long before he was sanctioned for execution.

Arrest warrants were issued for Tameleo and the others but Patriarca's right-hand man hadn't killed anyone, at least not Deegan. Instead, stone cold hired guns Vincent Jimmy "The Bear" Flemmi and Joe "The Animal" Barboza teamed up to spill the blood of the troublesome Deegan. In the aftermath, they pointed accusatory fingers at Tameleo and the others with the blessing of corrupt FBI agents, H. Paul Rico and Dennis Condon. Not only did the scandalous Rico and other agency officials condone railroading the innocent men, evidence was fabricated to make the bogus charges stick. It was all part of the rat-infested Bureau's nefarious scheme to cultivate mob informants, particularly Barboza, to aid in bringing down the top leadership of New England's La Cosa Nostra.

Despite Barboza's flimsy testimony, laced with obvious mistruths and flagrant inaccuracies, Tameleo and his co-defendants were convicted after a two month trial and sentenced to death by a Suffolk County jury. The framed defendants were imprisoned at MCI-Walpole to await execution by electrocution.

In 1972, the death penalty, which had never been popular in liberal Massachusetts, was overturned. Tameleo and the others saw their sentences automatically reduced to life imprisonment.

Fifteen years after his 1985 death, Tameleo would finally have his day in court. The FBI cover-up ultimately collapsed like a house of cards and the disgraced crimefighting agency revealed the details of the elaborate frame up.

Later, in 2007, a Boston federal judge awarded wrongful conviction damages in excess of one hundred million dollars, to be split equally between Limone and Salvati, who both served thirty-three years in prison, as well as the estates of Greco and Tameleo, who died behind bars.

Rocco sat and waited, contemplating. Time slowed to an agonizing crawl. The only sounds he could hear were his own raspy breathing and the steady drone of the Ford's motor. A putrid odor of exhaust infiltrated the car's interior. His head began to throb. Even though he'd long since shut off the heater, his shirt stuck to his sweaty chest. Rocco ached for a cigarette.

Glancing at the panel truck ahead, he wondered what Johnny might be thinking as he, too, awaited the light change.

In a defining moment, Rocco fought off an urge to follow Tameleo's lead and hightail it the hell out of there. Freedom was as close as his foot was to the accelerator. But that wasn't his style. Johnny was his friend and he would never be able to face the man's family, or his own, if he abandoned him. There was no way he would toss his partner to the wolves. Unlike the recently fled Tameleo, Rocco had every intention of following the code of conduct. If he and D'Angelo were going down, they would go together.

His imagination took hold and reckless thoughts crept into his mind. For a moment, he considered the loaded pistol stashed beneath the seat. "No need to carry a gun if you're not prepared to use it." Rocco had once overheard that comment in a Combat Zone nightclub frequented by wiseguys. He recalled it was a known mob assassin who'd made the remark. But he realized the man was probably just echoing something he'd heard at the local movie house. It was understood in organized crime circles, those who boasted about deadly exploits were usually pretenders. The real killers didn't much talk about executions. They just killed and cashed in.

Rocco Balliro certainly wasn't a killer but that didn't prevent his vivid delusions from running amuck. He envisioned a dangerous scenario that featured him leaping from the car and fleeing on foot, gun in hand.

The signal light changed to green and the truck ahead of him began to lurch forward. Rocco followed suit. The trio of remaining vehicles was on the move again but for how long?

Within a quarter mile of the intersection, the trailing patrol car came to life. The blue lights began to flash and the siren sounded a quick chirp. Rocco had anticipated that they would make the stop but the noise startled him nonetheless. He eased over to the right side of the roadway and angrily threw the shift lever into park but left the motor running. Optimistic to a fault, he hadn't fully ruled out the possibility of making a run for it.

Johnny also complied, angling the lumbering truck toward the side of the road just ahead of his partner.

Rocco again considered the gun stowed beneath the seat. Carefully, without shifting his upper body, he moved his left leg across the floor boards in a deliberate sweeping motion, attempting to determine if the weapon had slid into view. Thankfully, it hadn't moved. The gun, a lethal Browning 9mm pistol produced by Belgium manufacturers and a favorite of German infantry during World War II, remained concealed.

From his vantage point, Rocco was unable to determine how many cops were occupying the patrol car. It could have been just one guy, heading back to the station after making a coffee run. *Two at the most*, Rocco thought, as he again considered a dash to freedom.

Thoughts of Toby crossed his distraught mind. It made his heart ache. He longed for her. Instead of sitting in a car on a cold, depressing roadway in North Attleboro and about to be confronted by police, Rocco wished he was sitting on the familiar couch with his arms wrapped around her.

She had expressed trepidation that something might happen. Rocco pushed that thought aside. This was all just a terrible coincidence. He was just in the wrong place at the wrong time. What he did realize, however, was that dear Toby and her children would once again be alone if he was sent back to prison. He would be helpless to support her if he ended up behind bars. Toby would have a husband *and* a boyfriend in jail, and once again be forced to scrape enough together to feed her children.

The contents of his stomach churned and he fought off a wave of nausea. Rocco wished he hadn't gorged himself on pasta earlier that evening. It felt like days, not a couple of hours, had passed since he and Johnny had sat at that dinner table and finalized the details of their suddenly floundering expedition.

Squeezing his eyes tightly, Rocco rubbed them with the tips of his fingers until he saw dancing white stars. When his vision cleared, he took note of his surroundings.

Just ahead on the right was an isolated shopping plaza anchored by Stop & Shop. Although the huge supermarket had already closed for the evening, its nearly vacant parking lot remained awash with garish light from streetlamps. With that much light, it would not make for an advisable route of escape, should he make the attempt. Instead, Rocco schemed;

he might be better off running to his left, across all four lanes of highway, which were devoid of traffic, and into a strand of brush that fronted the northbound shoulder.

Just as the thought ran through his mind, Rocco looked in the rearview mirror and to his bewilderment saw not one or two, but rather four cops climb out of the cruiser and begin to make their way toward his idling car.

His breath caught in his throat and his mouth went dry. He felt that familiar rush of adrenaline. He sat perfectly still; so still, in fact, that his neck and upper back began to ache with tension.

"Shit," Rocco cursed aloud, hissing through tightly-clenched teeth. There would be no escape attempt on this night. Outnumbered four-to-one, any consideration of making a run for it now would be foolhardy. The odds were impossibly stacked against him. He was unquestionably heading for a jail cell.

When had such a promising enterprise gone so awry?

"Four cops," he moaned under his breath. "Four friggin' cops!"

CHAPTER 15

*"If you don't get caught, you deserve everything you
steal."* – Daniel Nayeri, Another Faust

Rocco Anthony Balliro intently watched as a pair of
uniformed policemen marched past his car, heading toward
the rental truck, which was idling about a hundred feet or so
ahead of him.

He wondered how Johnny was holding up. What was
going through his friend's mind as the officers approached?
Was he thinking the same thing – to make a run for it? Rocco
wished he had the means to communicate with his colleague,
to offer words of encouragement, but more importantly, to
corroborate their stories. He knew Johnny, like most of their
ilk, wasn't a fan of the cops. But say the wrong thing, the
night could get far worse for them.

Ultimately, the outcome hinged on the reasons behind the
traffic stop. Why had the cops pulled them over? Rocco failed
to recall bending any rules. He certainly wasn't speeding. If
they were facing a simple traffic violation, he figured, they'd
earn a ticket and soon be on the road to Providence again. No
harm done. They'd pay the fine and continue the delivery to
Patriarca's people. Later, he and Johnny would grab a beer or
two at a Federal Hill drinking establishment and share a good
laugh over their near miss.

Then again, he speculated, if the cops asked Johnny what
cargo he was transporting or insisted he produce a bill of
lading for the contents, he and his associate were doomed.

Several months prior to thwarting his so-called friend from inflicting further humiliation upon the innocent widow on Hanover Street, Rocco Anthony Balliro faced his first entanglement with the authorities.

In stark contrast to the goodwill he demonstrated by coming to the rescue of a helpless citizen, Rocco committed his first criminal deed by breaking and entering into the home of a North End resident to steal jewelry, keepsakes, and anything else he could haul away in a pillowcase.

While the Boston police were, at times, notoriously inadequate crimefighters, they did manage to capture young Anthony Balliro as he carried out a nighttime burglary of an apartment in his own neighborhood.

It was Tuesday, March 23, 1948, and the city of Boston was finally beginning to thaw from the snowiest winter on record when a young Anthony pried open a window that led to a first-floor bedroom, eased his rail-thin frame through the narrow gap, and once inside, began to gather anything he thought might be of value. He worked quickly but certainly not quietly. An eavesdropping elderly man in an adjacent apartment, aware that his neighbors were out for the evening, quickly dialed the police when he heard the commotion.

When the first-time burglar slipped back through the window opening, loot-filled pillowcase slung over his shoulder, two grinning Boston Police officers were patiently waiting for him, arms folded across their broad chests. One of the cops brusquely grabbed the stunned youth by the scruff of the neck.

"Whadda we have here?" the cop crooned sarcastically. He clamped a pair of cold, steel handcuffs to the scrawny wrists of an apologetic Anthony Balliro, who was seven months shy of his twelfth birthday.

During the five tumultuous years that followed, the youngster was charged with no less than ten criminal offenses. From the summer of 1948 to the autumn of 1953, his small-scale juvenile crime wave ran the gamut, from attempted larceny to the sale of stolen merchandise to disturbing the peace to the unauthorized use of a motor vehicle.

But perhaps the most heinous crime Rocco perpetrated before reaching adulthood was a vicious assault and battery on a man who did little more than comment about the clothing the teenager was wearing.

"If I had that night to do over again, I wouldn't lift a finger to harm that guy," a remorseful Rocco said many years later, as he shared a haunting description of his appalling actions of Wednesday, April 23, 1952.

In Rocco's inner circle, there existed fierce pride in appearance. Somewhat hypocritical perhaps, considering they spent many a night hellraising in places known more for squalor than sophistication. But he and his brood were usually decked out in the latest clothing trends and were always well-groomed. Their distinguished appearance drew respect from peers, and of course, the girls.

Billy Balliro, Rocco's elder brother, later agreed that he and his siblings were seldom seen in public unless they were dressed to the nines. "It didn't matter where me and my brothers were going or what we were doing," he admitted. "We almost always wore suits and ties."

On the night in question, Rocco was looking exceptionally dapper in his plaid cardigan sweater, a pair of new, dark blue dungarees cuffed at the ankle, and blue suede shoes, an accessory of which he was especially proud.

Along with a number of his delinquent companions, Rocco was hanging out on a train platform at Boston's North Station, which sat beneath the venerable Boston Garden.

The young punks were loitering alongside a concrete wall plastered with posters bearing announcements for upcoming Garden events.

Opposite was a bank of ticket windows, shuttered for the night. The last ticket to North Shore destinations had been sold an hour before. Nearby, several of the large hulking trains were parked idle, their diesel locomotives silent, awaiting the morning commute. To their right was a staircase with a rectangular sign reading CAUSEWAY STREET.

Trouble brewed when a man about forty years of age, clearly intoxicated, staggered toward the gang.

A breeze swept across the platform, stirring abandoned newspaper pages and other debris left behind by commuters. Growing restless and bored, the boys had been debating whether to wander over to the nearby North End to seek out a few of the girls they knew or perhaps, drift toward Scollay Square and grab a bottle of wine or two. As they discussed their options, the man appeared before them.

"Hey!" the stranger bellowed, his drunkenness unmistakable as he wavered on the platform. "Hey b-boys, whaz goin' on?"

"Get lost," one of Rocco's buddies harshly suggested.

"Yeah," another chimed in. "Get da fuck outta here before you get hurt."

The man failed to heed the sage advice of the young ruffians. He was far too drunk to fully comprehend the danger. Slurring his words, he said, "I ... just ... want to shay–"

"What ... do ... you ... want to shay?" Rocco echoed, mimicking the inebriated man, which elicited a round of laughter from his cohorts.

Identifying Rocco as the ringleader, the man shifted his attention to the tall, lanky, dark-haired boy. The group grew silent, stunned by the audacity – or stupidity – of this random individual who was invading their space. When he was within arm's length, the drunk leaned in. His stinking, alcohol-saturated breath washed over Rocco as he uttered, "Sonny, I tink ... you ... look, real, real ... nice in dem clothes."

Rocco's usually calm demeanor was instantly replaced with a rabid, diabolical fury. His short fuse ignited, he repeatedly clenched and unclenched his fists.

Was this guy out of his friggin' mind? Did he have a death wish? Was he one of those mentally diseased homosexuals the boys had been warned about in school? This guy had to be a queer. Why else would one man say to another man – or worse, a teenaged boy – that he looked "nice?"

As his friends looked on in amusement, Rocco rushed at the drunkard in a fit of unbridled rage. He slammed the flat of both hands into the man's bony chest with brute force. The boozer staggered backward and collapsed on the cold train platform. Unable to regain his feet, the man lay writhing as the boys gathered around him in a stormy, threatening semi-circle.

Rocco aligned himself with the man's head and without further provocation, delivered several vicious kicks to his skull. The man instantly went limp, falling unconscious. He laid motionless, blood spilling from a deep gash on his scalp. Rocco and the boys, meanwhile, made haste toward the station exit and Causeway Street below.

Later, when the cops gathered evidence and the hospitalized victim's account, the hotheaded young hellion was arrested and charged with assault and battery. Later, he was sentenced to a one year stay in the Shirley Industrial School for Boys.

There was no denying that Rocco Balliro committed the crime. When the cops later brought the not quite sixteen-year-old in for questioning, the drunkard's incriminating blood had stained the tip of one of Rocco's beloved blue suede shoes.

He was startled to attention by a loud tapping on the driver's side window. Rocco had been gazing forward, observing Johnny's roadside interrogation, which was taking place alongside the rental truck. Whipping his head around, he recognized the butt end of a flashlight through a thin layer of condensation that had accumulated on the glass.

Tap, tap, tap on the window again, louder and more insistent this time. The cop redirected the ray of light, shining it into Rocco's eyes. He instantly saw white dots and looked away as fumbled blindly for the handle so he could roll down the window. The cop thumped again, this time much harder, his mounting impatience evident.

"Jesus, you moron," Rocco mumbled under his breath. "You'll break the friggin' window." In defiance, he grasped and ever so slowly began to turn the handle. A crisp November gust rushed in through the widening opening.

Standing adjacent to the vehicle, a pair of cops warily peered in. Both were gripping the handles of their holstered revolvers. The officer nearest to the door crouched slightly to get a better look inside, sized up the occupant, and said, "License, please."

"Yeah, yeah, give me a sec," grunted Rocco as he reached down to retrieve the driver's license stashed in the console between the seats. As he did so, the cop aimed the flashlight into the car, carefully observing the occupant. Rocco decided that it was in his best interest not to make any sudden moves. He certainly didn't want to take a bullet from some jumpy, small-town cop.

He handed over the license. The cop trained the beam of light on the worn surface of the document and briefly inspected it.

"Any idea why we pulled you over tonight, Mr. D'Angelo?"

Mr. D'Angelo, Rocco thought, recalling when he last impersonated his buddy. But unlike that trying moment, when he squared off with the Boston cops in a dark alley and blurted out the first name that came to mind, this time the falsification was entirely intentional.

His reasoning was simple. He figured if they were stopped, Johnny would lie and say he forgot his license at home. He'd earn a citation for driving without one. Rocco, on the other hand, had no choice but to conceal his true identity. He was an ex-con driving on a suspended license. That alone was enough for the cops to haul him in.

Rocco shook his head and replied with a hint of sarcasm, "Not a clue, officer."

"We've been tailing you and the guy driving that truck," the cop said, gesturing toward the *actual* Johnny D'Angelo, who seemed to be facing intensifying scrutiny.

"You were observed weaving in and out of travel lanes for several miles," the officer said, lying through his crooked, tobacco-stained teeth.

Bullshit, Rocco thought. Rage began to simmer within him. He took a deep breath to cool the inner flames of fury. What the hell was this idiot spewing? Weaving in and out of lanes? C'mon! He and Johnny hadn't changed lanes since they passed through Norwood, a distance of at least fifteen miles.

Rocco resisted an overwhelming urge to ask the cop if he beat his wife but instead, calmly said, "Officer, you're mistaken, I haven't been drinking."

"Is that so?"

"That's so," he retorted, controlled yet defiant.

"Alright, Mr. D'Angelo– if that's your name," mocked the cop. "Let's step out of the car."

Rocco jerked on the handle, opened the door, and emerged into the night air, which had grown considerably chillier since they'd left Dedham an hour earlier.

The officer and his partner moved in quickly to grasp their subject's arms. Neither man looked particularly powerful, but in this instance, looks were deceiving. Their grips on his biceps were viselike.

Rocco noted his accuser's nametag which read Sgt. Bingham.

The uniformed tandem guided him toward their cruiser, the cylindrical beacons atop its roof flashing rhythmically on and off. It bathed the immediate surroundings in a garish blue light.

As he shuffled along the pavement sandwiched between the patrolmen, Rocco again pondered the accusation that he had been driving erratically, or as Sgt. Bingham claimed, "weaving in and out of travel lanes." He hadn't been drinking, at least not to excess. He and Johnny only had a couple beers during dinner – certainly not enough to impair them. And besides, he rationalized, that was more than two hours ago. He had drunk himself incoherent enough times in the past to know when he wasn't. No – there was something else afoot here. Perhaps their motive for making the traffic stop had something to do with the truck. Maybe they assumed the men were transporting something of value. A darkened stretch of obscure roadway in a remote town like North Attleboro provided a splendid opportunity for a shakedown. Criminally, Rocco considered, the only difference between himself and a police officer was that one of them wore a uniform to work.

"Alright. I'm just gonna pat you down."

"Sure, sure," Rocco complied. It was futile to resist. "Whatever you gotta do."

Sgt. Bingham leaned his captive over the hood of the patrol car. With the engine running beneath, Rocco was greeted by warmth through the hard, metal surface.

A trailer truck sped by, lifting a noxious concoction of dust and dirt. Rocco squeezed his eyes tightly closed against the road debris as his captor busied himself with a head to toe fishing expedition. Facing the roadway, Rocco failed to notice that the second cop had wandered off.

"Do you have any weapons?" Bingham asked, as he reached up under Rocco's jacket and then ran his hand down each leg, front and back.

"Huh?"

"Weapons," Bingham repeated. "Any weapons?"

"No."

"In your car?"

"No," the detainee snapped.

"No what?"

"No, there ain't any weapons in the car," lied Rocco as he thought about the handgun wedged beneath the driver's seat. How long would it be before they found it? It was only a matter of time before the weapon was discovered. It would considerably alter the dynamics of this roadside probe.

A new voice entered the conversation, and indignantly said, "What the hell do you call this?"

Rocco spun to face the opposite direction, toward the origin of the remark just in time to see a large, lethal hunting knife slammed against the hood of the car, inches from his nose. The metal on metal sound reverberated. *Dammit, I forgot about the knife*, he thought, annoyed by his carelessness. In his haste to ensure the pistol was securely concealed, he had all but overlooked the knife, which was ten inches in length, featured a razor-sharp steel blade, and could easily disembowel an adversary. Rocco had haphazardly tossed the blade to the floor of the passenger side of D'Angelo's car before they left Brighton.

"I asked you a question!" demanded Bingham's sidekick.

Awkwardly arched over the front of the squad car, knees resting against the chrome bumper, and legs splayed apart, Rocco was in no position to dispute the weapon or plead ignorance.

"Yeah, it's mine," he capitulated.

"What's it for?"

Rocco considered, for a moment, a smartass reply to yet another absurd question from this half-wit. *I clean my fingernails with it* was a response that briefly entered his mind. But he knew it was pointless to stoke this duo. His rebellious attitude was tempting fate and perhaps, physical harm, and would certainly hasten his trip to a lockup.

"It's for my protection," Rocco grumbled.

"Protection, huh?" The disbelieving cop sounded like he'd grown weary of the exchange.

Bingham didn't ask Rocco to expand on his explanation. Instead, he redirected his attention to a third cop who had just joined their group. This, Rocco recognized, was one of the guys who had been working Johnny over.

"Harry, you gotta see this," the new arrival said excitedly. Rocco turned to face him. He, too, had a silver name tag which flickered in the headlamp beam. It read Delaney.

"Sure, I'll be there in a minute," Bingham said as he readied his handcuffs. The police officer leaned forward, grasped his detainee's right arm, and pulled it around to the small of his back. He slapped a cuff on the first wrist and clicked it into place. The cold steel enclosure was a little too tight for Rocco's liking.

"Jesus!" he exclaimed. "Take it easy, will ya!"

Bingham responded to his prisoner's appeal by harshly yanking his left arm, fastening the second cuff a notch tighter than the first.

"Any more objections, D'Angelo?"

Rocco fought off an impulse to share a disparaging remark about Bingham's family. As pleasing as that might have been, it would likely have bought him a lump or two from a night stick, or worse. Instead, he bit his tongue and said nothing. Trussed up like the holiday bird that garnished the Zimmerman table a week before, a weary Rocco Balliro had little fight left in him.

CHAPTER 16

"The police must obey the law while enforcing the law."
– Supreme Court Justice Earl Warren

From the rear seat of the patrol car, where he sat side-by-side with Johnny D'Angelo, Rocco Balliro had a bird's-eye view of the goings-on inside the cargo box of the rental truck. Peering through the windshield, he observed as the quartet of police officers rifled through *his* collection of fur coats.

"These things are like a vise," Johnny complained.

"The cuffs?"

"Yeah," his partner answered, as he shifted his wrists bound behind his back, seeking relief. "They're cutting off my circulation."

"Careful, you'll just make them tighter," Rocco advised, knowing all too well from experience. The shackles attached to his wrists were chewing into his flesh as well.

"Bastards," Johnny spat with venom.

"What did they say?" Rocco asked.

Johnny glanced across the width of the seat and replied, "They asked for proof of ownership."

"Ownership? That's a new one."

"Yeah, I know"

"What'd you say?"

"I told them I lost the paperwork."

"Didn't fall for it, eh?"

Johnny grinned wanly and said, "No, not quite."

Rocco continued to watch the cops milling about in the truck. He had more than a sneaking suspicion about what they were up to.

"They asked where I was going with the coats," Johnny continued. "I said I was bringing them down to Rhode Island for a cleaning."

Rocco stifled a chuckle. He assumed, correctly as it was, that the two cops questioning his associate didn't find the answer believable or humorous, although Johnny wasn't intentionally attempting to be a wiseass.

"Yeah, I know," Johnny said. "As soon as the words came out of my mouth, I realized how stupid it sounded. Bringing a truckload of new coats with the price tags still attached to be cleaned." Johnny paused for a moment, shaking his head and added, "Dumb."

"Hey, don't worry about it," Rocco said. "You were under the gun, like me when I used your name in that alley."

"Yeah, guess so."

"Speaking of guns—"

"Jesus, don't tell me ..." Johnny's voice climbed an octave in distress. "They found it?"

"No, not yet," Rocco answered. "It's still stashed under the seat as far as I know. But when they impound the car, I'm sure they'll—"

"That's fuckin' great!"

"Take it easy."

"Take it easy?" his accomplice fumed. "That fuckin' car is registered in my name. They're gonna' pin the gun on me."

"Don't worry about it," Rocco insisted, attempting to allay Johnny's fears. "I'll take the rap. I'll probably be doing hard time for this shit anyway. Another year or two for the gun ain't gonna make much difference."

He suddenly wished he had the means to roll down the window and ventilate the interior of the car. A little fresh air would do them both a world of good.

The two men fell silent. For several minutes, the only sounds to be heard were the steady drone of the idling motor and occasional crackle of static emitted from the two-way radio mounted on the console.

Rocco was examining the interior of the cruiser, seeking a feasible means of escape when his attention was drawn back to the truck parked ahead of them.

"Hey, Johnny, would ya get a load of this," he said, gesturing with a nod of his head. "I don't fuckin' believe it."

Despondent over the dire circumstances, a sullen Johnny was gazing through the passenger window on his side of the car, in the general direction of the Stop & Shop supermarket.

"What is it?" he mumbled, sounding entirely disinterested.

"Look," Rocco urged. "In the rental."

Johnny turned to see a spectacle unfolding in the coat-laden compartment of the truck. Inside, the four rogue police officers were feverishly picking over the spoils of their traffic stop. Before long, the first of the cops emerged from the truck with a light-colored fur coat draped over his arm.

"Vultures," Johnny chaffed, hissing with disgust.

"I know," Rocco agreed, slowly shaking his head in disbelief. "We do all the heavy lifting and these dirty cops walk away with the goods."

A second patrolman, the man Rocco recognized as Delaney, clamored from the back of the truck with a dark mink tucked under his arm.

"Those worms are probably gonna give them coats to their fat wives for Christmas," Johnny snarled. He was verbally ruthless when provoked.

Christmas, thought Rocco, with pangs of longing that gripped at him. The meaningful holiday, his favorite as a young boy growing up in a staunchly Catholic household, hadn't crossed his mind on this harrowing night – that was, until Johnny mentioned it.

For several weeks, as November inexorably progressed toward December, Rocco envisioned how enjoyable it would be to bundle up the kids for a visit to downtown Boston to view some of the festive storefront window displays. Toby would guide the stroller sheltering her son while Rocco would tend to Bernice. They'd see reindeer and Santa Claus.

Mark, nearing his third Christmas and old enough now to truly cherish it, would shine with glee.

Later, to warm their bones, they might stop by Sophie's café for a mug of steaming hot chocolate and a slice of warm apple pie.

Rocco had so looked forward to lounging with Toby and the kids on Christmas morning in front of a huge tree decorated with ornaments and colored bulbs and strands of silver tinsel. Gifts galore would overflow from beneath the tree.

But now, thanks to these meddlesome North Attleboro cops, Rocco would be deprived. Instead of spending this joyous holiday with his beloved Toby, he would endure Christmas with jailed criminals and bitter guards who'd drawn the short straw for holiday duty.

Johnny continued to rant, insulting the despicable police officers and their family members. Rocco glanced out the window, which was somewhat fogged with condensation. He noticed Officer Bingham carrying a luxurious, full-length light brown fur coat. The thieving scoundrel walked around to the rear of the patrol car. Rocco heard the trunk click open. Within minutes, the remaining trio of miscreants joined Bingham at the rear of the car. From what Rocco could gather, each man was stashing one of the twice-stolen fur coats. Their task completed, the trunk lid was slammed shut.

The peculiar procession lumbered along the darkened, tranquil residential streets of North Attleboro, meandering past inviting homes. White spirals of smoke swirled from the crowns of chimneys, indicative of the late November chill that had descended upon this small southeastern Massachusetts community. Soon, winter would tighten its grip on the region and the tidy lawns would be shrouded in snow.

The cop driving the cruiser that held one Rocco Anthony Balliro and one Johnny D'Angelo was clad in the typical police-issue leather, minus the telltale nametag that his brethren Bingham and Delaney wore. His jacket, Rocco noted, was at least one size too small for his girth.

When the red-faced man slid his bulk across the front seat, after stashing his pillaged fur in the trunk with the others, he seemed winded. *Pathetic*, Rocco mused. *This character is one cheeseburger away from permanent desk duty or perhaps a twenty-one gun salute.*

Johnny's face grew clouded with anger and he glared as the overweight cop reached up with a beefy hand, yanked the shift, and urged the black and white forward. It was obvious to Rocco that this guy had made some disparaging remark to Johnny during his earlier roadside interrogation.

Seated to the right of the rotund cop was his partner, a middle-aged man of medium height and build, with thinning salt and pepper hair. From what Rocco could gather, this guy seemed to be the most level-headed member of the gang, although he certainly wasn't excluded from the feeding frenzy in the back of the rental truck.

The small flotilla of vehicles rolled steadily toward the center of town destined for the police station located on Mason Street.

Ahead of the patrol car, Officer Bingham led the pack, driving the commandeered rental truck while Delaney followed closely in the Ford.

The cruiser drove over a rut in the road, jostling Rocco and Johnny violently in the back seat. The jolt sent fresh waves of pain coursing through their bound wrists as the handcuffs dug deeper.

Rocco, who shifted on the seat seeking relief from the throbbing ache, surmised their driver purposely aimed for the pothole. His suspicions were substantiated when the fat cop turned and flashed a crooked, nicotine-stained smile seconds after propelling the vehicle over another rut.

Against his better judgment, Rocco took the bait. With an unmistakable undertone of sarcasm, he said, "So, officer, find everything you were looking for tonight?" The question achieved the desired results.

The cop's smile instantly faded and was replaced with a grimace of sheer fury. His brow grew furrowed. Raising his arm, he brandished a menacing, white-knuckled fist.

"I outta smack you right in the chops, wiseass," the irate flatfoot threatened with a gravelly two-pack-a-day voice.

Rocco understood he might have bought a beating. If not right there in the back of the patrol car, then certainly later in the hidden depths of the police station. Johnny smirked. Rocco had a knack for the verbal attack and wasn't afraid to use it. But to save his pretty face, and his dental work, he quickly resorted to damage control.

"Easy, big fella, easy," he soothed, trying to diffuse the lawman's wrath. "I was just kidding around. You can't take me seriously. Right, Johnny? Tell him."

"Uh huh," said his co-captive, not sounding at all convincing. "You're a kidder alright."

"Just keep your fuckin' yap shut or else you'll be missing a few Chiclets for your mugshot," the fat cop growled. His sidekick, meanwhile, stayed out of it.

Reaching the station, the three vehicles pulled into a small, cramped parking lot, one after another, and subsequently parked adjacent to a pair of white garage doors. The municipal building, a squat, single-story brick structure built in the early 1900s, was in a sorry state of disrepair.

As the fat cop and his partner climbed out of the car, Bingham and Delaney rejoined their colleagues. Bingham opened the rear door and beckoned for Rocco and Johnny to get out.

"Let's go, gentlemen," he commanded with an insidious smile hinting to the punitive treats that lied in wait. "It's time to see your accommodations for the evening."

CHAPTER 17

"I've always had a natural fear of the police, or abuse of their power." – Terrence Howard

Even though dressed in a pale yellow, rumpled sweatshirt and blue jeans with her hair knotted in a hurried ponytail, Toby was a striking beauty in Rocco's discerning eyes. In fact, he actually found her more appealing in this disheveled state than when she was wearing some of the lavish attire he'd acquired over the months. The only thing missing from the ensemble was the familiar black bandana she would frequently wrap around her pretty head when she was cleaning their apartment, fixing dinner, or relaxing in front of the television.

At that moment, however, she was anything but relaxed.

"I hate seeing you like this," she said, dabbing a damp eye with her sleeve.

"Trust me," he responded, forcing a weak smile as he peered at her through the inch-thick vertical iron bars. "I hate being stuck in this dump."

Toby stood in front of the drafty six-by-nine jail cell that held her boyfriend of nearly five months. She glanced downward and noticing her wrinkled shirt, used both hands to brush it smooth. He longed to embrace her and feel the warmth of her body against his.

"Honey, don't worry – you look great."

"I was in a hurry," she explained. "I threw on the first thing I could find."

He nodded and said, "Toby, you'd be gorgeous dressed in a paper bag."

Appreciative, she smiled in gratitude but changed the subject. "Tony, what happened tonight?"

"I'm still not sure," he answered, shrugging his broad shoulders. He directed his gaze to the stained, soiled floor beneath his feet and wondered how many men – and women – had bled and cried and spit and pissed on this floor over the decades. He wondered if his own blood might later be spilled on the crumbling surface by the fat cop, who was likely still fuming over their verbal sparring in the patrol car. *Imagine, Rocco thought, the cop being pissed off about being called a thief when he was, in fact, a thief.*

During the booking process, the officials were not pleased when it was discovered that the robbery suspect in their midst was not Johnny D'Angelo, as he had professed, but rather Rocco Anthony Balliro. According to the steady stream of teletype bulletins received by the North Attleboro police, he was well-known to both Boston and Brookline authorities.

One such teletype included a description of Rocco's older brother Frank.

ABOUT 1 OR 2 YEARS TPR JR ODONOVAN WHO STA HERE AT FRAM STOPPED A "FRANK" SAME ADDRESS ABOUT SAME AGE & DESC ACCORDING TO DIV-1 PD BSN – "FRANK BALLIRO" WAS CONSIDERED A VERY VERY VERY BAD SUBJECT IN BOSTON WUD JUST A SOON SHOOT THAT SPIT THAT MUST BE THE SAME ONE AS BROOKLINE PD STATED THAT WE ARE LUCKY TO BE WALKING.

There was some confusion as the police sorted out the teletypes and Rocco's true identity. He was amused and flattered that he was briefly mistaken for Frank, who was one of the tougher, more notorious of the Balliro brothers.

Rocco rested his forehead against the raw, cold metal bars and closed his eyes. He opened them when he felt Toby caressing the lingering reddened grooves on his wrists, a residual effect of the handcuffs.

He lowered his head in shame and remarked, "I guess I should've taken your advice."

"Which advice was that?"

"Providence."

"You mean about not going?"

"Yeah."

Toby continued to gently rub the indents on his wrists. The red welts were gradually beginning to fade.

"I'm sorry," he said in a nearly inaudible tone.

"Why'd they arrest you?" Toby asked.

Rocco didn't see any need to withhold the truth. He figured it was better to explain what took place than to have her read about it in the morning papers.

"Johnny and I were moving a truckload of coats to Providence," he said. "Remember, I mentioned it last night?"

"Yeah," she replied. "Just before you gave me the seal coat to take my mind off it."

He couldn't pull one over on her, for sure.

"Umm, yeah," he admitted. "Anyway, I sold them to some guys, and Johnny and I were making the drop tonight."

When Rocco mentioned his colleague's name, Toby turned to her right and gestured toward friend and neighbor, Maureen Lepore. Also an acquaintance of Johnny, Maureen had accompanied a distraught Toby for the trip from Brighton to North Attleboro while her younger sister agreed to watch over the babies.

Rocco could hear the soft murmur of voices several cells distant as Johnny and Maureen quietly chatted. By his count, this little jail could house a half-dozen prisoners.

"Toby, I'm sorry I dragged you down here." Actually, he was delighted to see her but felt selfish and guilty nonetheless. It was nearing midnight and she looked weary. She should be at home in their cozy apartment and not spending her evening in this damp, vile chamber.

"If I didn't love you, do you really think I would have come here tonight?" Indignant, she folded her arms across her chest.

"Alright, alright," he said, backing up a couple of steps into the depths of his cell.

Rocco was rather surprised that the North Attleboro cops had made an allowance for Toby to visit. During booking, he asked if he could make a quick phone call to let her know where he was. He didn't think they'd be sympathetic, particularly after he gave them lip during his arrest. But not only did they agree, Officer Bingham suggested he invite her to the station.

Rocco considered for a moment that perhaps these cops weren't so malevolent after all. But just as quickly, he pushed the thought from his mind. All he had to do was glimpse at the throbbing, red markings slowly fading from his wrists to realize that wasn't the case.

"So, Tony," she began, "what happened tonight?"

"I dunno, really," he answered with a shake of his head. "One minute, we're driving along and the next, we're getting dragged in here. There were four of them, Toby."

"I heard them talking about that," she shared.

"Whadda you mean?"

"The four cops," Toby responded. "I heard them talking about it."

A quizzical expression formed on his face. "What'd they say?" he asked.

"When we were waiting upstairs in the lobby," she recalled, "they were laughing. I guess they were dropping off some lunatic at the Foxboro Asylum."

Realization crept slowly toward Rocco and then it hit him, like a right hook to the jaw. "Jesus," he said.

"They sent extra cops in case he gave them trouble and— "

"—and that gave them the extra hands to grab me and Johnny," he said, finishing her comment.

Toby nodded.

Now he understood. No one tipped off the cops. He and Johnny hadn't been set up by someone trying to settle an old score with Tameleo, as he'd earlier theorized. Rocco's arrest was just a twist of fate – a sheer coincidence that placed him in the wrong place at the wrong time.

He considered the irony of his arrest.

Had there been just one officer manning the patrol car, which was the norm in small, suburban, low-crime communities like North Attleboro, he would likely never have stopped them on that dark, barren roadway. But four? That was a different story altogether. Cops were typically more brazen when numbers were in their favor.

It was fruitless to mull over the *what ifs* but Rocco realized that a minute or two difference would have altered his outcome. What if this so-called lunatic Toby heard the cops discussing had given them the slip in Foxboro? The guy might still be running. And Rocco and Johnny would be tipping back ice cold beers at one of the drinking establishments lining Atwells Avenue, celebrating a significant payday. Instead, he found himself caged in a rancid jail cell with a prison term hanging over his head.

He glanced upward at the harsh light bulb suspended above his sparse chamber that held little more than a metal toilet, a matching sink, and a rusting metal rack topped by a thin, moth-eaten mattress.

Rocco inhaled deeply, filling his lungs with musty, stagnant air.

"Have they set bail?" Toby asked.

"Fifty grand."

He knew Toby didn't have the means to raise that kind of money and didn't suggest she try. It would have been futile.

"So what's next?" she questioned.

"Arraignment," he replied, speaking the word as if he'd just eaten something rotten. "First thing in the morning at the Attleboro District Court. That's what they tell me anyway. After that, I don't know."

He did know. Unless his attorney, cousin Joe Balliro could spin a remarkable defense, doubtful under the circumstances,

Rocco would be heading back to prison after less than two years of freedom.

He craved a cigarette but noticed that Toby didn't have her purse. Not surprising. The police weren't about to allow her to bring it into the cellblock area for obvious reasons.

From several cells away, Rocco could now discern part of the conversation taking place between Johnny and Maureen. He overheard one comment in particular that caught his attention.

"When the cops pulled us over," Johnny said to her, "Rocco could have easily taken off. But he stuck with me. I'd trust him with my life."

Rocco grinned. His partner wasn't the type of guy who ever would lay blame when they set out to burglarize a Boston-area business, nobody was holding a gun to the man's head. Johnny understood that the rewards of criminal enterprise could be substantial, but so, too, were the inherent risks.

"What's so funny?" Toby asked, noticing his smirk. She hadn't heard Johnny's remark.

"Huh? Oh it's nothing. I was just thinking about something Johnny said."

Toby was just about to ask him to explain when she was distracted by the sound of someone approaching. Rounding the corner, his footfalls echoing, was Officer Bingham. He stopped and tipped his hat to Toby in greeting.

"Evenin', ma'am," he said.

Toby politely reciprocated with a guarded smile. "Good evening."

"Late night, officer?" Rocco interjected.

Bingham ignored him and instead, continued to scrutinize Toby. Rocco helplessly watched as the cop eyeballed his girlfriend, sizing her up like a fox in a henhouse. With nothing to lose, an infuriated Rocco might have slugged him. Bingham was fortunate to be separated from him by a set of iron bars.

"Ma'am, my apologies," he began. "But I'm afraid we have to end the visit. Time for you and your friend here to say goodnight."

"Sure," Toby said. "I understand. We can't thank you enough for letting us come down here tonight."

"No problem," Bingham said, leering at her. "Take a few more minutes and then come upstairs for your belongings."

Yeah, and maybe a little grab-ass, a seething Rocco thought.

The cop started to walk away but abruptly stopped in his tracks. He turned and said to Rocco, "By the way, Mr. Balliro, we've finished going over your car."

Rocco suddenly went numb. Despite the chill, beads of sweat instantly broke out on his forehead. *They found it*, he thought with apprehension. *They found the gun.*

"Nice wheels you have there," the police officer remarked with an expression that said he really didn't give a shit about the car but rather what his men discovered concealed inside. "After your lady friend leaves, we need to have a little talk."

CHAPTER 18

"The best way to escape from your problem is to solve it." – *Robert Anthony*

From the moment he first arrived at the New Bedford House of Corrections, a dreary and depressing structure which had cast foreboding shadows over Ash Street for nearly a century, Rocco Anthony Balliro began plotting his escape.

As he stepped from the patrol car into the early December chill, Rocco took the opportunity to scrutinize the sheer three-story granite exterior and imposing iron barriers crisscrossing the tall, rectangular windows on the lower floors. He noted that the third floor windows were free of the lattice. He knew that breaking out of the formidable jail would be daunting, but certainly not unthinkable.

His plan had already begun to take shape as he entered the musty foyer of the penitentiary. With a tandem of police officers cautiously trailing a stride behind, Rocco shuffled across the worn floor. The manacles shackling his wrists to a chain cinched around his waist jangled as he pressed forward. The drab room was sparsely decorated with several plastic plants and a faded American flag. Portraits of politicians were mounted on the surrounding walls.

Reaching the podium, Rocco stopped and stood at attention, silently awaiting further instructions. A bored-looking corrections officer, who was thumbing through a magazine, looked up to inspect the men who were interrupting his morning leisure.

One of the two cops handed the attendant a manila-colored sheath bulging with papers. *The story of my life in a cardboard folder*, thought Rocco morosely.

"Name?" asked the desk officer indifferently.

This guy needs to find another line of work, Rocco considered as he replied, "Rocco Anthony Balliro."

"Alright then, Mr. Balliro," the officer acknowledged as he slid off his stool, thumbed a pair of belt loops, and hiked up his sagging trousers. "Follow me."

"All set?" asked the cop who'd handed over the folder.

"Yep, we're good. You can pick up your cuffs next trip."

Without another word, the pair of North Attleboro police officers, neither of which was involved in his arrest the previous night, wheeled in unison and made for the exit.

No goodbye, Rocco thought. He resisted the urge to fling a sarcastic comment in their direction. You never knew when you might have a brush up with a father, brother, uncle, or cousin of an officer you'd pissed off in the past. Retribution for the offended relative was often swift.

As his guide keyed a huge, steel door that led to the inmate processing room, Rocco's thoughts drifted back to a day earlier when he was brought before Judge Francis J. Good, who presided over the Fourth District Court of Attleboro.

Along with co-defendant Johnny D'Angelo, Rocco Balliro was indicted for the November 28, 1962, heist of Worth's of Boston in Brookline, which yielded a cache of furs valued at more than thirteen thousand dollars. Additionally, he was found guilty of possessing a firearm without a permit, as well as an assortment of vehicular charges.

Rocco hadn't given his attorney, cousin Joseph Balliro, much room for legal wrangling. There was, however, good news for both defendants. As it turned out, the four arresting North Attleboro police officers committed a huge blunder.

"Your Honor," began Johnny's court-appointed public defender Edward J. Harrington, "the defense asks that the fur coats seized from the rental truck be removed from evidence."

"Explain, Mr. Harrington," Judge Good ordered, knowing full well the answer before he leveled the question.

"This evidence, Your Honor, was gathered by the North Attleboro police while conducting an illegal search of the defendant's vehicle."

The judge cleared his throat and said, "Go on."

"The arresting officers stopped the defendants for an alleged traffic violation," the defense attorney continued. "But the search of the—"

"Let me guess," a scowling Judge Good interrupted. "No just cause?"

"No, Your Honor," Harrington replied.

Out of the corner of his eye, Rocco saw the assistant prosecutor seated at an adjacent table turn pale. Judge Good just nodded in agreement. His hands were tied. Score one for the bad guys. The judge glanced over at the prosecutor with a look of disdain. For all intents and purposes, the search and seizure of the furs was illegal.

Rocco took obscene pleasure in the moment. He glanced at his co-defendant, who was grinning. Although his attorney was little more than a state worker, Harrington was worth his weight in gold at that moment. Their situation had just improved measurably, although Johnny was in better shape than his friend. Despite the success in taking the furs off the table, Rocco still faced the gun charge.

The New Bedford corrections officer ushered his newest inmate into the processing room and instructed him to take a seat. Rocco complied, easing his weary frame into a straight-backed chair placed against a cinder-block wall. There were a number of notices plastered to the surface, none that he could read from a distance, and several photos. Problem inmates, he assumed. He made it a point not to have his likeness added to this wall.

The attendant pulled up an identical chair, facing his subject, and placed the paperwork-laden folder on the scarred surface of an old desk. Twisting a knob at the base of a lamp, he illuminated the area. He then began to sift through the ream of documents.

"I see here, Mr. Balliro, that you served four years at Walpole," he stated matter-of-factly.

"Yes, sir," he replied.

His chaperone continued to flip through the document, raising a bushy eyebrow when he encountered something of interest.

"Hmmm, armed robbery?" he said.

"It was all a misunderstanding."

"Always is," the officer said dryly. "I've heard it a million times."

Rocco resisted the urge to comment.

"It also says here that you had some *difficulties* at Walpole," he continued.

"Another misunderstanding."

"That's not how I see it," the officer accused, tapping his fingers on the papers spread out before him. "Assault and battery on a corrections officer, for instance?"

Rocco slumped forward. He wasn't about to waste time and effort explaining the importance of defending one's heritage. It wouldn't matter in the least to this guy that the Walpole corrections officer in question earned a mouthful of knuckles for an unflattering comment about Italians. But while the beating of the guard earned Rocco acclaim from fellow inmates, he unfortunately had to savor his notoriety with a prolonged stay in solitary confinement.

Rocco figured it was best to play along with this charade. After a pause, he bowed his head and said, with phony remorse, "I learned my lesson, sir."

"Excuse me?"

"I did serious time in solitary," he explained. "Long enough to read a Webster's dictionary. I'd rather not do that again."

"Then I assume you'll have no problem adhering to our rules," said the interviewer.

"No, sir, no problem," Rocco answered.

Rocco, exhausted from lack of sleep in the North Attleboro lockup the night before, fought back the urge to close his eyes as the man spewed nonsense about what he could and could not do while incarcerated in the New Bedford House of Corrections.

"…and we don't issue uniforms here," the man added as his discourse came to a merciful close. "You can keep that leather coat. It gets cold at night and our heating system is a little old."

Yeah, like you, an expressionless Rocco thought. "Thank you, sir – much appreciated."

"Any questions?"

"None, sir."

"Well, then, let's go take a look at your quarters."

Like a caged animal, Rocco paced back-and-forth in his cell, trudging across the diminutive space with several strides. That's all it took with his long legs to navigate the nine-foot span from the bars at the front of the chamber to the rear wall. He covered the length, touched the cold, damp wall, pivoted in place, and promptly traipsed back to the iron bars. He repeated the dizzying sequence, over and over again.

As he went through his paces, he took care not to collide with the unforgiving metal edge of his bed or the toilet, which jutted obtrusively from the sidewall. He had a number of raised, bluish-yellow welts on his shins to prove the task was far easier said than done.

At regular intervals, Rocco would drop to the chilled concrete floor and perform a calisthenics routine, featuring a series of pushups and sit ups. This, he realized, was the best means to stay in shape while in confinement. And remaining fit was vital, particularly if he held out any hope of getting out of this despicable jail.

"Hey, Balliro!" reverberated a shout from the base of the staircase on the bottom tier, interrupting his workout.

"Yeah?" he hollered in response.

"Visitor!" yelled the voice belonging to one of the corrections officers tasked with guarding the facility's three hundred inmates. "Get yourself cleaned up!"

It must be Toby, he thought with a rush of anticipation. He sped through a wash, quickly scrubbing his face. He changed into a fresh white t-shirt and lastly, combed his hair.

He'd only been holed up in the deteriorating building for a couple of days, but he was already anxious to see Toby again. Deep inside, Rocco was suffering from paranoia. He knew she loved him. There was no question of that. But unless he furnished some semblance of hope that he would soon be free, by legal means or otherwise, Rocco wasn't sure how long Toby could remain devoted to him.

"Let's go, Balliro," beckoned the officer who had suddenly appeared in front of his cell. The uniformed man keyed the lock and swung open the narrow door. Rocco tucked in his shirt and stepped on to the catwalk.

"After you," the guard instructed. Rocco complied and wordlessly walked along the grated metal, glancing downward through the metal gaps to the level below.

Reaching the staircase, he gripped the banister as he negotiated the two flights, taking added care not to inadvertently catch the soles of his shoes on the grating. He had heard tale of men who had taken nasty spills on these treacherous stairs. A broken arm or leg would make an escape attempt, at least in the near term, improbable.

Twice, the guard ordered a halt so he could disengage a steel door and then secure it behind them after they passed through. The third and final door had a small sign affixed to it which read VISITOR'S ROOM. Rocco's heart began thumping madly as the officer slid a key into the slot.

As he opened the door and stepped aside to allow the inmate to pass, he advised, "Twenty minutes, Balliro."

"Yeah, okay."

"I'll let you know when there are five minutes left so you can say your goodbyes."

"Uh huh," Rocco muttered as he stepped across the threshold into the visiting area.

The room was square in shape: box-like, with poor lighting, a low ceiling, and no décor to speak of. Taking up most of the available space was a row of face to face individually-divided booths and chairs, separated along the length by an expanse of chicken wire. Other than fingertips, the thin wire prevented physical contact between inmate and visitor. Disappointing, certainly, but Rocco was grateful that no one else was in the room at the time, save for Toby.

She was a sight to behold. The last time he had seen her, at the North Attleboro police station several days earlier, Toby wore a frumpy, wrinkled sweatshirt and jeans. Her hair was unkempt and she looked the part of someone who had just rolled out of bed – which was the case. But as he told her, he was so glad to see her it didn't matter how she was dressed.

This time, however, she had ample time to prep for the visit and was perfectly stunning in a powder blue, button-down blouse with a matching calf-length navy skirt that clung to her like a glove. Toby's short, dark hairstyle was handsomely primped, and in an uncommon addition for her, she had liberally applied cherry red lipstick. She was radiant.

Rocco settled into a wooden chair midway along the row, which featured five identical positions. He imagined the room could grow awfully loud when the ten seats, five inmates and five visitors, were all occupied at once.

As Toby slid the chair from beneath the table opposite Rocco and sat, he smiled warmly and in his best impression of film actor Humphrey Bogart uttered, "Of all the gin joints in all the towns in all the world, she walks into mine."

"Hello, Mr. Bogart," she said with a sweet, girlish giggle. He loved her laugh.

He ached for her. "You look great."

"Oh, this thing," Toby said, downplaying her fetching ensemble. "It's just something I picked up at Turn Style."

"Did you pay for it?" he joked, recalling a story Toby once told him about her and sister-in-law Beverly getting picked up for shoplifting at Turn Style, a landmark department store in Brighton.

"Wise guy!"

"I'm just kidding," he said. "It's perfect."

"How are they treating you in here?" she asked, forcing a thin smile.

"Can't complain," he replied.

"You mean you won't complain."

She was right. It wasn't in his nature. But Rocco also knew that it would just add to her concern if he were to share that the aging jail was always ice cold, the food was inedible and often sickened inmates, and the corrections officers were a bunch of pompous illiterates who amused themselves by provoking guys just trying to do their time and stay out of trouble.

He changed the subject. "How're the kids?" he asked.

"Mark misses you," Toby said. Her eyes grew misty. "He keeps asking when Tony is coming home. He wants to drive your car again."

Toby was referring to the pleasant Sunday drive they'd taken to northern New Hampshire in mid-October to view the New England fall foliage. On one of the quieter, traffic-free roads, Rocco had positioned Mark on his lap, allowing the toddler to grip the steering wheel and "drive" the Olds. They all laughed as he exclaimed "vroom-vroom!" and implored Rocco to make the car go faster.

"That was hilarious," he admitted. "I miss him too."

The conversation carried on in a similar vein, with Toby sharing more vignettes from the home front. When she mentioned she was short on cash, Rocco told her where she could find a small stash he'd hidden in their apartment. It wasn't much but it would tide her over for a week or two. He also assured her that when funds ran low, his brothers would help.

"I'd feel guilty taking it," Toby said.

"Don't even think about it," he insisted. "You're family."

She raised her hand and placed it, palm forward, against the surface of the chicken wire. Rocco mirrored her, placing his splayed fingers against hers. Feeling the warmth of her tender skin through the metal mesh, he longed to wrap his arms around her. As he looked at the surface of his hand, pressing against hers, he caught a glimpse of something that sent what felt like an electric charge coursing through his body.

"Jesus," he whispered, restraining his voice in case the guards were eavesdropping in some way. "That's it."

"What?" Toby said, sounding alarmed. "What is it?"

"The chicken wire," he answered. "There's a space ..." He trailed off as he ran the tip of a finger along his find.

Toby shook her head and said, "I don't understand."

"Look," Rocco began. "I really need to get out of this place."

"Uh huh," she said. "Your lawyer is working on the case. Isn't he?"

"No, no," he said, waving off the comment. "I can't rely on him."

"A different lawyer, then?"

"No," he replied. "That wouldn't matter. The cops got me with a gun and some other charges. I'm facing serious time."

He paused and fixed his eyes on hers in a long, unblinking stare.

"Honey," she said, after a moment. "You're not thinking of—"

"Yeah, I am."

"But, how could you get away—"

"With your help," he said.

"My help?"

"Yeah."

"What can I do?"

Rocco looked around the room to reassure himself that they were truly alone, inched his chair closer to the leading edge of the table, and leaned forward.

"Listen," he began. Toby moved closer so she could hear what he had to say. Without pointing, Rocco gestured with a slight nod toward the honeycombed-patterned chicken wire that separated them. "You see this wire mesh, where it meets the edges of the booth?"

"Yeah."

"There's a small gap."

"Uh huh – I see it."

"It's narrow but looks wide enough, I think, to slip hacksaw blades through."

"Hacksaw blades?"

"Yeah," Rocco said.

Her face contorted in confusion, she asked, "What would you do with those?"

"Saw my way out of here," he bluntly answered.

"You're joking, right?"

His freedom hanging in the balance and time ticking away on their visit, Rocco grew impatient but withheld his emotions. He grinned, shook his head and inhaled deeply of the stale air that filled the poorly-ventilated chamber. It stunk of mildew and human perspiration. With a stony, emphatic expression, he said, "No, doll. I'm dead serious."

Toby stared at him, unblinking. "Alright, alright," she said calmly.

"Let me explain," he asserted. "But quickly, we're running out of time."

"Uh huh, sure."

"The bars on my cell," he began. "I'm pretty sure I can cut through them."

"With a little blade?"

"They're made from iron but it's old iron."

"Don't they watch you?" Toby asked, adding, "The guards, I mean?"

"Yeah, but only during the day," he answered. "At night, they sleep like babies. They make rounds but at the same time each night. Totally predictable."

"Uh huh."

"It'll take time," Rocco continued, gradually growing more animated as he expounded on his idea. He caught himself making a back-and-forth sawing motion at one point, to emphasize the verbal description. He could almost taste success as his plan took shape. "I'll cut the bars a little each night."

Toby looked down at her fingernails, pausing to absorb what he had just explained to her. It was overwhelming.

Rocco, for his part, leaned back in his chair and folded his hands, fingers laced together behind his head. He gazed at her, his lover and potential accomplice as she mulled over the request.

He felt a twinge of guilt but was desperate. He understood that, on any given day, he could be transferred elsewhere, including a return to the dreaded MCI-Walpole, from which escape was implausible. In the deepest recesses of his conscience, he knew it was wrong to ask Toby to risk her freedom so he might gain his.

Rocco had already decided, however, that if she declined to do as he asked, he wouldn't try to change her mind. It had to be Toby's decision entirely, without coercion. He was prepared to take no for an answer.

"Tony?" she whispered.

He sat upright. "Yeah?"

Before she could complete her comment, the door to the visiting room abruptly swung open and the corrections officer, who had earlier escorted Rocco down from the upper tier, intervened. "Five minutes, Balliro," he rudely announced.

Yeah, your mother, thought Rocco as he swiveled to face the intruder.

"Wrap it up," the man reiterated, checking his wristwatch.

"Yes, sir."

As the officer backed out of the room, Rocco raised his hand and unfurled a single-fingered sign of disrespect in the direction of the door.

He then returned his attention to Toby.

"Sorry," he said. "They get under my skin."

"I can see that."

He marveled at how well she held up under duress. It took a lot to rattle her. Like the night Gianni Saroni delivered the bad news, inaccurate as it turned out, that Rocco had been apprehended by the Boston Police following a pursuit.

He wondered which woman would make the decision regarding the procurement of hacksaw blades. Cool and calculating? Anxious and fearful?

"Tony?"

"Yeah?"

"I want you to get out of here," she said, adding, "and soon."

"Me too."

"I'll do it," she said, setting the wheels in motion for his escape attempt. "I'll get what you need."

CHAPTER 19

"The securest place is a prison cell, but there is no liberty." – Benjamin Franklin

Slathering a generous gob of Vaseline on his fingertips, Rocco Balliro knelt at the front of his cell and applied the substance to the base of one of the cast iron bars. He had found, since he began cutting through the inch-thick metal, that the petroleum jelly adequately dulled the noise made as he raked the hacksaw blade back-and-forth.

Rocco stood up and made his way to the sink mounted at the rear of his cell. Running the water at a trickle, he wet his hands, soaped up, and vigorously rubbed them together. Any Vaseline residue would make it difficult to grip the tool. The last thing he needed was to have a blade slip from his grasp and skitter to the catwalk, out of reach.

He toweled dry and returned to his work. Kneeling in a position in front of the bars that had grown familiar over the previous thirty-five days, he leaned forward, and lined up the teeth of the blade with the groove he'd made in the metal. As he pulled the thin blade toward him and then away, in a steady, rhythmic motion, Rocco's thoughts turned to the events that took place after Toby agreed to do his bidding.

"Where should I buy the blades?" she had asked as the final minutes wound down on her visit.

"Try Model Hardware in Allston," he suggested, recalling his recent purchase of the hanging rods and brackets. "I bought some stuff there last week."

"How many?"

"I figure four should do the trick," he answered, holding up his hand displaying four fingers for emphasis. "Ask someone in the store to help you. Tell them you need tempered steel blades, but flexible, not the all-hard type."

She echoed him in order to precisely commit the request to memory. "Steel ... flexible ... not all-hard."

"Exactly."

The couple fell silent. Before long, the corrections officer burst through the door a second time to retrieve his ward for the return to the cellblock.

"I'll see you in a couple of days," Toby promised.

Rocco turned and uttered "love you" over his shoulder as he stepped out of the room, uniformed escort trailing closely.

"I love—"

Her reply was cut short as the visiting room door slammed shut. When she returned several days later, Toby completed the sentiment.

"You know that I love you, honey?" she asked as she took up the same seat she had occupied during her first visit. Once again, they were alone, which was far more important now.

"Of course."

"Well, if it weren't for this cage separating us, I'd make you kiss me four times."

He was perplexed. "Why four?"

She smiled devilishly and stretched her arms straight out, resting them on the surface of the countertop. Palms down, flat on the smooth surface, she leaned closer to the wire grating. "One for each of the hacksaw blades I brought you."

His eyes grew round, like saucers. "You have them?" he asked excitedly.

"Yeah."

"I don't know what to say," Rocco said as he struggled to keep his emotions at bay. He had a lump in his throat. "You're unbelievable."

"Just say you'll get out of here soon, that's all."

"It's as good as done."

A knock sounded on the door behind Rocco and it opened slowly. This officer was far more polite than his predecessor.

"Five more minutes, folks."

"Thanks," Rocco said. There was no need to give this guy the finger.

After the guard left, he looked at Toby and said, "We need to hurry."

Without a word, she grasped the leading edge of one of her elbow-length silk gloves and began to peel back the material, rolling it down the length of her arm. As she did, the shiny, glinting steel surfaces of a pair of hacksaw blades were revealed. To Rocco, it was akin to discovering a thick vein in a gold mine. Treasure!

"I wondered how you'd manage to smuggle them in here," he said, proud of her ingenuity.

Toby nodded. "There was a scary moment when I signed in."

"Oh yeah?"

"The guard made me hang my coat in the lobby," she recalled. "He looked at the gloves and for a minute, I thought he was going to make me take them off."

"Jesus."

"I was so scared," she explained, "I nearly wet myself."

He chuckled lightly as Toby positioned the first blade upright and adjacent to the thin gap in the wire barrier. Carefully, she began to slide it through the narrow breach. Rocco grasped the receiving end as it reached his side of the screen and pulled it through, avoiding the sharp, serrated teeth. It would be difficult to explain a hand laceration to the corrections people. Toby repeated the procedure with the remaining three blades.

Within a minute, the guard would return to end the visit. Toby restored her gloves, stretching them along her slender arms. Rocco, meanwhile, rose from his chair and stuffed the blades down the front of his trousers.

Seeing this, Toby winced a little and warned, "Be careful there, Mr. Balliro."

He smiled as she left, knowing he would soon be leaving himself.

CHAPTER 20

"The best way to find out if you can trust somebody is to trust them." – Ernest Hemingway

Rocco Anthony Balliro and Johnny D'Angelo sat chatting, perched on hard, aluminum benches that were permanently welded to each of the four sides of a steel table. Individual chairs in the general population area of the New Bedford House of Corrections were frowned upon by officials. Loose furnishings had a tendency to become airborne during disturbances.

The pair was seated at the furthest reach of the indoor recreation area which abutted a staircase that led from the bottom floor of the cavernous enclosure to the upper housing tier.

Suspended from the ceiling were oval-shaped lamps, which gave off a murky incandescence and spawned bizarre shadows. The large space was cold, damp, and musty.

Nearby, several inmates were lifting barbells while others were anchored in front of a bank of payphones, likely chatting with loved ones – or their attorneys. There were a few guys reading books on loan from the institution library, as well as a pair of old-timers playing checkers.

Rocco lit up a smoke and drew deeply, relishing the nicotine rush. Cigarettes were tough to come by in the jail. He'd gone several days without, until finally scoring a pack in trade that morning. He generously extended the pack across the table, offering one to Johnny.

"How've you been?" Rocco asked, as his associate accepted the smoke and lit up. Both men generally kept to themselves, seldom venturing into this volatile area of the jail. There always seemed to be some knucklehead looking for a fistfight, which served no purpose other than to extend one's sentence.

"Not bad," Johnny replied. "How 'bout you?"

"I'm good."

"Seen Toby?"

"Yeah, she came in over the weekend."

"She's pretty crazy about you, coming all the way from Brighton like that."

If only he knew how devoted she really was, Rocco thought, nodding in agreement and saying, "Yeah, she's a special girl."

The conversation shifted. The two men complained to one another about the squalor in the jail. The conditions were deplorable. The showers were cold and for inmates who fell ill, medical care was virtually nonexistent. The staff prepared and served food that wasn't fit for human consumption but the choice remained to eat it or go hungry.

As advertised by the officer who processed Rocco in December, the winter drafts penetrated the walls of the aging jail. Except for sleep, Rocco seldom removed his jacket. He imagined that, during the dog days of New England summers, the building would grow unbearably torrid. Then again, he didn't intend to hang around long enough to find out. His work on the bars was progressing much more swiftly than anticipated. He figured it was a good time to let Johnny in on the escape gambit.

"There's something I've been meaning to tell you," Rocco began, as he stubbed out the remnants of his cigarette.

His friend leaned forward, rested his muscular forearms on the edge of the table and clasped his outstretched hands together, as if in prayer. It reminded Rocco of his days at St. Mary's in the North End of Boston, where he and his siblings attended parochial elementary school at the behest of their deeply religious parents. How long had it been since he sat at a wooden desk with his hands folded in similar fashion, praying to the dear Lord that the sister patrolling the ranks of students wouldn't thrash him with a wooden ruler again? Fifteen years? Certainly not long enough to forget the indiscriminate beatings handed down by vindictive nuns.

"What's that?" Johnny asked. "I'm all ears."

Rocco cut to the chase. "I'm getting outta here."

Johnny lifted his arms off the table and leaned back. His steely blue eyes were round and wide. He ran his hand through a thick growth of hair and cast a stunned glance across the table.

"Whadda you mean?"

"I mean, I'm breaking out."

"You're kidding, right?"

"No, I'm not kidd—"

Rocco cut short his reply as a corrections officer unexpectedly appeared from the shadow of the staircase and meandered toward their table. He slowed as he drew near and glared suspiciously at the duo.

"Up to no good, I assume?" he spat, directing his inquiry at Rocco.

"And good afternoon to you too, sir."

The screw barked, "You're a wiseass, Balliro."

"Yes, sir. I mean, no, sir. I mean ..."

"Knock it off," the guard said in disgust as he moved on.

Johnny waited until the officer had wandered out of earshot, then said, "It's a wonder they don't kick your ass more often."

Rocco grinned and said, "Hey, I gotta take my shots whenever I can these days."

"Yeah, like the *shot* you took with that cop in North Attleboro."

"You mean in the patrol car?"

"Yeah," said Johnny. "I thought he was gonna bust open your skull."

"Me too," Rocco agreed. "Guess I have a big mouth *and* I'm one lucky sonofabitch."

"So, you were saying?"

Rocco paused to light up another cigarette. "I said I'm getting out."

"When?"

"Coupla days, I figure," Rocco estimated, looking skyward to admire a smoke ring he'd just dispatched.

"How?" Johnny asked.

Rocco glanced around to ensure that no unwanted guests had crept close enough to hear their conversation. "I've been cutting the bars on my cell—"

"Jesus," his friend interrupted.

"—with hacksaw blades."

"Hacksaw blades?" he asked incredulously. "Where the hell did you get hacksaw blades?"

"Never mind that," Rocco replied, waving his hand to discard the question. "That's not important."

Actually, it was important. But there was no need to share every aspect of his plan. It wasn't that he didn't trust Johnny. Quite the contrary, in fact. But Rocco had to protect his girlfriend from the authorities — at all costs.

Certainly, after he made his daring escape, there would be an inquest. And Johnny, his long-time partner, would likely face rigorous questioning. What did you know, Mr. D'Angelo? How did your friend Balliro pull it off? Did you help him? If you didn't, who did?

That's where things could get dicey for Toby. While a trustworthy stalwart like Johnny would never, ever, intentionally rat her name to the authorities, he was still human and humans made mistakes. Had he known that it was she who supplied the blades, Johnny might slip and spill her name during the heat of an interrogation. The less he knew, the safer it would be for all three of them.

"Too bad I couldn't take you with me," Rocco said, after a brief pause.

"That wouldn't make much sense."

Rocco nodded, understanding fully. While he faced a lengthy sentence and probably an eventual transfer to a more secure facility such as MCI-Walpole, his co-conspirator would see the light of day much sooner. Bottom line: there was absolutely no need for Johnny to take a foolhardy risk and join in an escape try. As it turned out, Johnny was released in February 1963. Rocco ended up facing the more serious charges while Johnny did short time for motor vehicle violations.

Rocco was measurably relieved. Even as he made the suggestion to his comrade to join in the jail break, he doubted he could bring it about. His own effort had been grueling and involved more than five weeks of tedious work. It was farfetched to think that Johnny could duplicate the effort.

"So, a few days, huh?"

"Yeah, I'm close. Maybe Wednesday or Thursday."

"Anything I can do to help?"

Rocco shook his head

Johnny swiveled his legs off the seat and stood. He arched his back, stretching. Several nearby inmates abruptly stopped their activities, including the twosome playing checkers, and began to make their way toward the mess hall. Supper time approached.

"Gonna get a bite?"

"No, I socked away a can of tuna I got from the canteen," Rocco said, "I'm gonna have that with a few crackers."

"You're crackers," Johnny quipped.

Rocco chuckled lightly and rose to his feet. His joints protested; not surprising after weeks of kneeling on the concrete surface as he carved the bars.

"So I guess I'll see you when I get out," Johnny said.

Rocco stubbed out his cigarette and said to his colleague as he shuffled away, "Count on it."

CHAPTER 21

"I have been desperate to escape for so many years now, it is routine for me to try to escape." – Jack Henry Abbott

He detected footsteps, one after another, scuffling over the metal surface of the upper tier catwalk. It was a familiar cadence and one that arrived each night with punctuality. The sound of boots making contact with the grated floor indicated that it was nearing midnight and one of the graveyard shift corrections officers was presiding over the inmate head count in the New Bedford House of Corrections.

Right on time, Rocco thought, as he shrank deeper in concealment. The footfalls reached the adjacent cell and paused. While he couldn't see the guard, he knew from the repetitive nature of this nightly ritual that the man was aiming the beam of a flashlight into his neighbor's chamber, searching for any irregularities. That would include, amongst others, an unoccupied bunk.

At that perilous moment, seconds before the officer moved along the tier and reached his cell to perform a similar search, Rocco's cot was not occupied; at least not by him. Instead, beneath the flimsy, state-issued blanket was a carefully-fabricated body double, assembled with pillows, sheets, and rolled-up towels.

It had taken several weeks to accumulate the linens he would need to recreate his likeness. Rocco swapped a valuable pack of cigarettes for an extra pillow with a prisoner he'd befriended. A steady flow of candy bars were bartered with another inmate in exchange for a blanket. And most recently, he dealt away several girlie magazines for a couple of moth-eaten towels. It was prison commerce in its purest form.

"Hey, Roc, what's all the stuff for?" asked one inquisitive inmate as he munched on a bar of chocolate.

"It's cold in my room," Rocco answered, which was actually truthful. "I'm waking up every morning with a stiff neck."

"Ask the screws to move you somewhere else."

Rocco replied, "Naw, I don't want to move because the screws would be touching all my stuff."

Oh yeah, and I'd be walking away from weeks of sawing through the iron bars and have to start all over again in a new cell, he thought.

Some of the inmates he got to know over the weeks weren't bad guys, but Rocco kept them at arm's length. He shared the truth with Johnny D'Angelo, out of respect, but there was little need to confide in anyone else. The jail, he had found, was infested with rats, and not just the four-legged vermin that rampaged through the kitchen and mess hall.

Hiding at the foot of his bed, Rocco crouched lower. His legs were awkwardly contorted beneath him. He'd been there for ten minutes and his contracted muscles began to protest. He felt the beginnings of a cramp in his right calf but resisted the urge to reach down and knead it. As it turned out, it was the right decision. Somehow, he'd lost track of the guard's progress. Without warning, the uniformed silhouette materialized in front of the cell and directed the flashlight into the darkness.

Rocco instantly froze, like a block of granite. His breath caught in his throat, which quickly grew parched. *My kingdom for a sip of water*, he thought. As raw adrenaline surged through his body, an unpleasant metallic taste filled his mouth.

Without moving his head, Rocco cast his gaze downward, toward the concrete surface below. He feared that he might inadvertently stare into the ray of light flitting about his cell.

His reflection would mirror back to the officer and all would be lost.

A single bead of salty sweat formed at his hairline and broke loose, streaming down his forehead, coming to rest at his eyebrow. It triggered an itch he dared not scratch.

To make matters worse, he sensed a building sneeze. Fear gripped at him. *Jesus Christ, don't let me sneeze now*, he appealed.

Under a different set of circumstances, he might have found his plight amusing. He envisioned the morning headlines: "New Bedford inmate sneezes – escape attempt foiled."

Rocco could laugh about it later, when he shared the story with Toby and friends over sizzling steaks and cold beers. What he wouldn't give for an icy bottle at that moment.

He drew a deep breath and exhaled, squeezing his eyes tightly shut to fend off the sneeze. The ploy did the trick. Crisis averted.

Days before, Rocco performed a dress rehearsal. First and foremost, he had to ensure that there was sufficient cover at the foot of the bed to avoid detection. Secondly, he needed to make certain that the counterfeit likeness he'd constructed actually looked like a sleeping person. The run through went off without a hitch. It was flawless. But this time, something was amiss. The officer seemed to be spending more time than usual in front of his cell. Had he spotted an aberration that raised his suspicion? Would he enter for closer scrutiny?

Rocco remained hunkered down and entirely motionless. The prolonged probe clutched and grabbed at him. At any moment he expected the corrections officer to holler, "Hey, what's going on in there!"

But to Rocco's relief, the guard soon moved on to continue his rounds. If he remained true to form, he would wrap up his inspection of the remaining cells and then retire to the administrative office for some shuteye.

Anxious to stand upright, Rocco instead remained motionless for several moments, ensuring that the corrections officer was out of earshot. He had come too far to allow his scheme to unravel because of impatience. When he was confident the guard had finished his business, Rocco emerged from the shadows and crossed to the front of his cell.

Kneeling adjacent to the floor-to-ceiling bars that had confined him for forty days, and now forty nights, Rocco leaned forward and pressed his face flush against the cold iron. He peered along the darkened, drafty length of the upper tier, scouting to the right toward the staircase that led to the main level. He then turned his head to the left, his unshaven cheek flattened against the rigid iron, and strained from a difficult angle to explore the obscure reaches of the catwalk. All was quiet along the span.

Rocco lowered his gaze to the base of the bars where each night, he would wrap segments of black electrical tape to camouflage the deepening grooves.

He'd pilfered the tape from a toolbox left unattended by a maintenance worker. At the time, he found the petty theft rather ironic. Furnished with an opportunity to pocket a screwdriver or some other implement that could be used for protection, Rocco instead grabbed a non-lethal roll of tape. But the unexpected find proved far more significant than a weapon.

While he was accurate when he told Toby that the aging metal in the timeworn jail would yield to steel hacksaw blades, it was nonetheless painstaking work. His hands were evidence of that. In the dim lighting, he examined his palms and fingertips, which were covered with a patchwork of healing blisters and calluses.

It would all be worth it, Rocco thought, as he grasped the leading edge of a tape strip and peeled it off. Once he unraveled the first length, Rocco moved on to the second and lastly, the third bar.

Discarding the tape, he briefly paused to admire his work. Rocco gathered that if he made a through-and-through cut near the base of the cell door, relatively close to where the bars were bolted, he could use leverage to bend the pliable rods.

Standing upright, he stretched the weary muscles in his lower back. His joints cracked and snapped. It actually felt pretty good after spending so much time contorted like a pretzel. Without further delay, he gripped the iron bar just above the cut. Firmly planting his feet, Rocco leaned backward. Using his body weight as a lever, he began to coax the metal shaft, nudging it toward him with steady pressure.

To his delight, the iron gave way with ease, folding like butter. A huge sense of relief washed over him. Just like that, he was that much closer to freedom – and reuniting with Toby and his family.

Rocco promptly gripped the second and third bars and pulled them upward. As he paused to catch his breath, it wasn't lost on him that it had taken forty long nights to cut through the inch-thick iron but only forty seconds to dislodge the trio of bars.

Rocco grabbed his leather jacket, as well as the four hacksaw blades, which he'd stashed in the spine of a hardcover book. He also stuffed the last of his Nestle candy bars in his front shirt pocket. He had intentionally reserved a few not knowing when he'd eat again after reaching the streets of New Bedford.

Dropping to one knee, Rocco shoved his jacket through the opening. Rolling over on to his backside, he aligned himself beneath the twisted iron bars. Little by little, he began to shimmy across the floor, head first. When his shoulders reached the opening, he encountered an obstacle. Width-wise, it was a much tighter fit than he anticipated. Despite his effort to remain slim while in captivity, through frequent exercise and infrequent consumption, it appeared that three bars might not be enough to accommodate the breadth of his shoulders.

Bending both legs at the knee, he dug in his heels, urging himself ahead. He made little forward progress, however. For one terrifying moment, Rocco thought he might be wedged in place. Panic stricken, he was unable to move forward toward the tier, nor back into his cell. He cursed himself over the shortfall. *Four bars! I should have cut four bars!*

He imagined the stunned expressions of the corrections officers when daylight broke and they began morning rounds. Lo and behold, here's Rocco Balliro firmly wedged in the breach.

The visualization of that humiliation spurred him to redouble the effort. Taking a deep breath, he arched his back and rotated his arms, drawing both shoulders inward to their limits. Summoning strength from within, he plunged ahead, thrusting his frame through the outlet with near brute force. To his relief, he was able to finally break free. His slimmer lower body wriggled through with ease. He scooped up his jacket, and made haste toward the end of the tier.

He glanced in the cells he passed hoping he wouldn't stumble upon an inmate who happened to be awake. He wasn't quite sure what he would say – or do – if he was spotted by one of these men while roaming along the tier. Would they betray him? Without doubt, they would be just as startled as he. Fortunately, they all seemed to be sleeping soundly. Rocco hoped they stayed that way, at least for a few more minutes. Something as simple as a midnight visit to the john by any one of these guys could spell disaster for him.

Oddly enough, as he neared the limits of the tier, Rocco noticed several unoccupied cells, each with the door ajar. He wasn't expecting to see anything out of the ordinary but poked his head into one of the chambers. The interior was identical to his, save for the bare mattress and lack of personal effects.

Reaching the end of the catwalk, Rocco stood before a towering, rectangular window which faced toward darkened Ash Street below. It was the final barrier. Upbeat and motivated, he quickly set to work removing a wire mesh that encased this gateway to freedom.

The screen was made from a pliable chicken coop material similar to that used in the visiting room to prevent guests and inmates from making physical contact. *That hadn't been much of a deterrent*, Rocco concluded, *at least insofar as the hacksaw blade handoff from Toby*. And he didn't anticipate that the flimsy screen, which was affixed to the window frame by several screws, would pose much of a problem either.

Removing one of the trusty hacksaw blades from his pocket, Rocco slotted the end in the head of one of the screws and gave it a twist. He didn't need to undo all of the screws – just those along the base of the wooden frame and halfway up each side. Relieved of its bindings, he simply peeled the mesh upward to gain access to the window.

All that remained was a simple latch which fastened the bottom section of the window to the top. As he grasped the mechanism, Rocco found it more troublesome than he'd foreseen. It wouldn't budge. He surmised that the window hadn't been opened in some time. The latch seemed bound by years of rust.

Repositioning his body, Rocco added weight and leverage to the stubborn latch. As he leaned into it, the lock assembly unexpectedly broke free from its moorings. Before he could react, splintered metal shrapnel clattered to the grated catwalk resulting in a clamor that was loud enough to wake the dead.

Rocco froze. He held his breath, afraid to exhale. The pulses in his temples throbbed at a furious rate. Sweat broke out on his forehead.

All seemed lost. After the hardship he'd been through to get this far, had he really been outdone by a piece of metal no larger than a belt buckle?

There was nothing left to do now except wait for the corrections officers to storm up the staircase and take him into custody.

CHAPTER 22

"Stealing a man's wife, that's nothing, but stealing his car, that's larceny." –James M. Cain, in The Postman Always Rings Twice

After the metal shards impacted with the grated, steel surface, Rocco listened keenly for telltale signs of stirring in the cells along the tier. Surely, someone must have heard it.

He refused to budge. Seconds turned to agonizing minutes. It was only a matter of time. And yet, nothing. There were no guards rushing to capture him. Nor were there any inmates peering from their cells, craning their necks to determine where the noise came from.

Could it be that his blunder hadn't woken anyone? Had he dodged yet another bullet? It seemed he had.

Relieved, Rocco returned to work on the window. He slid his fingertips beneath the frame and carefully slid it upward, an inch at a time. He couldn't afford another slip up.

As he raised the window and the breach grew wider, chilly air surged inward. It was refreshing. Rocco savored the therapeutic qualities, breathing deep to clear his head.

Gripping the wide sill with both hands, he stuck his head through the opening. A blast of cold made his eyes water. When he could see clearly and got his first look outside, his heart sank.

"Dammit," he spat under his breath as he sized up a thirty, perhaps thirty-five foot drop to the surface below. With all his preparation, he hadn't planned for this.

The first possibility that crossed his mind was to scale the wall. But superhero, he wasn't. Admittedly, it would have been foolhardy and, likely, suicidal. While the timeworn surface furnished some footholds, the grooves between the granite bricks certainly weren't adequate for an unskilled climber.

He next considered a treacherous leap to the narrow patch of scrub grass that had sprouted near the base. Again, ill-advised. The soil beneath the thick grass was surely concrete-like following days on end of bitter cold. Rocco visualized himself lying prone on the ground, incapacitated by a pair of fractured ankles – or worse, paralyzed. *Better to land headfirst and die instantly,* he thought with a grimace, *than spend the next decade or more incarcerated in both prison and a wheelchair.*

What he needed was a length of rope or a substitute that could support his one hundred- eighty-five pound frame.

Rocco pondered the stockpile of sheets and blankets he left behind on his cot. While threadbare, he could have easily doubled or tripled lengths of the material to bolster it. An auspicious idea but he rejected it. There was no way he was returning to his cell, even if he could shimmy back beneath the bars.

Stepping back from the open window, he leaned against the adjacent wall and racked his mind for a solution. Rocco found himself staring at the trio of vacant cells located at the end of the tier. Then it hit him. Why hadn't he thought of it before? The mattresses! He could shred the mattresses with the hacksaw blade and piece together a rope using the strands of *cloth.*

The "rope trick" went very well, although he found one of the three spare mattresses tattered beyond use. That would result in a slight dilemma. As he cut long strips of cloth and knotted the material together in triple layers, he realized the rope would come up short. While preferable to an all-out leap of faith, there remained a roughly fifteen-foot drop that could prove hazardous.

Gathering his handiwork in his arms, Rocco crept soundlessly back to the window. Tying off an end of the rope to a radiator pipe, he shoved the remainder through the opening, allowing it to unfurl toward the ground below. Upon inspection, he determined that he would need another five feet or so to ensure a relatively safe landing. Frowning, he eyeballed the leather jacket which was rolled up in a ball beneath the sill. To his chagrin, the sacrifice had to be made.

Hauling the rudimentary rope back through the window, Rocco scooped up his jacket and quickly united the two, knotting a sleeve to the leading end of the woven mattress strips. Positioning the now-lengthened rope on the sill, he stuck his head through the opening, and dropped it a second time.

Taking a deep breath, Rocco urged the window higher. "Jesus," he moaned as the full brunt of a cold gust of wind penetrated the thin cloth of his shirt.

He scrambled onto the wide sill and sat on the edge with his legs dangling high above the frozen, unforgiving ground. Clinging for dear life, he inched his rear end forward. Pivoting slightly, Rocco freed one hand, and pulled the window down while balancing ever so carefully. Closing it might buy more time if a roving corrections officer made an unscheduled visit to the upper tier. Then again, the three disfigured iron bars on the front of Rocco's now-vacant cell would likely spark their interest.

It was now or never. Wrapping the rope around one leg and one wrist, he slid off while continuing to grip the ledge, deferring some of his body weight. Once he let go, Rocco would find out rather quickly if the knots he learned to tie as a child were true. If not, he would tumble to the unyielding ground below.

Closing his eyes and gritting his teeth until they ached, Rocco released his grip on the ledge. Under the strain, the rope yielded with a sudden, gut-wrenching lurch. He braced for impact, hoping it would be over quickly. He wondered how much time would pass before prison officials discovered his broken body, twisted and mutilated in a pool of frozen blood near the base of the jail's outer wall. Instead, he opened his eyes to find that the crudely-fashioned rope was, in fact, supporting his weight. It was strong and stout. But he couldn't tempt fate, not when he was this close. He began to make his way down. He understood that the further he descended, the more he taxed the capacity of the knots – he had to move quickly.

Less than a minute elapsed before he reached the terminating end of the rope – his leather jacket. At this juncture, suspended ten to twelve feet above the ground, Rocco had no other option but to simply let go of the sleeve.

As it turned out, the brief freefall into the tall outcropping of grass and weeds was not a problem. He touched down, sustaining little more than a slight tweak of his knee. It wasn't severe enough to hamper his ability to briskly walk – and walk he did, until he came upon means to get out of New Bedford.

Christmas 1962 arrived a couple of weeks late for Rocco Anthony Balliro but he certainly wasn't about to gripe about it. As he hurried along Ash Street, walking at a steady clip, he happened upon the best holiday gift a prison escapee could ever ask for.

There, parked along the curb, was a hulking '41 DeSoto. The tired sedan, nearly as old as Rocco himself, was covered in rust, dented from end to end, had a patchwork paintjob and a cracked windshield, and was lacking a rear bumper. But it was, nonetheless, a glorious sight to behold.

As he approached the car, Rocco briskly rubbed the exposed flesh on his arms in an attempt to fend off the stinging winter chill. He detected the faint, salty smells of the harbor, less than a mile to the east. A sudden gust of wind stirred road debris, flinging dust and dirt into his eyes. Rubbing them clear, he glanced back at the New Bedford House of

Corrections. In the diffused glow given off by security lighting surrounding the building, Rocco could still see the makeshift rope dangling from an upper window. Knotted at the end of the manmade tether was his leather jacket. Rocco shook his head in disappointment. He was quite fond of that jacket. It was a shame he had to leave it behind.

How could he complain, really? It was a small price to pay for his freedom. More so when taking into account the mishaps he overcame to get this far.

Reaching the DeSoto, Rocco grasped the door handle and pulled it open. He wasn't surprised to find it unlocked – who, really, would expect someone to steal a car in such disrepair? The corroded hinges groaned in protest. He slid in and gently closed the door against the biting wind that sliced along Ash Street.

The interior of the automobile was in no better condition than the outside. The vinyl seats were torn and yellowed stuffing was exposed. Aluminum floorboards were visible through remnants of frayed carpeting. A segment of the dashboard was tenuously held together with adhesive duct tape. And there was no avoiding the putrid, stagnant odors of cigarettes and beer. But none of that mattered to Rocco as long as he could get the old jalopy started and there was enough gas in the tank to reach the city.

And jackpot, another important find. In the cubby between the seats, Rocco found a couple bucks worth of loose change. That would surely come in handy to make phone calls later.

Thinking about home brought Toby to mind. She had visited several days prior and was thrilled to learn that he was close to reuniting with her.

"So when do you think?" she asked.

"Wednesday," Rocco replied, repeating the estimation he shared with Johnny earlier.

"I can't wait," Toby gushed.

"Me too."

"How are you getting home?"

"Not sure," he said. "I'm hoping I can find some wheels."

"I could come get you."

"Too risky," he said, shaking his head. "After they figure out I'm gone, the place will be crawling with cops."

She nodded in agreement, although he sensed a trace of disappointment in her expression.

"Look," he began. "Wait for me at the apartment. When I get back to the city, I'll send someone for you."

As they did at the close of each visit, Rocco and Toby said their goodbyes by pressing together the palms of their hands. Through the wire mesh, her skin was warm and welcome to the touch.

He could use some of that warmth right about now, as he prepared to start the DeSoto. While the wind was no longer a factor, the inside of the car was an icebox. He shivered violently enough to make his upper back and shoulders ache.

Prior to discovering the vehicle, enduring the frigid cold wasn't Rocco's primary concern. Rather, as he trekked along the streets with no coat, he feared drawing the attention of a patrol car. How would he explain his lack of a jacket on such a frigid night? Who in their right mind would be out walking about town without one? He might have to resort to flight on foot again. But in unfamiliar New Bedford, how far would he get before the local cops – or hypothermia – claimed him?

Rocco grinned at his ingenuity as he groped around in the darkness, feeling his way along the cold steel of the steering column until his numb fingers found the ignition. *No keys*, he thought, realizing that would have almost been too much to ask. "Not a problem," he uttered with the confidence of a man who was perfectly capable of starting a car without the benefit of a key, even as he fumbled with the ignition casing

The flimsy metal cover on the car's steering assembly broke lose after some gentle urging, exposing the ignition components.

"Hmmm, piece of cake," Rocco said as he examined the mechanism under diffused light from a nearby streetlamp.

He reached into his pocket and withdrew one of the chocolate bars, which was a little worse for wear following the daring descent down the rope.

Like a surgeon performing an intricate operation, Rocco rested the thin, rectangular candy bar on his thigh and unfolded the outer wrapper, revealing the foil hidden beneath. His fingers were swollen and numb from the cold, making it difficult to manipulate the thin paper. He discarded the red, white, and blue paper labeled Nestle and then peeled the foil itself away from the chocolate within.

Gingerly, Rocco smoothed out the wrinkles and rolled the delicate piece of aluminum into a tubular shape, like a drinking straw. He squeezed it flat, running his fingertips along the length. *Funny*, he thought, shaking his head in disbelief, but after all he'd been through to reach this point, *the success or failure of this escape relied on a simple candy wrapper.*

Leaning forward, Rocco located the three ignition contacts midway along the steering column. He applied the foil conductor to the first and then the next two. Just like that, with a spark, the car's engine roared to life. It was much louder than expected and would surely wake someone in a nearby residence, perhaps the owner himself.

He sprang into action. Grasping the shift lever, he threw the car into gear and punched the accelerator. Surprisingly, the DeSoto still had a few good horses under her hood and Rocco put them all to work. The car lurched forward into the New Bedford night, exhaust pouring from the rusted tailpipe.

Glancing at the glowing dashboard, he noted the fuel gauge hovered near full. The heater fan, cranked to maximum, sputtered briefly, and soon began to emit delicious heat from the outlet vents. Life was good.

Rocco snaked along quiet, traffic-free streets in search of a thoroughfare that would lead him to the highway, heeding stop signs and traffic signals. Before long, he caught a glimpse of a reflective green sign for Route 6 that would take him to the Fall River Expressway and, an hour's drive later, Boston.

Near daybreak, an elderly woman was walking her dog along Ash Street when she noticed something unusual about the New Bedford House of Corrections, which she passed each and every morning. The concerned citizen altered her route, detouring toward the main entrance of the imposing institution. Knotting the dog leash to a nearby tree, she made her way into the building. As the woman approached, the sole corrections officer on lobby duty raised his eyebrows over the curious pre-dawn visit.

"Good morning," the elderly woman called out as she shuffled across the dusty, tiled floor.

"Mornin', ma'am," the nightshift guard returned wearily. "How can I help you?"

"Actually, I think I can help *you*."

"How so?"

"There seems to be a rope of some sort hanging from one of your windows."

"I'm sorry?" the guard said as he stood up abruptly, nearly tipping over his chair. He cleared his throat nervously. "Did you say you saw a r–"

"I certainly did," interrupted the messenger. "A rope."

"Jesus…" murmured the distraught officer.

By the time he sounded the alarm, sending the jail into a frenzy of activity, escapee Rocco Anthony Balliro was already sound asleep in his Chelsea hideout.

CHAPTER 23

*"If my children were hungry, I should think I would steal
to feed them." – Ian Smith*

The heady aroma of freshly-brewed coffee wafted from
Polcari's grocery mart, infiltrating the surrounding
neighborhood via a brisk late January breeze which channeled
silently along Salem Street. Few could argue that Polcari's
blend was the finest in the city of Boston, perhaps all of New
England.

Standing on the corner of Salem Street opposite the well-
known North End shop, established three decades earlier in
1932, Rocco Anthony Balliro considered his surroundings as
he casually drew on a cigarette.

Locals awaited the return of summer and the fresh
produce piled on wooden pushcarts on Polcari's sidewalk.
Italian women, some dressed in decades old widow's weeds,
would deliberate the store's selection of imported pastas,
coffees, and cooking oils – all while gossiping with one
another in their native tongue.

Outside, adjacent to the pushcarts, would stand an old
wooden barrel filled with the most delectable sweet money
could buy. Rocco vividly remembered the visits he made
as a child to partake in the lemon-flavored ice scrapings,
liberally scooped into a paper cup by the shopkeeper. What a
refreshing treat it was on a hot summer's day. Rocco recalled
that, all too often, in his haste to ease a parched throat, he
would spoon the ice into his mouth far too quickly and suffer
a burning head rush. But once the ache cleared, he'd be at it
again, devouring the ice. Good memories, all.

He would have to make the trip to Polcari's with little Mark, who would turn two in about five weeks, on the 5th of March. Perhaps by July or August the authorities who sought Rocco would grow weary of the chase. Maybe they'd move on to bigger fish instead, namely the elusive Boston Strangler, who remained at large and continued to terrorize the city, having murdered nine women.

Rocco heard a noise. He wheeled around only to find it was an alley cat rummaging through a bag of garbage. He was getting antsy. It was time to move on. He had lingered on this street corner far too long. It was midday and Boston was bathed in thin, pale daylight. Sooner or later, someone would recognize him.

Two weeks removed from his brazen breakout from the New Bedford House of Corrections, the heat was still on. Anticipating that he might return to familiar stomping grounds, every cop in the city was on the lookout for him. It was risky to be out here and riskier still to remain in any one place for too long.

His brothers, who stuck their necks out and furnished an apartment hideaway in nearby Chelsea, certainly wouldn't approve of his gamble. He gathered that one or all of his five male siblings would likely remind him of his 1957 venture into the North End when he was, in fact, recognized during an ill-advised stick up.

But despite the peril, Rocco couldn't resist a visit to the place where he grew up in the late thirties and early forties. It occurred to him that if he were captured, he would be serving a long, onerous prison sentence. This could be his last chance to see home.

He glimpsed number Twenty Bartlett Place, the Balliro homestead where his mother Angela and father Rosario, Italian immigrants, reared twelve children – six boys and six girls – in a strict Catholic environment.

According to Rocco's sister Lucy, their "mama" delivered the majority of her children at home. "Our mother was terribly frightened of hospitals," she said. "They were reportedly losing babies or mixing them up in the nursery back in those days."

Anthony Balliro – he wouldn't be known as Rocco until he reached his late teens – had a promising academic start in life. His parents enrolled him in St. Mary's parochial school as a seven year old in 1943. Run by the Sisters of Notre Dame and the Jesuits, St. Mary's was located at 150 Endicott Street in the North End, adjacent to a church which shared its parish name. It was here that young Anthony would follow in the footsteps of his older brothers and accept a role as an altar boy. He recalled, with great pride, serving the priests and parishioners during the Sunday services.

Both St. Mary's School and the adjoining church were razed in 1977 to make room for construction of apartments to house a number of the elderly and infirm.

His junior high school years were relatively uneventful, although by the time he entered the eighth grade at the Michelangelo School, which structurally held an uncanny resemblance to the New Bedford House of Corrections, Anthony was already well-known to the police. His illustrious juvenile criminal record featured such wrongdoings as breaking and entering, attempted larceny, and the sale of stolen merchandise, all before his fourteenth birthday.

With most of his friends dropping out, Anthony chose to remain in school rather than face the wrath of his father. He persevered, despite the lure of the streets, and in 1952, graduated from Charlestown High School.

But while many graduates entered college, enlisted in the service, or made their way into the workforce, sixteen-year-old Anthony soon found himself on the way to the Shirley Industrial School for Boys to serve a one year sentence for the unprovoked beating of a drunken man.

As he recalled, his brother Billy, just back from a five year stint as an army corpsman in Korea, drove him to Shirley, a rural community an hour northwest of Boston.

In later years, Rocco was hesitant to discuss his days at this renowned reform school, one of four such institutions operating in Massachusetts until their closure in the mid-seventies. While not willing to offer details, talk of the school filled him with rage. It was rather obvious that he suffered abuse at the hands of the staff, like many others who were held there.

On the one hundredth anniversary of the school's founding, *Boston Globe* correspondent Julie Masis offered a glimpse into Shirley. She interviewed Jerome Miller, the former department of youth services commissioner, who was tasked with shutting down the facility.

"Miller said boys at the school were punished for running away by having their ring fingers bent back and broken," Masis wrote. "The conditions were so bad, he said, police hated to return runaways there because they'd hear them screaming. In the school's Cottage 9, where teenagers with disciplinary problems were held, the staff made them scrub floors with toothbrushes, he said, and the third floor held 'the tombs,' rooms without windows or toilets that runaways were thrown into naked as punishment."

Rocco left Shirley midway through his sentence, walking away from chronic abuse. "My first escape," he boasted.

On advice from the Balliro family, he wasted little time leaving the Massachusetts area – on the government's dime, no less. Making his way to the military recruiting office in Boston's Post Office Square, Rocco followed in his older brother Billy's footsteps and joined the army.

He understood that his criminal record would, under normal circumstances, prohibit enlistment. His legal birth certificate, however, listed him as Rocco Anthony Balliro. He pulled the wool over the recruiter's eyes by registering under the name listed on his birth record. Instead of Anthony, as he was known to the police and the court system, he *officially* became Rocco Balliro. He scribbled truck driver as his occupation. When army officials performed a background check, they would uncover a juvenile dossier free and clear of criminal offenses, arrests, and convictions. As far as the army was concerned, their new sharpshooter, who was assigned to the 364th Infantry, 9th Division, K Company, had never committed a crime in his life. To them, the strapping youth eagerly boarding a bus for Kilmer, New Jersey was a clean-cut, law-abiding kid in peak physical condition; exactly the type of soldier they required to restock a war-weary armed forces depleted by the Korean campaign, which came to an end in 1953.

Rocco's service to his country was short-lived, however. In January 1954, a matter of months after completing basic training at Fort Dix, New Jersey, he was handed an undesirable discharge.

"I was punished for trying to help a buddy who'd gone AWOL," Rocco recalled with bitterness over the lost opportunity. "He was drunk and I tried to sneak him back on the base before the MPs found him. They arrested the both of us and my army career was over."

Shortly after leaving the military, Rocco was sent away for his first prison tour. Arrested and convicted for a jewelry store break in, he soon found himself serving a two-and-a-half year stint at the Billerica House of Corrections.

Most of his next six years were spent behind bars at an assortment of Massachusetts facilities.

Rocco gazed longingly at Twenty Bartlett Place, which was located at the end of a narrow alleyway off Salem Street. It was a squat, three-story rectangular brick building, and similar to many of the structures in Boston's North End. It was proud and sturdy but, nonetheless, exhibited the wear and tear wrought by time and the region's unforgiving ocean climate.

In later years, long after the last of the Balliro clan had moved on to the suburbs and Rocco's older sister Flora Monteforte shuttered her popular Italian restaurant, Jenny's, located adjacent to the dwelling, the family followed a growing trend and converted Twenty Bartlett Place into individual condominium-style rentals.

Rocco was disheartened to learn that a pair of second floor windows of his childhood home were bricked in to add privacy for tenants.

"I guess I can understand why they might do that," he acknowledged, when told about the alterations made to what had once been his parents' bedroom. "Some of my brothers and me came of age at those windows. Across the alley, we could look into our neighbor's windows and they had beautiful, olive-skinned Italian daughters!"

Roughly a city block from where Rocco idly stood tempting fate was a notorious address – one that was filled with mystique and menace and instilled fear in most whose presence was requested inside its foreboding doors.

Number 98 Prince Street was the headquarters of the Angiulo crime family, which was made up of brothers Donato, Francesco, James, Niccolo, and Gennaro or Jerry, as he was better known. The five Angiulo brothers, headed by the elder Gennaro, held sway over organized criminal activities in and around Boston.

Rocco vividly recalled the Angiulo's dwelling, partly because he grew up in the shadows of the ominous four-story, brick-front building.

"We called it the Dog House," Rocco later shared. "If they ordered you to come in, it meant you were in the *doghouse* and in some sort of trouble." With a light chuckle, he added, "My brothers always seemed to be there trying to get me out of one jam or another."

Reputed underboss Gennaro Angiulo answered only to Raymond Patriarca in the hierarchy of the New England crime syndicate at the time, according to noted author

Stephen Puleo, who penned a detailed history of the North End entitled, *The Boston Italians*.

"In Boston, postwar mafia activity was in full swing by the mid-1950s," Puleo wrote. "Patriarca quickly named Gennaro 'Jerry' Angiulo to run the Boston rackets from his North End offices at 98 Prince Street. Angiulo consolidated power and controlled gambling, racketeering, and loansharking in the North End and throughout Boston for the Patriarca family."

As Rocco explained, the Balliro family of that era could be described as a faction working for the Angiulos and thus indirectly for Patriarca. Business dealings were brokered and his family paid a percentage of earnings up the administrative ladder until the money reached the top rung in Providence.

Rocco was soon on the move again, picking his way along Salem Street, covering ground with long strides. It was chilly – not cold – but he pulled the collar against his exposed neck. He despised this season. In New England, the winter seemed never ending. Rocco yearned to see his dear mother. The thought occurred to drop in but he set it aside. He knew that could put her in harm's way. He didn't think the cops were watching the house at that moment – if they were, he might already be in custody. But he knew the Boston Police were making regular visits to his family home to inquire about his whereabouts. He couldn't be captured in their midst. There was little doubt that the authorities would try to pin some half-baked charge on a family member, such as harboring a fugitive. And his parents certainly wouldn't be exempt from arrest.

As he left his neighborhood, Rocco took a last glance at Twenty Bartlett Place, before it disappeared from view. He wondered what his mother was doing. Cooking, perhaps? Or maybe she was relaxing in the living room and watching one of her shows.

He remembered the day their television arrived, to a lot of fanfare from family, friends, and of course, curious neighbors.

The Balliros were the first family on the block to have one of the remarkable TV sets and soon, everyone wanted one.

Rocco later discovered from his sister Lucy that their mother had purchased the television to serve as a distraction for her wayward boys. The mother of twelve hoped that the big wooden box with the moving pictures would grab their interest and keep them home watching shows instead of raising hell on the streets. It didn't quite work out that way. "They had other interests," Lucy said.

Reaching Cross Street, Rocco turned left, walked one block and then hooked a right on Hanover Street. His paced quickened as he neared his destination. Taking a deep breath, he fought off a bout of anxiety.

He ran his hand over his lower back, feeling beneath the leather. It eased his increasing paranoia. The gun was there.

As he turned right on to Blackstone Street, ominous, dark clouds formed overhead and the air grew dense with a threat of rain – or perhaps even snow. He eased up, shortening his stride as he neared the Puritan Meat Market, which was a popular butcher shop located less than a block from Haymarket. Thankfully, foot traffic in the area was light.

It was pride and necessity that drove him to this. While his caretakers had the best of intentions, Rocco had grown weary of his over-protective brothers providing for him since he went on the lam weeks earlier. It wasn't in his nature to accept handouts, even from family. And with the added mouths to feed – in this case, Toby, Mark, and Bernice – he felt even more burdensome. Rocco wanted to contribute. He wanted to support himself and his family and if possible, give something back to his generous brothers.

Pausing in front of the large display windows, he saw they were plastered with signs. He was grateful for the signage. It would obscure the interior from passersby, as well as roving automobiles and patrol cars.

Reaching the store entrance, Rocco grasped the door handle and burst into the butcher shop brandishing the weapon. He waved the gun from side to side, and barked orders.

"Alright, nobody move!"

"Christ," uttered a distressed voice from behind the chest-high counter at the rear of the store. Several customers froze, cowering where they stood. One man dropped a bottle of steak sauce, which shattered at his feet. Another customer, an elderly male, took a step backwards and nearly tripped over the edge of a floor mat. He pin-wheeled his arms for a few seconds before regaining his balance.

Rocco pointed the muzzle of the gun at him and hollered, "I said not to move!"

The old man turned ashen gray. He looked as if he might collapse at any moment. Rocco understood that if the old coot suffered a heart attack, the charges might include at least one count of murder, along with armed robbery. All the more reason to do his business and get out of the store quickly.

"Hey!" snapped a burly, middle-aged male from behind the counter. He was partly blocked from view by a chalkboard easel listing the day's specials. "Take it easy with that thing, will ya!"

Stepping forward to get a better look, Rocco raised the pistol. From ten feet away, he aimed it squarely between the eyes of a man wearing a stained apron and wielding a razor-sharp cleaver. He was obviously the butcher and it seemed that he'd been interrupted in the act of chopping meat.

Without taking his eyes off the chrome blade, which glinted beneath the fluorescent light suspended from the ceiling, Rocco uttered a directive, slow and concise. Between clenched teeth, he said, "Put. Down. The. Knife."

"What do you want? The money?"

"The knife," Rocco impatiently repeated. "I want you to lose that fuckin' knife. Put it on the counter where I can see it and step back."

The butcher failed to respond to his demands.

Rocco extended his arm and raised it, slowly and deliberately bringing the gun that much closer to his stubborn adversary.

"Yeah, yeah, relax," the butcher grumbled as he slammed the cleaver on the countertop and retreated to the rear wall.

Rocco took inventory. There were six men in the shop – five customers and the disobedient butcher. He turned his attention to the poor slob who stood in what was now a puddle of steak sauce, some of which had splattered on his shoes.

"Hey, mister, c'mere" Rocco insisted, gesturing with his gun hand for the man to approach.

"W-who, me?" the man stammered fearfully, pointing a finger at his own chest. His eyes grew wide.

"Listen, I'm not going to hurt you."

After a moment's hesitation, the man sidestepped the sauce pooled on the floor and inched toward the gunman.

Rocco glared icily at the establishment's proprietor, who had obediently stayed put. He was standing in front of a shelving unit stacked with paper goods.

"Hey, pal—"

"I'm not your pal," replied the belligerent butcher, whose thick, muscular tattooed arms were folded defiantly across his chest.

Rocco grinned. This character had a set of brass balls, no question. He respected that. At another time in another place, he'd probably enjoy hoisting a beer or two and swap stories with this tough guy.

"Gimme one of those bags," he ordered. "There, behind you on the shelf."

"These bags?" he said, pointing to the stack. It was obviously part of his overall resistance.

"Don't screw with me. Just do as I say."

The shopkeeper turned, pulled a folded brown grocery bag off the top of the pile, and placed it on the countertop. Rocco watched with a wary eye, ensuring he didn't lunge for the cleaver. He certainly didn't want to shoot anyone but if the guy made any sudden moves, all bets were off.

Rocco turned his attention back to the steak sauce guy. "What's your name?" he asked.

"Samuel," tentatively answered the man, who was tall and rail thin with a mane of white hair and a mustache to match. "Samuel Paulsen."

"Alright, Sam. I want you to take that bag and collect everyone's wallets. Quickly–"

"M-mine too?"

"Yeah, Sam," he replied, impatiently. "Yours too."

"Uh, okay."

Rocco's *assistant* reached for the bag and opened it. Sam first deposited his billfold and then made the rounds, fetching the wallets from each of the other four customers, including the elderly man whose color had thankfully improved.

The butcher, as expected, stonewalled. Rocco overheard Paulsen reasoning with the stubborn fool.

"This guy means business," he preached. "You really wanna get yourself shot over a few bucks?"

Hearing the comment, Rocco said, "He's right. Hand it over. And hurry up about it."

The hulking shopkeeper finally complied and relinquished his wallet, indignantly tossing it in the bag. Sam spun and began to walk toward Rocco. He was waved back with a flip of the gun.

"Don't forget the register."

"Uh huh — sure."

Following orders, Sam tucked the paper bag under his arm and positioned himself in front of the cash register. He stood for a moment staring at the panel of buttons but then shook his head.

"Help him," Rocco grunted.

Begrudgingly, the butcher stepped forward. He hesitated but then pressed a black button which released the money tray with a ringing bell. As Sam sprang into action, relieving the drawer of its cash, Rocco noticed the butcher was fixated on the cleaver.

"Don't even think about it," he warned.

"Alright, alright, take it easy."

Rocco's surrogate accomplice, meanwhile, completed his task, sealed the top of the bag, and handed it over without a word.

"Thank you."

"Um, you're welcome," Sam replied with a confused look. Rocco understood. He just thanked a man who was forced at gunpoint to help rob a bunch of strangers of their wallets – including his own.

With the proceeds from his visit to the Puritan Meat Market tucked safely under his arm, Rocco needed to put some distance between himself and the robbery victims. The last thing he needed was a confrontation out in the open and in broad daylight. And he wouldn't put it past the butcher to chase him.

As he weighed options, Rocco spotted salvation. His problem was solved. Off to the right, along a corridor that led to what looked like a storage area, was a rectangular sign suspended above a large metal door which read Cold Storage. *Perfect*, thought Rocco with relief.

"Alright, gentlemen," he said, gesturing for the men to move toward the door. "This way. C'mon, let's go."

All six complied, including the butcher who seemed as if the fight had finally gone out of him. He fell in with the small group quietly shuffling along, led by Paulsen. When they stood adjacent to the industrial walk-in freezer, Rocco signaled a stop. Paulsen, recognizing what was in store for them, spoke up.

"You can't do this," he said, fervently shaking his head. "This is cruel."

"C'mon, Sam."

"We'll freeze to death in there!"

"You're not gonna freeze," Rocco refuted. "You're all wearing winter coats. You'll be okay until someone comes along. Now, inside…" He waved the gun again.

Paulsen took a deep breath and grasped the handle with both hands. When he yanked it downward, the door swung open and the men were met with a rush of icy air.

"Jesus Christ," murmured one of the customers, a guy about forty, when the cold blast reached him.

There was also a tangy odor of raw beef mixed in with the artificial breeze. At the rear of the spacious freezer, massive livestock carcasses hung suspended from ceiling hooks. Affixed to the inner surface of the door was a handle – obviously, it could be opened from the inside. He would have to remember to lock it.

As the men filed into the freezer, with Sam leading the way and the butcher bringing up the rear, Rocco realized that he was wearing only a short-sleeved shirt beneath his apron. Muscles or not, his arms would be fully exposed to the cold.

"Do you want your coat?" he offered sympathetically.

"Fuck you," was the response.

"Suit yourself," Rocco said as he slammed the freezer door shut and slid the latch to secure it.

CHAPTER 24

"In our family we don't divorce our men – we bury them." – Ruth Gordon

Staring hungrily at the serving, Rocco Anthony Balliro dug his fork into the spaghetti and gave it several spins, gathering enough for a mouthful. But as he lifted the pasta to eat, he quickly backed it out, dropping the utensil to his plate with a loud clang.

"Shit, that's hot!" he exclaimed, grabbing for his beer and downing a few swigs to soothe the burn.

"Give it a few minutes to cool," suggested Toby as she busily stirred the contents of another small pan. "And wait for the sauce. It's almost ready."

"Sauce? Sauce? How many times have I told you it's not sauce," he halfheartedly scolded. "It's gravy!"

"Damn Italians," she said with a girlish giggle.

He just shook his head and finished off the beer. He had tried to explain the significance of calling pasta sauce gravy and not sauce. He knew Toby understood but enjoyed the friendly banter between them.

Rocco observed as she cooked, marveling at this beautiful specimen. He further contemplated her robe and wondered what she was wearing beneath it. *Perhaps nothing*, he thought. His slowly building fantasy was abruptly shredded when a small, shrill voice spilled from the living room.

"Mommy, Mommy," screamed Mark, who until that moment had been quietly playing with a yellow Tonka truck. A clanging metal-on-metal noise reverberated along the hallway.

"Mark, hush," Toby said, delivering the message sternly while not raising her voice. "You'll wake your sister."

A moment later, they heard him making his way along the hallway, his foot-pajamas scuffling over the worn floor. He coasted to a stop, short of entering the kitchen.

"Mommy?"

"What is it, sweetie?"

"Hey, little man," Rocco interjected.

Mark's face lit up brightly. "Hi, Tony," he sang. "Wanna play trucks?"

"Sure, buddy, sure. A little later, okay?"

"Okay." His smile could melt ice cubes. He was such a content kid. And smart as a whip, too.

Toby turned her attention back to Rocco for a moment. "Here's your *gravy*," she said, with a knowing grin as she scooped the sauce. "Say when."

"When," he muttered.

"Mommy?" said Mark, pointing at the plate of food in front of Rocco. "I want some sketti too."

"Sure, honey," she said. "Tony and I have to talk so why don't you go back in the living room and watch television. I'll bring your spaghetti in a sec."

"Okay, Mommy," he agreed with a tiny voice to match his equally tiny thirty-pound frame.

Rocco, meanwhile, was busy shoveling spaghetti into his mouth now that it had cooled. He paused and with his mouth half-full said, "So what did you want to talk about?"

"Nothing, really," she mumbled, which in Toby-speak was her way of saying she wasn't quite sure how to broach a difficult topic.

Rocco already knew what she was struggling to bring up. He'd been made aware of it a day or two after she and the kids joined him in Chelsea. Toby didn't reveal the news herself. Instead, he heard it through the ever-reliable underworld grapevine. In less than twenty-four hours, on February 1,

Toby's husband Barney Wagner would be released from jail and likely attempt to reclaim his family.

Rising soundlessly from his chair, Rocco crossed the kitchen. As Toby stood on her tiptoes, reaching for a serving bowl resting on a high shelf, he suddenly grasped her hips and pressed against her. She never heard his approach and was startled, stumbling awkwardly backward. Rocco tightened his grip on her, preventing a fall to the floor.

"Jesus!" Toby scolded. "You scared the shit out of me!"

"Guess I still got it," he snickered, referring to his catlike stealth. Spinning her in his arms so she was facing him, he encircled his forearm around her lower back, eliminating the divide between them. *This was so much better than touching palms through chicken wire in a visiting room of a jail*, he thought.

"Tony," she uttered. "Please don't sneak up on me like that. You're gonna give me a heart attack."

"Sorry," he said.

She reached to extinguish the flame on the stove and then relaxed, giving in to his embrace. Allowing herself to be enveloped in his muscular arms, she turned her face upward in anticipation of a kiss. But to his surprise, she suddenly, forcefully pushed him away. Rocco stepped back, stunned. Toby's face instantly grew crimson.

"Hey," was all he could say. "What gives?"

"Hey, yourself," she responded. Her eyes were trained squarely on his waistline. She stood with her hands on her hips, striking a defiant pose. "What's that for?"

He followed her gaze and realized then what had pissed her off.

"The piece?"

"Yeah."

He had forgotten to stash the gun. It was stuffed in the front waistband of his pants and obviously, Toby had felt its telltale outline when he embraced her.

"Toby, we've talked about this."

"I know, I know – it's for your protection," she groaned in frustration.

"Exactly."

"I just don't like them," she said. "Especially with the kids in the house. I wouldn't want Mark to–"

Toby broke off the comment. In his peripheral vision, Rocco saw that Mark had rejoined them. The little guy was once again standing in the doorway. He looked skittish. He couldn't have been standing there for very long but he had likely seen his mother grow upset with her friend Tony. Mark was far too young to comprehend the intricacies of her complicated relationship but he could sense distress.

"Mommy?"

"Mommy's alright, honey," she insisted, trying to ease Mark's concern. Rocco, in the meantime, retrieved the bowl she was unable to reach. She took it, spooned in a helping of pasta, and chopped it into smaller pieces with the fork.

Toby gave Rocco a sideways glance as she walked towards Mark and said, "Let me get him settled."

"Sure."

While he had an opportunity, Rocco removed his gun and quickly buried it under some dish towels in a drawer. He kept a strongbox in a kitchen cabinet but didn't have time to properly stash the handgun. Returning to the table, Rocco resumed eating just as Toby came back in the room.

She sat heavily in the chair opposite him and reached for their shared pack of cigarettes.

"Not eating anything?" he asked between mouthfuls.

"Maybe later," she said. "I'm not really hungry."

"You should have a little," he urged.

"Borrow your lighter?" she asked, an unlit smoke dangling from her lips. As he looked up from his plate, he noted her strained expression.

"Yeah," he replied, reaching into his pocket for the Zippo and flicking it for her. "Sorry."

"No problem," Toby said. "We both have a lot on our minds."

You can say that again, he wryly thought.

"I'm gonna grab a beer," he announced as he waltzed toward the fridge. "Want one?"

"No, thanks."

He noticed the beer supply was dwindling but wisely refrained from mentioning it. This was not the time. She was upset and discussing the need to resupply his vice would have been ill-advised.

Popping the top off, Rocco took a refreshing swig. He liked Toby's spaghetti sauce – gravy, rather – but it was a tad spicy and often left him with a killer thirst.

Instead of joining her again at the table, he crossed the room and paused in front of one of the windows that overlooked Washington Avenue. Setting the beer on the sill, Rocco raised the window for fresh air.

There was little activity on the street below, surely a result of a cold snap that had clamped down on Boston earlier in the week. It was the last day of January 1963, and the weather was frigid as the city stood on the brink of February.

As Rocco observed from the third floor apartment, a car drove slowly by the front of the Chelsea tenement. Instinctively, he stepped out of view, waiting for the vehicle to pass.

He thought back to several weeks earlier when Toby arrived in Chelsea. At first, she wasn't particularly comfortable. Compared with their place in Brighton, the Chelsea apartment was small and cramped. That, he found, didn't draw many complaints from her. She could deal with the temporary digs for a short time. The sparse, ragged furnishings, however, was a problem. She had grown used to nicer things. So he took matters into his own hands and robbed the Puritan Meat Market.

Meeting with his brother Bruno and his landlord the morning after, Rocco relinquished some of the proceeds from his brazen, daylight stick up.

"Guys, take this," he insisted, handing over the thick wad of cash. "Bring Toby somewhere and get some decent furniture for this place, will ya?"

"Where'd you get that?" a wide-eyed Bruno asked.

"Puritan Meat Market over on Blackstone Street," he answered matter-of-factly.

"You did that job?" the former cop, now their landlord, asked.

"Yeah, why?"

"I heard about that one," he said. "You locked those poor saps in the freezer!"

"Uh, yeah—" Rocco admitted, feeling slightly guilty over the outlandish act. "That was me. Were they okay?"

"Yep," he said. "Someone went in the store ten or fifteen minutes after you left."

"I didn't want to hurt anyone," he insisted.

Robbing that store was far less stressful than dealing with Toby, who remained silent as he continued to gaze out to the street below. She hadn't spoken a word for several minutes and was likely searching for the words to begin a dialogue.

For a moment, he considered letting her off the hook. But a confession would agitate her, especially if it came to light that he'd known for several days and yet allowed her to sweat it out. It was far better to feign ignorance.

Rocco was less than pleased with this unscheduled intrusion into their lives. Things were going well. He had yet to make any contacts or formal arrangements but he planned to leave the Boston area soon. San Francisco beckoned. He and Toby could start a new life and raise the children, three thousand miles from the pursuit of those who wanted to see him back behind bars.

It was getting colder in the kitchen as Rocco turned from the window to face her. The chilly breeze felt good on his back. Silence hung between them for several agonizing seconds.

Tapping her cigarette into the ashtray, Toby sighed and looked up at him.

"Honey," she began.

Rocco braced himself. It felt like those finals seconds just before the dentist's drill makes first contact with the surface of a tooth.

"Yeah?" he said as he scratched the itchy growth of beard on his chin.

"Are you gonna shave?" she commented, obviously stalling.

"Not right away," he replied with a smile, pointing at the stubble. "Disguise."

"Um … so … there's something I've been meaning to tell you."

"I figured that," he said.

"Huh?" She looked confused.

"You haven't been yourself, that's all."

She nodded and continued.

"Barney's getting out," she blurted.

Rocco joined Toby at the table. She absently twirled a pack of smokes round and round.

"Really?" he said. "When?"

"Tomorrow," she answered. Color seemed to be returning to her face. With the disclosure, the pressure receded. She was apparently relieved. "February first."

"Uh huh," he replied, trying to remain nonchalant. He couldn't reveal that he was in turmoil.

They fell silent until Toby reopened the channel. "I'll need to meet with him–"

"Yeah, sure. Understood."

What else could he say? At the end of the day, the man was her husband. There was no denying that simple fact.

"It's not what you think," she insisted.

"What do I think?" Rocco asked.

"That I'm going back with him?"

There it was, he thought. The comment was conveyed exactly as he anticipated over the months since he first become involved with this married woman – the woman he loved and cherished, along with her children. She was his girlfriend who was also someone else's wife.

"I never gave it a thought," Rocco lied. Deep inside, he was wishing that one of the other Concord inmates would give Wagner a fitting sendoff and drive a shank into his chest.

"I have," she admitted.

"I'll agree with any decision you make," he offered. It was an olive branch and he hoped Toby wouldn't accept it.

"I'm leaving him," she declared defiantly.

"I'm glad to hear that."

"Tomorrow morning, after he gets dropped off at his parent's house–"

"Brookline?" Rocco interjected. He recalled Toby once mentioning the Wagner family lived in the popular community that bordered Boston to the west – the home of Worth's department store, which he learned had retrieved many of its fur coats soon after his arrest.

"Yeah," she answered as she picked up his plate of half-eaten spaghetti and shuffled to the kitchen. "I'm asking for a divorce."

"Think he'll give you a problem?"

"Probably," she admitted, smiling grimly. She scraped the remaining food into a waste can and then ran the plate beneath a stream of water. "But I don't give a shit. He's no good and I'll be much better off without him."

Rocco was aware of some of the history in Toby's rocky relationship with Barney Wagner. He wasn't proud of the espionage but one night, while she went out with friends and he remained at home with the kids, Rocco unearthed a shoebox stuffed with cards and letters, as well as a diary she kept in 1960 when she was eighteen.

One of the entries was etched in his memory. When he read the revealing words, it spurred hatred for Toby's scoundrel of a husband. How could anyone treat this beautiful angel in such a way? The man was nothing more than a misguided, delinquent car thief and drug addict.

"As weeks went by, I watched Googsie steal, drink, and mostly treat me like a piece of dirt," Toby wrote, recalling in her diary the days in 1958 when she first began dating Wagner. "Everyone knew it. I knew it. But I loved him and I took it. I knew someday he'd get to love me."

Toby returned to her chair and when Rocco noticed her cinching the robe tighter and pulling the folds of the collar across her exposed neck, he closed the window.

Joining her at the table again, he withdrew a cigarette from the pack. He offered her one but she declined.

"Toby, let me go with you tomorrow," he said as he lit up.

She started to answer when Mark called from the living room. He had been well-behaved during their discussion.

"Mommy, I'm done with my sketti!" he shouted, forgetting his sleeping sister in the next room.

"I'll be right there."

She rose from her chair again. Leaning down, she pressed a kiss to Rocco's forehead.

"I appreciate the offer," she said. "But I don't think it would be a good idea."

"Why's that?"

"I know Barney. He'd be scared shitless of you."

"That's what I'd hoped."

"Funny."

"I'm worried about you, that's all."

"Yeah, I understand," she said. "But I need to do this on my terms."

"I just want to make sure he ... well ... ya know ... doesn't try to hurt you."

She smiled and said, "You're a phone call away."

With that, Toby turned and made her way toward the living room where the television droned and Mark waited patiently. She paused at the threshold, and turned toward him.

"Anthony?"

"Yeah?"

"Sauce," she said, grinning wryly.

"Gravy," he countered with a lighthearted chuckle.

CHAPTER 25

"A baby's cry is as serious as it sounds." – *Jean Liedloff*

It was just before seven in the evening when Rocco Anthony Balliro pulled up in front of the Roxbury apartment belonging to Bob "Buzzy" Adams, his young wife Mary, and their three small children.

Shifting the Oldsmobile into park, he snuffed out the headlights and sat back heavily. He was exhausted and his head throbbed. Rocco closed his eyes against the ache. Sleep didn't come easy the night before. Tossing and turning, he got an hour of shuteye, two at the most. As he battled insomnia, Rocco grew more and more uptight about Toby and the kids. How would this play out? What did the near future hold for them now that Barney Wagner would soon be back on the streets?

The sidewalks lining Center Street in Roxbury were strewn with heaping, waist-high snow, remnants of a nor'easter that battered the region several days earlier.

Rocco left the motor running for heat. Reaching into his pocket, he fished out a pack of cigarettes. Firing his Zippo, he examined his hands in the orange-blue flame. The calluses and blisters on his fingertips, rendered by forty nights of sawing through the irons bars in the New Bedford House of Corrections, were finally on the mend after three weeks on the outside. *Three weeks*, he thought. *It feels like three years.* So much had happened since his escape.

Thinking back, it had all seemed relatively easy. Even the ride along the highway was uneventful. Rocco was so relaxed during the hour-long drive, in fact, that he blared the radio in the old DeSoto – that was one part of the tired car that was in top-notch condition. He was in such good spirits, he found himself singing along with some of his favorite tunes.

Wheeling north along the Fall River Expressway, he estimated it was nearing two in the morning. The stretch of asphalt ahead was devoid of traffic. He had the road to himself. Anxious to reach familiar territory, Rocco was tempted to pick up the pace. But he fought the urge. There was always the chance that a Massachusetts State Trooper might be concealed in the thick brush on the median strip, grabbing a mid-shift snooze in his patrol car.

Before long, Rocco found himself back on his own turf, driving north along Blue Hill Avenue in Roxbury. He soon located an all-night gas station not far from Franklin Park in Jamaica Plain. Swinging the rust-bucket into the driveway, he glided to a stop in front of a payphone, taking note of the attendant in the cashier's booth. The man glanced up from a newspaper but went back to his reading when he realized the driver hadn't pulled in for a fill-up.

Rocco grabbed a fistful of loose change from the pigeonhole between the seats, silently thanking the nameless, faceless stranger who'd left it behind. Exiting the car, he walked over to the phone and dropped random coins into the slot. As he dialed, Rocco kept a watchful eye for a patrol car.

He assumed, accurately as it turned out, that the New Bedford House of Corrections officials had yet to find that their headcount was one less than it had been three hours before, at midnight. Rocco didn't recall a time during his brief incarceration when the guards had conducted an additional bed check. But he couldn't take chances. The meddlesome Boston cops might give pause to investigate an individual lurking in the shadows of a filling station at such a late hour, particularly a coatless man on a cold winter's night.

Pressing the receiver to his ear, Rocco listened. The phone rang a half dozen times before a groggy, male voice finally answered.

"Yeah?"

"Bruno?"

"Who the fuck is this?" indignantly asked his brother, the youngest of the Balliro clan. Like most, he wasn't one who appreciated being woken from a sound sleep.

"Bruno, it's me. Rocco."

"Jesus!" his sibling shouted as the fog of sleep lifted. "Where the hell are you?"

"Roxbury," Rocco replied. He looked around before he spoke again, as if someone might be eavesdropping. "I broke out tonight."

"Sonofabitch!" his brother exclaimed. "How'd you get to Roxbury?"

"I took the bus," he sarcastically quipped. "How the hell do you think I got here? I stole a car. I gotta ditch it though. I could use a lift."

"Where are you?"

"A Shell station on Blue Hill Ave," he replied. "Near Franklin Park."

"Stay put," Bruno ordered. "I'll be there in an hour."

It was more like half an hour, by Rocco's estimation. Bruno had obviously hauled ass to reach Roxbury.

After the Balliro brothers reunited, they quickly dumped the stolen vehicle in a remote wooded area near the Franklin Park Zoo and then drove across Boston to Chelsea, where a third-floor walk-up awaited Rocco.

The small apartment belonged to a former Chelsea cop who had befriended Bruno. He had realigned his loyalties after the police department he worked for fired him for undisclosed behavior unbefitting an officer.

The disgruntled cop, who lived on the first floor of the three-decker, not only provided a place for Rocco to go into hiding, but also brought his famished guest a welcome meal to celebrate his newfound freedom.

"Mmmph, this is delicious!" he exclaimed with delight, speaking with his mouth full.

"Easy," his brother urged.

"Easy, yourself," he replied, wiping his beard-covered face with the back of a sleeve. "I've been eating nothing but canned tuna. Finally – real food."

Later in the evening, the three men drank a few beers and swapped war stories. While they talked, the cop friend reached into his pocket and pulled out a .38 revolver, along with a small leather pouch. Rocco watched with rapt interest as the man dismantled his weapon, piece by piece, and carefully oiled each part before putting it back together.

"I never spent much time cleaning my guns," he said.

"Of course you have to clean them," said the former lawman. "What the hell good is a gun that jams when you need it most?"

"Man's got a point," Bruno remarked.

Rocco just shrugged, reached for another beer, and asked, "What time is it, anyway?"

"Five in the morning," his brother answered. Dawn would soon break over Chelsea and nearby Boston. "I need to get some shuteye."

"Same here but I gotta make a quick phone call."

"Yeah, go ahead," Bruno said with a smirk. "Wake up someone else in the middle of the night."

Rocco waved his brother off as he dialed. Both Bruno and his gun-cleaning associate left the apartment together.

After just a pair of rings, he heard someone fumbling with the phone for a few seconds and then greeted the caller with a gruff, "Yeah, who is it!"

"Jimmy?"

"Who wants to know?"

"Your mother," he replied.

"Rocco, that you?"

"Yeah, who the hell did you think it was?"

"I thought you were still in–"

"I was," he interrupted. "until about four or five hours ago."

"Holy shit!" a stunned Jimmy D'Angelo exclaimed. "You busted out!"

"Why don't you just put it on the front page?"

"How's my brother?" Jimmy asked.

"He's good."

"I'm guessing he didn't want to go with you?"

"Naw," Rocco said. "He'll be out soon enough. Jimmy, I need a favor."

"Sure, anything."

"Tomorrow, could you swing over to Brighton and pick up Toby and the kids?"

"Yeah," Jimmy agreed. "Where should I bring them?"

"I'm staying at Washington Avenue in Chelsea."

"Sure, sure, I'll take care of it. Count on me."

Jimmy D'Angelo later recounted the move from the Kelton Street apartment, which was achieved at breakneck speed. Jimmy helped Toby collect some belongings, filling to capacity a pair of old suitcases. Frantically, she gathered some of the children's things, understanding that the Brighton apartment might be off-limits for a while. Before long, the cops would be staking out the neighborhood. Jimmy ferried several armloads of clothing and other necessities while Toby ushered the children to the waiting car. The entire undertaking took less than a half hour.

When Toby arrived in Chelsea, she and Rocco met in an embrace. It was such a special feeling to once again clutch her warm body against his.

Little Mark squirmed between them and exclaimed, "Hi, Tony, where you been?"

Rocco and Toby glanced down at the little man with the unkempt dark hair and broke out in a fit of laughter over the innocent question. Mark soon joined in the happy chorus, not knowing exactly why.

It was one of those poignant moments that reminded Rocco why these three special people – Toby, Mark, and

Bernice – were so important to him and why he was seriously considering getting himself a legitimate gig.

But first, there was the problem of her husband. Something had to be done about Barney Wagner. If all went as planned and Wagner granted the divorce, Rocco and Toby would have the freedom to get married. Of course, they would have to relocate to a far-flung city somewhere – maybe on the West Coast – change their names, and hope the manhunt eventually tapered off. If Toby failed to convince Wagner to agree to the split, however, Rocco was prepared to step in and persuade him.

Rocco's stomach began to do flips as he sat in the idling Oldsmobile in front of the Centre Street apartment, where he'd hoped to find Toby. He couldn't quite put his finger on it but an odd sense of unease tugged at him. It was like trying to grab smoke. An undercurrent of anxiety steadily gathered momentum, much like the dull ache that throbbed in his skull.

He wasn't a believer of premonitions or anything like that. But his instincts told him to get out of there, far away from the Adams' apartment and this neighborhood. Something wasn't right. But much like he ignored Toby's intuition and her belief that his trip to Providence with the stolen furs was destined to sour, he also discounted the feeling that a dangerous path lie ahead.

Peering through the passenger side window at the apartment, which was on the bottom floor of a two-family house, Rocco saw that it was pitch black inside. Not a single lamp was lit. There was no indication that anyone was home.

She's not here, he thought. This was a waste of time. He sought out a small button on the driver's door handle and gave it a quick jab. As the power window lowered, cigarette smoke streamed out. A belt of chilly air replaced it.

He strained, listening for some sound, some sign of occupancy in the apartment. There was nothing, not a whisper. And then he heard something, faint at first, but growing louder. Rocco thought his mind might be playing tricks on him but carried across the stillness of the night, it sounded an awful lot like a crying baby.

He leaned forward, twisted the keys to shut off the Oldsmobile's rumbling motor and stepped out. Standing adjacent to his car and facing the Adams' apartment, Centre Street spanned to his left. Branching off Centre was Cedar Street which sloped downward toward Dudley Station.

Nightfall was deepening. Evenly-spaced streetlamps spilled a circular pool of muted light on the accumulation of snow below.

Rocco circled his car and stepped through a narrow passage carved into the towering manmade snow bank.

Zipping his jacket against the harsh cold, he carefully negotiated the patchwork of ice along the walkway. Reaching a small front porch, he ascended a pair of freshly-shoveled stairs.

Standing at the door, he listened intently. That's when he heard it again. From inside, Rocco detected the distinct wail of an infant. "I'm not going crazy," he uttered. And in the same breath, "Who in their right mind—"

He didn't finish the comment. Instead, he began knocking on the solid wooden door loudly.

"What the hell is going on here?" he said aloud.

It wasn't so much the high-pitched sound of a crying baby coming from the darkened interior of the apartment that troubled Rocco. Rather, it was the startling possibility that someone might have left a helpless child to fend for itself.

He had been knocking loud enough to wake the dead for a couple of minutes but to no avail. There was no response. First, he rapped on the wooden door itself and when that failed to yield results, he tried hammering with his fist on the ornamental glass that encircled the frame. Still, nothing. No one came to answer.

After each successive try, he paused to listen for any movement or sign that someone was at home. He tried to peer through the glass itself but the panes were opaque, the interior dark.

Perhaps someone was watching television or listening to the radio in a distant room and wasn't able to hear him pounding on the front door. Then again, who could ignore the cries of a baby in distress? Living with an infant for the previous seven months, he found that he could only tolerate the shrieking for a matter of minutes before giving in.

Frustrated and uncharacteristically at a loss, Rocco weighed his options carefully. Should he attempt to break into the apartment? It didn't look like it would take much to get past the door. Also, it had grown dark enough to provide sufficient cover from prying neighbors. If anyone nearby heard breaking glass, they might summon the police. But that wasn't necessarily a bad thing. At least the cops would tend to the crying baby, after he hightailed it out of there.

Rocco headed back to his car to retrieve a hammer from the satchel of tools stored in the trunk. Returning to the front door, he wasted no time swinging the metal head against a segment midway along the vertical glass panel. It shattered, leaving a gaping hole. Placing the hammer on the stoop, he reached through the opening, grasped the interior doorknob, and gave it a twist to disengage the lock. He then withdrew his arm, careful not to rake it along the sharp, ragged glass edges.

Entering through the now unlocked door, Rocco closed it behind him. He was struck by how dark it was inside the apartment. He couldn't see his own hand raised in front of him.

Rocco shuffled forward, arms outstretched before him. Within a few precarious steps, he encountered a table, positioned alongside a wall to his left. Feeling around, he discovered a small lamp on the smooth, wooden surface, which he lit without hesitation. The baby continued to cry in a distant room.

He paused for a moment, allowing his eyes to adjust. As he sized up the layout, Rocco realized that if the tenants came home unexpectedly, he would find himself in a perilous position. A broken window and trespass into their home? How would he explain himself? Then again, if Toby was with the Adams woman, as he suspected she would be – certainly she would understand his motives. And the window – he would pay for the damage. He had plenty of cash left over from the Puritan Meat Market hold up.

Rocco set off in the direction of the mystery baby. The wailing had tapered off but not ceased.

He stopped to peer into the first room that branched off the hallway and was met with a disturbing sight. Who could have done such a thing? Had these young mothers lost their minds? Under the paltry glow emanating from the small lamp in the foyer, Rocco was able to distinguish a pair of toddlers sleeping in beds clustered in the cramped bedroom. Wrapped in blankets, he wasn't able to determine if the children were boys or girls. But one thing was apparent. Their tiny shapes indicated they were very young, far too young to be left to care for themselves.

Rocco quietly backed out of the room, shaking his head in disbelief. He backtracked to the living room at the front of the dwelling, which offered egress to a spare room through a sliding door. Entering, he was again startled by what he discovered. If coming across two children asleep in their beds, in an apartment lacking adult supervision wasn't disconcerting enough, the sight of a baby lying on the cold, hard surface of a wood floor truly rattled him.

Understandably distressed, red-faced from crying, and covered head-to-toe in dust from the soiled floor, it was none other than Bernice Wagner, Toby's eleven-month-old daughter.

CHAPTER 26

"Worry does not mean fear, but readiness for the confrontation." – Bashar al-Assad

As he began to make his way out of the Centre Street apartment, Rocco Balliro caught sight of something he thought might be of use later. He hadn't noticed it when he lit the lamp, but resting on the telephone table was a pocket-sized address book. He figured that it might contain numbers of friends and family of Mary Adams and her husband Bob. He snatched the book.

Running a hand through his hair, Rocco looked back over his shoulder in the direction of the bedroom he'd just left. Thankfully, all remained quiet. All of the children, Bernice included, were sound asleep.

After getting over the initial shock and outrage of finding Toby's little girl lying prone on the floor, he sprang into action. He picked up the distressed child and gently placed her on a bed. Apparently, she had fallen from the crib. It was difficult to see in the ill-lighted residence but she appeared unhurt.

And as it turned out, she wasn't alone in the room. Sleeping soundly in an adjacent crib was an infant boy, roughly the same age as Bernice. Rocco couldn't fathom how the child continued to sleep through the shrill crying of his roommate. Obviously, the little guy belonged to Mary Adams, along with the two youngsters he found asleep in the adjacent bedroom. Rocco vaguely recalled Toby mentioning her sister-in-law had three children. The comment registered but until now, meant nothing to him. What mattered was that these two young mothers, Mary and Toby, had left four kids alone and not a single one of them was old enough, or capable enough, to fend for themselves.

Once he placed Bernice safely on the bed, Rocco fetched a facecloth, ducked into a nearby bathroom, and doused it with warm water. Returning to the baby, he gently dabbed with the damp cloth, wiping away the dirt and grime clinging to her skin.

Bernice soon fell into a lull as Rocco stroked her face. Her crying became a whimper, then stopped altogether. He thought perhaps his familiar, friendly face helped calm her. It wasn't long before the exhausted infant's eyes grew heavy and closed. Taking care not to disturb her slumber, Rocco surrounded her with pillows so she wouldn't roll off the bed.

After a pause to ensure that Bernice was asleep, Rocco turned to leave. He'd been in the apartment far too long. He didn't want to be there when the mothers of these children returned home. He didn't want to explain or justify the broken window. Additionally, he was afraid of what he might say, particularly to Toby. While he was searching for her and concerned for her well-being, he was upset about Bernice and needed some time to calm his nerves. He didn't want to confront her in front of Mary Adams. That discussion would come later, after he was certain no harm had come to her.

And where, Rocco thought as he retraced his steps along the narrow hallway, *was little Mark*? Toby had apparently taken him with her but left Bernice behind.

There were scores of unanswered questions. Where was Toby? Had something gone wrong? He should have heard from her by now. Rocco feared the worst. What if harm had befallen her? Granted, Barney Wagner was little more than a wannabe criminal; a despicable, low-level punk who stole cars and popped "bennies" for cheap highs. But Rocco knew that there was a history of abuse. Often strung out on drugs, Wagner was certainly capable of violence.

In her revealing diary, Toby wrote about Wagner's verbal attacks. For instance, on September 17, 1960, while six-months pregnant and suffering bouts of bleeding, Toby penned, "Barney got arrested in Roxbury for being drunk. They let him go this morning. Now he is asleep and doesn't remember a thing!!! So far, every time he comes around he tells me he hates me."

Approaching eight o' clock, nearly ten hours had passed since Rocco had last seen Toby. That morning, they had picked over a light breakfast in their Chelsea apartment. Understandably, neither had much of an appetite. The tension was palpable.

While tidying the kitchen together, Toby assured him that she would call within a few hours, right after she met with her soon-to-be ex-husband, as she described him.

"Are you sure you don't want me to go with you," he offered.

"We talked about this."

"I'm worried 'bout you, that's all," Rocco said, as he reached out and affectionately squeezed her arm.

"There's nothing to worry about," she insisted. "I'll be fine."

"If that asshole lays one finger on you, I swear—"

But he cut short the remark. Toby smiled weakly and walked away without another word. Perhaps it was better that Rocco didn't say what he had in store for Barney Wagner if Toby had one hair out of place after her meeting.

Moments later, she was readying the kids for the outdoors, applying layers of coats, hats, and gloves. She blew Rocco a kiss across the kitchen and, just like that, was gone.

As he grasped the door handle, preparing to leave the Adams' apartment, Rocco felt a slight twinge of guilt. While all four children were sleeping, he felt as if he, too, was deserting them, much like their mothers had before him.

Mentally, he began making excuses for the pair, particularly Toby. Perhaps, just before he arrived, they'd gone out for a few things at a nearby store. The women could already be on their way back to the apartment. Maybe the kids were sleeping and Toby and Mary Adams chose not to wake them. *They'll be back soon*, he assured himself. At least he was leaving Bernice in better condition than he found her.

Rocco exited the apartment, deftly sidestepping the shards of broken glass scattered across the threshold. As he picked up his hammer, a numbing gust brushed against the exposed skin of his face and neck.

"Man, it's cold," he said aloud, as he secured his collar. He realized that his headache had faded considerably. Hurrying along the slick stairs and sidewalk, he was anxious to get back to the warmth of his car. But as he neared the passage cut into the snowbank, Rocco glanced to his right and caught sight of a dark sedan idling roadside, just ahead of his Oldsmobile.

The street was shrouded in darkness and it was difficult to be certain, but Rocco thought he could make out a trio of shadowy figures inside, silhouetted against the vehicle's interior light. Two were seated in the front while a third occupied the rear. Could it be Toby?

He squinted, trying to clear his vision and get a better look. The interior windows were masked with condensation, further obscuring his view.

As Rocco observed, an individual in the front passenger seat rolled down the window and flicked out the remnants of a cigarette. Sharp, winter air poured into the car, instantly clearing the fog coating the windows.

Now Rocco saw that it wasn't Toby after all but rather three men. And he immediately recognized the fellow who disposed of the smoke.

During another of his espionage forays, he had seen the man's likeness in a number of photos Toby had tucked away in a dresser drawer. It was Barney Wagner, in the flesh.

Rocco remained motionless on the sidewalk, rooted in place. Slowly, he reached around to his lower back and felt for the .45 caliber handgun tucked into his belt. For several tense seconds, he thought he might have left the weapon behind while tending to Bernice.

"Phew," Rocco sighed in relief as he detected the telltale bulge beneath his jacket. Thankfully, the gun was still there.

Like a trip hammer engaged, his heart rate quickened. He felt the pulse pounding in his neck while the muscles in his upper back bunched and clenched with apprehension.

Without fully weighing the immediate repercussions, Rocco yelled, "Hey, Wagner!"

Calling out the man's name probably wasn't prudent but it elicited the desired response. Wagner stuck his head through the window and looked back to determine the source of the shouting. Seconds later, the door opened and he stepped out. As he exited, though, Wagner left the door ajar. He edged through another cut-through in the snowbank and firmly planted his feet on the ice-encrusted sidewalk. From Rocco's standpoint, it looked as if Wagner had positioned himself for a dash into the waiting car should the need arise.

It was an odd scene. Years later, Rocco compared it to one of the countless Old West gunfights he'd seen on television. Two cowboys, staring each other down across a distance. One flinches, ever so slightly, and the other draws his weapon and opens fire, fanning the hammer repeatedly until his opponent lay dead on the street.

Rocco had never met Wagner in person and the photos he saw during his midnight search of Toby's dresser drawers were, more or less, portrait-types or snapped from a distance. None portrayed his stature accurately, which was a rather frail-looking five-eight height.

"Hmmm, shorter than I expected," murmured Rocco under his breath as he sized up the man whose wife he had been sleeping with for the past seven months and to whose children he had been acting as surrogate father.

He wondered which revelation would infuriate Wagner more; learning that Rocco had been sleeping alongside his wife or the vision of his son Mark pretending to drive his foe's Oldsmobile, smiling joyfully as he manipulated the enormous steering wheel. He supposed both would be sufficient enough to trigger a murderous rage in most people, Wagner notwithstanding.

There was a time, early on, that Rocco had misgivings about his adulterous relationship. Certainly, he adored Toby and her kids and wanted nothing more than to spend the rest of his existence providing for them and loving them as if they were his own family. But somewhere inside, buried in the deepest crevices of his scruples, there was guilt.

At the time, Rocco put himself in Barney Wagner's shoes. It was an easy task considering his incarcerations, including a four-year stint at the loathsome Walpole State Prison. Among a wide array of demoralizing factors associated with long-term imprisonment, the inability to hold sway over one's wife or girlfriend while inside wreaked psychological havoc with many inmates. There was far too much idle time to ponder and fret. Where was she at that given moment? What was she doing? And, worst of all, who was she with?

Sure, for a couple of hours each Sunday afternoon, these women would pack up the kids and trek to the institution for a visit. She would stand by her man with love, loyalty, and the hope for a better life following his release. But the remaining six and a half days of the week, there was ample opportunity to roam unfettered by the restraints of a relationship or marriage. Many, like Toby, did just that.

If there was a degree of self-reproach in Rocco at the outset, it depreciated as his affair progressed, particularly as he learned more about the abuse she suffered. The more disdain Toby expressed for this poor example of a husband, who continued to stand motionless in the distance deciding between fight or flight, the more Rocco's blood boiled. He wanted nothing more than to break Wagner in two.

But first and foremost, he had to consider Toby's well-being. Rocco still didn't know her whereabouts or whether or not she was in danger. He had to move cautiously. Wagner could pay for his misdeeds later.

"Hey, Wagner, c'mere for a second," Rocco insisted, finally breaking the silent stalemate. Not surprisingly, the man stayed put.

In the enveloping darkness, Rocco watched as Wagner looked into the car. An unknown individual inside was saying something to him. He didn't respond but nodded in agreement.

"C'mon, Barney, I just want to talk with you for a few minutes," Rocco urged.

Whether it was the advice of his companions or his own decision, Wagner began to negotiate the treacherous sidewalk until the two men stood just several feet apart. Rocco, not usually at a loss for words, wasn't quite sure what to say.

"Let's get in," he finally suggested, pointing toward his parked car. "It's friggin' cold out here."

Wagner cast a wary glance but then soon followed through the cut in the snowbank, shuffling toward the Olds. Rocco climbed in behind the wheel and fired up the engine. Wagner slid into the passenger side and slammed the door with force. Under ordinary circumstances, Rocco would have suggested that his companion show more respect to his car. Instead, he bit his tongue. He didn't want to lose Wagner before he had a chance to get a few things out in the open.

Once both men had settled in and the heater was churning welcome warmth, Rocco sliced through the growing tension with a peace offering.

"Smoke?" he asked, extending a pack toward Wagner.

"No."

"Sure?"

"Yeah, I'm sure."

Rocco noted Wagner wasn't a bad-looking guy. He had a full head of sandy-colored hair topping soft, pale features including deep-set blue eyes, a thin, angular nose, and a firm, jutting chin. He looked weary but then, so did everyone who did time. Restful sleep in the joint was at a premium.

"I'm Rocco Balliro," he said as he lit a cigarette for himself.

"I know who you are."

Rocco couldn't resist a jab and said, "I'm the guy who's been feeding your kids."

"Yeah, and screwing my wife." *No baby steps here*, Rocco thought.

"Look, we need to fix this thing with Toby," he said.

Wagner, whose stare was fixed on the windshield, swiveled and said, "I don't give a shit about Toby."

Rocco expected Wagner to plead for Toby, to beg his rival to walk away from the sordid relationship and allow him and his wife to resume some semblance of the life they'd shared before he was shipped off to jail. He certainly wasn't expecting this comment about the woman they both loved.

"But she's your wife."

"She *was* my wife," Wagner spat, emphasizing the past tense in his response. His face was contorted in a scowl of fury. "I have no use for her anymore."

Deep down, Rocco was relieved. He had serious doubts Toby's marriage could be dissolved without a prolonged court battle. Now, it seemed, she could literally walk away from this maggot without a second thought. Rocco felt that much closer to realizing his scheme to take Toby and the kids to California, far away from Wagner, the ongoing pursuit of the police, and perhaps, the life of crime he had led for fifteen of his twenty-six years. But there was the matter of the children to be dealt with. He broached the subject with Wagner, point blank.

"What about your kids?" Rocco said.

"What about them?"

"Mark and Bernice? Remember them?"

"I just want my son. I want Mark. That's it!"

Interesting, Rocco mulled. Over the seven months he lived with her, Toby had exhibited an obvious favoritism toward her first-born. Mark was almost always by her side or in a carriage pushed along in front of her. Bernice, meanwhile, was often left behind with assorted caretakers. Bernice was a castaway, an inconvenience. And now, Barney Wagner was categorizing her in the same manner.

It wasn't the time or the place to ask why he'd excluded his daughter from the parental equation. Maybe he felt he had the capacity to manage a two-year-old boy but fell short with the resources to take custody of his daughter Bernice. Or perhaps it was something else altogether.

Rocco had his suspicions but would never raise the topic with Toby. He tried to complete a timeline on his own, calculating Wagner's incarceration versus Bernice's February 1962 birth. Could it be that Bernice was not fathered by the man who was fidgeting nervously in the passenger seat to his right?

At that moment, his reasoning didn't matter. It was just outright infuriating that Wagner would consider ripping Mark from the arms of his mother.

"You can't do that," Rocco admonished, raising his voice. He leaned in a little closer. "Don't even think about trying to take Mark away from Toby. I'm not about to let you do that. It would kill her."

Wagner recoiled. His waxen complexion turned a pastier shade of gray. His hands, resting in his lap like those of an obedient parochial school student, began to tremble.

Wagner was released from prison only hours before and returned home to find his marriage falling apart. And here he was, sitting in an unfamiliar car on a frigid night alongside the very man who brought this heartache to bear.

Edging forward in the seat, Rocco reached around to his lower back with his left hand, grasped the handle of the .45, and brought it into view. He reasoned that by allowing his companion to hold the handgun in safekeeping while they spoke, it might ease his apprehension. But when Wagner caught sight of the weapon, the brushed black enamel glinting in the dashboard light, his complexion blanched further and he stammered, "J-Jesus."

Rocco looked at the gun resting on the flat of his palm and then at the pale, drawn face of his guest and hastily exclaimed, "Whoa! Wait a minute. You have the wrong idea. Here, take it."

Deep inside, Rocco realized the move was sheer lunacy but he extended the gun, grip first. Still trembling, Wagner reached out to accept it, cautiously grasping the hefty weapon as if it was a scorpion about to strike. But then, without warning, he yanked his hand from harm's way.

"I don't want that," he snarled, refusing the offering. "I don't want your gun."

"I just want you to trust me," Rocco explained.

Wagner looked at him incredulously. "Trust? You want me to trust *you*?"

He was so engrossed in their verbal exchange, Rocco hadn't noticed a shadowy figure approaching until he tapped on the passenger side window. As Wagner sought a handle to roll the window down, Rocco slipped the gun under his leg. It was concealed but remained readily accessible. The man outside rapped on the glass again, this time with more urgency. Wagner, unable to figure out how to open the window, turned to look at his antagonist.

"Electric," Rocco explained, as he pressed the button on the driver's door panel. The glass pane rolled downward and the stranger who had crept along in the darkness came into full view. He stooped over and peered into the car.

Rocco didn't recognize him but his first impression of the intruder was dislike. Who did this guy think he was, barging in on their conversation? Rocco didn't appreciate the interruption. True, the discussion between himself and Wagner had grown strained – that was to be expected. But they were talking and that was the point. This disturbance could sever their attempt to reach a resolution.

"Googsie, you alright?" the new arrival asked in a gritty voice laced with a hint of a brogue.

"I'm okay," Wagner replied, sounding defeated. "We were just talking."

Realization came to Rocco. He now understood that whoever this guy might be, he was there for one reason and one reason alone – to act as muscle for Wagner. It was flattering for Rocco to learn that his tough guy reputation had preceded him and that Toby's husband felt the need to enlist the services of a bodyguard.

"I don't know who you are," Rocco interrupted. "But this is none of your business."

The man stared icily into the car. "I'm making it my fuckin' business," he snarled, like a vicious junkyard dog. "You got a problem with that?"

Rocco would later discover the man was actually Freeman "Punchy" Clifford, a low-level puke who was employed as an enforcer by Irish mob boss Edward "Wimpy" Bennett.

Clifford was a squat, muscular Irishman with a thick, reddish crop of hair. He sported a pale complexion with concave, green eyes that were set impossibly close together. His wide face framed a broad, flattened nose. His hands, which gripped the edge of the car door, were massive.

Clifford reached into the car, grasped Wagner's upper arm with a meaty hand and said, "C'mon, Googsie, let's go." Rocco slid his hand toward the button to activate the electric window upward but then noticed Wagner obediently submitted. Following Clifford's orders, he opened the door, stepped out, and closed it with a slam that reverberated through the hushed neighborhood.

"We weren't finished here!" Rocco yelled through the open window.

"Yeah, you were," declared Clifford as he and Wagner strode away.

Peering ahead, Rocco noted that the third individual, who had been sitting in the back seat of Clifford's vehicle, was now idly standing on the sidewalk. Though Clifford's car was dimly illuminated, Rocco recognized the man as Bob Adams, Wagner's brother-in-law and the tenant of the apartment he had broken into earlier.

When Clifford and Wagner rejoined him, the threesome consulted briefly. It was difficult to see but Rocco was able to make out Clifford pointing toward him. Obviously, he couldn't hear what was being said. He could only assume that it wasn't complimentary.

He resisted an overwhelming urge to get out of the car and confront Clifford a second time, on his terms. Rocco pulled the gun from beneath his leg and absently stroked the trigger with his forefinger. But a cooler head prevailed. He waited patiently for the men to get back in their vehicle and pull away from the curb.

Rocco looked in the direction of the apartment and thought of little baby Bernice and the other helpless children alone inside. And still no sign of their mothers. He shook his head, shifted the Oldsmobile into drive, and began to follow Wagner, Adams, and their bodyguard.

CHAPTER 27

*"He pulls a knife, you pull a gun. He sends one of yours
to the hospital, you send one of his to the morgue." –
Sean Connery as Jim Malone in* The Untouchables

Tailing Clifford through Roxbury, Rocco realized that he'd
ducked out of his Chelsea apartment without reloading his
gun.

Tightly gripping the steering wheel with one hand and
keeping his eyes trained on the lumbering vehicle ahead,
Rocco picked up the hefty weapon, which had been resting
on the console. He manipulated the magazine, detaching it
with his free hand. As he suspected, there remained only a
pair of cartridges.

"Dammit!" he cursed aloud. "Two fuckin' bullets!"

Rocco knew he was in big trouble if Clifford was leading
him into a trap.

By now, Wagner had tipped off his cohort about the
gun. Perhaps that was the topic of the trio's brief sidewalk
conference before they hopped in the car and took off. Armed
with that knowledge, but no gun of his own, the half-wit
Clifford was surely bent on getting his hands on one.

"Two bullets," Rocco reminded himself.

He was so engrossed with the daunting task that lie
ahead, Toby had momentarily slipped from his thoughts, even
though this evolving confrontation was all about her. Four
men – a husband, a boyfriend, a brother-in-law, and a hired
goon – were all about to wage war on the streets of Roxbury.

It wasn't lost on Rocco that his blood could be spilled
on the frozen, snow-coated pavement. But then, he didn't
need to be reminded that Toby had stuck her neck out for

him by smuggling the hacksaw blades into the New Bedford House of Corrections nearly two months earlier. She risked imprisonment and the loss of her children and he owed her for that. But it wasn't just his indebtedness that urged him along. Rocco truly loved Toby and was prepared to lay down his life for her.

Where was she? Was Mark with her? Perhaps she had dropped him off with her ex-sister-in-law Beverly or another babysitter while she dealt with her husband. That made sense but didn't explain Bernice. It wasn't like Toby to be so unpredictable. Or so callous. And what about Mary Adams? Not that it was any concern of his but she had left not one, but *three* children alone in that darkened apartment.

While he was anxious to hear the explanation for this uncharacteristic behavior, Rocco had more pressing problems. Just ahead of him, Clifford and his associates had arrived at their destination.

They came to a stop in front of an automotive garage on Dudley Street, which Rocco knew belonged to Bennett, who headed up the Roxbury-based Irish crime faction.

"I should have known," Rocco grunted aloud as he eased the Olds over to the opposite side of the street, roughly a half block behind Clifford and his companions. Tossing the shift lever into park, he pressed the power button, lowering the window about halfway. Icy air streamed in, jolting him to clarity.

His breathing quickened as he craned his neck and watched Clifford emerge from the sedan and pause briefly to cast a glance back in his direction. Under diffused light Rocco could have sworn he saw the Irish punk smirk at him.

"C'mere so I can wipe that fuckin' smile off your face," Rocco angrily muttered under his breath as he watched Clifford make his way into Bennett's garage. He was likely seeking weapons.

Rocco wasn't about to allow the lowly thug gain an upper hand in this potentially deadly chess match. Stuffing the

.45 caliber in his pocket, he stepped out of the car but left it running in case the need arose for a rapid retreat.

Crossing Dudley Street, he strode quickly toward Clifford's companions, who remained huddled in the car. Time was of the essence. Rocco figured if he could get Wagner alone again, away from the influence of the troublesome Clifford, they could resume their man-to-man and come to an understanding. There was no need for bloodshed.

But as Rocco drew nearer, the customer door to the garage opened. Clifford burst through the opening.

Rocco noticed he was empty-handed but that meant nothing – he might have a concealed handgun.

"Hey, Balliro!" Clifford shouted as he barreled headlong across the space between them. He was glaring menacingly. "What the fuck is your problem?"

"I told you," Rocco said evenly. "This ain't your beef."

"And I told you I was making it my beef!"

"This is between Wagner and me."

"He's all done with you."

"I want to hear it from him," Rocco demanded. The combatants both glanced toward the occupants of the car. There was no movement within, however.

"See?" said Clifford obstinately, flipping his head toward the car where Wagner and Adams cowered. Both listened intently to the escalating verbal sparring from the relative safety of the vehicle's interior. "Like I said, Googsie don't want to talk with you. Kill you, yeah. Talk, no."

Rocco saw red. He took a step closer. He was so enraged, in fact, he considered drawing his handgun right then and there and planting one of the two remaining bullets smack between Clifford's squirrelly eyes.

Rocco didn't think Clifford possessed the capacity to reason. In addition to the lack of anything resembling intelligence, the man didn't seem to have a non-violent bone in his body. Therefore, he was somewhat taken aback when Clifford briefly softened and said, almost pleadingly, "Listen,

Balliro, why don't you just leave Googsie be? He just wants to go back with his wife and go straight."

"His wife," Rocco replied with a sneer, "wants to be with me."

With that statement, Clifford's demeanor abruptly changed. He reached into his jacket pocket and pulled out a knife. The veins in his thick neck were bulging. He slashed at the air twice, back and forth, as if he were wielding a broadsword.

Was he kidding? Was this the best this insect could do? He couldn't find a gun in the headquarters of the Bennett brothers' crime family? A knife? A fuckin' steak knife?

Drawing his gun, a steely-eyed Rocco pointed it at Clifford's midsection. As expected, the Irishman abruptly ceased waving the feeble knife.

"Now what are you gonna do?" Rocco asked, his tone unwavering. Two bullets, as it turned out, were more than enough to settle this.

Clifford answered with his feet. He back-peddled toward his car, all the while keeping his eyes on the gun.

Rocco followed Clifford's every move with the pistol, keeping it trained on the man as he pulled open the driver's door and climbed in.

Despite his desire to end the life of this despicable piece of shit, Rocco decided against it, at least for the moment.

He returned to his Olds and waited for Clifford to make the next move. He hoped that whenever this fractured, stop-and-go confrontation came to an end, it would lead him to Toby.

Clifford was on the move again, pulling away from the sidewalk and heading south on Dudley. Rocco picked up where he left off moments before, tailing the hired hand and his two tagalongs.

Rocco was growing impatient. Clifford stood in the path of resolution and finding Toby. He should have shot him when he had the chance. The failed boxer needed to be removed from the equation.

The pursuit had been slow and deliberate, with Clifford driving at a crawl and intentionally allowing Rocco to keep up. The resumption of the cat-and-mouse game, however, quickened in pace and urgency. Without provocation, Clifford accelerated. For Rocco, the sudden change in the pattern was indicative of one thing – they were heading to Toby's location, wherever that might be, but they wanted to shake him first.

Rocco wasn't about to risk losing them. Despite stretches of hazardous, icy roadway, he punched the gas pedal and quickly closed the gap. Clifford upped the ante, again increasing his speed but his car was no match for the Oldsmobile. Rocco loomed, at times, a matter of inches off the rear bumper.

Careening around a bend at a high rate of speed, Clifford crossed a length of invisible black ice and began to wildly fishtail. Rocco couldn't see the driver but he imagined Clifford frantically attempting to regain control. The sedan jumped the curb and slammed headlong into a bank of frozen snow. He might as well have collided with a stone wall. The damage to the front end was substantial. Twisted metal wrapped around the wheels, taking the car entirely out of commission.

As he pulled alongside, Rocco noted a wisp of white smoke escaping from beneath the hood. "Next stop, scrapyard," he uttered with a malicious laugh.

Maneuvering closer to get a better look, Rocco saw that Clifford had rolled down his driver's window. Pressing the button to bring down the passenger side window of his own car, Rocco leaned over and said with a sneer, "Hey, asshole." Clifford glanced at him, dazed but unhurt. His two passengers looked a little worse for wear. Right about then, Wagner was likely wishing he was safe and sound back in the confines of his jail cell. His first night of freedom wasn't going very well.

As Rocco lined himself up with the rattled occupants of Clifford's car, he couldn't resist flashing a smile.

"Fuck you, Balliro!" Clifford spat.

"Your driving sucks!" Rocco shouted, his grin widening. "Call you a cab?"

"I'm gonna fuckin' kill you."

He laughed and said, "What are you gonna do, throw a snowball at me?"

An enraged Clifford opened the door and started to get out of the car. He had obviously forgotten that his adversary had a gun while he was unarmed, save for a knife. Rocco reacted instinctively, picked up his weapon which was resting on the seat next to him and with a steady hand, pointed it at Clifford. He was unable to restrain himself a second time.

When he fired a round through the open window, the report of the powerful weapon echoed off nearby buildings, sounding more like three or four shots instead of just one. Inside his car, Rocco was blinded for several seconds by the muzzle flash. An acrid odor of spent sulfur filled the vehicle interior.

Rocco surveyed the scene for damage rendered. Had he hit someone? Clifford? Wagner? Adams? Through the fading haze of burnt gunpowder, all three men looked to be intact. He'd missed. The bullet had evidently gone astray but served its purpose. It stopped a charging Clifford in his tracks.

Rocco entertained the thought of firing a second round. He had one bullet left and Clifford was a sitting duck, standing motionless beside his car. Once again raising the .45 caliber weapon, Rocco pointed it at his intended target. Clifford, trembling, waited for the end to come. But instead of shooting the vulnerable Irish enforcer, Rocco again lowered the weapon, sparing the goon's miserable life. He slammed the accelerator pedal, spinning the wheels, churning up chunks of road debris in his wake.

Once he was out of sight of the collision, he slowed to a more sedate speed – there was no need to end up like Clifford and his boys. Roxbury was soon in Rocco's rearview mirror.

Firing a round at Clifford had definitely changed the pattern for Rocco. In addition to felonious escape, the police would likely tack on an attempted murder charge. If they captured him, Rocco would be sent away for a long, long time. There was more urgency now to gather Toby and the kids, and get out of the Boston area. But he needed help. Clifford and his misfit duo would certainly be better prepared if they locked horns with Rocco again.

But Clifford wasn't the only one craving another crack at him to save face. There were at least two cops, in particular, who wanted nothing more than to get their hands on Rocco Balliro after they allowed him to slip from their grasp.

As he maneuvered the Oldsmobile along Atlantic Avenue, Rocco was unable to avoid a chunk of metal debris in the roadway. "Shit!" he exclaimed as he heard the telltale *pop* of a blown tire. Pulling over, he got out to inspect the damage and found the driver's side front tire shredded beyond repair.

Even if he had the time, Rocco couldn't change the flat. In November, prior to the Worth's burglary, he and Saroni had emptied the trunk to make room to stash more fur coats. That included the spare tire. He could have kicked himself for not putting it back.

Rocco was mulling over his next move when Boston's finest made it for him. A patrol car appeared out of the darkness, rounding a corner from Northern Avenue. The cops pulled up behind his disabled car.

"Shit," he hissed. "Not again."

He felt that familiar rush of adrenaline. His muscles tensed, spring-loaded like an Olympic sprinter preparing to burst from the starting blocks. But then Rocco noticed that neither of the two cops who approached had drawn a weapon. It was a telltale sign that they weren't seeking him. At least not yet. Apparently, they had no clue as to whom was in their midst.

The .45 caliber handgun was safely tucked away at the small of his back, stowed out of sight. Not that the gun would do him much good even if he was crazy enough to engage this pair. He had a single slug left.

"Eve'n', sir," said the first police officer, tall and gangly.

"Good evening, officer," Rocco greeted in kind.

"Everything alright here?"

"Flat tire," he said to the officer, gesturing toward the obvious.

"Spare?"

"Um, no," he replied. "Left it at home."

The second of the duo joined in the conversation. "Where's home?" he pried. The lawman didn't sound suspicious – just curious.

"Revere," Rocco lied without hesitation.

"My brother lives in Revere," one of the lawmen shared.

"Oh yeah?" Rocco responded, trying to sound genuinely interested but all the while, pushing back a huge surge of anxiety. He felt that familiar pit in his stomach. What would he say if the officer asked him to elaborate? Sure, he knew plenty of wise guys from the coastal community, which bustled with beaches, barrooms, clubs, and assorted mob hangouts. But he'd be hard-pressed to produce a false address that he was certain actually existed.

Thankfully, the line of conversation ended. Nothing further was said about Revere.

"So you need a lift?" asked the cop as he directed a flashlight beam on the mangled tire.

Rocco swallowed hard. He couldn't believe what was happening. Here he was, an escaped prisoner and more recently, an attempted murderer, chatting amicably with a pair of Boston cops who were offering him a ride home. Not to a cold jail cell at the precinct. Not to a temporary lockup at the nearby Charles Street Jail. But home! He fought an urge to laugh.

"Um, no thanks, officer," Rocco said. "There's a cab stand just up the street. I'm just gonna grab a taxi."

"You sure?"

"Yeah," he replied. "Alright if I leave the car here until I get back with a tire and some help?"

The cop determined there was room for vehicles to pass. "Sure, but not too long, okay?"

"Yeah," Rocco agreed. "An hour at the most."

"Any more than that, we'll have to send a tow truck and you'll have to shell out for storage."

"Understood, officer," he said. "Thanks again."

Rocco inhaled deeply and sighed with relief. He was like a fish that had just managed to wriggle off a hook. He had been right under the noses of a pair of Boston cops and they'd let him slip away. No chase. No running. He simply walked away from the pair and hailed a cab.

He concluded the men would likely be chastised by their superiors and fellow officers once the near miss came to light. But clearly, he couldn't risk another encounter like it. He might not be so fortunate the next time around.

CHAPTER 28

*"You can get much farther with a kind word and a gun
than you can with a kind word alone." – Al Capone*

A taxicab dropped off a solitary passenger near the intersection
of Union and Carter Streets on the west side of Chelsea,
roughly a mile from the hulking span of the Mystic River
Bridge, which linked Boston with North Shore communities.

The tall, slender man with dark, weary eyes paid the fare
and stood immobile on the sidewalk as the cab pulled away.
Wrapping his collar tightly against the bitter cold, he waited
and watched as the vehicle haltingly motored toward Route
1, which would take him back to the city. It was perilous
to allow the driver to catch sight of which direction his
passenger traveled on foot. If Rocco Anthony Balliro had
learned anything over the years, it was to never trust a cabbie.

Many of the hacks who worked in Boston were notoriously
quick to spill their guts to prying police. By doing so, they
might dodge a speeding ticket or two at a later time. Then
again, if the victim of these rats was able to determine which
one dropped a dime, that particular cabbie might be dodging
angry bullets instead of traffic tickets.

Memories of the taxi driver who fingered him soon after
his drunken North End holdup were still fresh in Rocco's
mind. How could he forget? He did a hard prison stretch at
Walpole partly because of that worm.

Once the taxi was out of sight, Rocco started a brisk
walk toward his Washington Avenue apartment. He was
also wary of passing patrol cars. Since he busted out of the
New Bedford House of Corrections, the dragnet for him had

intensified and would no doubt increase twofold once word of his most recent scrape reached the authorities.

Rocco's pace quickened along Washington Avenue. Reaching the front of his building, he burst through the front entrance and bounded up the stairs two at a time.

How long had it been since he broke into the home of Bob Adams and his young wife Mary? Four hours? Five? He had lost concept of time.

As he keyed the door to his apartment, Rocco wondered if Toby had tried to reach him while he was out. Better still, maybe she had come home in his absence. Wishful thinking on his part, but he hoped to see her sitting at the kitchen table, the familiar black kerchief framing her pretty face.

He flipped the wall switch, flooding the small apartment with light. As his eyes adjusted, he was disappointed but not surprised to find that Toby wasn't there. Nor was there was any sign that she had been there recently. The place was exactly as he left it three hours before, according to the clock mounted on a wall. It read ten o'clock. A dozen hours had passed since he and Toby shared a hastily-prepared breakfast followed by her departure, with the kids, to seek out her husband.

Rocco tossed his car keys on the table and added the handgun. He marched to the fridge for a beer and grabbed an apple from a large bowl of fruit. As he bit into it, Rocco realized he hadn't eaten anything since early morning. He was famished but stopped short of fixing a meal.

While it was fresh in his mind, Rocco crouched to open a small cabinet beneath the sink. Stretching his arm to its limit, he reached in and withdrew the strongbox stashed there.

The silence in the apartment was deafening. As he downed his beer, Rocco found that he actually longed for the happy sounds of *his* family. He'd grown accustomed to the clatter over the seven months he'd spent with Toby and her kids. It was like music. He wished he could hear little Mark playing with his toys, laughing merrily at just about everything. And

Toby, with her frequent, hearty sarcasm. She always managed to come up with some crass but comical remark to take him out of the doldrums. Oddly enough, he even found himself missing Bernice's incessant fussing when she demanded a bottle, diaper change, or some form of attention.

Opening the lockbox, Rocco peered inside, glimpsing at the guns and boxes of ammunition. Removing the individual items, he lined them in a neat, orderly row across the table. One by one, he reloaded the assortment of weapons, starting with the nearly spent .45 caliber pistol he fired at Clifford.

One of the rounds rolled off the table to the floor. As Rocco bent to retrieve it, the address book he'd taken from the Adams apartment fell out of his back pocket. He'd forgotten about it.

Fetching the phone, he dialed the number he found on the inner cover of the address book. **Bob and Mary Adams and Family**, it read, in neat cursive handwriting.

As the receiver rang in his ear, Rocco took a quick swig of his beer. He nearly spilled it when he heard a female voice on the other end tentatively say, "Hello?" He wasn't expecting anyone to pick up. He assumed it was Mary Adams, although he had never spoken with her and wouldn't recognize her voice.

Holding the phone close to his ear, Rocco cupped the mouthpiece with his free hand and paused. His senses were on full alert. He listened for sounds in the background that might reveal what was taking place in the Roxbury apartment he had left several hours before. Was Toby there? Barney Wagner? His thug pal Clifford? He couldn't discern any recognizable sounds save for the breathing of the woman on the telephone.

"Hello? Anyone there?"

He knew he had to respond within the next few seconds or she'd hang up and likely not answer if he tried to call again.

"Hello," she said a third time, the frustration now evident in her tone.

Finally, he broke his silence.

"This is Tony Russo," he said, borrowing the name of an old Walpole cellmate.

"Rocco?"

He went mute again. So much for the fake name.

"Rocco? I know it's you," Mary insisted.

"Put Toby on the phone."

"You shot at my husband!" she claimed indignantly, adding, "And my brother!"

"I didn't shoot anyone," he weakly refuted.

"Really?" she said, her voice intensifying. "Really? How do you explain the bullet that almost hit Barney?"

Better luck next time, Rocco thought. But he said nothing to her about the random round he fired into Clifford's car. There was no need to incriminate himself with this half-crazed woman.

Nor did he need to remind himself that Mary was Barney Wagner's sister. She would support her brother, regardless of any explanation he furnished. It made no difference whatsoever that her sister-in-law Toby participated equally in the extramarital affair – like any true sibling, Mary would still blame Rocco entirely for her brother's failed marriage. In her distorted view, Barney could do no wrong.

"And you broke into my house," she continued, shrieking. "What the hell were you thinking? There's glass everywhere! I have children!"

He resisted the overwhelming urge to point out that yes, he did break into the apartment. And yes, he left behind a pile of glass shards. But he did so to render aid to small children that were left alone by their irresponsible mothers. How would she explain that? He should be the one asking questions. *What kind of mother are you anyway*, he could hear himself say.

But he wasn't about to get into a debate with Mary Adams about the rights and wrongs of motherhood. He didn't really care about her opinion or her explanation. None of that mattered now. Time was of the essence. He sensed Toby was in imminent danger.

"Let me speak with her."

Mary said nothing further. Rocco thought she might hang up the phone but when he heard a loud bang, he realized that she'd slammed the receiver on a table in a fit of rage.

Rocco nearly hung up himself. He didn't actually need to speak with Toby to know she was there. He'd wasted enough time verbally tangling with Mary Adams. He should already be halfway to Roxbury. Then he remembered: no wheels. By now, his prized Oldsmobile was locked up in a Boston police impound yard.

As his mind rambled through options, a meek voice came across the telephone line that stopped him cold. The hair stood up on the nape of his neck. His tortured stomach was flip-flopping again.

"Tony," she began.

"Honey, are you alright?" he asked, trying not to sound alarmed.

"Tony, please don't come here," she pleaded.

She sounded frightened. He sensed somebody was listening to their conversation. Wagner? Clifford? The Adams guy?

"What's going on? What do you mean don't c–"

"Don't come here," Toby repeated, in a low tone that was almost a whisper. She obviously didn't want to be heard. "Don't do anything crazy. They're waiting for you."

The line went dead. There was silence followed by the steady drone of a dial tone.

The Boston cops got their long-awaited break at around eleven-thirty on the night of Friday, February 1, 1963, when Mary Adams returned home from a visit with her parents in Brookline to find shattered glass littering the floor of the foyer. Apparently, her Roxbury apartment had been broken into. After a brief discussion with Toby, who'd gone with her to Brookline, the police were contacted.

Several officers from nearby Roxbury Crossing Station were dispatched to investigate the break-in.

When Boston Police Sergeant Frederick J. Lovett, Detective Thomas J. Calnan, and Patrolman Robert Ryan descended upon the scene, Mary Adams was quick to blame Rocco Balliro, Toby's boyfriend, for the fractured pane of glass. She didn't hazard a guess, when asked, as to why he might have broken into her apartment but did point out to the trio of responding officers that nothing was taken.

Mary Adams said nothing to the police about leaving the children alone while she and her sister-in-law Toby went out to run errands and visit family members. Such an admission would only cloud her condemnation of the alleged perpetrator.

When the police learned that fugitive Rocco Balliro might pay another visit, they summoned additional manpower to the scene. Joining the contingent was Patrolman John Hoffman and Sergeant Hippolit Piatkowski, a forty-one year-old decorated World War II veteran, who immediately took control of the crime scene.

"We've been looking for him," the sergeant said to the two young women.

Piatkowski, along with plainclothesmen Lovett and Calnan, set about sizing up the apartment, which was on the street-level of a top-and-bottom duplex. The second floor tenants were not at home.

Officers Hoffman and Ryan, meanwhile, were dispatched to guard the exterior of the home from an unmarked car. They took up a position overlooking Cedar Street.

As the officers studied the layout of the apartment interior, the telephone in the foyer rang shrilly. Mary Adams looked warily at Piatkowski, as if seeking his permission to answer it. The grizzled cop wordlessly nodded. She strode to the little table in the foyer, where hours before Rocco had taken her address book, and lifted the receiver.

"Hello?" Mary greeted the caller. She paused for a response.

All in attendance waited and watched for her reaction. It wasn't Rocco Balliro, as they thought it might be. Rather, Mary's brother Barney was calling from the Wagner home in nearby Brookline.

"Barney," she said, noticeably relieved to hear from him. "Are you alright?"

The trio of cops stood idly by, listening to her side of the conversation.

After a pause, she cried, "He did what? Jesus Christ!"

Piatkowski moved closer, preparing to take the phone from her when she abruptly ended the call.

"Barney, the cops are here – in the apartment," she hurriedly said. "I'll tell them what happened."

"Who was that?" Sergeant Lovett asked as she hung up, fumbling with the receiver.

"My brother," Mary replied, glancing toward Toby to gather a reaction as she spoke. "Rocco shot at them."

The cops sprang into action. They shifted furniture in the living room, repositioned chairs, slid a coffee table aside, and moved the couch to provide adequate concealment from intruders.

They pulled down the shades, located light fixtures, and began to extinguish each, one by one. They left a single lamp in the living room illuminated so they could continue with their work.

Piatkowski broke from the group for a moment and made his way along a long hallway that dissected the apartment down the middle. On the right, as he walked from the front to the rear of the rectangular-shaped dwelling, he noted three bedrooms with the first split from the living room by a sliding door. The other two had individual entrances off the main corridor. To his left, Sergeant Piatkowski found a spare room and the kitchen.

Without delay, he returned to the waiting group. He was a proven cop, with a decorated military background, but was about to make a costly error in judgment.

"Mrs. Adams?" he began, according to several witnesses who later recapped courtroom testimony.

"Yes?"

"I want you to stay with your children," he said, gesturing toward the bedroom where two-year-old Robert Jr. and three-year-old Cheryl were sound asleep. "Detective Calnan will be with you. Don't come out, no matter what happens. You got it?"

She nodded.

He then turned in Toby's direction and noticed she had retrieved her son Mark. Perched on her hip, he was resting his sleepy head against her shoulder.

"Mrs. Wagner, listen carefully," he commanded.

"Yes?" Her voice was subdued, partly for the boy falling fast to sleep in her arms and partly in compliance with the police officer.

"I want you and your son in the back bedroom," the cop instructed. He spoke with a stern, even tone. "If this Balliro guy shows up here, I don't want him to see you. Understood?"

It was futile to question the man's authority. He meant business.

"Yes," she replied.

"I need to use the phone," the sergeant said. "I need to see about getting more men."

"Sure," said Mary.

Time slowed to a crawl. The three cops occupied themselves by making small talk with the two young mothers in the cramped living room. They kept voices muted so they wouldn't wake the children sleeping in nearby bedrooms. Toby had returned Mark to bed as well.

Boredom set in but suddenly, the phone rang again, shattering the stillness and startling the group.

Piatkowski aimed the flashlight to guide Mary Adams as she raced to answer before it could ring a second time and awaken the children.

The air was suddenly electric. All five participants were thrust into an adrenaline rush.

"Hello?" Mary said.

She turned to look over her shoulder and found all eyes intently focused on her, police officers and Toby alike.

"Hello? Anyone there?"

Her greeting was followed by silence both on the phone and in the apartment around her. It was quiet enough to hear a pin drop.

Instinctively, Sergeant Piatkowski drew closer, prepared to relieve her of the phone if it became necessary. It was obvious who was on the other end of the line.

"Hello?" Mary repeated, her voice now laced with unfiltered irritation.

She paused again. Still no response from the caller.

"Rocco?"

There was continued silence.

"Rocco? I know it's you."

The caller apparently responded to that direct inference because Mary Adams launched into a tirade, scolding the individual on the other end of the line for taking a shot at her husband and her brother and breaking into her home, leaving a dangerous mess of sharp, broken glass in his wake.

After a moment, Mary Adams pivoted to face her sister-in-law Toby, who had turned noticeably pale.

Holding the phone at arm's length, Mary said, "He wants to speak with you."

Toby glanced toward Piatkowski who nodded his approval. Walking slowly across the room toward Mary, Toby uncertainly picked up the receiver, handling it like a dangerous cobra, and placed it against her ear. Cupping her hand over the mouthpiece, she spoke silently so the nearby police officers couldn't clearly discern what she was saying.

"Tony?" she began hesitantly.

Behind her in the living room, one of the three cops extinguished the last lamp in the living room, immersing the apartment into thick, total darkness.

Over the din of the busy nightclub, the barkeep shouted across the room, "Hey, Rudy, you got a call!"

"Who is it?"

"Your brother," he replied. "He sounds upset."

Rocco listened impatiently as the bartender, who doubled as a Boston police officer when he wasn't pouring drinks at the club, flagged down Rudy.

"Yeah? Hello?"

"Rudy, it's me."

"Rocco, how the hell are you?"

"I need your help." There was desperation in his tone and sensing it, Rudy turned serious.

"Sure, sure," his paternal twin brother said. "What's up?"

"Toby's in trouble."

"What kind of trouble?"

"It's a long story," Rocco answered impatiently. "I'll explain when you get here."

"Okay," Rudy calmly replied. "I'll pick you up in an hour. I just have to finish up here."

But Rocco had already hung up. He was busy preparing the four guns he'd spread across the kitchen table.

CHAPTER 29

*"The police are not here to create disorder, they're here
to preserve disorder." – Richard J. Daley*

After telephoning his brother Rudy at the club, Rocco readied
the guns, loading each to capacity. There were four weapons,
including his personal favorite – a Colt .25. Sitting at the
kitchen table in the cramped Chelsea apartment he'd shared
with Toby and the kids since his escape from jail, he pondered
the task that lie ahead.

Rocco was certain that Toby was in serious jeopardy.
There was no doubt in his mind. Barney Wagner was pissed
off, understandably. His wife of three years had stepped out
on him while he was jailed in the Concord Reformatory.
Wagner's comment about wanting only his son and not giving
a shit about Toby rang in Rocco's ears, repeating itself over
and over, like a skipping record album. "She was my wife,"
the spurned Wagner had remarked during their discussion in
the Olds. "But I have no use for her anymore."

The hatred was palatable. It was a recipe for disaster. In
Rocco's opinion, Wagner had been painted into a corner and
during a fit of rage, was capable of anything. There was no
time to waste. He had to rescue Toby from her husband and
the man's despicable ally Clifford before something terrible
happened.

Standing in the shadows of the kitchen, Rocco watched for
his brother Rudy from the window. It was nearing midnight
when the familiar Chevrolet Impala pulled up to the front of
the building. He couldn't be certain but from the distance, it
looked as if there was a man riding shotgun in the passenger

seat. It was likely that Rudy had brought along an extra hand. There was strength in numbers.

Stuffing the guns in his pockets, two in each, Rocco zipped his leather and left the apartment.

"Man, it's fuckin' cold," he remarked as he slid across the back seat of the warm vehicle and rubbed his hands together. He looked up to see that his brother did, in fact, bring along another man to help out. It was none other than Al "Slim" Ciocco, all-purpose lounge hand and gangster strong-arm. The thirty-three year old was good to have around if a fight broke out.

"How's it goin', Slim?"

"Good, Rocco. Good"

"Where to, little brother?" Rudy impatiently interjected.

"Roxbury. 107 Centre Street. Know where it is?

"Yeah."

Rocco's sibling tossed the shift lever into drive and pulled away from the curb. A twenty minute drive lie ahead. "So what's going on?" he asked.

"We need to help Toby."

"She's in trouble?"

"Her asshole husband got out of jail this morning," he answered. "He's pissed that she's been with me while he was away."

Rudy turned to glance back at his brother and frowned.

Rocco grimaced and said, "Yeah, yeah, I know what you're thinking. But she wants to be with me." Pausing, he added, "The guy's a loser."

Tossing in his two cents, Slim asked, "So what's he gonna do to her?"

"I dunno," Rocco replied with a shake of his head. "I just have a bad feeling 'bout this, that's all. He's got a friend with him too. One of Bennett's guys."

"Have you talked with her?" Rudy questioned as he maneuvered the big Chevy on roads overlaid with an icy sheen.

"Yeah. For a few seconds. On the phone."

"What'd she say?"

"Not much," Rocco replied. "She sounded scared shitless, like someone was listening to her."

"Husband?" Slim suggested.

"Yeah, could've been."

The trio abruptly fell silent for the remainder of the trip across the city. Rocco, left to his thoughts, mulled what he might do after successfully liberating Toby from the clutches of her soon-to-be ex-husband.

Of course, there could be no delay in leaving the Boston area. Once the cops got wind of his altercation with Clifford and the fact that he fired a round at the contemptible Irish enforcer, there would certainly be renewed interest in his apprehension, as if escape from jail wasn't reason enough.

Rocco closed his eyes for a moment but was jolted sharply back when Rudy stated, almost nonchalantly, "We're here."

He killed the headlights and brought the Impala to a stop in front of the two-family dwelling. Both Rocco and Slim rubbed away a thin film of condensation which had built up on the windows.

"You sure she's here?" Rudy asked as he peered through the streaky glass at an apartment conspicuously void of light. It looked vacant.

"I dunno. She was here an hour ago – when I called on the phone."

"Think they took her someplace else?"

"Could be," Rocco answered. "They knew I was coming here."

"What now?"

"Let's check the apartment."

"Alright," Rudy agreed as he eased his foot off the brake pedal, allowing the high-idling vehicle to coast forward toward the intersection of Cedar Street.

Ahead, the narrow roadway was lined with waist-high snowbanks, revealed beneath diffused illumination from distant streetlamps. There was an eerie, almost surreal glow to the street, as if it was a fabricated stage set for an Alfred Hitchcock thriller. Turning right onto Cedar, Rudy parked adjacent to a cleft in the snow and silenced the engine.

Rocco, meanwhile, had removed all but one of the handguns from his pockets. "Slim, take this," he said, handing over a .45 caliber pistol.

He wrapped his thick fingers around the grip and stashed the firearm inside his coat.

Rudy pivoted in the front seat and extended his hand toward his brother. Rocco obliged, slapping a gun firmly on his palm.

The three men got out and quickly made their way through a narrow manmade channel carved in the snow. Footfalls crunched on the residual ice-snow mixture coating the sidewalk. Rocco shuddered and led the trio as they marched single file. Visible clouds of frosty breath escaped from their mouths as they labored, ascending a grade on Cedar Street and then turning left on Centre.

Reaching the walkway that led to the apartment, the men paused briefly, but then moved without further hesitation to the front door.

Rocco pointed out the cardboard covering the glass pane he'd shattered to gain access to crying Bernice earlier. His companions nodded and withdrew their concealed weapons.

He'd been relatively calm during the brief ride from Chelsea, but as he and his associates prepared to enter the pitch dark dwelling and face a possible ambush from Toby's captors, Rocco's senses kicked into overdrive. Raw adrenaline coursed through his veins and his mouth went dry. The collar of the t-shirt he wore beneath his jacket seemed as if it were tightening around his throat, like a miniature boa constrictor.

Despite the bitter cold, small beads of sweat formed on his forehead. Drawing a prolonged breath and then exhaling, Rocco crouched and pulled away the cardboard patch. Reaching through the gap, he located the deadbolt and gave it a spin. It made a loud click. If there was anyone in the apartment, they would surely have heard it. The element of surprise was no longer in his favor, if it ever was.

"Are you guys ready for this?" Rocco uttered as he stood upright and grasped the doorknob. He leveled the question even though he knew there was no turning back now.

Both men nodded and readied their handguns. Rocco did the same, palming the trusty .25 caliber in his jacket pocket.

With further delay, he twisted the knob and forcibly shouldered the door, unintentionally splintering the wooden jamb. Bursting headlong into the pitch black foyer, Rudy and Slim were close on his heels. An icy wind gust followed them in.

From a darkened, obscure corner of the living room, a menacing shout immediately met the three intruders.

"This is the police! Drop your guns!"

Bedlam erupted in the apartment.

Straining to see, Rocco blindly opened fire in the direction of the voice, spraying bullets in a pattern left to right until his Colt was nearly spent. It was pure instinct. If he was going to be killed on this night, he wasn't going alone.

From within the deepest recesses of his mind, he hastily replayed what he'd heard before the shooting commenced. Did the unseen voice shout, "This is the police?" Perhaps. But if so, it was likely nothing more than Clifford or Wagner impersonating a cop to gain the upper hand. Had Rocco really believed what he'd heard, it might have given him pause which could have proved deadly.

Beside him, he could hear the rapid fire clicking and report of a weapon as Rudy engaged the unseen attacker, who was now returning their fire.

Rocco's ears were ringing and the acrid odor of spent gunpowder wafted through the air. It permeated rooms where, hours before, young children cavorted and climbed on furniture, furniture which was now riddled with searing, smoking chunks of lead.

Another hidden adversary joined the fray, shooting at them from the corridor. And then a third. *How many are there?* thought a fearful Rocco as he squeezed the trigger yet again. *Are we outnumbered? Outgunned? Had Clifford gathered more men?*

Slim trained his pistol toward the second gunman, concealed in the obscurity of the dark hallway, which Rocco knew led to the bedrooms and the kitchen, and began blasting away. They were all firing in unison now.

Under a deadly volley from two or perhaps three shooters, Rocco braced for the inevitable. Exposed and vulnerable in the open foyer, it was only a matter of time before one or all of them took a bullet. They were pinned down. There was no refuge from the torrent of lead whizzing by their heads, save for the envelope of darkness.

The .25 caliber was empty so Rocco felt around for the second gun stored in his pocket but then thought better of it. There was a lull in the shooting and the hail of scorching slugs crisscrossing the apartment came to a halt. An eerie silence replaced the ear-splitting gunfire. As suddenly as the gun battle had begun, it was over. But from the murky recesses of the apartment, Rocco heard a vague, yet unmistakable sound. It made his blood curdle. It sounded like the unseen gunmen were reloading. "Jesus Christ!"

Raw survival instincts took over.

"C'mon!" he hissed through clenched teeth. "Let's get the fuck outta here!"

There was no hesitation. The three men bolted from the apartment, retracing their steps through the open doorway and along the narrow path.

Slick with ice, the concrete walkway had proven difficult to navigate at a pedestrian pace. Running proved outright treacherous.

As they awkwardly bolted for the car, Rocco and his companions believed they were seconds from escape. But the threat was far from over. Coming up behind them, a pair of men gave chase on foot.

Rocco gathered these pursuers hadn't come from inside the apartment. They were still some distance along Centre Street. More of Clifford's pals, arriving late to help out? They were shouting something as they closed the gap, but it was unintelligible amid the commotion.

Without so much as a hint of what he was about to do, Slim brandished his weapon, came to a sliding stop, and turned to face the onrushing duo. Rocco thought the weapon, like his, was empty. He was wrong. Slim raised the gun and fired a pair of rapid bursts in the direction of the two men. It was obvious that he wasn't shooting *at* them – they were nothing more than warning shots fired over their heads. The tactic worked. Both men came to an abrupt stop and then turned tail and ran in the opposite direction. It was a strange scene.

Rocco heard more gunfire coming from inside the apartment.

"What the hell is going on?" he said. "Who the fuck are they shooting at in there?"

"I dunno," said Rudy, gasping. He was breathing heavily from the exertion of their getaway. "But we need to get outta here! C'mon!"

As Rocco scrutinized the scene unfolding on the undulating roadway behind their speeding car, a torrent of despair surged through his body. His stomach roiled with anxiety and he fought off a bout of nausea. He could feel his heartbeat pounding in his throat. Not trusting his own eyes, Rocco risked another glance. To his dismay, the scene hadn't changed.

"Oh God!" he exclaimed as the revelation washed over him.

"What is it?" Rudy shouted over the din of the Chevrolet's racing engine.

Careening around treacherous, icy bends in the road at death-defying speeds, Rocco was anchored in the back seat, hanging on for dear life. For leverage, both of his feet were wedged beneath the front seat and he clung with a white-knuckled death grip to the door handle. Ill-advised, perhaps, but he stretched his body upward from a protective crouch to take yet another look out the rear window. The blood drained from his face. He felt as if someone had punched him in the midsection. It was difficult to catch a breath.

"Fuck!" he gasped.

"Rocco, what's going on!" Rudy hollered as he worked the steering wheel.

"I can't fuckin' believe this!"

"What is it? Who's chasing us?"

"They're cops!" Rocco yelled without turning to face the driver. He didn't dare look away. His eyes were glued to the vehicle in tenacious pursuit over the Roxbury streets, its flashing blue light affixed to the roof on the driver's side. "We were shooting at fuckin' cops!"

"What are we gonna do?"

"I don't know!" Rocco responded over the clamor. "We need to lose them! Step on it!"

On his brother's frantic suggestion, Rudy hit the accelerator and the Chevy reacted, lurching violently forward. The transmission screamed in protest and fumes of heated metal permeated upward through the floorboards.

Searing hot slugs impacted with the exterior of the Chevy. The sound reminded Rocco of hail pelting off a metal roof during a storm. But unlike hailstones, one of these bullets could instantly snuff out his life or the life of one of his two comrades in the front seat.

Rocco hunkered down. Silently, he prayed that the metal structure of the trunk and the stuffing in the seats would be of sufficient thickness to stop, or at least slow, a round colliding with the rear end of his brother's Impala. He braced himself for the impact of a bullet, hoping that if he was hit, it wasn't anywhere vital.

How the hell did he end up like this? Reeling, he went over it in his mind. Minutes before, he had laid siege in the apartment, bent on rescuing Toby and her kids from the clutches of her infuriated husband. Rocco had gathered, by her words of caution during their brief telephone exchange, that Toby was being held against her will by Wagner and Clifford.

When Rocco and his associates burst into that dark foyer and were immediately met with the guttural order to "drop your guns," it was instinctual to fire their weapons defensively. They'd walked into an ambush, likely set up by Clifford in retribution for the earlier embarrassment Rocco dished out.

Instead, he now understood it wasn't Clifford and his gang lying in wait in that pitch black apartment. Rather, it was the cops. Rocco, his brother Rudy, and Slim Ciocco had just engaged in a tremendous firefight with the police, all the time believing they were exchanging gunfire with "a bunch of bad guys," as he later described it.

Sure, whoever shouted for them to drop their weapons identified themselves as the police, but that was meaningless. Rocco heard it but, at the moment, discarded it as a ruse by Clifford and company.

Nausea resumed twofold when it occurred to Rocco that, in all that shooting in the apartment, they might have hit one of the cops concealed in the darkness.

Worse still, he and his associates could have easily been brought down by a stray bullet. It was a small miracle that the three of them emerged unscathed after such an intense gunfight. Could the same be said for the cops? How many were there? Had one of them taken a bullet? Had one of them been killed?

Rocco gathered his wits and pressed into action, despite the chaos enveloping him and his colleagues in the speeding car.

"Rudy! Slim!"

"Yeah?" the two men replied simultaneously.

The bullets were still flying in their direction. Keeping his head down, Rocco loosened his viselike grip on the door handle and slid forward on the seat. He imagined, again, what it might feel like if a slug met his flesh.

"Gimme your guns!" he insisted. "We gotta ditch them."

Yanking his weapon from the front of his pants, Slim handed it over to Rocco. The muzzle was still warm from the recent firing.

Rudy seemed to be in a state of shock, staring straight ahead, unblinking. The burning tires of the Impala screamed as he cut the wheel into a bend in the road and punched the pedal again. There was ice everywhere and it wasn't lost on Rocco that they could all be killed in a collision. Death by a police bullet or death by shredded steel after impacting with an immovable object, such as a tree or utility pole. Did it really matter?

"Slim!"

"Yeah, I'll get it, Roc!"

Raising his voice to be heard over the turmoil, Slim warned, "Rudy, I'm gonna take your gun, okay?" There was no response. He was entirely focused on the road ahead.

"C'mon, guys, hurry!" Rocco cried out.

Slim reached across the car but stopped shy of grabbing the pistol that was protruding from Rudy's gaping jacket pocket. It was clearly in view but it was perilous to interfere with his driving, especially at their current rate of speed.

"Rudy, your g–"

Rocco's brother suddenly snapped out of it and shouted, "Go ahead – take it! Take the fuckin' thing!"

Slim leaned in and grasped the pistol grip. He warily withdrew the gun, taking great care under the circumstances.

The assumption was the weapon was spent, like the rest. But one could never be sure if there was a bullet left in the chamber that could discharge if they ran over a pothole.

Once the gun was safely removed from Rudy's pocket, Slim handed it back to Rocco. He added it to the others, which included his .25 caliber Colt and the .45 caliber.

Rudy veered around another slight turn and the guns slipped from Rocco's reach, scattering across the slick seat. Leveraging his feet against the door for balance, he leaned to collect the strewn hardware. The car's interior was full with the stench of spent gunpowder. Acrid fumes stung his eyes. He tasted blood in his mouth and realized he bit his tongue.

Balancing the four guns on his lap, Rocco grasped the window knob and began to spin it rapidly, lowering the glass. Biting cold air poured in through the opening. As his brother leaned into a hard turn, Rocco scooped the guns off his lap with both hands and tossed them. He detected a faint clatter as the pistols met the pavement.

With one mission accomplished, Rocco set his sights on the next task. He had to get out of the car.

"Rudy, listen up!"

"Yeah!"

"We need to split up!" he shouted over the din. "We need to spl–"

Rocco never finished the comment. His train of thought was abruptly severed when he heard the unmistakable *plink* of a slug striking the metal crossbar just above his head.

"Ouch!" hollered Rudy in distress. "What the fu–"

"What is it?"

Rudy freed a hand from the steering wheel and reached around to the back of his head. Rocco, observing as his brother felt around with his fingertips, was startled to see Rudy's hand come away coated with bright red blood.

"Jesus Christ!" he cried. "I'm hit, Rocco. I've been fuckin' shot!"

"Shit! How bad?"

"I dunno! I can't tell!"

"Slim, see if you can find something to stop the bleeding," Rocco implored.

"I can feel it!" Rudy bellowed as he manipulated the Chevrolet with one hand and inspected the wound with the other. "I can feel the bullet! I think it's under the skin!"

Slim opened the glove box and rifled through the contents. He found a handkerchief and handed it over.

"Are you alright?" Rocco grilled.

"Yeah, yeah, I'm okay," his twin answered as he applied the cloth to the wound. A quarter-sized stain of red formed. "Christ, I'm one lucky sonofabitch!"

The irony of the moment struck Rocco. Moments before, the three men had faced a torrent of bullets during a frenetic exchange of gunfire in the now-distant Centre Street apartment with an unknown number of assailants – police officers, apparently – and had somehow emerged unscathed. If that wasn't enough, they drew yet another salvo while retreating to their car, again escaping without a scratch. Luck finally ran out, however, as a wayward slug found its way into their speeding automobile and the back of Rudy's skull.

Rocco speculated that the stray bullet had penetrated the canvas of the soft-top and impacted with the metal crossbar support. The ricochet steered the deadly slug in a downward trajectory toward the back of Rudy's head. It was a terribly close call. Had he been leaning back any further, even a matter of inches, Rudy would surely have been killed and Rocco and Slim would have been left at the mercy of a careening, driverless vehicle.

"Are you sure you're alright?"

"Yeah, yeah!" Rudy acknowledged. He was unwavering; seemingly not overly concerned about the close shave that nearly consigned him to the city morgue. "It's nothing, Rocco. Just a flesh wound!"

"I should stay with–"

"Don't worry about me," his brother interrupted. "We gotta get you outta here!"

Rudy jabbed the accelerator sharply and the Chevy lunged forward. The eight cylinders toiled, all barrels opened wide as the car hastened headlong toward Dudley Square. Rocco grasped the top edge of the rear seat and hauled himself up to have another look.

Sizing up the trailing police, Rocco saw that the cops were falling back. Their standard issue Ford was clearly no match for Rudy's modified Impala.

"You're losin' them!" he shouted in encouragement over the roar of the motor. "Find somewhere to pull over!"

"Get ready!"

As they rounded a slight bend in the roadway, their pursuers dropped from sight. Rocco exclaimed, "They can't see us! Pull over! Now!"

Rudy cut the wheel hard right, navigating toward the curb with the skill and dexterity of an Indy 500 competitor working the oval. The tires screeched in dissent over the sudden deceleration. Odors of burnt rubber and exhaust permeated the interior of the vehicle.

Rocco, hand at the ready on the handle, gave it a jerk and kicked the door aside with the flat of a boot-clad foot. As he leapt from the car, he shouted to his companions, "I'll catch up with you guys later!"

Neither man replied. The Impala's tires chirped, found traction, and Rudy and Slim were gone in an instant, hurtling along the slick, slumbering Roxbury streets.

Shivering as icy air met sweat-dampened clothing, Rocco broke into a sprint, taking care not to slip and fall on the residual snow coating the walkways. The cops would reach him in seconds. His senses on full alert, he darted in the direction of a towering hedgerow that encircled a nearby apartment building.

He was fortunate to stumble upon cover so quickly. Like many of the neighborhoods on the outskirts of Boston, tenement rows dominated the landscape and for the most part, there was little greenery. Coincidence, perhaps, but Rudy had dropped him off at one of the few locations that offered concealment.

Reaching the row of shrubbery, he wedged his thin frame through a narrow breach and crouched. Not a moment too soon. A split second later, the cops who'd been chasing the trio whipped around the corner and sped by.

How much time had passed since he, Rudy, and Slim bolted from the apartment? Was it five minutes? Ten? Either way, it was sufficient enough for the police to deploy reinforcements. Before long, these Roxbury streets would be crawling with cops, all hunting for him.

With utter dismay, Rocco considered what had just occurred. Until moments ago, he had been nothing more than a small-time crook who robbed jewelry stores and stole women's furs, among other minor criminal exploits. But now, following the assault on 107 Centre Street, he would be highly sought after by the authorities. And if a cop took a bullet during the melee, he and his cohorts would be only slightly less relevant than the city's current most wanted, the notorious Boston Strangler.

Rocco stood up and stretched his legs and lower back. He stomped his feet to dislodge some of the snow from his shoes; beneath the hedge, it was ankle deep.

All seemed quiet. The dragnet had yet to intensify. For all the cops knew, he was still in the car with his brother Rudy. They had no reason to search this neighborhood, at least not yet.

He needed to find suitable refuge, sheltered from the bitter cold, so he could rest and sort things out. Behind him was a three-story, red brick apartment building. Rocco made his way to the entrance and tried the door, frequently glancing over his shoulder for approaching patrol cars. Finding it unlocked, he stepped inside the foyer and was met with warmth from a small, hissing radiator.

Wending his way through narrow corridors, Rocco ascended a staircase two flights, stepping lightly. He happened upon an unlocked door that read **SUPERINTENDENT** and stepped inside.

There was a small filament bulb suspended from the ceiling. Rocco moved several brooms and mops aside, creating sufficient space to rest his weary bones. He sat heavily, his back flat against the wall and knees folded to his chest. He closed his eyes against deepening fatigue.

In the meantime, several blocks away, Rudy Balliro lost control of the speeding Impala and broadsided a taxicab near the intersection of Westland and Massachusetts Avenues. The cabbie was unhurt, but in the collision, both vehicles were damaged beyond repair.

Rudy and Slim fled on foot, with Boston police officers in close pursuit. Rudy, with the bullet wound to the back of his head still seeping blood, managed to elude the cops. Slim, however, was not as fortunate. He was apprehended trying to board a bus at the Dudley Square commuter depot.

At the precinct, the cops found that two stray bullets had pierced his outer coat, but Slim's only wound was a scraped face sustained during the collision with the taxicab.

Rocco, meanwhile, had already drifted off to sleep in his cramped hideout.

CHAPTER 30

"Nobody ever did, or ever will, escape the consequences of his choices." Alfred A. Montapert

Toby Wagner's ex-sister-in-law Beverly Zimmerman was returning home after a night out with friends when she first learned about the shootings.

Earlier, she'd gone out for cocktails at a newly-opened joint in Lynn, followed by drinks at their traditional Brighton haunt, the Lincoln Café.

After they had their fill, Beverly and company piled back in the car for the brief trip to her apartment on Delaware Place, which was located adjacent to the ornate St. Columbkille Parish church on Market Street.

Riding in the front seat, she heard a radio announcer break into the music program with a special report.

"Shhh," she said sharply, in an attempt to hush her chattering companions in the rear seat. "I want to hear this."

The car fell silent. She leaned across the seat and fumbled with the knob on the radio, adjusting the volume.

This report just in. There has been a double shooting in Roxbury. During an intense gun battle between the Boston Police and several unidentified assailants, Toby Wagner, 21, and her young son Mark were caught in the crossfire. Both victims have been transported to area hospitals suffering from gunshot wounds. Mother and child are reported to be in grave condition.

"Pull the car over," Beverly insisted.

"What is it? Why?"

"Please," she urged. The dashboard light revealed her pale face. "Please – just pull the car over. I think I'm gonna be sick."

Perplexed, her companions anxiously awaited an explanation. Beverly drew a deep breath as the sedan glided to a stop. She reached for the knob on the door, winding down the passenger window. Leaning out, she was met by a rush of welcome February air which also spilled into the stuffy car. The occupants in the back seat huddled against the chill but didn't complain.

Beverly exhaled with a sigh and slowly shook her head in disbelief.

"What's wrong?" asked one her friends.

"That was my sister-in-law and nephew he was talking about," she uttered, her stare now fixated on the green-tinged glow of the radio dial. "They've been shot."

Had he not been in such a dire situation, the task before Rocco Balliro would have seemed entirely absurd. Here he stood, in a darkened alleyway, wielding a stone roughly the size of a baseball, preparing to smash the window of his brother's sandwich shop.

It was nearing three in the morning. The dark of night was rapidly slipping away. In a matter of hours, dawn would break over Chelsea and his freedom of movement would be rendered impossible.

He'd slept fitfully for a little more than an hour, holed up in the darkened janitor's closet. Oddly enough, when he emerged from the Roxbury apartment building, there was no activity in the street beyond. There were no patrol cars in sight, no cops racing by on foot, no barking search dogs – nothing to indicate a monumental gunfight had taken place just blocks away. It was unnerving.

Rocco gathered his bearings and began to walk briskly toward Dudley Square. Idle buses and trains awaited Saturday morning passengers. Rocco looked for a cab.

Thankfully, he wasn't as far from the commuter terminal as he'd first thought. Rocco reached Dudley Station and a few minutes later, the warmth of a taxicab.

"Where to, pal?"

"Chelsea," Rocco uttered through numb lips. "Washington Avenue."

"What brings you out at this hour of night?"

Great, a chatty driver, Rocco thought. He would have preferred that the guy just shut up and turn on the radio instead. Maybe there'd be some news about the gun battle.

"Card game with a few buddies," he answered.

"Win anything?"

"Naw, not much."

"Too bad," the cabbie said. "Hey, alright if I put on the radio?"

"You read my mind," Rocco replied.

The driver spun the tuner dial, eventually coming to rest on a station featuring jazz. Rocco leaned back in the plush seat and tightly closed his eyes. Wending their way over the darkened streets of Boston, it wasn't long before a broadcaster interrupted the music program with breaking news.

"Hey, turn this up, will ya?"

"Boston police are currently seeking Rocco Balliro, believed to have been involved in a shootout in a Roxbury apartment that wounded a young woman and her child. Both have been taken to City Hospital for treatment. The suspect remains at large and is armed and dangerous."

Rocco's stomach churned and he tasted bile as it bubbled upward. He swallowed hard. Toby? Mark? Wounded? "Jesus Christ," he muttered under his breath.

Reaching over to crack the window for fresh air, he fought back another bout of nausea. Droplets of perspiration broke out on his forehead, despite the cold breeze.

"You okay, pal?" the driver asked. "You don't look so good."

"Yeah, I'm okay," Rocco lied. "Must've been something I ate."

"Uh huh."

"Mind if I the open window a little more?"

"Sure, buddy," said the cabbie. "G'head – I have the heater on."

"Thanks a lot," Rocco said. He lowered the glass several more inches.

"Shame," began the driver, shaking his head.

Rocco glanced at the man's reflection. "Yeah," he said.

"That young girl and her kid – getting hurt and all. Hope they're gonna be alright."

"Yeah," Rocco responded after a pause, averting his glance so the driver couldn't look him in the eye. "Yeah – me too."

"I hope they catch this Rocky guy they're talking about," the driver added.

Rocky? Rocco fought the urge to correct him.

A few tense seconds passed before the cabbie went back to spinning the radio dial. He said nothing further, leaving his passenger to his thoughts.

Toby and Mark hurt? What were their injuries? What condition were they in? What the hell were they doing in that apartment? What were those ignorant cops thinking, setting a trap for Rocco but failing to safeguard women and children?

The radio report, while brief, made no mention of police officers killed during the violent clash. *Small consolation*, he thought, but at least he wouldn't face murder charges, after all.

Or would he?

Clenching his fists until his knuckles whitened, Rocco pushed aside heightening anguish. It tugged at the very fabric of his being. What if Toby and Mark were ... what if they had been ... dear God, no!

At first, Rocco considered returning to his Chelsea apartment so he could regroup. He needed to contact his brothers. Maybe they had more news. Certainly, they could press their contacts for more information.

If nothing else, he could determine the fate of his brother Rudy. Did he manage to get away from the cops? Was the bullet wound to his head worse than originally suspected?

Rocco had to get to a phone.

Reaching Chelsea, he instructed the taxi driver to pull over along Washington Avenue, several blocks shy of Bruno's business. He paid the two dollar fare with a sawbuck.

"Hang on, let me get your change."

"Keep it."

"Geez, thanks pal," the wide-eyed driver said. "Take some milk of magnesia for that stomach, okay?"

Once the bright yellow car had slipped from view, Rocco made double-time to Bruno's sandwich shop. He circled to the rear of the building. Wielding a stone found near a pile of brush, he wasted no time shattering one of the rectangular window panes on the delivery door, reached through the breach, and twisted the deadbolt to gain entry.

Once inside, Rocco went straight for the telephone and dialed Rudy's apartment. It rang once.

"Hello? Paula?"

"Yes?"

"Paula, it's me – Rocco."

"Anthony," she said. "Where are you?"

"Chelsea, at Bruno's store."

"Are you alright?"

"Don't worry 'bout me," he insisted. "Have you heard from Rudy?"

"Yeah," replied his sister-in-law, who sounded as if she was about to burst out crying. "He called a few minutes ago."

Rocco tried to remain calm, for her sake. She was at least eight months pregnant with her first child. As he spoke, his voice remained even and measured. He grasped the enormity of the situation but tried to suppress the growing panic within.

"Is he ... um ... okay?"

"I think so," she answered. "He said he wasn't hurt in the accident."

"Accident?" Rocco asked, suddenly alarmed. Could this night unravel any further? "What accident?"

"He said he crashed the car."

"Jesus!" Rocco exclaimed. He was careful not to slip up and say anything about the bullet wound to his brother's head. It was apparent Rudy hadn't disclosed that bit of news to his wife, for obvious reasons.

"Do you know where he is?"

"I'm not sure," Paula said. "He mumbled something about your brother Joe taking him to a doctor just to get checked out. I think the name was–"

"Shapiro?"

"Yes," she said. "That's it."

"Okay, Paula," Rocco said. "I know where to find him."

"Anthony, what's going on?" she asked. "I'm really worried."

There was no question the tears had begun to flow now. He could hear the sobbing in her troubled voice. For the first of many times to come, Rocco felt a wave of guilt wash over him. It was his fault that his brother was hurt. And he would also be to blame if this special woman's husband was ultimately marched off to prison.

"Don't worry," he said, knowing the words were empty. "I'll call you later."

Rocco exchanged goodbyes, hung up the phone, and turned to make his way out of Bruno's shop. As treacherous as it was to do so, he was heading back to Roxbury.

CHAPTER 31

"When I was just a baby, my mama told me, son, always be a good boy, don't ever play with guns." – *"Folsom Prison Blues", Johnny Cash*

Gingerly, Dr. Leo Shapiro positioned a small, rectangular-shaped segment of cotton gauze on his patient's scalp and applied pressure to staunch the blood.

The man who, until that moment, had been sitting perfectly immobile on a dinette chair, instinctively flinched when the pad made contact with the bullet wound. Startled, Shapiro fumbled and dropped the sterile bandage to the floor.

"Dammit!" he exclaimed as he stepped back from his skittish patient.

"C'mon, Rudy," coaxed a calming voice from the shadows of the room. "Relax and let the doctor do his job."

"Sorry, Joe," Rudy said to his elder brother. Twisting his head to look behind him, he added, "Sorry, doc."

"Alright, I'm going to start again," warned Shapiro as grasped his patient's shoulder and guided him back into the chair. "Try to stay still."

Standing idle behind the pair, Rocco Anthony Balliro had remained mum for several moments, mindful of the doctor's need for concentration. He broke his silence and asked, "Anything I can do to help, doc?"

He noticed his brother Joe glancing at him from a sentry position. Across the room, Joe gave his younger sibling one of those *you've already done enough* looks. *A verbal scolding was preferable to that expression*, thought Rocco as he bowed his head, wracked with remorse.

"I'm all set," Shapiro said.

Thankfully, Joe had turned his attention back to keeping watch over the darkened streets of Roxbury. He was peering through a seam in the curtains.

Rocco had arrived at the Blue Hill Avenue office of Dr. Shapiro some twenty minutes earlier, after a brief crosstown taxi trip from Chelsea. Rudy filled him in on the fate of their associate, as well as that of the Impala.

"I think I hit a patch of ice," he recalled, slamming the fist of one hand into the palm of the other to illustrate the collision. "I couldn't stop it – we were going too fast."

"Car wrecked?"

"Total wreck," Rudy responded. "We hit him pretty good. I'm surprised me and Slim walked away from it – well, I mean, ran away from it."

Rocco thought about Clifford's crash earlier that evening, the one that triggered this irreversible chain of events. It seemed like days, not hours. "What happened to Slim?" he asked.

"I heard the cops picked him up over at Dudley Station."

"Shit!" Rocco hissed. More guilt. Thanks to his actions, Slim might now have to watch his two kids grow up through a glass panel in the MCI-Walpole visiting room.

"I don't know what he was thinking," Rudy said, shaking his head while he still could. "He should've gone with me."

"Okay," Dr. Shapiro interrupted. "I'm ready to start again."

Rudy tilted his head forward and tucked his chin into his chest. Shapiro adjusted a light, concentrating the beam on the hole in Rudy's skull. The location of the slug was readily apparent. A small, clearly-defined lump, roughly the size and shape of a marble, protruded midway between the nape of Rudy's neck and the top of his head. It was lodged just beneath the surface of the skin. Shapiro, who was known in organized crime circles as tight-lipped and loyal, had already cut away some of the hair that obscured the wound.

"Rudy, I'm going to give you a numbing agent."

"Sure, doc, go ahead."

Shapiro picked up a syringe, displaced the air, and leaned in to inject the anesthesia. This time, Rudy remained still as the needle found its mark. Shapiro, a slight, balding sixty-year old, stepped back to allow it to take effect.

"I'll say it again," said the doctor as he readied a pair of forceps. "You are one lucky bastard."

"Yeah, sure – preserve me long enough for the executioner to finish the job later," Rudy said.

Rocco shuddered. The comment, while sarcastic, truly hit home. Just hours before, he and his brother had shot it out with the Boston police. *A gun battle with cops, for Crissake,* he thought with incredulity. While still starkly fresh in his mind, it was difficult to grasp. He wasn't ignorant to the fact that they were in serious trouble. Nor was it lost on his brother Joe, who continued to watch the street for police activity.

Rocco observed as Dr. Shapiro inserted the tip of the forceps into the wound and began to dig for the slug. A small bead of blood formed and ran down the back of Rudy's neck. Shapiro dabbed it dry with gauze.

Feeling suddenly queasy, Rocco sought to occupy himself elsewhere when Joe called out to him.

"C'mere for a second," the elder Balliro beckoned, summoning his sibling by wagging a curled index finger. Without hesitation, Rocco complied and shuffled across the room. Joe, nine years his senior, grasped his shoulders and leaned in to kiss him on both cheeks, one after the other, in a time-worn Italian greeting. Joe, tall, slim, and good-looking, stepped back and for a moment, didn't say a word. He didn't need to; the expression on his face said it all. An admonishment was inevitable. Rocco took the initiative and stepped in front of the onrushing freight train.

"I'm sorry," Rocco began, averting direct eye contact.

"What were you thinking?" Joe asked, lowering his tone so that Rudy couldn't overhear the exchange. "A fuckin' shootout? With cops?"

"It was … was … um … because of Toby."

"Yeah, I figured it had something to do with a broad."

"I thought she was in trouble."

"Yeah," replied Joe, shaking his head in disgust. "And now you're in deep shit and she's in the hospital. Along with her little boy–"

"But–"

Rocco paused, unsure how to finish his response. He glanced toward the floor, seeking an answer.

" –all thanks to you."

He had no idea how badly Toby and Mark were hurt. What happened in that apartment after he left? He recalled, as he and his associates hastily retreated to the waiting Chevy, hearing an additional burst of gunfire coming from inside.

For a terrifying moment, Rocco considered the worst. Had Toby and little Mark been inadvertently shot by the cops, who were staked out in the darkness?

What the hell were Toby and Mark doing in that apartment in the first place? When he first decided to go there, he thought she was being held by Barney and his buddy Clifford. But the fact that it was the Boston police in that apartment, and not Wagner, changed everything. If the cops were inclined to set a trap to ensnare their prey – escaped convict Rocco Balliro – what would possess them to leave innocent women and children in harm's way?

Did those simpletons *really* stake out the Adams' apartment with his girlfriend Toby, her sister-in-law Mary Adams, and their combined five children still inside? *Those fuckin' cops*, he thought, seething with rage.

Not that he would ever give the likes of Clifford a scintilla of credit for anything but even that moron would've had brains enough to clear the house, at least the children anyway, prior to staging an ambush. The cops, on the other hand …

Rocco shook his head.

"What is it?" Joe asked.

"Nothing," he answered. "I was just thinking about–"

"Oh, so now you're thinking?"

Rocco ignored the sarcasm. He was fixated on Toby and little Mark. If something had gone terribly wrong in the hallways or rooms of that pitch black apartment, certainly the cops would share the blame for not ushering the occupants to a safe place.

Joe shattered his train of thought.

"Now you're looking at hard prison time," the Balliro family boss lashed, cutting to the chase. "Did you really want them to drag your ass back to Walpole?"

"I know," Rocco said, lowering his gaze. "I know I fucked up."

"You fucked up alright," chastised the elder Balliro. "But did you have to drag your brother into it?

Both men looked over at Rudy, who remained still as Shapiro buttoned up the bullet wound.

Joe Balliro turned his attention to the drapes again, separating them further to gain a wider view of Blue Hill Avenue. Rocco waited for the reprimand to resume. It made him feel guilty to think such thoughts but he suddenly felt hunger pangs. A hundred years had passed, it seemed, since he sat down to breakfast with Toby on Friday morning. It was now nearing Saturday morning and the only thing he'd put in his stomach was a beer and a bite of an apple.

"What're you gonna do now?"

"I dunno," Rocco answered. "I'm working on that."

"You should go with your brother," Joe advised.

"With Rudy? To Jersey?"

"Yeah."

Rocco nodded unconvincingly. That was out of the question. The Balliro family had people in New Jersey, friends who would provide refuge until the heat was off. These folks would house and feed them. But there was no way he was leaving Boston, not as long as Toby was in the hospital. He wasn't about to walk away, at least not without her – and the children – at his side.

During the twenty-minute cab ride from Chelsea to Dr. Shapiro's office, Rocco hatched a plan to visit with Toby and perhaps, if she was well enough to travel, whisk her away from the hospital. Together, they would then locate Mark and soon after, take flight. San Francisco would be a perfect place for his girlfriend to recuperate.

His scheme was simple. While in Bruno's sandwich shop, Rocco had spotted several freshly-cleaned white uniforms hanging in the storeroom. Bruno would wear the white pants and matching shirts while in the kitchen. He kept extras on hand.

Rocco plotted to grab a set of the whites, which closely resembled uniforms worn by hospital orderlies, and in this simple disguise, sneak into Boston City Hospital as a staff member. He would slip in, right under the noses of the doctors and nurses, and slip out with his girlfriend and her son.

His brother Joe abruptly yanked the curtains closed and cursed.

"What is it?" Rocco asked.

"Cops."

"Did they stop?"

"No, just driving by," Joe replied, "but slowly."

He risked another look outside, spreading the drapes no more than an inch apart. Rocco noted that the first light of dawn was breaking.

"Hey doc," Joe hailed.

"Almost done," Shapiro responded, answering the question before it was asked. "A couple more sutures and he'll be good as new."

Rocco turned to walk away but Joe stopped him in his tracks.

"Hey."

"Yeah?"

"So you going?"

Rocco knew right well what Joe meant but feigned ignorance and asked anyway. "Going where?"

"Jersey, with your brother."

"Um – no," Rocco answered, tentatively. Honesty was the best policy in this instance. "I think I'm gonna stay 'round here for a coupla days."

"You're asking for trouble."

"I'll be okay."

"Alright," Joe said as he unfurled a roll of currency and forked over a wad of twenties. "But if you change your mind–"

"I'll call you."

Stuffing the bills in his pocket, he made his way to Rudy, who was now standing upright and looked much better. Like Dr. Shapiro had declared, he was good as new.

"Hey, little brother."

"Hey, big brother," was Rocco's response. He forced a grin.

"Long night, huh?"

"I'll say."

"I heard you talking with Joe."

"You always had big ears."

"Uh huh," Rudy said, adjusting his shirt collar. "So you ain't going to Jersey with me?"

"Not right away."

"Later?"

"Yeah, maybe."

Rudy paused, looked him square in the eye, and said, "You're going to see Toby at the hospital, aren't you?"

Rocco looked over his shoulder at Joe, who continued to keep watch over Blue Hill Avenue.

"Don't let Joe hear you," he said. "He'd kill me if he knew."

"You know the cops are gonna be watching that place," Rudy warned.

Rocco nodded and thought again about his plan. He had even considered arriving at the hospital near seven o'clock in the morning so he could safely blend in with the staff arriving for the day shift. He figured the place would be so busy with comings and goings, nobody would notice an extra orderly.

"I have a plan," he appealed.

"You had a plan earlier tonight," Rudy blurted sarcastically.

His brother's comment was mixed with equal parts acid and bitterness. Another wave of guilt slammed into him like a five pound hammer. He shifted his gaze, unable to look his brother in the eye. He couldn't quite find the words to apologize, once again, for dragging his twin into this sordid mess. Thankfully, Rudy rescued him. Like all siblings, they had their beefs but couldn't stay angry for long.

"Sorry, Rocco," he said. "I didn't mean it."

"I deserve it."

"Hey, you thought Toby was in trouble," Rudy reminded him. "I would have done the same thing."

"Yeah, I know, but–"

"And who knew the cops would be there?" his brother added.

Rocco nodded. He knew his brother was consoling him as best he could. Under the dire circumstances, it was welcome.

"Yeah, I guess you're right."

"You thought it was those maggots Clifford and Wagner who was waiting for us, remember?"

"Uh huh."

His brother was right. None of them would have run into that dwelling with guns drawn if they knew cops were waiting in ambush. That would have been downright crazy.

"Hey, look at the bright side," Rudy said, as he pulled on his jacket and zipped it.

"Yeah?"

"At least nobody got killed."

The emergency ward at City Hospital was remarkably quiet for a Friday night. Typically, the gritty streets of Boston produced a wide array of walking wounded, along with those souls rushed through the doors on ambulance gurneys, writhing in pain from gunshot wounds, stabbings, motor vehicle accidents, as well as non-trauma-related medical issues such as chest pain and difficulty breathing. There was seldom a lack of some daunting acute crisis to challenge the highly-skilled staff of this top-notch hospital which was located on Albany Street in Boston's South End.

But as Friday became Saturday, and the first day of February became the second, the corps of bored doctors, nurses, and support personnel manning the graveyard shift, wiled away the long hours swapping ER war stories of lives saved and lives lost.

They were abruptly swept from sedentary lounging into heart-pounding activity near one-thirty in the morning when the wide ambulance bay doors suddenly swung apart and a bevy of shouting police officers surrounding a wheeled stretcher burst into the department. A rush of cold air trailed them through the opening as nurses and doctors sprang from chairs and raced to render aid.

"In here!" frantically shouted the ER chief physician, pointing at the trauma room. "Bring the victim in here! Hurry!"

A trio of cops complied, following his orders and maneuvered the gurney into a cramped, brightly lit room as additional staff rapidly gathered.

"What happened to her?" the doctor questioned as he tugged on a pair of sterile surgical gloves and began a rapid examination. His white lab coat was soon stained red with blood.

"Gunshot," answered one of the officers gruffly. "To the head."

Their job done, the grim-faced policemen stepped out of the way, yielding the precious space as more medical staff streamed in to assist. Within seconds, all hands were participating in the frenzied, but highly choreographed, delivery of treatment to the young woman, who was unconscious and ashen.

Doctors rigorously barked orders, nurses jabbed intravenous lines into her arms and performed rescue breathing with a specially-fitted face mask.

The prolonged effort was valiant and exhausting but to no avail. There was simply no hope; the trauma was too severe. Like a conductor bringing an orchestra to a silent close, the chief physician stepped back from his patient, aborting the effort in defeat.

The weary staff retreated from the room, one by one. The last person to leave, a young nurse, perhaps a year or two older than the lifeless women on the gurney, shut off the lights and gently closed the door behind her.

Across town, in a similar antiseptic emergency room at Boston Children's Hospital, a little boy, not yet two years old, succumbed to a single gunshot wound to the abdomen, despite heroic efforts by a team of skilled surgeons to save his life.

The police officer who had rushed him to the hospital in a patrol car stood over the tiny shape shrouded beneath a sterile white bed sheet and failed to fight back tears.

CHAPTER 32

"I'm not against the police; I'm just afraid of them." –
Alfred Hitchcock

A persistent mid-winter cold spell finally lifted on the morning of February 2, 1963, granting a welcome respite for snow-weary New Englanders. It was Saturday and the streets of Chelsea were rife with weekend traffic, pedestrian and automobile alike, as folks patronized area businesses, restaurants, and cafés.

Customers who stopped by the little sandwich shop on Washington Avenue, however, found the shades drawn and a handwritten sign reading **closed** hanging in the window.

Inside, a haggard, solitary figure sat in a booth and silently mulled the glowing tip of a cigarette.

Rocco Anthony Balliro shook his head in denial. A single, salty tear ran down his beard-covered cheek. Until that moment in time, he didn't think it was possible to cry anymore.

Sick to his stomach, Rocco took a deep breath to fend off the nausea that had plagued him for hours. Still, as lousy as he felt, he was also famished. Nearly thirty-six hours had passed since he'd eaten breakfast with Toby in the kitchen of their Chelsea apartment.

"Dear God. Toby," he said. The stark realization hit home yet again. Yesterday morning, they were sharing a plate of buttered toast and today, she was…

But she can't be! She was only twenty-one, for God's sake! So young and radiant. They were running away together to San Francisco. They were getting married; after her divorce was finalized, of course. Maybe they'd have more kids. They'd talked about that possibility. The couple even laughed about the black hair their future offspring would likely possess. Dark like little Mark's scruff of hair. Now, there was nothing. No plans, no possibilities. No Toby.

And her adorable little boy? Not even two. His second birthday was still a month away. But now, March would come and go and there would be no birthday party. There would be no cake. No candles. No celebration of that special childhood milestone, turning two. Instead, Mark would be a year and eleven months forever, locked at that age for all time. All the wonders and joy of a long life were taken from him. Gone in an instant. Gone in a flash of gunfire.

Little Mark succumbed to a bullet wound to the abdomen, according to the static-filled radio broadcasts regularly emanating from a flimsy transistor radio in Bruno's backroom.

"Sweet Jesus, what have I done?" he said through clenched teeth.

Even though he didn't kill them with his own hands, Rocco concluded that his actions brought about their deaths. If only he hadn't gone to that Roxbury apartment, none of this would have happened. Toby and Mark would still be alive. Rocco would still be on the run for the escape from the New Bedford House of Corrections. But certainly not for a double murder. He should have stayed away, remained in Chelsea and waited for his girlfriend to return with news of her upcoming divorce from Barney Wagner. Even if it was bad news – even if she'd decided, after meeting with Barney, to go back with the poor excuse for a human being – that would've been far better than the alternative.

But there was no justification for what he had done. Nor could he bring them back. Rocco wiped another singular tear from his face with the backside of his hand. His beloved Toby – *his* family – gone in an instant.

In his bestselling book *A Death in Belmont*, author Sebastian Junger shared a unique perspective on the typical traits of a murderer. "The very pinnacle of the homicide pyramid – the very worst crime a person can commit, the only crime that regularly rates the death penalty – is murder in the first degree," Junger wrote. "Under most state statutes, murder in the first degree is defined as murder that is premeditated and deliberate. Like 'malice,' the term 'premeditated' means that the idea of killing entered the mind of the killer beforehand, and the term 'deliberate' means the killer went on to weigh its merits and ultimately decided it was a good thing to do. The murder was committed with 'cool purpose' rather than with 'hot blood'; it was a conscious, rational decision by someone who did not value human life."

Could Rocco Anthony Balliro be labeled a murderer – a cold-blooded killer – based on this expert opinion? Certainly, it wasn't in his character to plan a killing, especially that of a loved one. He was a thief, not a hit man. He stole furs, jewelry. Until he took his final breath, Rocco would insist that he went to that apartment to rescue his beloved Toby, not kill her. He had no reason to commit such a heinous crime.

Rocco stabbed out the smoldering cigarette in an ashtray. A new mental state gradually took hold, substituting the grief that racked him to the foundation.

Since he'd reached the restaurant an hour or so earlier, he'd found his emotions running the gamut. Sorrow was predominant as he mourned and struggled to come to grips with the deaths of Toby and Mark. But from sorrow, mixed with filtered shame, Rocco transcended to unbridled wrath. Slowly at first, then steadily, it climbed to a violent crescendo and began to consume him.

Enraged, he abruptly slammed his fist on the tabletop, nearly toppling the ashtray. He steadied it and climbed wearily to his feet.

Somewhere in the area – perhaps right under his nose here in Chelsea, that worthless thug, Freeman Clifford, roamed the streets under his namesake, a free man – while Rocco was sought by every cop in the city. If that parasite hadn't interfered with diplomacy, none of this would have occurred. Rocco and Barney Wagner surely would have been able to iron out their differences like grown men and come to an understanding over Toby. They were attempting to do just that when Clifford intervened with a knock on the window of the Oldsmobile.

He instigated and elevated the conflict, provoking Rocco to heightened levels of hostility. From shooting blindly at the trio after Clifford crashed his car into the frozen snow bank to the ill-conceived confrontation in the Roxbury apartment, Rocco was driven to unreasonable conduct by his newfound adversary.

The dispute was never meant to take place between Rocco and the Boston cops but rather, he and Clifford. Wagner played a role, sure, but he was little more than a puppet under the control of Clifford. In essence, some of the blame for the deaths of Toby and Mark, perhaps most of it, should fall squarely on the Irish enforcer. Rocco knew it wouldn't bring his girlfriend and her son back but he promised himself that he would somehow settle the score with Clifford.

Reaching the stockroom in the back of the restaurant, Rocco made his way to an industrial-sized refrigerator and pulled the lever to open it. He reached into the fridge and lifted the foil covering a ceramic bowl to inspect the contents, which turned out to be tuna fish.

During his incarcerations, Rocco regularly purchased and consumed canned goods from the prison canteen in order to avoid the loathsome, rancid prison food. It was often tainted with rat droppings and at times, human excrement introduced as an ingredient by disgruntled inmate cooks. While at Walpole and later, the New Bedford House of Corrections, he grew quite fond of tuna.

He found a loaf of bread on the countertop, scooped a generous helping of tuna on the surface of one slice, and slammed the other on top of it. Ravenous, Rocco wolfed down the sandwich in several bites, chasing it with a can of cola. A beer would have been better but there was none to be found.

Rocco pulled the chair from beneath his brother's desk and sat heavily. Leaning back, he rubbed bloodshot eyes. Grief stricken, he fought back another round of tears as he considered his bleak future.

What now? What to do next? His girlfriend and her son were dead. His brother Rudy, by now, had reached New Jersey and was in hiding. Every cop in the City of Boston, whether in a patrol car or walking a beat, was carrying a mugshot of Rocco Balliro. Embarrassed by their inability to bring the Boston Strangler to justice, the cops all wanted to be a hero and apprehend the fugitive who went berserk and shot it out with their brethren in that darkened Roxbury apartment. It wasn't a matter of *if* Rocco would be arrested for alleged misdeeds, but rather when. The odds were stacked against him.

Leading the manhunt, Police Commissioner Edmund L. McNamara enlisted Hans Reppenning in the effort. Reppenning, a detective with the West Berlin, Germany police, had traveled overseas with his specially trained dog to aid his counterparts in the hunt for the Boston Strangler. The dog was quickly pressed into service to search for one Rocco Anthony Balliro. The dragnet spanned the entire city and some of the suburbs beyond. No stone was left unturned.

Pushing aside a pile of invoices, menus, and other paperwork pertinent to his brother's business, Rocco reached for the telephone resting on the corner of the desk. Lifting the receiver off the cradle, he dialed a familiar number. The phone rang only once before it was picked up at the other end.

"Rocco?"

The eldest Balliro brother had obviously anticipated receiving the call.

"Hey, Joe."

"Where the hell are you?"

"The restaurant."

"Bruno's joint?" Joe asked. "In Chelsea?"

"Yeah."

Rocco debated telling Joe that he had to break a window to gain entry but reconsidered. It wasn't important.

"Bruno with you?"

Joe seemed remarkably calm and collected. And he didn't sound angry. At least not like he had earlier at Dr. Shapiro's office.

"No," Rocco answered with a sigh of fatigue. "I'm alone."

Joe went silent, as if he were weighing his next comment. Rocco knew what was coming next but paused long enough to determine if he and Joe were on a similar wavelength.

"Little brother, can I give you some advice?"

"No need."

"Oh yeah, why's that?" Joe asked.

"Cause, if you were gonna say I should turn myself in," Rocco ventured, pausing to clear his throat before continuing, "I've already decided."

"Uh huh."

"Can you pick me up?"

"Sure," Joe replied. "Where we going?"

"I need a ride," said Rocco, "to the police station."

CHAPTER 33

"I know there were many good policemen who died doing their duty. Some of the cops were even friends of ours. But a cop can go both ways." Martin Scorsese

Nearly one month prior to the shootings which occurred between Rocco Anthony Balliro and the Boston Police, twenty-three year old Patricia Bissette was found dead in a small apartment she shared in Boston's Back Bay.

Concerned for her well-being, Bissette's employer stopped by her place on the morning of Monday, December 31, 1962, to determine if everything was alright. She worked as a secretary for his Boston engineering firm and had failed to report that morning, which was uncharacteristic. According to a number of accounts, she was seldom late for work. When her boss arrived and rang the doorbell, then loudly knocked, there was no answer, so he walked away from the building.

As the day wore on, however, Bissette's boss grew increasingly anxious and impatient. Soon, he gave in to the apprehension and returned to her apartment for another attempt. This time, with assistance from the property superintendent, he finally gained access. Prying open a window, he warily made his way into her bedroom. He was joined by the superintendent.

At first glance, it looked as though she was simply sleeping. But when the two men peeled back the bed covers to reveal her pale, ashen corpse and the nylon stockings cinched tightly around her crushed neck, it became apparent that Bissette, who was later found to be pregnant during an autopsy, had earned her place in the annals of serial murder history as the eighth victim of the notorious Boston Strangler.

Obviously, there was no correlation between the deaths of Toby and Mark Wagner and the multiple brutalized victims of the Strangler, save for the early sixties timeframe and the Boston locale. But there was one aspect the killings held in common. The crimes were handled or rather, mishandled, by one of the most inept police forces of the era.

The Boston Police Department drew sharp criticism from across the nation for shoddy investigatory work and chronic inability to apprehend a suspect who, over a two-year span, sexually mutilated and murdered thirteen women, ranging in age from nineteen to eighty-five.

Ultimately, the Boston police had little to do with solving the serial murder case in 1964. The culprit, Albert DeSalvo, was in custody for an attempted rape in the distant suburb of Bridgewater, Massachusetts, and confessed to the carnage in the city. In 1973, he was found murdered in his cell while serving life at MCI-Walpole, and in 2014, newly discovered DNA evidence linked him to the sixties homicides – there had previously been doubt that DeSalvo was actually the killer.

In the midst of the floundering Strangler investigation in 1963, however, Boston law enforcement was vilified and plunged deeper into a swirling cauldron of scrutiny following the shootings in Roxbury. Following the deaths of Toby and Mark Wagner, mother and child, the Boston Police Department's credibility worsened. In the aftermath of the tragic events of February 2, 1963, tight-lipped police officials were unable to fend off prying reporters and before long, the department was under fire for the botched, overzealous stakeout.

The situation grew further inflamed as accounts trickled in from officials and media outlets.

WBZ-TV news photographer Nat Whittemore, for instance, was an eyewitness to the aftermath of the carnage.

"I was having a bite to eat at an all-night café with my crew," recalled the cameraman, who spent five decades recording Boston news. "We heard there was a shooting on

Centre Street. I got there as a police officer was carrying the little boy to a waiting patrol car."

The little boy, not-quite two-year-old Mark Wagner, was featured the next morning on the front page of newspapers nationwide clutched in the arms of Boston Patrolman Richard Milan. In the heart-wrenching, grisly photograph, Mark's face is contorted in a painful grimace and his shirt is soaked with blood.

"As they ran past me, I heard the boy say, over and over, 'me hurt, me hurt,'" Whittemore claimed. "It was a long time ago but that's something I'll never forget."

Toby Wagner, meanwhile, lay dying in a pool of blood seeping from a bullet wound to her head. According to the police report, she was "taken in the District 10 RL ambulette, Patrolmen Milan and Raffle assisting to the Boston City Hospital."

Accusations were leveled and department spokesmen scrambled to explain what would have prompted the unthinkable; a small contingent of renegade police officers setting a trap to snare an escaped convict but failing to clear the dwelling of two young women and five small children. It proved to be a deadly blunder.

California defense attorney Michael H. Metzger later commented, "There was incredible negligence on the part of the police with respect to their construction of a stratagem likely to produce bloodshed, not to mention the inexplicable fact that the dead civilians had been left at a place in the apartment which would be (and obviously was) extraordinarily dangerous."

Lawyers and high-ranking police officials alike questioned the thinking behind the ill-advised, unsanctioned sting devised to nab the escapee.

"We want to know why these three men (the policemen) were positioned where they say they were and why the outside stakeout apparently wasn't in a position to stop Rocco Balliro before he got into the house," said Boston Police Captain Joseph J. Cummings during a press conference.

Despite frequent visits to their homes and places of businesses by officials, which bordered on harassment, the tight-knit Balliro family refused to cooperate with investigators. Informants were scarce, at least those who were willing to share what they knew. And the fugitive himself followed strict orders and remained under wraps in his Chelsea hideout, save for a brief trip to the Puritan Meat Market in the North End.

Certainly, Rocco Balliro was a trophy worthy of an ambitious police operation. He'd been on the lam for several weeks after a brazen escape from the New Bedford House of Corrections, but until the fateful February night, frustrated authorities had failed to turn up any clues to his whereabouts which could have led to a peaceful arrest.

It was Rocco who eventually surrendered and became a sacrificial lamb, affording the Boston Police Department an opportunity to save face.

CHAPTER 34

"The most anxious man in a prison is the governor." –
George Bernard Shaw

Consumed with vivid, horrific nightmares, one after another, Rocco Anthony Balliro awoke with a start, jolted from fitful sleep. Disoriented, he was unsure of exactly where he was for a few fuzzy seconds. He sat bolt upright, nearly striking his head on the metal supports framing the top bunk above. He painfully wrenched his neck while trying to ward off a skull-to-steel impact.

"Jesus," he groaned, while rubbing the strained muscles near the base of his neck. He found his t-shirt was soaked with sweat and plastered to his skin.

Swinging around to the edge of the cot and dropping his bare feet to the drafty, concrete floor, the cobwebs of sleep began to dissipate.

Unsteady, he rose from his bed and shuffled across the width of the cell, reaching the wall-mounted aluminum sink. Running the faucet at a trickle, Rocco cupped his hands, and gathered cold water. He took a sip and then splashed the remainder on his scruffy face. He hadn't shaved in weeks, which wasn't typical. But the beard had been part of his disguise since the escape. He supposed he could shave it off now.

Retreating to his rack, he sat on the edge of the thin mattress. Dismayed, Rocco shook his head.

It was tough to grasp, even for someone who'd been in and out of assorted jails and prisons for a number of years that he could be back in a cell so soon. A mere three weeks separated Rocco from his unscheduled departure from the

New Bedford House of Corrections and his arrival at his new digs: the Charles Street Jail in Boston.

Actually, there was nothing at all *new* about Charles Street.

Better known to native Bostonians and many of its reluctant guests as the Suffolk County Jail, this prison facility first opened for business in 1851 after a three-year construction project. Assembled from huge, chiseled granite blocks cut from the nearby Quincy quarries, the front of the building faced northwest, overlooking the banks of the flatwater Charles River, which separated Boston from neighboring Cambridge. Flanking it to the rear was the world-renowned Massachusetts General Hospital, which later expanded tenfold to nearly surround the imposing prison structure.

During the jail's heyday, a number of the eight by ten-foot cells were occupied by illustrious accused wrongdoers such as Ferdinando Sacco and Bartolomeo Vanzetti, the duo convicted of murder and later executed following a trial that had been characterized as prejudicial and inadequately defended.

Also confined was former Boston mayor James Curley, equal rights activist Malcolm X, and the entire crew of German submarine U234, which surrendered to US Navy warships off the Grand Banks near the end of World War II.

In 1973, inmates fed up with increasing squalor and overcrowding filed a lawsuit claiming that conditions in the festering facility infringed on their basic human rights. The United States District Court agreed. Immediate closure was ordered but because of limited alternative housing elsewhere within the Massachusetts Correctional system, the Charles Street Jail persisted for an additional seventeen years.

Massachusetts General Hospital later acquired the property and in 2007, following a multi-million dollar renovation, the decrepit building emerged as The Liberty Hotel, one of Boston's most luxurious accommodations.

It was a far cry from the quarters of nearly five decades before, when jailed criminals would compete with insects, pigeons, and rats for living space and dined on inedible entrees of fried bologna and mashed potatoes.

Rocco strode to a shelving unit and retrieved a neatly-folded, fresh t-shirt from a stack of clothing. Peeling off the sweat-soaked shirt, he tossed it in the corner and pulled the replacement over his head, careful not to jar his aching neck.

He wasn't sure of the exact time but sensed it was three, perhaps four in the morning. In a couple of hours, dawn would break over the City of Boston, the jail would come to life, and Rocco Anthony Balliro would begin his sentence in earnest.

Feeling a little better in a dry t-shirt, he stretched out his lanky six foot frame. Perhaps he could grab an hour's snooze before the prison woke up. As he closed his eyes and faded into restless sleep, Rocco's thoughts turned to the whirlwind of events that had taken place over the previous twenty-four hours.

After placing the call to his brother Joe from Bruno's Chelsea diner, he leaned back in the office chair and propped his feet on the corner of the desk, careful not to damage anything. When he later opened for business, Bruno already faced repair of a broken window. Rocco didn't want to add any more headaches for the youngest of his five brothers.

As much as he would've like to, there wasn't time to squeeze in a nap. It was a brief drive from the North End to Chelsea and Joe was a stickler for timeliness. If the man said fifteen minutes, then it would be fifteen. Rocco slid into his jacket and stepped into the alley through the delivery door.

Rocco circled the building and reached the street just as his brother Joe arrived. He wasn't alone. Seated in the passenger seat, dressed in a neatly-pressed, expensive suit was another Joe: cousin and family attorney, Joseph Balliro.

Rocco opened the rear door of the dark sedan and climbed in. Sitting in the back seat, behind his brother, was attorney Neil Colicchio. He nodded at Rocco, who returned the wordless gesture. The interior of the car smelled of cigarettes which triggered a craving. Cracking the window, he lit up and took a deep, fulfilling draw. Rocco offered one to his rear seat companion who shook his head.

Cousin Joe was the first to break the silence.

"How're you doing, Anthony?" asked the good-looking attorney riding shotgun. Joe adjusted the rearview mirror, angling it so he could see his cousin without turning around.

Rocco replied, "I've had better days."

"I'm sure."

"So whadda you think?"

"I think you're making the right decision," his newly-retained lawyer answered, nodding slowly, as if to convince himself.

In his peripheral vision, Rocco saw Colicchio tipping his head in silent agreement, like a puppet.

"Yeah, I guess so," he murmured. He took another drag on his smoke, realizing it could be the last for some time.

While he accepted the mutual advice to turn himself in and put his fate in the hands of the court system, Rocco had his doubts. He wasn't confident he'd get a fair shake in the defendant's chair. He was, after all, an ex-convict and a prison escapee. He had ties with organized crime, which would surely be made known to a jury by a prosecutor. Why not pile on a murder charge or two? He was the ideal fall guy for the cops and the district attorney.

Emotions ran hot in Boston. At an alarming rate, vulnerable women were being raped and slaughtered across the city and yet the incapable police had failed to come up with a suspect. And now a twenty-one-year-old woman and her toddler son lie dead in the city morgue. Someone, anyone, had to be held accountable for their killings. Rocco Balliro and his associates had guns. They entered that apartment and fired those guns. Two people died. End of story. Throw away the key, Your Honor.

Of course, few would believe, or care, that Rocco was deeply in love with Toby Wagner and would never harm a hair on her head. The authorities weren't going to listen to his explanation. Rescue mission? Held against her will by her own husband? "Nonsense," they would likely say. "Nothing but the foolish rants of a desperate, hopeless man."

The media certainly didn't help. A number of area newspaper reporters had already tried and convicted the accused in a series of malicious articles. All that remained, based on their accounts, was for someone to throw the switch and rid the world of one Rocco Anthony Balliro. A trial? Mitigating circumstances? Police misconduct? It was more like a witch hunt.

There were supporters, however, who raised the specter of doubt and gave Rocco a glimmer of hope when all seemed lost.

For instance, *Globe* reporter Frank Mahoney wrote, "How were three gunmen able to burst into the middle of a stakeout, kill two persons and walk out the way they entered?"

Rocco knew the answer to that pointed question, of course. They *weren't* able. In his firsthand account, the two Balliro brothers, along with sidekick Slim Ciocco, never advanced into the apartment. They engaged the unseen adversaries – cops, not Wagner and his pals – from just inside the front door. They hunkered down in the foyer and fired their weapons. And then they left, at a dead run. Thirty seconds inside, thirty-five at best.

And there was something else nagging at him again; something peculiar that took place as he and his companions fled the scene after the shootout. Precariously sprinting along the treacherous, icy sidewalk, hotly pursued by a pair of men who'd leapt from a nearby parked car, Rocco heard another burst of gunfire coming from inside the apartment. It was unmistakable. The men remaining inside were shooting again. But at whom? Why were they firing their weapons? Did they think the intruders, Rocco and his gang, were still inside?

He again thought about his chances in a murder trial. Surely there was evidence, contrary to the damning hearsay in the newspapers, which could exonerate him. If not complete acquittal, perhaps he'd earn a reduced sentence. His cousin Joe seemed hopeful. If not, why suggest that Rocco turn himself in? Why advise that he stand trial for a crime he did not commit? Why send him to the gallows?

But it was far too late to change his mind about surrender. It would embarrass his brother Joe if he ditched at this stage. An agreement had already been made with Garrett Byrne, the Suffolk County District Attorney.

The elder Balliro broke the silence in the car. "Hey, Rocco?"

"Yeah, Joe?"

"I contacted Rudy and told him you were turning yourself in."

"And?"

"He's coming back from Jersey," Joe said, "to do the same."

"Uh huh."

Without further comment, Joe Balliro revved the motor, threw the gear shift, and eased his car into the Washington Avenue travel lane. It was three in the afternoon and traffic was light. Resigned, Rocco slumped back in the seat and closed his eyes. The muscles in his neck were knotted and a dull throbbing ache had found its way into his head. Again, he wondered if turning himself in was the right decision. Not that it mattered. There was no turning back.

Before long, the Balliro trio and Colicchio reached their destination on a remote segment of Main Street in nearby Everett. Rocco was last to emerge from the car. He took a final drag on his cigarette and flicked the smoldering filter. He waited for his brother and the two lawyers to greet Boston

Deputy Superintendent Edward W. Mannix and Detective John Doyle, who were encircled by a small contingent of uniformed police officers. To a man, they were taut with unease. It showed in their faces. But there was no need for concern. Their soon-to-be detainee wasn't going anywhere.

After a prison escape, police shootout, and high-speed car chases, his arrest was anticlimactic. A submissive Rocco Anthony Balliro was handcuffed by one Everett cop, frisked for weapons by another, and hastily ushered to a waiting patrol car.

CHAPTER 35

"If you tell the truth you don't have to remember anything." – Mark Twain

Rocco Balliro's gaze was trained on the Mystic River Bridge as his police motorcade crossed it. Beacons atop the vehicles flashed blue against the fading light, eerily reflecting off the steel bridge supports.

To his left, Rocco looked down upon the North End, which sloped from the fringe of historic Charlestown to the waters of Boston Harbor. Steam from cooking stoves rose from many of the rooftops before disappearing into the dusky winter sky.

He wondered if his dear mother Angela was preparing a meal for his dad. In his mind's eye, Rocco could smell the aroma of cooked pasta and gravy; he could taste the savory, garlic-laced meatballs. He and his brothers never left the table hungry.

While Angela Balliro was the best cook in all the North End in Rocco's estimation, Mother Anna's on Hanover Street ran a very close second.

Month's earlier, he and Toby had ventured into the North End to take part in the Feast of St. Anthony. After indulging in a sumptuous meal at Anna's, the young lovers joined scores of jubilant well-wishers in pinning dollar bills to a likeness of St. Anthony of Padua as it was paraded through the streets. Later, after dark, they sipped coffee at the popular Café Pompeii followed by a moonlit stroll along streets jammed with revelers.

The warm memories triggered more heartache. Two days had passed since he learned of the deaths of Toby and Mark.

Near constant badgering since his arrest in Everett certainly didn't ease his fragile state of mind.

"Where are you taking me?" Rocco asked as two men guided him, handcuffed and with leg irons binding his ankles, along a corridor in the Everett police station.

Seconds later, he was deposited on a cold, metal chair in a windowless interrogation room. Leaning forward, elbows on the table in front of him, he rested his weary head on clasped hands. He felt grimy and was in desperate need of a shower.

"So Mr. Balliro, after you're booked for murder–"

Rocco jerked his head around and cast a menacing scowl. As he did, the chains encapsulating his wrists jangled. The cop, standing behind him with arms folded across his chest, flinched slightly.

"Murder?"

"You're responsible for the deaths of Toby Wagner and her son," the lead detective accused. He was monotone, as if reading from a script.

Murder? Rocco recoiled at the mere suggestion that anyone, even the misguided cops who arrested him, would consider he was capable of killing the woman he loved. And her son? It sickened him.

"Got a cigarette?"

"No, I don't smoke."

"Figures."

"So what do have to say for yourself?"

"'Bout what?"

"The charges against you?"

"I didn't kill no one."

"'Scuse me?"

"I didn't kill them," Rocco said. Instead of leaning forward, he slid back in the chair and slouched with his feet crossed at the ankle. Toby again crept into his thoughts. He missed her terribly.

"Okay, Mr. Balliro, if it wasn't you, who did it?"

Rocco nearly said what was on his mind. *The cops did it, you sarcastic little maggot. The Boston cops shot them. Your brothers in blue.* But he resisted the urge, biting his tongue. He knew it didn't matter what he said to this stiff. Obviously, he was just seeking his moment in the limelight, his fifteen minutes of fame. He would later brag to a throng of reporters that he was first to interrogate notorious killer and prison escapee Rocco Anthony Balliro.

The detective was getting on his nerves and Rocco was on the verge of blurting out something derogatory when the door to the interrogation room swung open and a pair of uniforms rumbled in. As much as he didn't want to admit it, their arrival likely saved Rocco a bloody lip, or worse.

"On your feet, Balliro," one of the cops gruffly ordered. "Time to go for a little ride."

Rocco complied. Resisting made no sense. He'd just get popped on the head for his troubles.

"Where you taking him?" asked the young detective.

The cop gave his plainclothes associate a disdainful look as if he couldn't be bothered and mumbled, "We're handing him over to the Boston people."

Before long, Rocco and his chaperones were navigating across the Mystic River Bridge and heading to the Roxbury Crossing police station.

"Officer?"

The cop driving the vehicle looked in the rear view mirror. Their passenger hadn't uttered a word since leaving Everett. "Yeah, what is it?"

"I want to see her."

"See who?"

"Toby."

"You're kidding, right?"

"She was my love," Rocco professed. "I just want to see her one last time before they bury her."

"You're nuts," said the cop in disgust as he punched the accelerator.

The Boston police, not surprisingly, proved to be far more proficient interrogators than their Everett counterparts. Booked for suspicion of murder, Rocco Balliro was fed a light meal and then ushered into an interview room for what proved to be an exacting, punishing round of questioning.

Unbeknownst to the weary suspect, as he sat alone awaiting the inquest, there was a pair of visitors scrutinizing him from a vestibule behind a one-way mirror.

"Here, take this," said a burly cop to one of the two men, whose face was red with rage.

Herman Zimmerman looked at the offering, a shiny, black baton, and asked, "What the hell would I do with that?"

The barbaric cop grinned maliciously and tipped his head toward the glass panel separating them from the subject and said, "I'll turn my back and look the other way while you, um, take care of business."

Zimmerman exhibited his displeasure over the suggestion. "No, I'm not going to do that," he scowled.

"I'll do it!"

A distraught Herman Zimmerman turned and glanced at his outspoken companion; twenty-four-year-old son Malcolm, who was far too eager to pay retribution to his sister Toby's alleged killer.

"C'mon," said the elder Zimmerman, shaking his head. "Let's get outta here. I've seen enough."

As Toby's family members departed, three detectives subsequently joined Rocco Balliro, who was handcuffed to a steel table in the interview room. Only one, a middle-aged man with a Marine-style crew cut and deep-set eyes, did the questioning. The other two silently stood by, stone-faced, like a pair of thugs for hire.

"Tell us, Mr. Balliro," the ringleader began, without introducing himself. "What took place at 107 Centre Street, Roxbury last Friday night?"

Rocco mulled his response. There was absolutely no denying he and his co-defendants, Rudy and Slim, laid siege to that apartment. They burst through the door, weapons drawn. They fired those weapons. But engage the police in a gun battle? It was crazy to think he'd do something so absurd intentionally. Even these seasoned cops had to believe that anyone in his right mind would never wage such a battle. Virtually sightless in the depths of darkness, they had no way of knowing they were exchanging gunfire with a trio of cops. Had he known there were police officers lying in wait, Rocco wouldn't have ventured within a hundred miles of that apartment.

"I thought my girlfriend Toby was in trouble."

"Trouble?"

"Yeah," answered Rocco with a nod.

"What kind of trouble?"

"I thought she was being held against her will by her husband."

"Why would he do that?"

"I spoke with him earlier–"

"You mean you shot at him," the detective interjected.

"I spoke with him," repeated Rocco, showing restraint. "And he was unhappy over his wife leaving him for me."

"Really?" The detective glanced at his cohorts with raised eyebrows and sarcastically ridiculed their detainee. "The man, he says, was *unhappy* about his wife leaving?"

The duo chuckled in response. Rocco instantly grew incensed. His face turned crimson with fury but somehow, he kept his internal composure and restrained himself. Verbally lashing out was ill-advised. Instead, he yielded to his emotions.

"I loved her," he said, clearing his dry, parched throat. He could use a drink, a glass of water would do, but didn't ask. He doubted the cops would accommodate him, regardless.

"Is that so?"

"Yeah, and she returned my love."

"Oh yeah?"

"Yeah."

"I guess we can't argue with that."

"What's that supposed to mean?" Rocco asked, hesitantly.

"I understand she also paid you a visit or two while you were in jail in New Bedford." his interrogator leveled.

Rocco immediately clammed up and looked down at the floor. He shifted in the uncomfortable chair. As he did the length of chain attaching the handcuffs jingled, like a pocketful of loose change. Over his dead body would he ever allow this cop, or anyone for that matter, to lure him into revealing Toby's involvement in his New Bedford escape. They might be able to siphon other information from him over time but there was no way Rocco would allow Toby's good name to be tarnished.

The detective, realizing that he wouldn't get very far with this line of questioning, changed his tact.

"So, Mr. Balliro," he charged, raising his voice for added effect, "a shootout with the police? Forty bullets were found in that apartment."

Rocco didn't hesitate, stating, "It was too dark to see. We thought we was shooting it out with Wagner and his pals."

"The report I have here," said the detective, frowning as he rifled through a folder stuffed with documents, "states the officers identified themselves as such."

"Yeah, maybe," he replied with a shrug.

"And yet you opened fire?"

Leaning forward in the chair, Rocco Balliro glared fiercely at his interrogator and shrewdly implied, "In the dark, anyone can *say* they're cops."

It was then that the detective breathed a loud sigh of frustration. He pulled out a chair and sat, facing his subject. It was going to be a long day.

CHAPTER 36

"They're not supposed to show prison films in prison.
Especially ones that are about escaping." — Steve
Buscemi

Elmer "Trigger" Burke, who was handy with a machine gun
and made his living in the forties and fifties as a hit man for
hire, was locked up in the Charles Street Jail in 1954, charged
with the attempted murder of Joseph O'Keefe.

O'Keefe, according to lore, was one of the masterminds
behind the infamous 1950 Brinks robbery which yielded
nearly three million in cash and checks and took place at the
former Brinks building located on the corner of Prince and
Commercial Streets in the North End of Boston.

A number of organized crime figures who played a role
in the robbery feared O'Keefe would eventually fold under
pressure and flap his gums to authorities. He was the type,
they believed, who would quickly capitulate under the threat
of jail time. That left only one option.

Burke made the trip from New York to Boston where, for
a fee of one thousand dollars, agreed to rubout the rat-to-be
O'Keefe with a quick burst of machine gun fire.

Tracking down O'Keefe in Dorchester, Burke blasted
away at his mark after a lengthy foot chase. But O'Keefe
survived to tell the tale and Burke was soon captured,
tried, and ferried off to Charles Street. He wasn't there for
long, however. On August 28, 1954, a pair of gun-wielding
intruders, dressed in prison guard's uniforms, infiltrated the
jail and led Burke to freedom.

Recaptured a year later, Burke was tried and convicted for
an earlier killing in New York and in 1958, fried in the Sing

Sing prison electric chair affectionately known by inmates as "Old Sparky."

Burke wasn't the first to escape the Charles Street facility. According to a 1906 *New York Times* article, con artist George H. Gaskill was the benefactor of a wayward prison guard. Not only did the eager officer leave Gaskill's cell door unlocked, he also arranged for a storeroom to remain unsecured, affording the inmate access to items needed to hasten his departure.

"It is thought that the prisoner went from his cell on the fourth floor to the storeroom, where he obtained a ladder and pulley tackles," read the *Times* story. "With the latter he lowered himself and the ladder from the unbarred window of the storeroom to the ground, raised the ladder to the prison wall and scaled it. After gaining his freedom on the Fruit Street side of the wall he removed his prison clothes and threw them back in the yard."

Fifty-seven years later, Rocco Anthony Balliro followed in the proverbial footsteps of Mr. Gaskill, taking his leave from the Charles Street Jail in much the same manner, just months after arriving for a pre-trial stay.

Even the great Harry Houdini would have to applaud the relative ease with which Rocco devised and carried out a pair of newsworthy escapes from a pair of Massachusetts prison facilities in 1963. Although unlike Houdini, who incorporated sleight of hand and visual illusion to thrill audiences with his dramatic escapes, Rocco would gain unauthorized furloughs simply by wielding a smuggled hacksaw blade or two.

Considering their detainee's penchant for breaking out of jail, one would have expected the authorities to remain more vigilant. Rocco's midnight defection from the New Bedford House of Corrections, staged five months before, was still fresh in the minds of a number of red-faced sentinels. Even more embarrassing for the Charles Street officials, Rocco Balliro gave them the slip via his trademark method: sawing through iron bars.

The brazen escape also gave rise to a local urban legend. In June 2007, just as the jail-turned-four-star-hotel was about to open for business, WBUR news radio carried an interview by Boston-based reporter David Boeri with developers Marty Coleman and Richard Friedman, along with former Suffolk County sheriff Robert Rufo who, for many years, was embattled in court for double-bunking inmates to ease overcrowding.

"Back when the Lockdown wasn't for cocktails, there were numerous escapes," recounted Boeri during the broadcast. "Coleman recalls one involving a killer named Rocco Balliro."

"One guard smuggled the hacksaw blade in and Rocco went right through," said Coleman. "Of course, the iron was from way back in 1851. It went like butter, whoop, and he bent back the bars and walked right out."

Not exactly. Coleman had it partly correct. There was, in fact, a guard who was paid off and played a substantial role in the escape by affixing black adhesive tape to a locking mechanism on a door which led to an unoccupied section of the aging facility. It opened a pathway to escape.

The hacksaw blades mentioned during the interview were actually delivered by an associate who owed Rocco a favor. Unlike its New Bedford counterpart, the Charles Street Jail allowed less restrictive, face to face visits. This liberal policy afforded Rocco's visitor a chance to simply hand over the implements when the guard's attention was occupied elsewhere.

Prior to the receipt of the hacksaw blades, Rocco spent several weeks fashioning other tools he thought he might need, including a counterfeit "revolver," carved from the hard plastic casing of a transistor radio.

Additionally, he whittled another piece of the plastic into a key. Like the bogus pistol, which officials later said could have easily been mistaken for authentic under the cloak of darkness, the key proved unnecessary. But Rocco was

quite proud of the devices he'd honed from the rudimentary supplies at his disposal.

"Even though I hated the food, I'd go to the cafeteria every day for lunch," he later explained. "I sat at a table close to a guard station so I could study the keys hanging from his belt. Then I'd go back to my cell and carve my own key from memory."

While pleased that the insider left the critical door unsecured, as planned, Rocco recalled a slight pang of disappointment when he couldn't try the counterfeit key. "It would've worked," he boasted confidently.

Both Slim Ciocco and Rudy Balliro were also held at Charles Street, pending a trial slated for June 24, 1963. Rudy was in a cell on the same third tier not far from his brother. Slim, meanwhile, was confined in another section of the jail.

Soon after returning from a "sanity check" at Bridgewater State Hospital, Rocco had a chance to speak with his twin during recreation hour in the atrium. Typically, the men were allowed to exercise in the yard but that day, inclement weather kept the population indoors.

Sidestepping droppings from the scores of nesting pigeons perched high above their heads in the ceiling structure, the two men walked and talked, voices subdued. There was a guard at every turn.

"How've ya been, little brother?" Rudy asked.

"Not bad," Rocco replied, "Now that I know I'm not insane."

The comment drew slight laughter. "I'm surprised they didn't keep you there longer, just to make sure."

"Food was better in Bridgewater," Rocco praised. "I was getting tired of eating canned tuna all the time."

"Yeah." Rudy nodded. "And I'm sure there's no pigeon shit in it like this cesspool."

"How's your head?" asked Rocco, referring to the gunshot wound Rudy sustained during the Roxbury car chase.

"Okay, I guess. Gonna be a scar there but it's better than being dead."

Both men ceased their conversation when a corrections officer crossed their path. Once he was far enough away, they resumed their discussion.

"Did you hear they searched my place in Roslindale?" Rudy asked.

"Christ!" Rocco exclaimed. "What'd they find?"

"Guns," his brother replied with a nervous laugh. "Lots of guns."

"Paula okay?"

"Yeah. They took the guns but left the wife."

Rocco laughed and Rudy soon joined him. A nearby guard eyed them suspiciously for a moment but then went back to ignoring the inmate brothers.

"And the baby?"

"She sent a picture of him," was the reply. "Kid's got his dad's good looks."

Rudy's face suddenly clouded. Rocco understood the forlorn expression and felt the familiar stab of guilt and anguish. There was a distinct possibility that his brother might have to watch the child grow up during jailhouse visits and it would be Rocco's fault. He thought it best to change the subject.

"Seen Slim?" he asked.

"Yeah," said Rudy. "A few days ago."

"How's he doin'?"

"Oh ya know," his sibling answered with his trademark sarcasm. "Pretty good, 'cept for the whole jail thing."

Rocco chuckled but time was slipping away on the recreation hour.

"So, the trial–"

"Uh huh."

"–in a few weeks."

"Yeah?"

"I'm thinking of gettin' the fuck out of here before then."

Rudy shook his head and said, "You *are* crazy."

"What do I got to lose?"

Rocco's brother paused and then nodded, acknowledging the dire circumstances they faced in the form of long prison sentences. And dare they consider it, however slight the chance, a death penalty sentence was in the offing.

"You wanna go with me?"

"What, break out?"

"No, run out for an ice cream," Rocco quipped. "Whadda think?"

Rudy mulled it over for a few seconds but then shook his head. "Naw, I'll take my chances in court."

Without saying it aloud, Rudy was pointing out the obvious by declining the invite. Depending on his attorney's plan of attack, the older Balliro twin could earn a lighter sentence with a plea deal. The court might extend leniency because he had a wife and now a kid. Rocco, on the hand, was likely doomed to face life in jail – or death.

"Yeah, I don't blame you," said Rocco as he reached out and gripped his brother's shoulder.

"So what's the plan?"

"Same as New Bedford," he shared with a telling grin. Pausing, he looked around to ensure there was no one within earshot and said, "I'm cutting the bars on my cell window."

"Noisy?"

"Yeah, but the Vaseline dulls it."

"Where'd you get that?"

"The clinic," he replied. "Told the guards I had a stomach ache so they took me down to see the nurse. I squeezed some Vaseline in a paper cup when she stepped away."

Rudy shook his head at his brother's ingenuity and resourcefulness.

"Better question?" he said. "Where'd you get the hacksaw blades?"

Flashing a mischievous grin, Rocco replied, "A family friend. And we have a guard in our pocket."

"You're something else."

"Yeah," acknowledged Rocco. "Yeah, I guess I am."

"Where you gonna go if you make it out?"

"I dunno. Still working on that."

"Our friends in Jersey?"

"Naw," Rocco said with a shake of his head. "Florida or California maybe."

"The farther, the better, eh?"

"Yeah."

Five minutes remained on the recreation hour so the Balliro brothers said their goodbyes with an embrace. A nearby guard, noticing the close contact between them shook his head, silently pointing out that it was against the rules. Rocco shot back a look as if to say, "go fuck yourself."

As Rudy strode toward the staircase that led to the upper tiers and his jail cell, Rocco paused for a moment before following suit. Rudy turned and called out to his brother.

"Hey, Roc?"

"Yeah?"

"See you in church if the windows are clean."

Rocco grinned widely. He never grew tired of that line.

According to newspaper accounts, sources leaked that the three accused Roxbury gunmen were plotting a breakout, but not from the old jail. Rumors floated by Rocco Balliro himself reported that something might take place during the transport from the Charles Street Jail to the Suffolk Superior Court in Pemberton Square, or at the courthouse itself.

All Rocco had to do to ensure word reached the authorities was strike up a conversation with an inmate who was known to have a big mouth and *voila*, rat express straight to the warden's office. The false tip triggered an extensive, and expensive, security buildup at the courthouse.

Rocco, meanwhile, was putting the finishing touches on his plan. It was June 23, 1963, and the trial was the next morning. He figured the most opportune night to escape would be Sunday, when the streets around the institution would likely be uncrowded.

Returning to his cell following a meal, Rocco had a few hours to kill. He stretched out on his rack and thumbed through a tattered copy of *Life*. The magazine cover photo featured Pope John XXIII who had died several weeks earlier.

Despite his Catholic upbringing and years spent in parochial school, Rocco Balliro wasn't much of a religious man. But he wasn't beyond prayer. Closing his eyes, he silently prayed for Toby and little Mark, who he knew were angels in Heaven looking down upon him. He wondered, if they had the opportunity, what they might say to him. Would he be forgiven? Toby had to know he meant no harm. She had to know that he worshiped the both of them. Months had passed since the shootings and still, the ache of losing *his* family had barely faded.

And what ever happened to Bernice? Where was the orphaned daughter who'd survived the torrent of bullets? Clearly, the Boston Children's Aid people would never hand that dear child over to the likes of Barney Wagner, an ex-convict and drug addict. He certainly didn't have the means to raise a one year old on his own, even if he managed to stay out of jail.

Wagner readily admitted that fact himself, in a letter he later wrote to Hilda Zimmerman regarding Toby's surviving daughter. Like Toby, Barney also called her Wendy.

Dear Hilda,

I received word from my mother that you are seeking custody of Wendy. I want more than anything to see her have a good home. At the present time I'm not very capable of providing a home for her because I don't even have one myself.

My mother was going to care for her but as you must already know, she couldn't wait to get rid of her.

Hilda, I love Wendy very much not just because she is my daughter but also because she is part of Toby. I know that she would have a good home with you but I realize it would be kind of hard on you, where she is still a baby. I would appreciate it if you would write or have Mal write me and let me know what you'd like to do.

As always,
Barney

Rocco's thoughts of Bernice were interrupted by approaching footsteps of the guard making a headcount. As the officer trudged along the steel catwalk, Rocco warily glanced at the vertical, three-quarter-inch bars that made up a window on the front of his cell. They were spaced several inches apart and he had cut two of them close to the framework.

An inquisitive guard with a keen eye might have noticed the grooves in the iron. But in his favor, Rocco understood these often complacent men were required to check over two hundred inmates in a short period of time under dull lighting. They seldom paused for more than a few seconds before moving on.

Unlike the punishing sawing at the New Bedford House of Corrections, he had found these bars were far easier to cut. He could work standing upright which was more productive than awkwardly kneeling.

Additionally, the aging wrought iron proved pliant, almost soft, as he applied Vaseline and raked the hacksaw blades back and forth. Contrary to the forty days in New Bedford, Rocco wrapped-up in less than a week's time. And the damage to his hands was minor in comparison.

After the guard made his pass, Rocco stood up. His joints groaned in protest but he wasted no time heading for the rear of the cell and dropping to his knees adjacent to the toilet.

His jailers would be making another bed check in a matter of hours. Time was of the essence.

Unscrewing several bolts, he removed a metal plate, revealing the plumbing works for the sink and toilet. In between the pipes, he had found ample space to store the tools of his trade: hacksaw blades, the phony gun and the key carved from his radio. He'd also stashed several blankets which he hoped were of sufficient length, when tied together, to scale the exterior wall. Rocco recalled, vividly, the treacherous drop from the upper floor of the New Bedford House of Corrections when a makeshift rope fell shy.

Stuffing the supplies in a pillow case, Rocco screwed the plate back in place, hand-tightened the bolts, and made his way to the front of the narrow cell. Glancing back, everything seemed in order except, of course, his empty cot.

Opening the bag, Rocco removed one of the hacksaw blades and dabbed Vaseline on the surface. He then set to work, sawing through the last millimeters of iron that held the two bars in place. Top first, then bottom, he tightly gripped the rusting metal as it came free after several strokes of the blade. *Like butter*, he thought with a grin.

Placing the bars gently on the floor, Rocco lowered his bag of supplies to the catwalk and followed, wriggling through the opening. There was ample space; there would be no getting stuck this time.

Adrenaline surged as he made double-time along the tier, toward a security door. Everything was falling into place; Rocco could already taste sweet success. But his confidence waned slightly as he approached the steel door. What if their insider had developed a case of cold feet and failed to render the door? Rocco wouldn't have time to saw through another set of bars. He'd be unable to go forward and certainly couldn't go back. He'd be trapped like one of the rats in the kitchen at night. His fears proved unfounded, however. The rogue guard had done as promised. Reaching the sturdy gate, Rocco found that the locking mechanism had not engaged.

It was covered with several strips of adhesive tape which prevented the latch from securing.

Once through the gate, Rocco found himself standing in an uninhabited segment of the facility. All that separated Rocco from the outside was a window made up of more of the familiar pliable iron bars. He withdrew one of the hacksaw blades, liberally applied Vaseline, and began to cut away the window latch, which like most of the metal in the jail, had grown porous during the one hundred-twelve years since the building was first constructed.

It took ten, perhaps fifteen minutes, to finish the cut. Detached from its mooring, he grasped the window framework, and pulled it aside with minimal effort. He stashed the remainder of his supplies behind a radiator.

Rocco quickened his pace. He knotted the blankets together end to end. He was confident that the material would support his weight. But he was somewhat concerned, much like he'd been when he absconded from New Bedford, that the length of the makeshift rope wouldn't be sufficient.

One thing was for sure; it didn't matter that he was wearing just a t-shirt on this night. It was late June and as he raised the window to make an exit, Rocco was met with the warmth of an early summer breeze.

Gathering the homemade rope, he tossed it out the window to a rooftop below and was preparing to go out after it when he heard a rustling noise coming from a distant corner of the room behind him.

"Shit," he hissed as his head whipped around to determine the origin. What the hell was that? Was it a guard? If so, what the hell was he doing here? This was an empty dormitory. There was no need for anyone to be snooping around.

Again, a faint shuffling, a little more pronounced this time. Rocco braced himself. Would it be fight or flight? Fight was the only option, really. There was no way he could outrun a pursuit, once an escape alarm was sounded. He could leap from the window he was perched on, certainly, but he wouldn't reach the wall, never mind have time to climb over it.

As his heart slammed inside his chest and his stomach threatened revolt, the source of the mysterious noise revealed itself.

"Jesus Christ," Rocco whispered to himself as he watched a whitish-gray creature waddle into view. He had to stifle a laugh when he saw what had nearly given him a heart attack. "A pigeon," he said aloud. "Nothing but a fuckin' pigeon."

CHAPTER 37

"Love is how you stay alive, even after you're gone." –
Mitch Albom

Rocco Anthony Balliro extended a foot to the gravel surface beneath the car and paused to take a final drag on his smoke. Running a hand through his thick crop of hair, he suddenly felt very weary. It was well after midnight as he prepared to carry out one of two tasks that had gnawed at him during his abbreviated stay in the Charles Street Jail.

Nearly six months had passed since the shootings. He had thought the anguish might fade with the passage of time but it hadn't. Not in the least. The burning ache in his heart was as strong now, if not stronger, than it was when he first learned of their deaths.

He tried so hard while imprisoned, during days that wore on endlessly, to erase the haunting images of her final moments of life. Instead, he visualized some of the more pleasant moments he and Toby spent together.

They cherished romantic, candlelit meals in quaint North End cafes, for instance. She also took pleasure in their visits to an intimate Coolidge Corner club to savor a nightcap. And there was the occasional indulgence in a potent Pineapple Passion drink at one of the countless Chinatown eateries. Even some of the nights spent in loud, boisterous Combat Zone lounges made for stirring memories. Whether they were downing a beer at Izzy Ort's Golden Nugget where, according to one patron, "a shooting was just part of the evening's festivities," or sipping a cocktail at a club, they seldom lacked the means to enjoy one another's company. When they were out on the town together, Toby always seemed content.

But reminiscing only made the heartache worse. A day hadn't passed during which his reflections of their brief time together weren't filled with visions of precious Toby lying dead in a widening pool of blood. It was impossible to shake the fact that his actions had contributed to her death and that of her baby boy.

Pivoting to face the windshield, Rocco noticed the newspapers resting on the dashboard. Both *The Boston Globe* and *The Boston Herald American* trumpeted his escape with glaring headlines. The *Herald* featured a diagram of his route out of the jail, as well as a photo of his crudely-fashioned rope dangling from the top of the wall. Rocco took great pleasure in the embarrassment suffered by Charles Street Jail officials.

In the aftermath, a number of high-ranking brass had egg on their faces, including Sheriff Frederick Sullivan, who was also in charge of the facility years earlier when Elmer Burke broke out with the help of gunmen. Hours after the discovery of Rocco's dash to freedom, Sullivan was deeply immersed in damage control and ordered to conduct probes in conjunction with the Boston Police Department, the district attorney's office, the Prisons Committee, and the Boston City Council, as well as the FBI, which had already taken over the investigation of the prisoner's disappearance.

Despite the circumstances, there was no denying Rocco reveled in the notoriety. *For Crissake, the front page,* he thought. With photos! Everyone in the city was reading all about him, Rocco Balliro. Prison escape artist! Two breakouts in less than five months! Manhunts for the elusive prisoner!

His considerable ego inflated like never before, he found himself smiling.

"Something funny?"

"Huh?" He swung his head around to see Bruno, the youngest of the six Balliro boys, who was leaning against the steering wheel and staring at him. "Uh, nothing, just thinking about some of the stuff they wrote about me in the papers."

"Yeah," Bruno said. "You're famous."

Rocco smiled again and nodded in agreement. He silently mouthed the word famous.

The *Herald* account read, "The murder suspect dropped 15 feet down to a roof from which he was able to scale the prison wall leading to Fruit St. in the West End opposite the Massachusetts Eye and Ear Infirmary."

While the articles boosted his self-admiration, Rocco didn't appreciate being called a murderer. But he also understood it sold far more newspapers.

The *Herald* reporter made the escape sound easy. Not quite. Following his encounter with the roving pigeon, Rocco climbed through the dormitory window, feet first. Suspended from the height, he gripped the sill for a few scary seconds, and then simply let go, falling to the surface below. The impact of shoe leather with the roof made quite a clatter but he knew, from concise planning, that the kitchen below would be unoccupied at that late hour.

Scooping up the blanket-rope, Rocco sped across the roof, crouched low to minimize his shadow against security lighting. Reaching the wall, which on the interior was only several feet in height, Rocco tied off an end of the strand to a barbed wire lattice support. Once satisfied the knot would support his weight, Rocco lowered the rope to the exterior.

Carefully negotiating the razor-sharp wire, he followed, scrambling down the rope. The descent reminded him of the drills he was ordered to perform during his brief stint in the army.

Rocco thought, for a moment, about what he might say to a passing pedestrian. Unlike New Bedford, this was a major city. People were out and about at all hours of the night. But as he lowered himself down, Rocco found there wasn't a soul in sight. The street was thankfully deserted.

As he had feared, the flimsy patchwork rope rendered from blankets came up short and he was forced to plummet some fifteen feet to the sidewalk below. Reaching the limit of the rope, Rocco released his grip. Bracing for impact, he was relieved to land without injury. *Piece of cake*, he silently mulled, wiping the sweat from his forehead with the front of his shirt.

Bruno's urging brought him back to the task at hand. "C'mon, whadda you say we get going?"

"Yeah, sure," Rocco replied as he emerged from the car and paused to briefly survey their surroundings.

To the left, a long row of densely-packed homes stood hushed, darkened against the midnight hour save for the soft glow of a random porch light.

Bruno circled the car and joined his brother. He was right about the need to get out of there. They had to move it along. At any moment, someone could emerge from one of these homes and summon the police. The brothers strode briskly forward toward their destination. A resourceful Bruno produced a pair of flashlights.

"So, any idea where we should look?" he asked.

"Yeah," Rocco replied. "I think so."

Crossing beneath a sturdy, stone archway that marked the northern boundary of the sprawling Woodlawn Cemetery, Rocco wondered if he was doing the right thing.

He had come to this place, barely a day after his gutsy escape from the confines of the Charles Street Jail, to find the gravesite of Toby and pay his last respects. It was foolhardy, to say the least, with every Boston cop hot on his trail. What would the headlines read if notorious jail breaker Rocco Balliro was pinched while wandering in a graveyard?

Did he really want to see her burial site? He thought it might give him some peace, some closure. Then again, a visit like this wasn't going to change anything. Toby was gone and his life was ripped apart. Despite the indecision, he pressed ahead.

Bruno suggested they split up. They could cover more ground.

"Yeah, good idea," Rocco agreed.

"I'll go this way," Bruno indicated, gesturing toward a narrow footpath leading toward a congested segment of gravestones.

"Sure."

"If you find it, aim your light in my direction," Bruno instructed. "But be careful not to hit any of these houses with the beam."

Rocco marveled at the maturity of his brother, the youngest of the Balliro clan. Bruno had already proven that he was virtually fearless and fiercely loyal to Rocco.

He regretted asking Bruno to aid in this misguided endeavor. If an Everett police cruiser stumbled upon them, both would promptly be hauled off to jail. Rocco, permanently. But on the other hand, he was grateful for the help and support. Bruno understood what his older brother was doing. The older Balliro siblings, Joe, Frank, and Billy, would likely put a boot in Rocco's ass and kick him the hell out of town. New Jersey. Florida. Anywhere but Boston, they would say.

A thought crossed Rocco's mind that made him feel like retching but, admittedly, could aid in their search.

"Hey, Bruno."

"Yeah?"

"Toby's grave will be … um … brand new."

Bruno didn't reply. He didn't have to. He just nodded as he walked into the depths of the cemetery.

Moving catlike along rows of graves, Rocco wondered if he'd ever find what he was looking for amidst more than a hundred thousand souls.

Here was an infant, taken from her family after barely a month of existence. Several gravesites further along the same row, a four-year-old boy was buried beneath an ornate marble stone that held his photograph, a puppy at his feet.

Under the beam of the flashlight, Rocco came across the gravesite of a five-year-old girl and her young mother, laid to rest on the same summer day in 1923. It brought to mind little Mark, whose life was snuffed out like the candles on a second birthday cake that he would never enjoy.

Rocco wondered if Toby's parents, Hilda and Herman Zimmerman, had seen fit to bury little Mark alongside his mother where he spent so much time when he was alive.

As he continued to search the countless plots, Rocco came upon a small sign on a rusted chain link fence. It read **Beth Israel Cemetery**. A sudden realization struck him.

"That's it," he said aloud. "Jewish."

Toby's family was of Jewish descent. It stood to reason that she might have been laid to rest here.

Energized by his find, Rocco hastily made his way along a sloping driveway, ever wary of the aged, uneven pavement beneath his feet.

The entrance gate was slightly ajar. Rocco slipped through the breach and began checking grave markers.

A voice startled him.

"Any luck?"

"Yeah, I think I'm close."

"Want some help?"

"I'd rather do this alone, if you don't mind."

"Yeah, I understand. I'll wait in the car."

Bruno left Rocco to finish his search for Toby's gravesite. It didn't take long.

His first emotion was anger.

"What the f–" he started to say but stopped short of cursing, remembering where he was.

Nestled in a remote, secluded corner of the Beth Israel graveyard, Toby Wagner's burial plot stood out from those around it, but not in a good way. It was, simply put, an eyesore.

While nearby graves were manicured and well-kept, covered with neatly-trimmed sod, Toby was laid to rest beneath a raw, ugly rectangular patch of exposed soil, slightly sunken after recent rainstorms. Instead of an engraved stone, the site was identified by a nondescript wooden marker with her name scribbled across the surface in handwritten, block letters.

Salty drops streamed down Rocco's unshaven face. He couldn't recall the last time he wept like this. He missed Toby terribly. He yearned to turn back the clock.

Granted, it wouldn't change the fact that he was an escaped convict but he never doubted his ability to give the authorities the slip, with Toby and the kids in tow, and make a new life for his family.

Rocco Balliro crossed himself. As he did, he realized he was wearing a shirt that Toby had bought for him the October before, in celebration of his twenty-sixth birthday. It was a splendid collared shirt, button-down, featuring narrow, pencil-thin blue stripes. Toby loved this shirt and he made a point to wear it for her often.

On a whim, he dropped to the ground at the edge of Toby's grassless grave and began, with his bare hands, to scoop aside soil. The dirt was soft and pliable and before long, he had dug a small excavation, perhaps a foot in depth.

Brushing the soil from his hands, Rocco unbuttoned and took off the shirt. Bare-chested, he rolled it into a ball and placed it lovingly into the hole. He then gently covered it. Climbing to his feet, Rocco dusted off and mumbled a quick prayer before leaving. He walked double-time back to the waiting car.

Bruno looked on in mild amusement as his brother emerged from the shadows of the darkened cemetery half-dressed.

"Where the hell is your shirt?" he asked, bewildered.

"I'll explain later," Rocco replied as he climbed in the car and closed the door. "C'mon, let's get outta here."

The phone rang six or seven times and he nearly hung up in frustration when finally someone answered.

"Hello?" said the female voice at the other end, sounding weary and depressed.

"Hilda?"

"Yes, who's this?"

"Roc – um, I mean Anthony. Anthony Balliro."

There was an uncomfortable silence after he identified himself. Rocco got the sense Toby's mother was deciding whether or not she wanted to speak with him. He waited for the drone of a disconnect, which he figured was inevitable.

"I'm sorry to bother you," he continued when she didn't say anything, "But I was–"

She cleared her throat as if she was prepared to say something but then remained silent.

"–I was at Toby's gravesite last night."

Hilda took a deep breath and said, "The police are looking for you. They came to our house and asked if we'd heard from you."

He didn't ask what she said to the cops. It didn't matter. The authorities had likely spoken with anyone and everyone who had even the slightest bit of contact with their elusive prey. He knew they would leave no stone unturned until he was carted back to jail.

"Hilda," he said. "The grave ... it's got no stone or grass. There's nothing. Is it money? I can get you the money."

"Anthony," she began with a sigh. "We've ordered the stone but it's traditional not to unveil it until just before the first anniversary of death."

Now it made sense. Jewish traditions. He felt much better after hearing her explanation. The Zimmerman family had intentionally left their dear daughter's grave bare; but with good reason.

It wasn't lost on Rocco that Hilda was so willing to speak with him. She could have easily hung up upon hearing his voice. It was obvious she didn't think he killed her daughter.

She knew there was more to the story than that told by the police and the newspapers. They'd vilified him. Despite her grief, Hilda knew Rocco loved Toby. *Small victory*, he thought, but a victory nonetheless.

"Is ... um ... Mark–" he started and then broke off, not sure how to phrase the delicate question.

Hilda understood.

"No, he's not buried with Toby."

"Huh? Why the hell not?"

Rocco realized he came across indignant but Hilda caught him off guard.

"He's not Jewish," she calmly explained. "We tried, but the cemetery people wouldn't allow it. It's against their rules."

So many rules and traditions, thought Rocco. "Where is he?"

"In West Roxbury," she answered. After a long pause, she added, "With other children."

He didn't press for more. It was understandably a tender subject, discussing the burial site of her grandson.

"Hilda," he said, his voice wavering as he spoke. "I miss them."

"We *all* miss them, Anthony."

CHAPTER 38

*"If anything in life is certain, if history has taught us
anything, it is that you can kill anyone." – Al Pacino as
Michael Corleone in* The Godfather, Part II

While acutely aware that the best plan would be to get out
of Boston, Rocco Anthony Balliro lingered on the outskirts
of the city, in places like Everett, Chelsea, and Revere, but
avoided his regular haunts. The previous night's sojourn to
Toby's gravesite furnished a modicum of emotional solace
but it also made his blood boil. He wouldn't be content until
he confronted Freeman Clifford, the man he held partly
responsible for events that led to the deaths of Toby and Mark.

In a borrowed car, he motored across the city, avoiding
the main Boston thoroughfares as much as practicable. The
hour was edging toward midnight when Rocco rounded a turn
to Dudley Street and eased the car to a stop opposite Walter's
Lounge, which was a popular Roxbury establishment owned
by the Bennett brothers.

It wasn't lost on him that he was, at that moment, merely
blocks away from Centre Street and the scene of the February
carnage. It made him queasy to realize he was so close to the
place where his girlfriend and her son were slaughtered.

Rocco was considering how he could get a word to
Bennett when he spotted a patron walking toward the
entrance of the watering hole. Now, perhaps, he wouldn't
have to barge headlong into the bar. Leaning across the front
seat, Rocco quickly rolled down the passenger side window
and called out to the stranger.

"Hey!" he shouted.

The man turned and hesitantly answered, "Uh, yeah ... what's up?"

"Do me a favor?"

"Uh huh?"

"Could you ask Bennett to come out and see me?"

"Who should I tell him is asking?"

"Tell him a friend is here to see him."

He understood such an ambiguous message might alarm Bennett. A number of his brethren from Somerville and Charlestown had had their blood spilled since the Summer of 1961 as the Irish gang war escalated. But Rocco had no alternative. He wasn't about to furnish his real name. For all he knew, this guy doing him a favor was an off-duty cop.

"Alright," agreed the man, sounding suspicious. "I'll let him know."

Rocco lit up a smoke and settled back in the seat. He scratched his face. At times, the itch was unbearable. He detested the beard he'd grown since leaving New Bedford but it was part of a simple disguise. He was startled when a hand reached through the open window of his car.

"Jesus!"

"Hey there," exclaimed Edward 'Wimpy' Bennett as he grasped Rocco's shoulder. "What the hell are you doing here?"

"How've ya been, Eddie?"

"Never mind me! How 'bout you?"

Rocco should his head. "I've had better days, I guess."

"You okay?"

"Yeah, yeah ..."

"I read 'bout you in the papers," the excitable Irish mob boss said.

"Oh yeah?"

"Gotta admit," Bennett said, shaking his head. "You got a set of balls, kid."

Talk about balls, thought Rocco. It was rumored in many circles that Bennett was part of the gang that carried out the hugely successful 1950 Brinks robbery. While authorities didn't officially link him to the crime, Bennett did a year in prison after he was found in possession of sixty thousand in marked bills.

"You're crazy coming to this neck of the woods," Bennett stressed, gesturing to the quiet street stretched out before them. "I seen cops all over the place."

"Oh yeah?"

"Yeah. Looking for you, I bet."

Rocco nodded and said, "I'm staying one step ahead."

"So, what brings you down here?"

"I'm looking for Clifford."

"He's not here," Bennett said, nodding in the direction of Walter's Lounge in the backdrop. Subdued music and muffled laughter could be heard from the interior.

"I need a favor."

Bennett leaned in closer, lowered his voice, and said, "Sure."

Rocco didn't mince his words. His expression was cold sober and resolute. "I want him clipped," he said in a low, hushed tone.

"Clifford?"

"Yeah."

Rocco looked into the wisdom-filled eyes of Bennett, sizing up the man who maintained a stronghold on loansharking and bookmaking operations in Roxbury and Dorchester.

Bennett was a short, slightly pudgy Irishman with a pasty, rotund face. In his early forties, he was prematurely balding but it was a feature that made him look friendly and good-natured.

Rocco had no way of knowing, of course, but the man who stood before him would be dead in four short years.

Bennett, it was later discovered, met his untimely end in a Dorchester garage he co-owned with his two older brothers, shot point-blank in the face by mob assassin Stephen "The Rifleman" Flemmi.

Reputed crime boss Francis "Cadillac" Salemme apparently had designs on the Bennett brothers lucrative shylocking and bookmaking businesses, as well as their popular Roxbury lounge, and took part in the gangland-style hit.

Three months later, in April 1967, the two killers unceremoniously took out a second Bennett who swore vengeance for his slain younger brother.

Walter Bennett, fifty-five, was strangled to death by Flemmi for making threatening overtures.

Neither of the men's remains, purportedly buried beneath the soil of a barren Hopkinton, Massachusetts, shooting range, has ever been recovered.

The Flemmi-Salemme killing spree was far from over, however. In December 1967, as Christmas drew near, the oldest of the clan, William "Billy" Bennett, was kidnapped and shot four times in the chest. Thrown from a speeding vehicle, he was left to die in a Dorchester snow bank, which turned bright red with blood.

"Look, Rocco," began Bennett, "I know you didn't ki–"

"I know what you're gonna say ... that I didn't kill the girl."

"Yeah."

"I've heard it before," Rocco shared.

"They're letting those cops get away with murder," Bennett declared, slamming his hand against the roof of the car in disgust.

"And Clifford."

"Huh?"

"And Clifford too."

"Yeah, and Clifford," echoed Bennett. "For interfering. I get it, pal."

"So you'll help me?" asked Rocco, appreciative of the verbal support but trying to urge the conversation forward. He had been parked there too long.

"I'll see what I can do."

"Thanks."

"Here, take this," said Bennett, as he fished a bankroll from his pocket and handed it to Rocco, who later counted out two hundred bucks.

"Thanks again," uttered Rocco as he started the car, bid Bennett goodbye, and pulled away.

With the last of the loose ends tied up, it was high time he got out of Boston.

If he actually intended to carry out Rocco's request to execute Freeman "Punchy" Clifford, Bennett never got the chance. But Clifford ultimately met his end in mid-1974 via a shotgun blast to the midsection over a loan-sharking dispute with a business partner.

CHAPTER 39

"If you want to understand the causes of aggression,
study police officers." – Steven Magee

Beverly Zimmerman heard the comment but was distracted and failed to acknowledge. She was lost in deep thought.

"I think we're being followed," her alarmed companion remarked.

As the car came to an abrupt stop at a red light, Beverly saw they were yielding so a young mother could push a baby carriage across busy Commonwealth Avenue. The woman, she noticed, resembled her late sister-in-law Toby. It was uncanny, actually. The girl had the same petite figure and the same flowing, jet black hair. The same pretty face as well. And in the carriage was a boy, perhaps two. Mark's age, or at least the age he would be if he were still alive.

The empty ache of loss returned with a vengeance. How long had it been since they were killed? Four months? Five? She'd lost count. She absently wondered what had become of Mark's belongings. His carriage? His crib? His toys? All the trappings of a little boy who would no longer need them.

"Bev?" said her friend as he gradually nosed the car forward across the intersection. "Did you hear me? I think there's someone following us."

She snapped out of her lethargy and glanced at him.

"Huh?" she said. "Following us?"

"Yeah. The same car has been behind us for a while."

She shifted in the passenger seat of the big sedan as if to turn and look back.

"No, don't!" exclaimed her young male friend who had gone pale. He reached across and grabbed her wrist. "Don't look at them. Use the mirrors."

Beverly inched downward in the seat, positioning herself to get a view from the side mirror.

"Do you know them?" he asked. "Do you recognize them?"

"No," she replied, shaking her head. "Maybe they're friends of ..." she began but tailed off.

"Friends of who?"

"Never mind."

Thankfully, they had reached her Delaware Place apartment building.

"Friends of who?" her friend impatiently repeated when he failed to get a response.

"I'll explain later," she said, as she climbed out of the car and closed the door. As her friend backed out of the driveway, Beverly risked a glimpse toward Arlington Street. She noted the car that had been following them was now parked across the street, directly in front of St. Columbkille Church. From the distance, she could see there was a pair of shadowy figures in the front seat.

Could it be? Were these friends of Rocco Balliro? She'd read in the papers that he'd escaped from jail and was on the run. Did his people think she knew something about his whereabouts? Maybe they thought Toby had mentioned possible hideouts and these guys were here to shut her up. Farfetched, perhaps, but who could say they wouldn't go to great lengths to conceal their associate's whereabouts.

Bounding up the stairs, Beverly reached her second-floor apartment and made it inside after briefly fumbling with the keys. Flipping the bolt, she heard telltale footfalls climbing the staircase, trailing her. She channeled the security chain with trembling fingers and slid it into place, knowing full well that the flimsy metal would do little to halt an intruder.

Placing her ear against the door, Beverly listened intently. Her breath caught in her throat as she heard muffled voices and then three taps on the outside of the door, spaced evenly. *Knock-knock-knock.*

She drew a deep, prolonged breath. Beverly was thankful for her babysitter, who'd agreed to keep her two-year-old son overnight. He wouldn't have to see the harm that was about to befall her.

Her imagination running wild, Beverly wondered what it felt like to get shot. Just as quickly, she pushed the thought from her mind.

Spinning the deadbolt but leaving the chain engaged Beverly peered through the narrow gap between the door and the surrounding frame. A pair of men, clean-cut and dressed in business suits and neckties, gazed back at her.

"Beverly Zimmerman?"

"Y-yes," she stammered.

"Boston police," the plainclothes detective said. "Mind if we come and ask you a few questions?"

She didn't respond right away.

"Ma'am?" the taller of the two detectives urged.

"Oh I'm sorry," she said, detaching the chain and opening the door for the two men. "Please come in."

"Thank you, ma'am."

"I'm only twenty-four," Beverly said with a smile, flipping her long, black hair back over her shoulder. "I'm *far* from a ma'am."

Neither of the detectives responded to her attempt at levity so she gestured toward the small kitchen table, inviting them to sit.

"Can I get you anything?"

"No, thank you, ma'am," the lead detective said as he and his partner pulled out chairs, each upholstered with bright, flowery patterns. Each man withdrew a pen and notebook from their suit jacket's interior pocket and flipped the covers. "This shouldn't take long."

Beverly didn't join them at the table. Instead, she began to tidy some of the clutter that had gathered on the kitchen countertop. Keeping her hands busy took the edge off the anxiety.

Without any precursor or introduction to open their interview, the taller of the two detectives rattled off his first question.

"Do you know Toby Wagner?" the ill-mannered cop blurted.

The question itself wasn't shocking but she was taken aback by the blunt, tactless delivery.

"You mean *did* I know Toby Wagner," Beverly replied sarcastically. It must have hit a nerve because the detective who asked the question looked up and nodded apologetically.

"Yeah, she was my sister-in-law," Beverly continued. "Ex-sister-in-law, actually. I was married to her older brother Malcolm."

"How 'bout Rocco Balliro," the second detective asked, joining the conversation for the first time.

"No, I don't," she replied sharply, unwavering.

He raised his eyebrows, skeptically. "Are you sure?"

Beverly stood with her back to the counter, arms folded defiantly across her chest, and glared menacingly at the detective. She ached for a cigarette but couldn't recall where she'd left the pack. An earlier breakfast at a Brighton café began to boil over as heartburn.

"What I meant to say," she elaborated, "was that I didn't know him personally. I knew who he was and I knew he was seeing Toby but that's it. I only saw him in person once and–"

"When was that?" interrupted the lead detective, his interest captured.

"I don't remember, exactly," she replied. "Last November, I think it was. Yeah, November. Rocco was playing cards with his buddies in Toby's apartment."

"In Brighton? Kelton Street?"

"Yeah."

"Did you recognize any of the other men?"

"Nope."

"What did Balliro have to say?"

"'Hi, Bev.'"

"That's it? 'Hi, Bev'?"

Both men scribbled notes.

"Anything else to add?"

"No," she answered.

The detectives got up from their chairs and prepared to leave. They were clearly disappointed. They'd wasted their time.

"Detective, I have a question for you," she said.

"Yeah, what's that?"

"I heard a rumor that Rocco Balliro didn't shoot Toby and Mark."

"Oh yeah? Where'd you hear that?"

She sensed by his tone that a line had been crossed but she continued, nonetheless.

"Um, just some friends talking about the case, that's all."

The detective responded indignantly. "If he didn't shoot them, who did?"

"Well, um, I heard it could have been the pol–"

Cutting her off before she could finish the statement, the detective caustically snapped, "Ma'am, here's my business card. Call me if Balliro tries to contact you, alright?"

"Sure," Beverly agreed, knowing that would never happen.

"And ma'am?"

"Yeah?"

"Some advice," he said, leaning in closer and casting a threatening scowl. "Don't believe everything you hear."

CHAPTER 40

"An utterly fearless man is a far more dangerous
comrade than a coward." – Herman Melville

Lining the mile-long parade route of the quaint, seaside community known as Lordship, Connecticut, were scores of revelers enjoying marching bands, fire trucks, clowns, and the local little league baseball teams riding atop carefully-crafted, vibrantly-colored floats.

It was a picture-perfect July 4th afternoon and the weather, which was typically hot and muggy this time of year in southwestern Connecticut, featured gentle breezes wafting across the waters of nearby Atlantic Ocean.

As was the tradition, the military representation drew a rousing cheer from the flag-waving throng while a passing politician would impel polite applause and a random, half-hearted heckle.

But one of the most anticipated displays in Lordship's annual Independence Day parade was the antique cars driven by folks dressed in vintage garb of the roaring twenties. Adults and children alike enjoyed the dark, imposing vehicles and the gangster impersonators.

At regular intervals, several of these characters would leap from the slowly moving cars brandishing mock Tommy machine guns. To the delight of many spectators, these men would pause to reenact gangster battles, complete with the *rat-a-tat-tat* sound effects derived from their phony weapons. Young children would plug their ears against the noise but joyous smiles never left their faces.

For the adult observers, it was the preserved automobiles, hand-waxed and glistening brightly beneath the July sun, that truly impressed. Many of the retirees, in their mid-sixties, had once owned similar vehicles and reminisced about some of the long drives they took with their girls.

Included in the mix were a 1928 Dodge Victory Six, a 1927 Studebaker Dictator Sedan, and a V-16 Cadillac touring car, among others. Riding in the passenger seat of the burly V-16 which, according to historians, was a preferred model of ruthless Chicago gangster Al Capone, was none other than the dashing Rocco Anthony Balliro. He was wearing a slick, pin-striped suit and a fedora.

Waving to the adoring crowd as the car paced slowly along the parade route, Rocco and his co-actors tossed out handfuls of hard candy for the children who dashed madly into the street to gather the sweets.

Many folks snapped photographs of the spectacle with Kodak Brownie cameras, none realizing at the time that the man waving from the vintage Cadillac, whose grinning mug would likely end up in their keepsake photo albums, was a fugitive from justice vigorously sought by a number of law enforcement agencies, including the Boston Police, the Massachusetts Department of Corrections, and of course, the FBI.

"So, where to next?"

"Rhode Island, I think," Rocco replied, pausing to drain the remainder of a cold beer, which was the perfect antidote to cleanse parade dust and dirt. "Yeah, I think I'll head up to Providence."

Rocco was chatting with his host of the past few weeks, Jimmy DelMaggio, who was known in semi-professional boxing circles as the Pattern Leather Kid. The two men were leaning against the Caddy and tipping bottles from an ice chest that had been stored in the trunk of the car. It was Jimmy who'd invited Rocco to join a group of his buddies in the parade.

Years earlier, DelMaggio did a stint in the Charlestown Jail with Rocco's older brother Frank, who at the time was nearing the end of a sentence for truck hijacking. DelMaggio, who was in for assault, was paying back a jailhouse favor by harboring his former cellmate's fugitive sibling.

"You can stay longer if you'd like," DelMaggio offered. The invitation was genuine but Rocco had no choice but to move on.

"Thanks, Jimmy," he said to his host, who was small in stature but powerfully built. DelMaggio would top a short list of guys Rocco would want at his side in a bar fight. "But I'll be outta your hair first thing in the morning."

Neither man brought up the fact that Rocco had worn out his welcome with some of the local mobsters. They didn't appreciate the Bostonian's singular, unsanctioned activities that were cutting into their profits. It wasn't a lot of money but it ruffled feathers, nonetheless. Running a small numbers game funded with some seed money he'd acquired, Rocco brought unwanted heat on himself and raised the ire of the Connecticut faction, which had ties to the Genovese crime family out of New York.

"They're just talking 'bout you, that's all," DelMaggio had professed over a friendly card game several days earlier.

But Rocco knew better. He'd seen enough mob retribution to understand what happens to those who cross the bosses. Within most organizations, talk usually turned to action, especially when there was money or reputation at stake. Even a paltry sum could result in bodily harm. As much as he wanted to remain holed up in the pleasant seaside community, it was time to go. It was time to heed his brother's advice.

"You can't stay in one place for long, brother," Frank had sternly lectured during their earlier drive to Lordship. "Got it?"

"Got it," was Rocco's simple reply. There was no arguing the point.

"A coupla weeks, no more," Frank continued.

"Sure, sure."

Rocco knew his brother was right. Common sense said that if he became too comfortable; too complacent, the authorities searching for him would surely pick up the trail. He had to keep moving and stay ahead of them.

Originally, Rocco had suggested that he should trend further south, even as far as Florida. Southwestern Connecticut, a mere three-hour drive from Boston, seemed too close for comfort. But while a Florida hideout might have stretched the long arm of the law, Frank stressed that the distance would also make it burdensome for the Balliro family to funnel money and other support.

A beer held in front of his face brought Rocco back to Lordship. He grasped the neck of the bottle and took it from DelMaggio.

"You know you're welcome here anytime," invited the former amateur prize-fighter.

"Yeah," Rocco acknowledged. "I appreciate that."

At dawn, Rocco tossed his meager belongings in the borrowed sedan, said his goodbyes to DelMaggio and his wife, and hit the road. It was already warm and promised to be a scorcher.

The drive from DelMaggio's place to Providence, Rhode Island, took a little more than two hours. Rocco heeded the speed limit; not that he had much choice in the old car he was driving. It reminded him of the DeSoto he'd stolen for the flight from New Bedford after his first jailbreak.

Before long, the City of Providence loomed in the distance. Reaching downtown, Rocco made his way over to Federal Hill, which was home to many Italian transplants, sumptuous restaurants and cafés, and of course, a prominent mafia presence. Mob boss Raymond Patriarca, who was generous to his men but ruthless to his enemies, kept his headquarters in this tiny, tight-knit slice of Providence, at 161 Atwells Avenue.

Across the many layers of the New England underworld hierarchy, Rocco Balliro worked for Patriarca, although indirectly. In Boston, he and his brother Rudy were considered enforcers for the organization, falling under the Angiulos who, in turn, answered to Patriarca.

According to academic.ru, an Internet research website, producer David Chase recognized the Balliro brothers when developing characters for a new television mini-series, *The Sopranos*, which ultimately enjoyed a hugely successful broadcast run from 1999-2007 on cable network HBO. Chase, according to the article, fashioned many of his New Jersey-based mafia characters in the likeness of actual mobsters and their associates.

"Pasquale and his twin brother Phil Parisi," the account read, "were based on real-life Patriarca crime family mob associates Rocco and Salvatore Balliro from Roxbury, Massachusetts."

Rocco steered clear of the building which housed Patricarca's headquarters, glancing warily through the windows as he cruised by.

Unbeknownst to any of the occupants, the feds had infiltrated the Patriarca organization and were two years into an electronic surveillance operation. A listening device had been installed by the FBI on March 6, 1962, and was continually recording incriminating conversations between the head of the New England La Cosa Nostra and countless visitors.

Rocco pulled over in front of a no-name bar a couple of blocks from the popular Acorn Social Club. It was nearing ten a.m. when he stepped from the car, stretched his cramped muscles, and made his way into the dingy barroom. The room stank of stale beer and body odor, clearly a low rent establishment. A bell attached to the top of the door jingled, signaling his arrival. It reminded him of Sophie's place in Brighton and triggered another bout of heartache.

He missed the breakfasts he shared with Toby in that cozy little café. They'd eat, sip coffee, and talk for hours about nothing. He could almost hear Toby's voice and smell the freshly-baked apple pie.

Dimly lit, the small room was vacant save for a bored-looking bartender and a reclusive figure sitting in the shadows. Rocco smiled as he recognized the individual and strode over to greet him.

"Seat taken?" he asked the man, sliding a wobbly chair from beneath the equally shaky table before receiving an answer.

"Mr. Balliro, my friend."

"Been a long time," said Rocco as he reached out to shake hands.

"Too long," said Paulie Colicci, who looked far younger than his thirty-eight birthdays. "Whatcha drinking buddy?"

"Beer."

"Hey, Sal," Colicci called out to the bartender, "beer for my friend?"

The barkeep nodded, popped the top off a bottle of Schlitz, and delivered it to their table.

"So where you been?" Colicci asked as Rocco tilted the bottle.

"Lordship, Connecticut. Nice little town. I was staying with Jimmy DelMaggio."

"DelMaggio?"

"Yeah," said Rocco. "The Pattern Leather Kid."

"Oh yeah, I've heard of that guy. Good fighter."

Rocco nodded in agreement and said, "None better. Did time with my brother Frank in Charlestown"

Colicci took a swig of his beer and wiped his mouth with the back of a sleeve. He looked at his table guest with a smirk and said, "I heard a few things 'bout you too."

"Oh yeah?"

"Read it in the papers."

"Which one?"

"*Herald American*," answered Colicci. "A guy left a copy at the bar. They had pictures of you and a rope hanging from the wall of some jail."

Rocco chuckled and nodded.

Colicci raised his empty beer bottle to get the barkeep's attention, wordlessly seeking a replacement. The man prepared another round.

"I guess you have this thing about climbing over walls in the middle of the night," Colicci continued.

"Uh huh, getting to be a habit," Rocco stated.

"So this whole shooting thing?"

Rocco paused to light a smoke and offered one to his tablemate who shook his head.

"What about it?"

"In the apartment," Colicci began. "What do you think happened?"

"I think," Rocco said, taking a prolonged drag on the smoke, "that the cops shot Toby and her boy. Not intentional or nothing like that. By mistake."

"Uh huh."

"After the shooting stopped, me, Rudy, and Slim took off. But after, I dunno, ten seconds maybe, there was more gunfire inside. We were already outside running for the car when I heard it."

"So the cops–"

"So the cops were shooting again, yeah." furnished Rocco, finishing Colicci's comment. "At each other! After we left. Can you fuckin' believe it?"

"And your girlfriend?"

"I wasn't sure if she was there; there were two girls, Toby and Mary Adams and five kids stashed in the bedrooms while the cops waited on me."

"What the fuck!" Colicci exclaimed.

Rocco nodded in agreement, took a swig of his beer, and continued. "I think after the first round of shooting Toby must've thought it was over and tried to get the fuck outta there. They said she was carrying Mark in her arms when–"

"When the asshole cops started firing again?"

"Yeah," said Rocco, getting a little choked up as he finished telling Colicci the story. "Toby ... um ... took one in the head and Mark was ... was shot in the stomach."

"Christ, Roc," Colicci said, "the whole thing sucks. And you take the rap!"

The two men fell silent and drank their beers without saying a word for a few moments. Rocco absently peeled the label off his bottle while Colicci cleaned his fingernails with a pocket knife.

Like Rocco, Paul J. Colicci had a long rap sheet and had been in and out of prison over a criminal career spanning more than two decades. His claim to fame was a 1947 quarter-million dollar heist of well-to-do socialite Mrs. Richard Coffin, who was the wife of late author Damon Runyon.

Colicci robbed the South Dartmouth, Massachusetts, home of Coffin but was later apprehended and sent up to MCI-Walpole.

"So we have a place for you to stay," Colicci said, breaking the silence.

"Yeah?"

"Decent room in a nearby hotel. Clean, anyway."

Colicci insisted his charge try to lay low and stay out of trouble during his stay in the Providence area. He was, after all, on the lam from multiple agencies. But there was another reason; he was just trying to protect his friend, that's all. This was Patriarca's territory and out of respect, his guests were expected to keep their noses clean and not bring unwanted attention to the enclave.

"Sure, Paulie," he responded with a crooked grin and a wink at the fatherly advice. "No need to worry 'bout me."

Colicci raised a one-handed stop sign and shook his head, knowing right well that keeping his ward under wraps for any length of time would be a tall task, indeed.

For the most part though, Rocco did as he was asked. He endured boredom and kept a low profile for the sake of his friend. If he wasn't hanging out in a bar nursing a beer, he could be found resting in his hotel room, watching television. Out of sight, out of trouble was the intent. There was one night, however, when Rocco had no choice but to step outside the persona he'd adopted during his stay in Providence.

Returning to his Atwells Avenue hotel on foot after a visit to one of the local establishments, he encountered a young woman who appeared to be in serious trouble. While he had several drinks on board, Rocco was certainly cognizant enough to recognize when someone was in dire need of help.

The woman, no more than twenty, was pinned against the side of a building by a pair of men in white uniforms, apparently sailors on shore leave. They were grabbing and groping her and it became evident, as Rocco drew near and got a better look, that she wasn't the slightest bit interested in their advances. She struggled to break free but one of the men was nearly twice her size and overpowered her with ease.

The near-midnight air was viscous and drenched with humidity. Moving quickly, Rocco advanced toward them. All the muscles in his upper body grew taut and the hairs were raised on the back of his neck. His pace quickened as he closed the gap between himself and the assailants.

Rocco's blood boiled when he caught sight of one of the men violently groping the woman's crotch. The dirty maggot yanked up the front of her skirt and jammed his hand between her legs. She yelped loudly at the violation. The other guy clamped a meaty paw over her mouth to silence her.

"Hey, asshole, let her go!" shouted an infuriated Rocco.

Startled, the scarlet-faced, thickset sailor covering the girl's mouth released his victim for a few seconds. It was long enough for her to plead in anguish, "Help me, please, help me! They're gonna kill me!"

Rocco was close enough now to get a good look at her. Beneath the diffused light given off by a nearby floodlight, he saw that her eyes, wide and terrified, were bloodshot from crying. Mascara-stained tears ran down her pale, drawn face. Her long, light brunette hair was matted and in disarray and perspiration glistened on her forehead. Several buttons were torn off her dark-colored blouse, revealing a white brassiere beneath. He saw that she was slender, almost frail, beneath the torn, tattered clothing.

Red-face's partner-in-crime snarled at the new arrival. "Get da' fuck outta here!" A string of spittle flew from his mouth. Turning to face the wall, he retrieved an empty beer bottle and smashed it against the concrete surface of the building. Shards of brown glass rained in all directions. Slashing the sharp remnants of the bottle back and forth, the drunken attacker brayed, "Get yer fuckin' ass outta here or I'll cut yer throat!"

"Let. Her. Go," Rocco uttered coolly through tightly-clenched teeth, pausing between each word.

"Fuck you," said the bottle-wielding sailor as he lunged forward with the man-made weapon. Rocco stood his ground and the man warily paused.

While the pint-sized drunkard menaced, the other sailor, much bigger and stronger, let go of his victim, who collapsed to the sidewalk in an exhausted heap. Her chest was heaving as if she had just run a long distance.

The burly sailor advanced a step toward Rocco, his beefy hands balled in fists of fury. "I'm gonna kill you," he growled.

But suddenly, like a vicious guard dog yanked backyard by a short leash run, the man froze in his tracks. Eyes bulging with fear, his sweaty upper lip began to tremble and twitch as he stared down the dark, blue steel barrel of a .45 caliber handgun aimed squarely at the middle of his ample forehead.

His hand steady and unwavering, Rocco sneered, "You want some of this?"

"N-no," the sailor stammered as he back-pedaled.

"C'mon, give me a reason," Rocco urged.

"T-take it easy, man."

Rocco derived a bizarre sense of amusement in what occurred next. As his hefty, would-be attacker raised his hands skyward in surrender, a large, wet spot began forming on the front of his pearly white uniform pants. The big, tough sailor, who likely won far more fistfights in barrooms than he lost, was pissing himself. The pungent odor of urine filled the air. Rocco smirked. How would this guy explain the yellowish stain to his sailor buddies when he got back to the ship?

"I ought to shoot the both of you."

"We didn't mean nuthin' by it," the sailor implored. "We wasn't gonna hurt her."

"You're a fuckin' liar," Rocco said. "Get outta here before I end your miserable fuckin' lives."

In a flash, the two men were gone – running along Atwells Avenue toward downtown Providence and the distant harbor. Their night of reckless drinking and assaulting defenseless girls was over, at least in this city. Rocco watched as they faded into the distance and then turned to the expressionless girl, who was staring straight ahead. She looked as if she had gone into shock.

"Hey, you alright?" he asked. She didn't respond.

Slipping the trusty .45 into his waistband, he walked over to her. She remained sitting, propped up against the building with her legs folded beneath her. Rocco reached down, grasped her arm, and gently helped her regain her feet.

Up close, Rocco found her very attractive, despite her disheveled state.

"You alright?" he repeated. She began to come out of the trancelike state.

"Thank you," she said in a weakened, traumatized tone. It was almost a whisper.

"How'd you get mixed up with those animals?"

She shook her head and gazed down at her feet in shame, weeping. "I-I just s-stopped in the club for a drink on my way home from work," she explained. Her voice was still hitching somewhat as her tears abated. "I should never have done that.

They s-started bothering me as soon as they came in and n-no one in that place would lift a hand to s-stop them."

"People keep to themselves in this neighborhood," Rocco pointed out. He didn't know what else to say. If he were in that bar, he certainly would've put a stop to the sailor's abuse. Unlike most people, who didn't like to get involved, Rocco seldom hesitated to render aid to someone in trouble, particularly a helpless girl.

"I guess so."

She paused to collect herself, wiping away the mascara stain that had tracked down her cheeks. "When I left the bar, they followed me," she continued.

"Well, you're fine now."

"I don't know what would have happened if you didn't come along when you did," she said.

"It was nothing."

"I owe you my life."

"You don't owe me anything."

"How can I ever repay you?"

Rocco looked at her and then glanced along the long, darkened stretch of Atwells Avenue, where his hotel was several blocks in the distance.

He later recalled she had an adorable smile, pretty blue eyes, and cooked an amazing breakfast in the morning.

CHAPTER 41

"I think our police are excellent, probably because
I have not done anything that has occasioned being
beaten up by these good men." – Clement Freud

Rocco Anthony Balliro couldn't quite remember when Chinese food tasted so good. Perhaps it had something to do with his dining companions, three very attractive young women, who were joining him in the takeout indulgence. Or maybe it was because he was finally back in the Boston area, Chelsea, actually, after two months on the lam in Connecticut and Rhode Island.

Growing stir crazy after a couple of weeks in Providence, Rocco decided it was time to pull up stakes and head north. Homesick, he yearned to see family and friends. Packing the few possessions he'd accumulated, he said his goodbyes to Paulie Colicci, who'd stopped by the hotel with some cash to tide his friend over. They walked together to retrieve Rocco's borrowed car, which had been stashed in a nearby vacant lot.

"So ... Boston?" asked Colicci. "You're going back?"

"Yeah."

"You think that's wise?"

"No," replied Rocco honestly. "But I gotta make some money. And I can't do it here. The Man would have a shit-fit."

"Uh huh." Colicci had to agree. The often ruthless Patriarca wouldn't take kindly to a low-level enforcer the likes of Rocco Balliro setting up shop literally under his nose. Patriarca and Tameleo were sympathetic to Rocco's plight and allowed him to take refuge in Providence. But there was a limit to their generosity.

"Stay in touch, Paulie," Rocco said as he pulled open the car door with a rusty creak.

"Sure. I'll give you a call."

Paulie Colicci never made that phone call. It was the last time Rocco would see his friend alive.

Colicci was arrested later that summer for a minor parole violation and wound up back behind bars. It was Paulie's opinion that the charges against him were bogus and he figured he'd be out in no time. To be certain, though, he reached out to his boss, Raymond Patriarca. Colicci was of the belief that The Man could conjure a little magic, have the charges overturned, and spring him from jail sooner than later. The request, however, fell on deaf ears. Patriarca, as Rocco later recalled hearing, "didn't give a shit."

As weeks grew into months, Colicci became increasingly frustrated with the lack of response from Federal Hill. As he simmered in a cell at the Rhode Island State Penitentiary in Cranston, Colicci believed that Patriarca had neglected him. He expressed this rebellious thought in a letter. His anger unrestrained, Colicci described the highly-respected and feared mob boss as a "fag" in the correspondence. He might as well have penned his own obituary.

Colicci was eventually released from prison but the stage was set. Patriarca was not a particularly happy man. As others would attest, if their tongues weren't silenced by fear of deadly retribution, The Man did not take kindly to insults, especially from the likes of Colicci, a lowly soldier in his organization.

On the afternoon of July 21, 1964, a guest of the Sheraton Motor Inn in Quincy, Massachusetts was walking his dog in the sun-baked parking lot when the animal began to incessantly bark at a parked car.

Stooping over to inspect under the vehicle, the dog-walker noticed a pool of brownish substance pooling beneath the trunk. It had the thick texture of gravy and was steadily dripping from the vehicle. There was also a fetid odor which seemed to be coming from somewhere inside the car.

Baffled, the man summoned the motel manager who, in turn, contacted the Quincy police. When the authorities arrived and forced open the trunk, a pair of rotting, bloated corpses was revealed. The overwhelming stench sickened the cops unfortunate enough to be standing nearby.

The body of thirty-nine year old Colicci was discovered tightly wedged in the depths of the trunk. In the sweltering heat, which had gripped the Boston area for several days, decomposition had accelerated rapidly. His remains were unrecognizable.

Joining Colicci in the trunk-turned-coffin of the Chevrolet Impala was Vincent Bisesi, age forty. Bisesi, also of Rhode Island, was an incidental victim. Simply put, he was in the wrong place at the wrong time when assassins came calling.

According to the Associated Press account published July 24, 1964, a cause of death was quickly established. "Medical examiner George Dalton ordered the men removed to a Quincy funeral home for an autopsy," the article recounted. "A policeman who asked that his name be withheld said one of the men appeared to have been shot in the back of the head."

The killers of Colicci and Bisesi were never brought to justice for the brutal murders. In later years, Colicci's name was unceremoniously added as the sixth victim on a list of sixty-one men killed during the infamous Boston Irish gang wars that endured from 1961 to 1967.

"Anthony, honey, want some more?"

Rocco snapped out of a daze and glanced up from the couch to see a pretty face hovering over him. Rail thin and dressed in a pale yellow, snuggly-fitting sweater, twenty-three-year-old Jeannette McDonough was the married girlfriend of Jimmy D'Angelo. Jimmy, the younger brother of Rocco's fur-transporting cohort Johnny D'Angelo, was doing a stint for robbery. Jeannette's estranged husband William was likewise jailed, serving a stretch at Deer Island for assault and battery.

"More rice?" she repeated. In one hand, she balanced a white container overflowing with fried rice and in the other, a serving spoon.

"Uh, yeah, sure," he finally replied, lifting the dinner plate that was resting on his lap. "I'm starved."

Not quite starved, he thought as he watched Jeannette ladle spoonfuls of steaming rice. The night before, Rocco had virtually gorged himself on a fried seafood dinner prepared by Jess Jackson, a close friend of the Balliro brothers. Jackson owned a restaurant on Massachusetts Avenue in the bustling South End and had generously arranged for Rocco to camp out for several days in a vacant apartment above his popular establishment. The accommodations were a welcome upgrade to the Federal Hill hotel room, which had grown dreary and depressing.

"Say when," said Jeannette, her hair teased skyward in a huge beehive.

"When."

"There ya go," she said, her eyes twinkling behind a pair of fashionable eyeglasses. "*Mangia*."

"Thanks."

"Another beer?"

Rocco, with a forkful of rice poised at his mouth, glanced at the near-empty bottle resting on the edge of the coffee table and nodded.

"Okay, honey, right back," she assured.

Jeannette retreated toward the kitchen, her perfect rear end dancing in a pair of skintight blue jeans topped by an impossibly narrow waistline. Her petite, hourglass figure somewhat reminded him of Toby, which triggered a twinge of pain. Rocco could not foresee a time, even after years had gone by, that he would ever cease mourning the loss of his girlfriend and her son. He would always be haunted by the events of that dreadful night back in February. The ache in his heart, he was afraid, had become a fixture.

It was Friday, August 2, 1963, and six months had passed since the shootings by the Boston Police. The felonious Boston Police that is, at least in the opinion held by many who were close to the case. And it wasn't just friends and family raising the specter of police misconduct. Others, without ties to the Balliro family, questioned the audacity of police officers casually placing seven innocent women and children in harm's way during a potentially perilous operation, unsanctioned, to nab an escaped convict. There wasn't a semblance of common sense in their absurd scheme. An intentionally darkened apartment set up to trap and apprehend Rocco Balliro? The potential for violence and gunfire? Mothers, and their babies sleeping nearby? Common sense? More like it outright stupidity.

The Boston Police, as part of damage control, claimed the officers weren't staking out the apartment as disclosed but rather, were there to protect Toby, Mary Adams, and the children should Rocco Balliro decide pay a visit. If that unsupported claim was truthful, however, then why were the lights in the dwelling extinguished and why were the men hidden in the darkness?

Of course, as long as he avoided capture, Rocco couldn't dispute charges or describe what *really* took place that night. He couldn't tell a judge and jury about the gunshots he heard coming from inside the apartment as he and his associates fled.

Rocco was convinced that it was police bullets that killed Toby and little Mark. There had to be evidence, ballistics, perhaps, that would exonerate him. Witnesses? Maybe one of the three cops who were staked out in the apartment that night, consumed with guilt, would come forward. *Yeah, sure,* Rocco thought, *an honest cop? Gimme a break.*

What charges would he face? While Rocco never denied storming the apartment and engaging the police, he wouldn't admit to killing anyone, much less the woman he loved. A first-degree murder charge could bring the death penalty, but more likely life behind bars without the possibility of parole. He wouldn't accept that. But a manslaughter rap for sparking the chain of events? Fifteen, maybe twenty years. That's prison time he could do. He'd be out in his mid-forties, earlier with good behavior.

Jamming the fork into the half-eaten mound of fried rice, Rocco leaned forward and set the plate on the table. His eyes, it seemed, were bigger than his stomach. Sliding back into the couch, he closed his eyes and tried to tune out the drone of the television. In the distant kitchen, he detected the muffled chatter of his three hosts but couldn't discern what they were saying. Not that it mattered. He was dog tired. Forty days on the run had taken a toll on him.

Rocco was startled by a knock at the apartment door.

"Jesus, who the hell is that?"

Jeannette emerged from the kitchen and scurried toward the door.

"Stay put, Anthony," she whispered, touching a finger to her lips to silence him. "I'll see."

Instinctively, Rocco reached around to his lower back and wrapped his fingers around the grip of his .45. His heart rate accelerated in anticipation of yet another confrontation. Was it the cops? Not likely; he would've heard them coming up the rickety staircase. From where he sat, he had a clear view of the door and watched anxiously as Jeannette undid the chain and twisted the lock. She opened the door a sliver, peering into the dim hallway beyond. Rocco braced. Once again, he was caught between fight or flight.

"Hey, Jeannette," said an unfamiliar female voice from beyond the door.

A woman, Rocco thought. *No threat there.* He loosened his grip on the weapon.

"Hello, Helen," was the return greeting from Jeannette, cold and standoffish. Rocco sensed that the unseen woman was not welcome.

"Can we come in and hang out with you?"

We? More than one person out there, Rocco presumed.

"We're kinda busy," Jeannette sourly replied.

"I smell Chinese food. Can we join you?"

"Um, no–"

Before Jeanette could get the words out of her mouth, the woman in the hallway shoved the door inward and barged into the apartment. Jeanette stumbled backward but caught her balance in time to guide the uninvited individual back across the threshold. But it was too late. She'd already caught a glimpse of the guest sitting on the couch.

"Hey, isn't that Roc–"

"Another time, okay?" Jeannette snapped as she brusquely closed and bolted the door. Lowering her head, she inhaled deeply and then glanced at her houseguest, who sported an expression of mild amusement.

"Who was that," he quizzed.

"Nobody."

"You don't like this person I take it?"

"She's a trouble making bitch."

"She saw me," Rocco nonchalantly pointed out. "I think she knew who I was."

"Don't worry about it."

"Is she gonna be a problem?"

"Meaning?"

"You wouldn't let her in," Rocco said. "She must be pissed off."

Jeannette put her hands on her slender hips, dipped her head, and gave him one of those looks. Her expression said it all.

"Okay, okay," he succumbed. "I'll shut up."

"Uh huh. Oh shit, I forgot your beer."

Again, Rocco took notice as she sashayed toward the kitchen. *Jimmy D'Angelo snared a one-of-a-kind with this beauty*, he thought. *What a knockout.*

Retrieving the dinner plate, he balanced it on his lap, and resumed his original position on the plush couch. The rice had gone cold but he began to eat again anyway.

Time was inexorably slipping by and Rocco was again growing weary. Sinking into the comfortable couch, it was unlikely he'd stay awake for long. He'd already decided to crash for the night right where he was. Jeannette and her sister were not opposed.

It was just after eight-thirty and darkness had settled over Chelsea. August nights were typically hot and humid in the Boston-area, making for uncomfortable sleep. But this night was unseasonably pleasant. A light breeze rustled the leaves on the tree just outside the second floor apartment. Rocco, his eyes half-closed, found himself fading into sleep.

Jeannette had long since brought his beer and promptly returned to the kitchen to take up another round of gossip with her nineteen-year-old sister, Joanna Cefala, who shared the apartment, and Mary Viola, a friend from East Boston.

On the television, Ed Sullivan was cracking jokes for a studio audience. The volume was too low for Rocco to hear but he wasn't much interested. What did catch his attention, however, was the sound of activity in the street below. It was unmistakably car doors slamming shut, lots of them.

Rocco's heart sank, like a ship's anchor to the sea bottom. *No, it can't be*, he thought, with growing alarm. Suddenly, he was sweating profusely. He rose from the couch and made his way over to the window facing out to Chestnut Street. Rocco turned to see if Jeannette and the girls had heard him get up. They remained in the kitchen, out of sight.

With a trembling hand, he grasped the thin, sheer curtain framing the window and pulled it aside several inches, taking great care not to reveal himself to those outside. Leaning slightly forward to get a better look, his suspicions were confirmed. He froze, spellbound by the gripping exhibition unfolding on the street below.

"Anthony?"

Startled, he released the curtain and spun around. Jeannette was standing behind him.

"What's the matter?" she asked. Deep concern overspread her pretty face.

"The whole fuckin' Chelsea police force is out there," he hissed through clenched teeth.

Jeannette, now joined by Joanna and Mary, turned pale with fear but said nothing. The trio, their faces drawn, remained silent as Rocco risked another look.

"Jesus," he moaned, his throat hoarse and raspy as dread firmly took hold. "There's gotta be a hundred cops out there."

"Anthony, I'm so s-sorry," Jeannette stammered. Tears were forming in her eyes.

"For what?"

"Helen."

"Who?"

"Helen," she repeated. "That bitch I kicked out of here. She must've recognized you and called the police."

Jeannette, as it turned out, hit the nail on the head. The shunned woman had, in fact, tipped off the cops.

"An unidentified woman called Chelsea police headquarters and told Patrolman Henry Kwiatkowski: if you want Rocco Balliro, come here now," wrote reporter Robert Bassett for the morning edition. "It's 219 Chestnut Street. Balliro is here. Then she hung up."

With only minutes to spare, Rocco sprang to action. He had to protect the girls.

"Listen up," he insisted. He circled the coffee table. The three young women remained speechless. Their faces were pale with fear. "Look, girls, the cops will say you was hiding me. I'm gonna tell them I was holding you hostage. Stick to that story, okay?"

At the base of the staircase, there was a dreadful commotion. The police were assembling. There was no attempt made by the contingent to mask their imminent approach.

Jeannette broke her silence. "But Anthony, what–" she began but he cut her short.

"Just do as I say!" he shouted above the din of the gathering storm at the base of the stairs. "I'll take the heat."

The cops had begun to file up the staircase, their heavy combat boots thudding loudly against the wooden steps. Muffled voices resonated from beyond the apartment walls, closing fast. There was also, Rocco noted with a shudder, the telltale metallic clicking sound as the lawmen chambered shotguns with deadly shells.

Rocco brandished his .45 caliber and disengaged the safety. Unlike the night he encountered Clifford on the icy streets of Roxbury, when he had just two bullets to work with, his weapon was now fully loaded.

Jeannette looked warily at the gun.

"Hostages, right?" he asked as he popped the clip and examined the contents. "*Capiche?*"

The girls nodded in unison.

An instant later, all hell broke loose. A police officer kicked in the door, which splintered off the hinges and slammed violently against the inner wall. Shattered shards of wood flew in all directions. Several plainclothes policemen, guns drawn, swarmed into the apartment like a wave of angry hornets. But the cagey jail breaker they sought had already fled, bolting from the room. He sprinted through the kitchen and burst through another egress that led to an exterior porch at the rear of the triple-decker.

The cops hurriedly pursued, led by a veteran Chelsea lawman later identified as Captain Robert Renfrew. He dashed through the apartment with shotgun lowered, ready to blast away. In the distant background, babies were wailing. The assault on the apartment had woken Jeannette McDonough's children.

"Balliro, this is the police!" Renfrew shouted.

Rocco realized he was hopelessly trapped. The only means to escape the cramped porch, he quickly discovered, was to leap over a three foot, picket fence railing. Feasible, certainly, but the building was surrounded by heavily-armed police. Surely, there were officers positioned somewhere in the alley below who would pounce once he reached the ground. That was *after* he sustained broken bones on impact with the asphalt surface.

Detecting another door to his left, Rocco reached for the knob, and gave it a twist. It was a storage closet, unlocked and filled with mops, brooms, and other cleaning materials. He quickly ducked inside and closed the door behind him. It was pitch black inside the tiny space. Holding his breath, Rocco listened intently. Within seconds, the unmistakable sound of thudding boots could be heard on the porch, inches away. The fugitive was out of sight but cornered. There was nowhere to run.

Closing his eyes tightly, Rocco hastily weighed his options. There were two. He could burst out the broom closet and go down shooting in a final, deadly act of defiance. Or he could give up and let the courts decide his fate.

Feeling around in the darkness, Rocco sought the one item that might save his life. His hand came upon a piece of cloth, which he'd glimpsed just before pulling the door shut. Drawing a deep breath, he opened the closet door several inches and extended his hand outward. In it, he waved a white rag of surrender. For a second, he braced, half-expecting a cop with an itchy trigger finger to blow his hand off.

Rocco later found out that he had good reason to worry. The Chelsea police who were dispatched to apprehend the wanted man were issued shoot to kill orders. The dragnet would take him dead or alive. And they were armed to the teeth, prepared to wage a mini-war in the quiet urban neighborhood, if necessary. According to newspaper accounts, police hardware included assorted shotguns, carbines, sub-machine guns, and gas bombs. If their quarry so much as flinched, it would've cost him his life.

Rocco wasn't aware of it at the time but tensions amongst the Chelsea police contingent were taut following a tragic event that occurred literally hours before. In nearby Boston, forty-six-year-old police patrolman James B. O'Leary was shot and killed during a foot pursuit of several liquor store robbery suspects. The death of their *brother* in the line of duty still freshly imprinted on their minds, these Chelsea police officers were taking no chances with the apprehension of the escape artist.

"Alright, Balliro, come out of there. Now!" barked Renfrew, who was stationed several feet from the meager hiding place.

"Easy," Rocco responded. He tried to swallow but was unable; his constricted throat was completely parched. "Don't shoot. I'm gonna slide my gun out, okay?"

"Do it slowly! Don't try anything stupid."

Stooping down inside the closet, Rocco edged the door open wider, and placed the .45 caliber handgun flat on the wooden porch surface. He gave the weapon a little shove with his fingertips, sliding it toward the waiting police officers. He then stood upright and slowly emerged into the open to find several scowling uniformed men glaring at him. Each was aiming a shotgun at his midsection.

"I think the Chelsea police did a good job," Rocco Balliro casually remarked to an assembly of reporters in a standing-room-only squad room soon after he was booked and placed in custody. "A lot better than the police in Roxbury did."

Described as "haggard" by observers, the twenty-six year old, wearing black pants and a white, button-down dress shirt, looked more like forty. He had aged. Pale and gaunt, his hair had grayed near the temples. He claimed that he had not grown a scruffy goatee and dyed his hair as part of a disguise. "It's just worry," the accused insisted to the throng of reporters, representing both newsprint and television. Men scribbled in notebooks and cameras whirred as he spoke.

Meanwhile, nearly two hundred curious residents had congregated in the street outside the walls of the Chelsea police station, hoping to catch sight of the man characterized as "one of the most dangerous criminals ever the object of search by local law enforcement agencies." Of course, the ill-informed individual who made that farfetched claim left a certain Boston Strangler out of the equation.

Rocco was asked why he returned to the Boston area when he could've remained on the loose.

"I came back to clear my name," he declared. He cast his eyes downward and added, "I knew the cards were stacked against me, that I wouldn't get a fair shake, and that I'd go to the can for something I didn't do. That's why I broke out."

From the back of the room, Rocco heard one of the interviewers murmuring Toby's name.

"I didn't shoot her," he declared defiantly. One of television reporters latched on to the tense moment and asked, "Who did kill them, Rocco?"

"You know *who* killed them," was his answer. The comment was carefully measured, but steady and sure. It resulted in a brief, yet powerful pause to the interview.

Several of the Chelsea cops on hand chafed at the insinuation that their Boston counterparts had killed a young woman and her child in cold blood. Rocco glanced around the small, cramped room and studied the faces of the lawmen. He was met with harsh, unblinking scowls. There was unbridled rage in their eyes – had they returned to the Chelsea porch at that pivotal moment, the outcome might have been different.

The scuttlebutt had long since been floated that Rocco Balliro and his supporters had enlisted inside help in the jail break but when asked, he refuted the hearsay. "No. I did it alone and I didn't have any help from anyone," he lied. "And I didn't have any help from anyone all the time I was out. I took care of myself. I didn't impose on anybody."

Another reporter leveled the obvious follow-up question, asking why Rocco broke out of the Charles Street Jail on that particular June night. If he was, in fact, innocent of the crime as he vehemently insisted, why flee the day before his trial and an opportunity to profess innocence?

"Because I didn't have a chance," the prisoner explained, shrugging. "They all know me." Rocco was, of course, referring to his underworld ties. There was no denying his wise guy pedigree. Which jury, no matter how impartial, could ignore the life he'd led prior to the shootings? For all intents and purposes, he was an incident just waiting to happen.

He adjusted handcuffs that burrowed deeply into his wrists, leaving them reddened and sore. A watchful detective eyed him suspiciously.

An intrepid newsman drilled deeper, asking about a rumor raised that Rocco was not going to be taken alive in Chelsea, that he intended to shoot it out with the cops.

"Yes, of course I would have," he asserted. "I wasn't carrying the .45 caliber for nothing. But I was holding these people hostage. I gave up because I didn't want the same thing to happen that happened in Roxbury."

Rocco later learned that Jeannette McDonough had complied with his advice and claimed under police scrutiny that she and her companions were held hostage. "He told me to keep my mouth shut or he would kill my eight-month-old son," she maintained.

Along with her sister and friend, Jeannette was brought in by the Chelsea police, who were fully aware that the three women were friends with the wanted man and their hostage story was fraudulent. The authorities, led by Chelsea police Chief Abraham Burgin, rejected the notion that Rocco Balliro had held the women against their will. They believed their prey had visited the McDonough apartment a number of times. They also dismissed the gossip that he'd traveled "halfway across the country," as Rocco claimed, believing instead that he remained local, drifting from one friend's apartment to another.

The women were charged as accessories for harboring a fugitive and held on ten thousand dollars bail each. The court was lenient, however, due to their young age and the fact that Jeannette had three small children under her care. Release from the lock-up soon followed with some legal wrangling from defense attorney Joseph J. Balliro, Rocco's cousin.

Following the press conference and a round of questioning by detectives, Rocco was transported back to the festering Charles Street jail. He was placed in a segregation cell, away from the inmate population. His only companions were pigeons, rats, and a mute guard. Despite his pleas, he was not allowed to see his brother Rudy.

Corrections officials, under fire in the aftermath of the daring escape, were taking no chances with their clever, calculating inmate. Rocco Balliro was placed under twenty-four hour guard, both inside and outside the jail; cops were actually tasked with patrolling the exterior of the walls, conducting surveillance day and night.

Seventeen years would pass before Rocco Anthony Balliro engineered another successful prison escape.

CHAPTER 42

"A lawyer with his briefcase can steal more than a hundred men with guns." – Mario Puzo.

On a chilly September afternoon in 1963, defendants Rocco Balliro, his brother Salvatore, and their co-defendant Albert Ciocco were found guilty of first-degree murder in the deaths of Toby and Mark Wagner, mother and child.

The Suffolk Superior Court jury set aside the death penalty and the trio was sentenced to life imprisonment for their crimes. Guilty verdicts were also returned on the lesser indictment of breaking and entering into a dwelling in the night with intent to commit an assault by means of a dangerous weapon.

The convictions marked the end of a trial that lasted only fifteen days.

In the midst of a slow-paced judicial system rife with delays, lapses, and attorneys wrangling for continuances, the trial of Rocco Balliro and his two co-defendants was swift, indeed.

"One minute, I was in the Charles Street Jail awaiting trial," said the defendant in disbelief, "and the next, I was doing hard time at Walpole. It was all too quick. And the case against us was weak. There were a lot of holes in witness testimony."

One of "holes" Rocco referred to was none other than twenty-one-year-old Mary Adams, who was purportedly an eye witness to an execution. She claimed, under oath, that she saw Rocco Balliro walk over to Toby Wagner and fire a bullet point blank into her head. He also shot Mark in the stomach, she insisted.

Rocco Balliro's defense attorney made a mockery out of Mary Adams. As part of his opening statement, Neil Colicchio pointed out to the jury that the Adams woman had been held in custody by the police for a number of months and he strongly suspected she was coached. The authorities insisted she was held for her own protection, but the defense team claimed it also gave the cops unfettered access to her, to ensure she got her story straight while on the witness stand.

Oddly enough, pending drug charges against her husband Bob were mysteriously dropped while she was in custody. "Something to sweeten the pot for providing damning eyewitness testimony perhaps," insinuated one official who was close to the case but preferred to remain anonymous.

In later years, Boston Police Detective Sergeant Matthew King, who was in charge of the police internal investigation, said in an affidavit, "Mary Adams' testimony was always suspect due to her relationship to the parties."

"Mrs. Adams," began Colicchio, "the man you describe as having fired a bullet into the head of Toby Wagner, is he in this courtroom today?"

"Yes," she meekly replied.

"And the man you claim shot Mrs. Wagner's son Mark, is he in this courtroom?"

"It's the same guy."

"For the court, would you please point to him?"

Tentatively, Mary Adams leveled a trembling hand and index finger in the direction of the defendant. Rocco simply stared back at her, expressionless.

"And you're sure that's the man you saw in your apartment on the night in question?"

"Yes."

"You saw him kill your sister-in-law in cold blood. Is that correct, ma'am?"

"Yes."

"According to your statement to the police, he shot her in the head?"

"Yes."

"And her son?"

"Yes. Both of them. He shot both of them."

"Mrs. Adams," he continued, skillfully luring the witness toward perjury like a spider spinning a web. "That night, in your apartment, it was dark. Pitch dark. Am I correct?"

"Y-yes," she stammered in response. "But I ... I could s-see."

"Really, Mrs. Adams? *You* could see?"

The twenty-one year old began to show her youth under the heat of a cross examination. "Uh huh. Yes."

"You could see, but the police officers couldn't?"

"Uh, no. I mean, yes?"

"Is that an answer or a question, Mrs. Adams?"

"Yes, I could see." She was unraveling.

Rocco, who recounted the tense exchange, said he began to feel better about his chances as his lawyer pressed the prosecution's witness.

Colicchio walked over to the defendant's table and retrieved a document that was resting on top of a stack of notebooks and folders. Returning to the witness stand, he cleared his throat for effect and pretended to read even though he knew, word-for-word, what was written.

"Mrs. Adams," he began, "I have here the Boston police report which describes in some detail the events that took place on February 2, 1963. While you were in protective custody, do you recall reading this narrative?"

"No."

"Well, I won't trouble you and this court by sharing the entire account," the lawyer said. "But there is one passage that caught my attention. Your Honor, may I?"

"Go ahead," the judge grunted.

"It describes the officers aiming their weapons and firing at gun flashes. I assume this was because they couldn't see who was holding those guns in the darkness."

"Mary Adams was like a panicked rabbit hunted by a skulk of foxes," said Bill Balliro, on hand to support his brother.

Her face had gone pale and she reached for the glass of water positioned in front of her. As she picked it up and took a sip, her hand was noticeably trembling.

"Mrs. Adams, I'll say it again, so we're sure we all understand."

She glanced desperately toward the prosecuting attorney who lowered his head, conceding he'd lost his witness. Her credibility had dipped to zero.

"I'll repeat: it was so dark in your apartment that the Boston Police admitted they were aiming at gun flashes," the attorney reminded her, as if she could have forgotten. "They couldn't see anything or anyone. And yet you profess some sort of superior eyesight that allowed you to see my client shoot Toby Wagner point blank. And you did this from behind a couch, no less?"

Colicchio didn't wait for a response. He had this witness on the ropes and went in for the finish. Rocco Balliro, meanwhile, was thoroughly enjoying watching her squirm.

"Mrs. Adams?"

"Yes?"

"Let us agree that you could see in the dark," the crafty lawyer continued, firmly planting a seed of doubt in the jury. "Are you sure that this is the man you saw fire a weapon?"

"Yes, I'm sure."

"Could you describe him to the court?"

"What?"

Colicchio repeated, "I want you to describe him to me."

Mary Adams looked frantically toward the judge, who came to her aid. "Are you going somewhere with this line of questioning, Mr. Colicchio?"

"Yes, Your Honor."

"Get on with it, then."

"Sorry, Your Honor," he said. "Mrs. Adams, to please the court, would you describe the defendant."

Taking a deep breath and fighting back tears, she began, "He's tall and ... um ... thin. He has a full head of hair. It's a little gray on the sides."

"Go on."

"What else do you want me to say?"

"His face," the lawyer gruffly urged. "I want you to describe his face."

"He's handsome, good looking," she said. "And, um, clean-shaven."

"I'm sorry, could you repeat that for the jury, a little louder please."

"He's clean-shaven?"

"And this is the very same *clean-shaven* man you saw, clearly, in your dark apartment that night?"

"Yes."

"This is the man you claim shot Toby Wagner? And Mark Wagner?"

"Yes!" she shouted, her frustration having reached a crescendo.

Attorney Colicchio wheeled and returned again to his overflowing briefcase, rummaged for a minute, and produced an 8x10 black-and-white photograph. The tension in the courtroom was thick. He prepared to finish off the prosecution's star witness.

"Your Honor and members of the jury, if I may," he said, holding up an enlarged mugshot photo of Rocco for all to see. It had been taken soon after he turned himself in to the Everett police. In the photo, the defendant had a thick, dark beard on his face. He'd begun to grow it after escaping from the New Bedford House of Corrections as a means to conceal his identity. "This, you might recognize, is Rocco Anthony Balliro. With a full beard. It is a beard, I might add, that was on his face the night of the shootings."

Preceding his murder trial, in early August 1963, Rocco stood before Suffolk Superior Courthouse Judge Robert Sullivan to answer to the escape charge.

As if the bright lights and television cameras in his face during the impromptu Chelsea news conference weren't enough, his ego was stroked further during the trip from the Charles Street Jail for this court appearance. Rocco was transported by a heavily-armed police detail numbering at least twenty men. The authorities took serious his ingenuity and ability to outwit captors. They weren't taking any chances.

Manacled at ankles and wrists, the restrictive chains jangled as Rocco entered the court building and trudged up two flights of stairs. It was hot in the foyer and he broke into a sweat with the effort. Reaching the courtroom, brimming with reporters and spectators as well as several family members, Rocco stood mute when asked to enter a plea. Judge Sullivan looked to the defendant's attorney, Neil Colicchio, for clarification.

"Does your client wish to enter a plea?"

"No, Your Honor," Colicchio replied, glancing up from his briefs. "He does not."

"Well, then," Sullivan said, "the court will enter one for him: not guilty in the indictment for escape. Understood?"

Colicchio answered for his client. "Yes, Your Honor, Mr. Balliro understands."

Rocco, meanwhile, was fuming. He'd learned from a note slipped to him during a recess that his father, Rosario Balliro, was facing arraignment on bomb charges, literally steps away in a courtroom on the main floor of the same building.

Rocco was incensed that the Boston police department had embarked on what he termed a "witch hunt" following his Chelsea capture. Glory-seeking District Attorney Garrett

Byrne wasn't satisfied with just one Balliro in custody; he wanted to see the entire clan behind bars.

On the morning of August 5, 1963, a police detachment was dispatched to the Balliro home at 20 Bartlett Place in the North End. They frightened Angela, rifled through drawers, ripped apart boxes, and left much of the family belongings in disarray. Byrne later claimed he was probing for incriminating evidence tied to those who helped the fugitive evade arrest.

Collared in the pre-dawn raid was the sixty-seven-year-old family patriarch, along with the youngest of the six Balliro brothers, twenty-one-year-old Bruno. The elder was brought in for possession of explosives. Three homemade bombs were found in the search which, according to Sergeant Thomas Johnston, had the capacity to render substantial damage if ignited, intentionally or otherwise.

"The three of them were made out of what appeared to be juice cans," described Johnston, head of the Boston Police Bomb Squad. "The cans were wrapped with masking tape covered by friction tape. They contained an extremely fast explosive and had a fast fuse, something like a firecracker fuse but larger. It took us three hours to dismantle the bombs."

Also recovered during the raid was a .357 Magnum revolver, which was hidden in the bottom of a fishing wader. Police officials tied the powerful weapon to Bruno Balliro. One informative cop told a reporter that the gun could "shoot out an engine block."

Bruno was later released while his father made bail. Both returned home to the North End to reunite with family.

Rocco, meanwhile, was brought back to Charles Street to await trial for murder.

Several days after his arrest in Chelsea, a brief conversation regarding Rocco Balliro was picked up by the FBI via the microphone surveillance planted in the

Providence office of Raymond Patriarca. The conversation, officials believed, took place between the reputed mob boss and one of his underlings.

"On 8/8/63," the transcription of the exchange read, "the informant advised than an unman (unknown man) was of the opinion that Rocco Balliro did not kill the child in Roxbury, Mass., several months ago for which crime Balliro is now being held. He is of the opinion that police officers who were trying to apprehend Balliro at the time were responsible for the death of the child."

It was regrettable that Rocco's own flesh and blood failed to share a similar standpoint.

After winning an appeal of the 1963 convictions because the judge in that trial erred in denying the defense team interview access to a number of key witnesses, Rocco Balliro and his colleagues were granted a new trial which commenced nearly two years later, on August 18, 1965. In hindsight, Rocco might have been better served to sidestep further legal proceedings and certain lawyers, particularly those with an agenda.

Like an urban legend that flourishes with the passage of time, there will often be variations and embellishments in the verbal portrayal of events that took place five decades ago. But one aspect remained a constant in 1965 and beyond: Rocco Anthony Balliro was coerced by his cousin Joseph J. Balliro Jr. into accepting a plea of first-degree murder, and in doing so, essentially signed on the dotted line agreeing to a lifelong stay in the Massachusetts Correctional system.

The reason behind the arm twisting had to do with a hasty bargaining session conducted between the principal attorney and a judge who was seeking the easy way out of what promised to be a long, drawn out trial.

Rudy Balliro was represented by cousin Joe while Rocco was paired with Neil Colicchio.

As Rocco recalled, he was locked up in a pre-trial holding cell of the Suffolk Superior Court when he was approached by the tandem of lawyers.

"Well, I was called over to the screen," Rocco recounted. "I was told by attorney Joseph Balliro that there was talk between them and the presiding judge, Mr. Felix Forte. And they told me, he was willing to reduce the charges of my brother and my co-defendant, Ciocco, to manslaughter if I would agree to plead guilty to the original indictment of murder in the first degree."

Rocco, of course, resisted. He wasn't about to capitulate to such a preposterous arrangement. He didn't care that it was his highly-respected cousin Joe who had brokered the deal. The bargain was no bargain for Rocco. It certainly wasn't negotiated with *his* best interest in mind. In essence, he'd be conceding guilt to a crime he didn't commit. Admit to killing Toby and Mark? Never. He would never yield.

Distraught and angered, Rocco backed up in the holding cage. Behind him, sitting quietly on a steel bench, were Rudy and Slim. Neither man spoke. They averted their gaze and waited.

"No fuckin' way, Joe," Rocco said. He was seething. "I'm not gonna do it."

"Wait a minute," his cousin urged. "Let me talk to you."

"You're wasting your time."

"Anthony, now listen to me," the family attorney insisted. "Quiet down."

"C'mon, Rocco, you gotta listen to what he has to say," Colicchio interjected.

The comment earned the lawyer a scornful look from his rebellious client. Rocco knew the man was nothing more than a puppet to be manipulated by the influential Joseph J. Balliro Jr. It was no secret that Colicchio had been mentored for a number of years by the defendant's domineering cousin. As attorney Balliro's protégé, he had no choice but to agree with a deal that would send his client to prison for life. There would be no rebuttal on his part.

"But I ain't guilty of murder!"

"I know," said his cousin Joe in a soft, comforting voice. "But–"

"I don't think I should do this," Rocco interrupted. He leaned in closer and laced his fingers through the chicken-wire screen. Lowering his voice, he glared menacingly at the pair of attorneys with their fancy suits and added, "In fact, I am not going to do this."

"Anthony–"

"I'm not guilty."

"You're not guilty of the murders, Anthony," his cousin agreed with a nod, "but this was your beef and you did ask your brother to go with you to that apartment."

Rocco felt the noose tightening.

"Jesus, this is fuckin' crazy!"

"Your brother is married," the attorney said, ignoring the rants. "He has a wife and child at home. You should do the right thing."

Joe Balliro wielded an unfair advantage over his cousin. A day earlier, Rocco had appeared in this same courtroom under the influence of narcotics. A court-appointed physician, Dr. Ford, took a blood sample and visually examined the accused, who was determined unfit to stand trial. He described the defendant as "crocked" and the matter was continued for twenty-four hours. But Rocco recalled that he was still coming down from the high when he was brought back to the courthouse the next morning. "It was like having a hangover," he explained.

Rocco gazed downward and said nothing for a moment. When he looked up again, his older brother Joe had appeared and was now standing next to Colicchio. There was suddenly a bitter, acidic taste in his mouth. He couldn't remember what he had for breakfast that morning but whatever it was, it made his stomach roil. His intimidating sibling, stone-faced, said nothing. But his presence alone gave Rocco pause. Cousin Joe had brought out the big guns and was pushing all the right emotional buttons. He could be very convincing. Even at a young age, in his late twenties, Joe Balliro Jr. was already a much sought-after criminal attorney. Still, Rocco defied him, although his resolve was weakening under the pressure.

"I can't believe this is happening," he moaned, his shoulders slumping. "I'm innocent."

"It's your duty to get your brother off the hook, Anthony," his cousin asserted, adding more shame to the mix.

"Yeah, I get that."

Rocco abruptly discontinued the conversation and stormed away, retreating to the rear of the cage. He hated to admit it but Joe was right about a few things. Toby Wagner was dead. Her son Mark was dead. He'd lost *his* family. He'd selfishly dragged his brother into this sordid mess; it was now up to him to get his twin out of it. He should make the sacrifice for the sake of both Rudy and Al Ciocco, so they wouldn't be deprived time spent with their families.

"Hey, brother?"

Rocco hadn't seen Rudy approach from behind.

"You gotta listen to them, Roc," Rudy suggested.

"This is crazy. I ain't guilty."

"I know, brother. I was there," his twin agreed. "But maybe this is the best thing."

Rocco closed his weary eyes and nodded. How could he disagree? His back was against the wall and determination was wavering. He might have been capable of withstanding the persuasion of cousin Joe, and perhaps brother Joe as well, but Rudy was another story altogether.

"Yeah," Rocco finally agreed, lowering his head in a shameful posture. "Maybe you're right."

As much as an hour had passed since attorney Joseph Balliro first approached the dreary holding cell with his dubious proposal.

With brother Rudy at his side, Rocco set his jaw and looked squarely in the eyes of his cousin.

"Go ahead," he finally submitted. "Make the deal."

CHAPTER 43

"True heroism is remarkably sober, very un-dramatic. It is not the urge to surpass all others at whatever cost, but the urge to serve others at whatever cost." – Arthur Ashe

Walpole State Prison was a powder keg just waiting to ignite during the dog days of summer 1966. After months of growing tensions between Department of Corrections officials and the inmate population over poor living conditions, coupled with an unabated flow of narcotics, the fuse was lit for a confrontation.

On a sweltering Friday night in mid-August, the notorious prison, which housed some of the most violent felons in the state, finally reached a boiling point. A riot broke out that quickly escalated and transformed the grounds and a number of buildings into a war zone.

On the exterior, heavily-armed Massachusetts State Troopers, assisting prison officials and corrections officers, ringed the wall and helped man the watch turrets.

Inside, meanwhile, scores of inmates were hurt in the bedlam that ensued. Injuries ran the gamut, from minor cuts and bruises to more serious fractures and lacerations. Most went untreated until after the facility was stabilized.

Fifteen corrections officers were also injured while trying to regain control of the facility that bore the name of a quiet, bedroom community in southeastern Massachusetts. Several guards were hospitalized, including Officer Robert Hayden, twenty-four, who was rushed to the emergency ward at nearby Norwood Hospital suffering from stab wounds. Hayden was knifed in the back multiple times by an unknown assailant, but survived the attack.

There were no fatalities during the uprising. This might not have been the case if not for the actions of an unlikely hero who emerged from the shadows of a tier under siege and risked his own life to save another.

During the early years of his incarceration at MCI-Walpole, Rocco Anthony Balliro was, admittedly, a trouble maker. He frequently got into scrapes with inmates. Worse still, he was often verbally abusive to corrections officers and made threats. He often questioned authority. Regularly spurning the prison rules, Rocco's misconduct bought him the deprivation of several lonesome stretches in solitary confinement, where he claims to have read a large Webster's dictionary cover to cover to occupy his mind.

"I wasn't a model prisoner," he conceded. "I was always high on drugs and did and said a lot of stupid things. I'm not proud of the way I acted during those early years in the can."

On August 12, 1966, Rocco offset some of his prison misdeeds with an act of sheer integrity and bravery. The twenty-nine-year-old inmate, serving the third year of a life sentence, took steps to prevent bloodshed when a corrections officer found himself trapped behind "enemy lines."

According to corrections officer Joseph Guarino, who later in his career was promoted to the rank of deputy superintendent, there was a number of roving inmate gangs destroying prison property and wreaking havoc. Many were armed with hastily rendered weapons fashioned from broken furniture. Shattered table and chair legs, the business end sharpened to a stabbing point, were wielded by a number of prisoners. Others had set small controlled fires and acrid, black smoke billowed from several cells.

Along with a squad of officers, Guarino was dispatched to restore order to the chaotic maximum security section. In the midst of the mayhem, he found himself separated from his men. With little warning and no time to reach safety, Guarino was cornered by an angry pack of about twenty-five to thirty inmates, shouting, "Let's get the screw and kill him!"

Along with another unnamed inmate, Rocco Balliro placed himself in front of Guarino, shielding the heavily outnumbered prison guard from the deadly, rampaging horde. It was a foolhardy move on his part. The inmates, like a pack of ferocious wolves, would surely tear him to shreds. They closed in. But Rocco remained steadfast.

"Don't do it!" he said to them with a stern, unwavering voice.

The throng gave pause, suspicious. Surely, one of their own would not risk life and limb to protect a lowly guard. The let up in their advance, no more than a few seconds, proved enough.

Rocco turned to the officer cowering behind him and muttered, "Get out of here while you can."

At that moment, officers in the inner control station disengaged the huge steel door allowing Guarino to slip through. It immediately closed behind him with a loud clang. He was visibly shaken but unharmed.

"Inmate Rocco Balliro's intervention may well have saved my life that evening," Guarino later wrote in a letter drafted for use in a 1990 commutation petition.

Rocco was also commended by then deputy superintendent Fred Butterworth who, in the aftermath of the revolt, told a *Boston Herald American* reporter that "the North End bad boy" successfully urged a number of inmates to lay down their weapons and return to their cells.

In the days following the mutiny, while prison officials were praising his effort, Rocco was suffering grave consequences for his collaborative role. He was ostracized and his life was threatened. Most days, he needed eyes in the back of his head and was certain that the menacing sideways glances from the men on his tier would be followed by a deadly attack with a crudely-fashioned blade; it was only a matter of time, he figured, before they killed him for colluding with the guards.

His only trustworthy companion was a feral cat, aptly named Max. The guards allowed Rocco to take the animal into the unit and feed it. Aside from his pet, however, Rocco Balliro lived a miserable, paranoid existence for at least a year after the riot.

"In the wake of what I consider to have been a brave act and one that perhaps was deserving of some reward, my life instead became filled with verbal and physical assaults by the inmates with whom, of necessity, I had to live," he wrote years later for a commutation hearing. "Directly or indirectly, I was branded by the inmates of the Massachusetts Correctional System for having saved the life of this young correctional officer."

The Commonwealth cited the need for immediate reform after the incident. Officials sought a remedy that would curtail prison strife and acts of violence on the part of inmates gone berserk. There was far little correction in the *corrections* system, believed many on the outside of the walls.

Reporters sought out Officer Hayden, who was recuperating at home, and asked what he thought might have sparked the disturbance at MCI-Walpole. He suggested that the cause was likely related to an infiltration of contraband drugs. Guarino even went so far as to give the uprising a name – The Pill Riot.

The drug of choice, according to corrections officials, was Talwin which was a popular pain killer similar to morphine and known to produce euphoria. The narcotic pipeline flowed unabated into the prison.

Rocco Balliro, who spent much of his first decade in prison under the influence of one substance or another, couldn't agree more.

"I'm not exaggerating when I say that it was easier to get drugs in prison than on the street back then," Rocco imparted. "There was money to made and a lot of the corrupt guards were in on it."

According to author Jamie Bissonette, who penned *When the Prisoners Ran Walpole: A True Story in the Movement for Prison Abolition*, Talwin distribution was used as a means to subdue the prison population. But there were other methods, according to Bissonette.

"There were no written rules," she claimed. "Guards acted with impunity, and decided policy and punishment arbitrarily. Beatings were a regular part of prison life."

Massachusetts Correctional Institution-Walpole grew out of a need to replace aging facilities elsewhere in the state, including the Charlestown State Prison which, at the time, was the oldest prison in the country. Construction of the sprawling penitentiary in Walpole, which cost nine million dollars, was completed in 1955 and a year later, nearly six hundred inmates had taken up residence inside its fifteen-foot walls topped with wires charged with electricity.

A total of nine observation towers are perched strategically around the perimeter of the intimidating wall affording a bird's-eye view of the interior. From these turret-like structures, corrections officers oversee a dozen housing units, the foundry buildings, and the yard, where inmates congregate and exercise when conditions allowed. The towers were also designed to establish sharpshooters in the event of an uprising.

True to its maximum-security designation, a sixty-bed segregation unit dubbed "Ten Block" was added in 1959 to house those incorrigible prisoners deemed too lethal to mix with the general population.

It was a fetid segment of the prison, loathed by inmates and corrections officers alike. In the midst of this unit was a pair of "blue rooms," used to confine the worst offenders.

"These rooms were regular cells without bed, toilet, sink, chair, or desk," described former corrections officer Michael McLaughlin in his 1989 novel *Screw*, which described in detail the life of a Walpole State Prison guard. "Each had a hole in the floor into which the occupant could urinate and defecate. They also had a solid steel door in addition to the normal grill door. Basically cold and featureless, they seemed like throwbacks to the Dark Ages."

Upset that the renowned prison was associated with the town and a growing detriment to the community's reputation and home values, fed up Walpole residents banded together in the mid-eighties, seeking a new name for the thirty-year-old facility. The townspeople held a contest and after legislation was filed and approved, renamed the prison MCI-Cedar Junction, after a defunct Walpole railroad depot. The new name didn't stick.

Rocco didn't much care what they called the place. He just wanted out. The ink was barely dry on the newspaper accounts of his brief sojourn into heroism, saving Officer Joseph Guarino from an all-but-certain death, when Rocco Balliro resumed what he knew best: planning prison breaks.

Some of his escape schemes were offbeat; others the rantings of a man desperate to taste freedom again.

His brother Rosario "Billy" Balliro shared one of Rocco's more cockamamie plots.

"He once asked me to blow up the supports of the water tower that stood next to the prison wall at Walpole," recalled Billy with a chuckle. "He figured that the tower would fall forward and crush the wall and he would simply run out through the opening."

In 1967, Rocco earned one of the highly sought-after jobs in the foundry, where inmates would emboss license plates for the Massachusetts Registry of Motor Vehicles. It was grueling, dangerous work and the laborers earned a paltry fifty cents a day. But it wasn't a few bucks to spend at the canteen that attracted Rocco and a number of fellow inmates to the hot, smoky foundry.

"Hey, Balliro! C'mere for a minute?"

He didn't glance up from the metal press machine right away. Many a prisoner had lost tips of fingers over of a few seconds of distraction. Closing the lid on the aluminum segment, Rocco slid the locking mechanism across the top of the machine, securing it in place, and applied the press. He stepped back, still wary, and rubbed his hands together, displacing some of the metal shavings that were attached to his thick machinist's gloves.

"Yeah, what's up, Mario?"

Mario, a short but muscular middle-aged Italian guy with thick, dark hair, was one of the first inmates to enter the hallowed halls of MCI-Walpole when it opened for business twelve years before in 1955. He'd been there since, now serving the tail end of a fifteen-year stint for holding up a filling station in East Boston. Beginning his sentence at the one-hundred-fifty year old Charlestown jail, Mario was later transferred from the crumbling city-based jail to the brand new facility built in a suburb thirty miles south of Boston.

He'd been a close pal of Frank Balliro while at Charlestown and later became fast friends with Rocco, assuring Frank that he'd watch over the younger Balliro boy. Easier said than done, he later found.

"We're thinking about getting the fuck outta here."

Rocco's interest was immediately piqued. Escape talk was always music to his ears. "Oh yeah?"

Mario looked over his shoulder, ensuring that a nearby guard tasked with watching the inmate workers wasn't paying attention, as usual. He was sitting with his feet propped up on an old desk, absorbed in a paperback.

"Yeah."

"What's the lowdown?" Rocco asked.

"A tunnel," Mario answering simply.

"You're kidding."

"No," said Mario, resolutely. "I'm not kidding."

"You're gonna dig a fuckin' tunnel?" Rocco queried, a little too loudly.

Mario whipped his head around to see if the officer had heard. To his relief, the man was still buried in his book. "Yeah, that's exactly what we plan to do."

"Where to?"

Mario gave Rocco a sarcastic look and replied, "To my cell, for rainy days." After a pause, he added, "Under the wall, where else?"

"Jesus. That's gotta be more than a hundred yards."

"Don't act so surprised."

"Huh?"

"Who woulda believed you were going to saw through them iron bars?"

Rocco chuckled and said, "Yeah, I guess you're right."

Later, during lunch, Mario shared the plan. The element of trust with Rocco Balliro was assured. After all, he had planned and executed two escapes on his own and spoke only with his most trustworthy confident, Johnny D'Angelo, prior to the New Bedford break, and his brother Rudy before cutting his way out of the Charles Street Jail. This stuff was right up his alley.

"So we found this little room that leads to a sub-basement below the foundry," Mario explained. He twirled and shoveled a forkful of foul-looking pasta into his mouth and loudly chewed as Rocco, who wasn't eating, patiently waited for his brother's friend to go on.

Mario grinned and continued. "The floor is concrete but it's only a thin layer to the soil below."

It was Rocco's turn to smile. "They made it easy for us."

"Yeah."

"I'm ready. I'll dig the whole fuckin' tunnel myself to get out of this place."

"Good."

"When do we get started?"

"No need to wait," Mario replied, cautiously looking over his shoulder to ensure the guard hadn't crept closer. "We start tonight."

The tunnel try by Rocco Balliro and friends wasn't the first of this nature. Several years earlier, in late April 1964, a trio of detainees tried to abbreviate their Walpole prison sentences by digging from the same foundry building. Inmates James DeCoste, William Schubert, and James McDonald didn't get very far, however, according to newspaper accounts.

"The convicts had broken through a five-inch thick concrete floor in a tool shed of the prison foundry and had gone eight feet down and then burrowed eleven feet in the direction of an outside wall," read an AP article published in the *Lewiston Daily Sun*. "Authorities said they had been aware of the escape attempt for six weeks. The tunneling was halted when authorities discovered that an electric jackhammer was to be used."

Rocco's gang, according to his memory, was more successful, reaching much deeper into the yard than their predecessors.

"There were four of us digging," he recalled years later. "We'd take turns scooping soil with hand shovels we made in the foundry. We'd spread the dirt all around the foundry. We even put some in trashcans."

The excavation went on for a number of weeks. It was death-defying work, to say the least. The collaborators were exposed to all sorts of hazards including potential asphyxiation due to lack of oxygen in the narrow, confined space. And, of course, collapse loomed large. Ultimately, however, the crew met with failure due an unforeseen obstacle.

"They ran into a brick wall," answered Peter Limone when asked years later.

Limone was sitting with a pair of friends at a corner table in his restaurant Antonio's which is located on Cambridge Street in Boston. The prominent dining establishment is bustling, typical for a summer evening. Across the street, a steady parade of ambulances deliver patients to the Massachusetts General Hospital's emergency room. Adjacent to the MGH, the Liberty Hotel, formerly the Charles Street Jail, is welcoming guests. Its foreboding exterior granite walls are in full view through the windows at the front of

Antonio's. Some hotel patrons will shell out hundreds just to spend the night in one of ten cells that were converted to luxurious hotel rooms during the renovation.

"A brick wall?" Limone was asked by one of his dinner guests.

"Yeah," he responded with his trademark piercing smile and twinkling eyes. "A brick wall!"

Limone, the reputed former head of La Cosa Nostra in New England for two years, through 2009, was alluding to a deterrent that he claimed was added to MCI-Walpole when the prison was constructed in 1955. Save for the design architects and a few close-mouthed bricklayers, he shared, very few individuals were aware that an actual *wall* had been built beneath the surface at a substantial depth to prevent such tunnel diggers from reaching the prison perimeter.

"How many guys did Rocco say were with him?" Limone asked. Four was the answer he was given. "Four!" he shouted incredulously, drawing the attention of several nearby diners. Laughing, he added, "Maybe he meant there were four guys on *his* shift. There were at least sixty guys working on that tunnel more or less 'round the clock."

If anyone could be described as an expert in the inner workings of MCI-Walpole, it would be Peter Limone, who passed away in the summer of 2017. Wrongly accused of the 1965 gangland hit of Edward "Teddy" Deegan, Limone spent thirty-three years in prison. He was part of the foursome sent to jail based on the FBI-backed, perjured testimony of killer-turned-rat Joe Barboza.

Limone was released in 2001, and later, along with Joseph Salvati, and the estates of Henry Tameleo, Ronald Cassesso, and Louis Greco, split more than a hundred million dollar settlement in a successful lawsuit against the federal government. Oddly enough, the defense attorney who helped to win the two-month long case was none other than Juliane Balliro, the daughter of Joe Balliro Jr.

When asked how one manages to survive thirty-three years behind bars, Limone leaned back in his chair, folded his hands across his midsection, and again shared an infectious smile that could only belong to a man who truly cherishes his freedom. "You have to able to judge the character of those around you and mostly, the corrections officers," he said, as he again observed the patrons in his popular Italian eatery. "You have to separate those who might give you a bad time and try to drag you into a problem from those who were just trying to make a living."

Sage advice, indeed, but Rocco chose to travel a contentious path. His belligerent ways seldom worked out in his favor. Instead of attempting to establish a rapport with corrections officers, like his friend Peter Limone, Rocco Balliro chose instead to provoke the prison staff, at least until the mid-seventies when he finally saw the light and the promise of furloughs.

For his involvement in the outlandish escape attempt, Rocco Balliro was charged and later, transferred to a maximum security state penitentiary in Cranston, Rhode Island.

In his book, author McLaughlin described this interstate compact.

"It allowed the department to trade inmates with another state," he wrote. "It ran on the theory that if a powerful, troublemaking inmate is transferred to a prison where no one knows him, he becomes everyone else until he can build a reputation."

Of course, there was a flaw in the system with many of the organized crime figures, including Rocco Balliro.

While incarcerated at Cranston, for instance, he ran into a number of Federal Hill-based wise guys, including Rudolph Sciarra, who was a high-ranking capo in the Patriarca *borgata* and according to one source, was known as a "feared, ruthless individual on the street and struck fear in people." Rocco knew Sciarra as one of Patriarca's top hitmen.

"So, what brings you here?" Sciarra asked as the two men sat loafing on a bench in the sprawling recreation yard at Cranston.

"Got kicked out," Rocco answered with a laugh. He ran the fingers of both hands through his thick hair and then rubbed his eyes. Since arriving at Cranston, he hadn't gotten much sleep. The accommodations, he found, weren't quite as tolerable as those at MCI-Walpole. Or perhaps it was because he hadn't yet grown used to his new surroundings.

"Kicked out?"

"Yeah."

Sciarra paused to light up a smoke and offered one to his companion. Rocco hadn't had a cigarette in weeks and relished it as he inhaled deeply.

"How the fuck did you get thrown out of Walpole?"

Rocco shook his head, took another prolonged drag on the smoke, and said with a chuckle, "Guess you could say they didn't appreciate the landscaping work I did to their property."

Sciarra grinned and nodded, understanding. "I had a feeling you might've been in on that."

The conversation waned and the two men sat quietly, taking in the activities around them. A dozen bare-chested, tattooed men were lifting weights while several inmates jogged in single file along a worn, narrow track that encircled the yard. Corrections officers observed the activity through open windows from distant turrets.

It was a pleasant afternoon and temperatures warmed into the seventies. There wasn't a cloud in the sky, which was a deep, azure blue. Rocco raised his face toward the glow of sunlight. As the warmth soothed his skin, he was a million miles and a hundred years from the shootings that claimed the lives of his beloved Toby and her little Mark. He missed them dearly but the anguish wrought from their deaths had eased during four years of imprisonment.

"The Man is coming in soon," announced Sciarra, interrupting his thoughts.

"Patriarca?"

"Yeah. In a week or two. He's gotta do a month, I hear."

"What the hell for?"

"I dunno for sure," said the Rhode Island killer. "I think it might be for taxes or something fucked up liked that."

Rocco's friend Paulie Colicci instantly came to mind. It had been nearly three years since his body had been discovered in the trunk of a car in Quincy. Through prison channels, Rocco heard about the killing of this humble man who offered him guidance and companionship while he spent a few weeks on the lam in Providence. But the logic behind the slaying? What had he done to deserve execution? Rocco had no idea that Colicci was murdered for characterizing mafia kingpin Patriarca in a disparaging tone.

"Well, I'm glad to hear that," Rocco said.

"What? Patriarca coming in?"

"Yeah."

"Why's that?"

Rocco took the last draw on the cigarette, which had dwindled down to the filter. Stabbing out the embers on the edge of the bench, he turned to Sciarra and said, "I'll be able to give him my sympathies."

"Sympathy? Who the fuck for?"

"Paulie."

"Paulie who?"

"Colicci," he answered.

Sciarra suddenly looked uncomfortable. His face turned beet red and his brow furrowed. Standing up abruptly, he folded his arms across his chest. "Don't do it, Rocco," he advised with a stern voice that was part suggestion but mostly warning.

"What?"

"Kid, do yourself a favor and don't mention Colicci to Patriarca if you see him."

Rocco looked up and asked, "Uh, problem?"

"I'm just telling you," Sciarra declared, "It'd be a really bad idea."

"Um, sure … okay," Rocco reluctantly agreed.

"See you around," the Rhode Island capo said as he marched off toward the prison tiers without another word.

As Rocco watched Rudolph Sciarra fade into the distance, it became abundantly evident that the hired killer had something to do with Colicci's demise. If he didn't pull the trigger himself, at the very least he knew how Rocco's friend met his end. Nonetheless, he would heed the man's advice and withhold his sympathies. Whatever the reason behind Sciarra's admonishment, there was no reason to piss off the volatile Patriarca.

CHAPTER 44

*"If you want total security, go to prison. There you're
fed, clothed, given medical care and so on. The only
thing lacking ... is freedom." – Dwight D. Eisenhower*

Squirming in the hard, wooden chair centered in a conference
room in the administration building of MCI-Walpole, Rocco
Anthony Balliro cleared his throat and answered the question
that had just been leveled by one of the board members.

"Yes, sir," he proudly responded. "I've been married five
years; it'll be six in December."

"A good woman, no doubt," remarked spokesperson
Bernard Miller, who was flanked by Robert Drucker, and
corrections officer John Brown.

"Yes, sir," replied Rocco. "Ellen is a good woman."

"It says here," began Miller as he adjusted his eyeglasses
and shuffled some papers on the table in front of him, "that
you've been housed in the SECC since ..."

"September 7, 1977," Rocco interrupted. "Just over eight
months, sir."

"Uh huh," Miller said. "And you continue to improve, uh,
behavior-wise, according to this report."

"Yes, sir," Rocco agreed. "I've been working in the
library and taking classes."

Drucker, who'd quietly observed while his cohort
questioned the inmate, finally chimed in. "Mr. Balliro?"

"Yes, sir?"

"I understand you're seeking a furlough?"

"Yes, sir."

"You've been denied previous requests?"

"Uh, yes, sir. They didn't think I was, ya know, ready."

"You're ready now?"

"Yes, sir," Rocco answered.

"And the purpose, I imagine, is to spend time with your wife?"

"My wife and family."

"Family?"

"Yes, sir," he answered with an audible sigh. "My mama died five years ago and my brother Frank four years before that. I wasn't allowed to go to their funerals. I'd appreciate a chance to spend time with my remaining brothers and sisters."

As Drucker scribbled notes on a tablet, Rocco thought about Frank. He missed his brother terribly. Pinned to the wall of his cell in Walpole was a yellowing *Boston Globe* article published on January 2, 1969. He'd read it so many times, Rocco could recite the brief chronicle nearly word for word. It was inexorably burned into his memory.

New Year's Day in New England was stained yesterday with tragic, often bizarre accidents on the highways and roadways. Ice and snow-covered roads appeared to be a factor in several fatal crashes. Among the crash victims was Boston underworld figure Frank Balliro, 40, killed at 4:14 a.m. yesterday when his car swerved off McLellan highway, East Boston, and hit a retaining wall. Papers in Balliro's pockets listed addresses at 111 Shore Dr., Winthrop and 617 Park Av., Revere. He was alone in the car. It took firemen half an hour to extricate him from the wreckage. Balliro, part owner of the Intermission Lounge on Washington St., downtown Boston, has a long police record. His brothers, twins Rocco and Salvatore Balliro, are serving life sentences for the murder of a Roxbury woman and her son.

The last sentence never failed to leave a bitter taste in his mouth. *Damn reporters*, he thought. Was it really necessary to link his brother Frank, a victim of a terrible motor vehicle accident, to Rocco's highly questionable murder rap?

His brow furrowed in anger but then he recalled an anecdotal tale his sister Lucy told him a matter of days after their dear mother Angela passed away in 1973.

"Anthony, you won't believe what happened when we got to the cemetery," she shared during a prison visit soon after the Balliro matriarch's funeral. "The gravediggers opened the wrong grave for mama! They dug on poor Frank's grave. We were angry at first but then we all began to laugh."

Rocco grinned at the touching memory.

"Something funny, Mr. Balliro?"

He looked up to see Drucker sporting a quizzical expression.

"No, sir ... uh ... yes, sir," Rocco answered. "I was just thinking about my family."

"I see," said Drucker. He paused to look at the documents in front of him and jabbed a pointed finger at one in particular. "Your application mentions an upcoming commutation try."

"Yes, sir."

"And if granted, a furlough will help you in this respect?"

"Yes," Rocco replied. "It will."

"How so?"

In a well-rehearsed response, Rocco recited, "I need the furlough to prove to society and the Department of Corrections that I can be trusted."

Brown, a long time corrections officer, added his two cents to the interview.

"Mr. Balliro?"

"Yes, sir?"

"You've been working down on the farm at MCI-Bridgewater, it reads here."

"Yes, sir, I've been driving a tractor."

"You enjoy your work on the farm?"

"Yes, sir."

"And is it fair to say that your behavior has taken a complete about-face?"

"Yes, sir!" he jubilantly answered. After a series of refusals over the previous months, Rocco felt confident that he was on the precipice of finally earning a furlough. He was *that* close, it seemed. He could almost taste it. "I haven't had a poor score since '75. That was my last *D*."

Miller leaned over and muttered something to Brown that Rocco couldn't hear. Brown nodded. Miller also looked toward Drucker, at the far end of the long rectangular table, who also nodded in the affirmative.

"Well, Mr. Balliro," said Mr. Miller, "it seems that my colleagues concur and I see no reason why we shouldn't grant your furlough."

Drucker and Brown, their faces expressionless, nodded in agreement again.

"We'll just need time to draw up some paperwork," Miller explained. Lowering his glasses to the tip of his nose, he glanced over the top of the rims and said, "I'd suggest, Mr. Balliro, that you keep your nose clean until then."

Rocco could barely contain himself. Success! He'd done the work and finally earned a long-awaited furlough. He had watched other inmates enjoy the benefit since Massachusetts Governor Francis Sargent established the program in 1972 with the hope that it would inspire improved conduct. Sargent thought holding out the carrot instead of the stick could accomplish this. And now, Rocco would have his turn. Soon, he'd be free of confinement, at least for the weekends. The North End and his family beckoned. He couldn't wait to paint the town. And finally, he could spend a few romantic nights with his wife on the outside!

"You can count on it, sir," Rocco pledged with a gleaming smile.

CHAPTER 45

"Always forgive your enemies; nothing annoys them so much." – Oscar Wilde

It wasn't a spur of the moment decision by any means. Suffice to say, he'd thought long and hard about the repercussions of the actions he was poised to take. But when the opportunity presented itself, Rocco Anthony Balliro took it. One minute, he was driving a big green-and-yellow John Deere tractor, tending to rows of crops at the MCI-Bridgewater farm complex and the next he was a passenger in a friend's car on the way to South Station in Boston and a waiting passenger train.

Separated from his 1963 escapes by seventeen years, Rocco had, once again, decamped from a prison. His breakout this time, however, didn't require subterfuge or smuggled hacksaw blades. There were no iron bars to cut. There were no walls to scale. There were no subterranean tunnels to dig. Instead, he simply dismounted the tractor, gathered a few belongings, and casually walked away from his work assignment on the farm at the Southeast Correctional Center at MCI-Bridgewater.

In just a few seconds, the forty-three year old Rocco had transformed himself from a model inmate, who'd shown great promise, to a wanted fugitive. Instead of trending toward a reduced sentence and release, he was, once again, vigorously sought by multiple law enforcement agencies, including the FBI.

The June 6, 1980, edition of the *Boston Globe* carried a brief piece describing a possible reason behind the jailhouse walk-away. "Balliro began receiving furloughs last year after he was transferred to Bridgewater from Walpole state prison," reporter Paul Feeney wrote. "When he failed to return to the prison, there was speculation that Balliro was upset because a furlough request the previous week had been turned down without any reason given."

The reporter had it almost right. True, there was no reason given by prison officials but Rocco knew why the upcoming furlough was denied. He knew why the program was under curtailment, at least for him. He was certain his wife Ellen was behind it. She dealt him a losing hand through her lobbying influence with both state house and prison officials. She could be very convincing and used that skill to manipulate the furlough program, effectively ending her husband's participation.

Rocco saw it coming, however, beginning with an argument he'd had with her on a Monday morning after spending a weekend with his brothers and friends hanging out in the Combat Zone. She'd come into the prison to pay him a visit, as she often did. They were sitting alone, just the two of them, in a small multi-purpose room. In the background, a television mounted on the wall droned.

Rocco twisted a half-smoked cigarette into a metal ashtray. Ellen didn't like the smoke; she said it bothered her sinuses. From the look on her face, Rocco sensed he was in some sort of hot water. Her initial statement confirmed just that.

"Anthony," she began, "I didn't see much of you this weekend."

"Yeah," he admitted. "Sorry 'bout that."

Rocco had learned, with Ellen, that offering short answers was usually the safest avenue. Discussions between them would occasionally escalate to full-blown arguments but sometimes he could diffuse her by letting her dictate the conversation.

"That's two weekends."

"I know."

"Actually, three," she corrected.

"My brother's wedding? Remember?"

She nodded, recalling that he'd attended the wedding reception for the youngest of the Balliro boys, Bruno.

Ellen was, if nothing else, persistent. "Where'd you go Saturday night?" she pressed.

"The North End," he lied. He was actually roaming the Zone, drinking to excess in a few strip clubs with several associates. She could never find out that he spent most of the evening with half-naked strippers draped all over him.

"We were supposed to have dinner," Ellen pressed. "Remember?"

"Uh, yeah. Sorry, but–"

"Anthony, I'm tired of the excuses."

A warning bell went off in his head. *Tread carefully*, Rocco thought. They'd been married for nearly eight years, since December 21, 1971, when corrections officials granted permission for the couple to recite their vows in the prison chapel; the jailhouse wedding was the first of its kind at MCI-Walpole. During the time since, Rocco had grown very adept at maneuvering the obstacle course that had become his marriage. He could do the dance as well as any husband even though his practice was limited to visits like this one and furloughs. When he spent them with her, of course.

"Ellen, I swear–"

"Don't waste my time."

"No, really," Rocco insisted. "Next time they let me out, I'm all yours."

"You can say that again," she uttered under her breath.

"Whadda you mean by that?"

Ellen clammed up and didn't answer. Instead, she turned her attention to the television

Rocco felt a chill run up his spine. Something was amiss but he couldn't quite put his finger on it. There was something devious about Ellen's comment. It wasn't just words. What was the meaning? Was the furlough program in jeopardy? Did she know something? Was she withholding information from him? It was troubling and for several weeks, Rocco battled near-constant paranoia. Before long, he found out what Ellen had meant and it wasn't good news.

Returning from a day working in the fields, Rocco entered his room in the SCC Penthouse, which was a wing in the MCI-Bridgewater administration building. Rocco likened the exclusive rooms to a luxury motel, at least when compared to a typical jail cell. There were ten rooms for ten deserving men, based on good behavior, pursuit of educational improvement via classes and training, and of course, notable positive social adjustment. Rocco Balliro, on the basis of his well-documented turnaround, had earned one of these exclusive prison accommodations in addition to the coveted farming job.

He was covered with dirt and grime and could barely wait to hit the showers. As he grabbed a towel off a shelf and turned to head for the unit's communal showers, Rocco spotted an envelope resting on the corner of his desk. On the upper left corner, it was embossed with the familiar Commonwealth of Massachusetts insignia. He recognized it as the envelope used to deliver his furlough dates and related instructions. With trepidation, Rocco lifted the flap and removed a single-page document.

As he read it, his face turned crimson with rage. He was absolutely livid. He couldn't believe what he was reading and couldn't recall the last time he was this angry.

"What the fuck!" Rocco cursed to the empty space around him as he reread the letter:

Mr. Balliro,
During your next scheduled furlough, travel will be restricted to locations no further north than Brockton, Massachusetts. We anticipate you will adhere to this condition so that future furlough requests may be looked upon favorably.

Submitted,
Bernard Miller
Department of Corrections

"Are they fuckin' kidding me?" Rocco growled as he tossed the correspondence on the desk. The letter slipped off the edge and fell to the floor. He gave it the boot. "Brockton? Jesus!"

This was all Ellen, he thought. She was behind this. There was no question. Now he understood what she'd meant by the scurrilous comment she'd made. Determined to fix it so he wouldn't be able to travel into Boston any longer, she'd obviously peddled her influence with prison officials. He was certain it was his wife who'd convinced the Department of Corrections to impose restrictions on him and in doing so, completely undermined his ability to meet with family and friends. No more Combat Zone. No more North End. Ellen would be his warden.

That conniving, controlling bitch, he thought. He so wanted to confront her but it was paramount that he keep a level head. Lashing out at her would just make matters worse. Rocco wondered how much further she might carry this crusade to keep him under her thumb. He would find out weeks later, when the two of them drove up Route 24 to the Westgate Mall in Brockton, which had opened in 1963, the same year he was sent up for murder.

"Not hungry?" Ellen asked.

"Nuh uh," Rocco mumbled as he stared at a half-eaten cheeseburger and a batch of untouched french fries.

They were having lunch in a small café that overlooked the mall parking lot. It was midday and brightly sunny, but chilly. Soon, it would be spring and warmth would swap places with the snow and ice that had gripped the region for the last four months.

"Such a waste," she said.

"What?"

"The food. It'll be a shame to throw it away."

As ill-advised as it was, he couldn't resist unfavorable feedback and stated with a sneer, "Food's lousy here. North End's much better."

His wife slowly lowered her fork. Leaning back in her chair, she brushed back her long, blonde hair with both hands and then folded her arms across her chest.

Ellen was an attractive thirty-year-old woman with deep, blue-green eyes, voluptuous red lips, and a pale, Cleopatra-like skin tone.

There was a time when he did love her. He even had her name tattooed across his upper chest as a permanent tribute. But there were problems, exacerbated by her possessiveness and desire to control him. She needed to know where he was and what he was doing at every waking moment, even though most of those moments were spent between prison walls.

But the number one obstacle in their relationship, as far as he was concerned, was her utter disdain for the lounge scene. Of course, he didn't dare venture into the Combat Zone with her at his side but there were plenty of places to indulge in the North End and throughout the city. Ellen told him that she didn't like to drink and had no tolerance for those who drank in her vicinity, including her husband. She much preferred spending Rocco's limited furlough time strolling in a park or like this, eating cheeseburgers in some suburban mall restaurant.

Rocco recalled one comment he'd made, in the not too distant past that really set her off. They'd just left a downtown Boston lounge. The entire time spent there, Ellen did nothing but roll her eyes and complain about the foul stench of the cigarette and cigar smoke. As they walked along a sidewalk damp with moisture from an earlier rainfall, Rocco suddenly wheeled and grunted, "Listen!"

"Don't *listen* me," she snapped, mimicking his abrasive tone. Her voice was like fingernails on a chalkboard.

"My brothers hang out here."

"And?"

"And ... I want to hang with them without hearing any bullshit about it," he explained in a stern tone.

"What about me?"

"What about you?"

"You'd choose your brothers over your wife?"

Dead on, he wholeheartedly agreed, but understandably avoided sharing his innermost thoughts with her. That could prove hazardous to his health. Instead, he diplomatically retorted, "I shouldn't have to choose. I can make time for both."

It was a dispute they never resolved. Climbing into the car, Ellen drove while Rocco fiddled with the radio tuner. He added more volume, loud enough to deter Ellen should she want to continue their heated discussion. He also rolled down the passenger side window for fresh air which he knew aggravated her. "It messes my hair," she would always complain. When Ellen dropped him off at the SCC in Bridgewater about thirty minutes later, Rocco had to admit it was one of the few times he was glad to be back at the prison.

Now they were bickering again and over a second-rate restaurant in the Westgate Mall, no less. He sensed Ellen was glaring at him but avoided making direct eye contact. Instead, Rocco lifted his coffee mug and took a few sips.

The café's lone waitress, a pretty little brunette no more than twenty, sashayed past their table. Rocco hadn't noticed when she'd taken their order but now he saw that she held a remarkable resemblance to Toby, right down to the deep, dark eyes and the facial dimples. Memories of his beloved hadn't faded entirely, even after the passage of seventeen years. "Prison does that to you," Rocco once explained. "You see the same thing, day after day, and it freezes your memory of people and things before incarceration."

The brief glimpse of this fine young specimen, wrapped in a colorful apron, stirred nostalgic flashbacks of some of the pleasant moments he and Toby spent together in some of popular Boston eating establishments. It didn't matter whether it was a simple mug of coffee at Sophie's little place in Coolidge Corner, Toby and Rocco always got along famously. He couldn't recall ever having an argument with her, not a shouted word between them. They loved and respected one another and there was never a reason to raise their voices. Absent was the petty squabbling that he and Ellen frequently engaged in. Toby wasn't controlling or meddlesome. Sure, she would try to gently twist his arm for his own good, such as the time she attempted to talk him out of going to Providence to fence the cache of stolen fur coats, but she always relented and gave Rocco his space.

The bittersweet thought of what could have been, a life devoted to his first true love and her two beautiful children. It left a pit in his stomach. If only he could turn back the clock and right the wrongs. Without realizing, Rocco shook his head, ever so gently.

"Is there a problem, Mr. Balliro?"

Ellen only addressed him by his last name when she was pissed off about something. He returned her stare and didn't like what he saw. It was an unmistakable look of reproach.

"No," he lied, lowering his gaze. "No problem."

He didn't know it then, but that was to be the last time he would see Ellen. In May 1980, Rocco submitted a request to the board for a weekend furlough near the end of month to attend a family gathering in Boston. If approved, it would've marked his fourteenth such temporary release. He was denied. The furlough board did not cite the reason; they didn't have to. He knew why they shot him down.

Several weeks later, Rocco Anthony Balliro was standing in the shadows of the Golden Gate Bridge. The furthest reach of the span, connecting San Francisco with Marin County, was swallowed by a deep, gray fog. Photos he'd seen of the bridge didn't do it justice. In person, it was simply indescribable. He stood for a time, drinking of its beauty, as well as that of the city behind him. A smile spread across his face as he silently reflected. Much of the weariness that had gripped him for nearly two decades lifted. At long last, Rocco had reached the city of his dreams.

CHAPTER 46

"Leaving San Francisco is like saying goodbye to an old sweetheart. You want to linger as long as possible." –
Walter Kronkite

By all means, under the circumstances, an airplane would have been the most expeditious method to reach San Francisco. Rocco Balliro understood that. And with virtually every lawman in Massachusetts on the lookout for him, speed was of the essence. He needed to get far away from the Boston area and do so quickly. But he was afraid to fly, always had been. The thought of boarding an airplane made him sick to his stomach. "There was no way I was getting in one of those tin cans and flying all the way across the country," Rocco later said. "No way!"

Instead, he traveled via train and did so indirectly. A point-to-point trip would have been far too easy for the authorities to track. Instead, he traveled via a circuitous, zig-zagging route that took him through Dallas, Chicago, Salt Lake City, Phoenix, and finally, with the help of former partner Gianni Saroni, into the San Francisco area. Along each leg of the journey, Rocco would pause for a day or two, icing the trail. He had friends who put him up in Chicago. In the other whistle-stops, where he lacked trustworthy contacts, he'd check into an off-the-beaten-path, fleabag motel under the alias Louis Monteforte, which would be the name he would assume permanently upon arriving on the West Coast.

Gianni Saroni, his accomplice in a number of criminal exploits while back in Boston, had relocated to California years earlier and taken up a legitimate trade as a hairdresser. He actually did quite well, cutting the hair of film actor Robert

Duvall for his role in the George Lucas science fiction classic *THX1138*. He also styled the hair for a number of Hollywood starlets, including pop music icon Joan Baez. Saroni married an attractive Asian woman by the name of Fran, also a successful hairdresser, and the couple had a daughter.

Rocco settled in, taking full advantage of the Saroni family's generosity, much like he had with the DelMaggios in Connecticut while on the lam in 1963. There was one difference, however. As tempting as it was to get back in the shylocking game and make a few quick bucks while in San Francisco, Rocco opted to keep his nose clean while a guest in the Saroni home, which was located on Grant Avenue in the Telegraph Hill community. He didn't want to bring the cops down on his friend's family.

Along with the fake name Louis Monteforte, Rocco donned another temporary alias: Nicholas Tzannos. It would further confuse the authorities seeking him.

The weeks passed and Rocco grew more comfortable, fully enjoying the sights and sounds of the vibrant West Coast city. He was particularly enchanted with the Golden Gate Bridge.

At forty-three, the bridge was nearly the same age as Rocco himself, having opened to vehicular traffic on May 28, 1937, a matter of months after his first birthday.

The span was such a spectacular sight to behold and it never failed to impress him during his stay. Whether it was a simple drive across the expanse or admiring it from a number of vantage points, the sight of the Golden Gate Bridge always left Rocco awestruck. *There's nothing like it back in Boston*, he thought as he drew a deep, cleansing breath of salt-laden air during one of his many visits to Golden Gate Park.

Thinking of home made him feel melancholy. Not that he'd ever trade his newfound freedom for a jail cell but at least while locked up, his family could pay him a visit here and there.

Rocco had spoken with his brother Billy earlier, which deepened the homesickness. The Balliro brothers caught up with the news from both coasts. As they spoke, it was around dinner time in California which meant it was about eight o'clock back east.

"How's it going, brother?"

"Good, Billy, good," Rocco replied. It was heartening to hear a familiar voice, even though separated by several thousand miles. "How's the rest of the family?"

"Not bad," his older sibling answered. "Joe's over at the club tonight."

Billy was referring to the family-owned Intermission Lounge which was located at 699 Washington Street in Boston's Combat Zone. In its heyday, the Intermish would pack them in. Patrons thirsted for such feature acts as Roger Pace and the Pacemakers, whose specialty was "high energy" jazz, as it was described.

An urban tale was propagated in later years about Pace and his unexpected exodus from the Intermission Lounge. It seems a competitor within the confines of the Zone had lured Pace and his band away from the Balliro family, promising to sweeten their payday. Upon hearing this, Billy Balliro paid a visit to the thieving club owner and demanded the immediate return of the popular music act. When his inquiry was soundly revoked with a "get da fuck outta my joint," Billy reportedly retrieved a 12 gauge shotgun from his car, located the club owner's Cadillac parked in an alleyway, and opened fire, pumping searing lead slugs into the custom beauty. He fired a last round into the engine block, effectively turning the once resplendent automobile into a heaping pile of scrap metal.

When asked if this tale was accurate, Billy Balliro grinned mischievously and simply replied, "Roger Pace came back to the Intermish the next night."

The Intermission Lounge, like many other clubs located in the seedy adult entertainment quarter of Boston, fell on hard times after the 1976 stabbing murder of Harvard student

Andrew Puopolo. Following the highly publicized, grisly killing of the rising football star, city officials began a crusade to clean up the grimy streets and rid the ten-block tract of its entrenched parasites. The Boston Police Department was tasked with clamping down on scores of venues scattered across the formerly designated red light district, including pornographic movie houses, adult book and novelty stores, and of course, the multitude of strip joints and night clubs. Cops who'd previously looked the other way as pimps, prostitutes, and drug dealers plied their wares were now routinely making arrests. The Combat Zone shrank rapidly and the filth would soon disappear altogether, supplanted by legitimate retail businesses and residential properties.

"How's Rudy?" Rocco asked.

"Doing well," Billy confirmed. "Can you believe it? His oldest is in high school already."

"Jesus," Rocco said. "Where has the time gone?"

Rocco's fraternal twin Salvatore "Rudy" Balliro had earned parole from the Plymouth House of Corrections in the mid-seventies after serving just ten brief years for a manslaughter charge. Rudy and Al Ciocco, the family friend who joined the brothers in storming the Roxbury apartment during the winter of 1963, saw their sentences substantially reduced after Rocco succumbed to the coercion of his cousin and attorney Joe Balliro Jr., agreeing to plead guilty to first-degree murder prior to the trio's 1965 retrial.

"And Bruno?"

"He talks about you constantly," Billy shared. "Rocco this and Rocco that. Drives us crazy."

"Yeah, I miss him too," said Rocco. He could've talked with Billy for hours but he was starting to get a little choked up and didn't want his brother to hear the emotion in his voice. Rocco hastened the phone call along.

"Billy, I gotta get going, okay?"

"Yeah, sure," he agreed hesitantly. "You alright, Roc? You don't sound so good."

"I'm fine," he lied. His heart ached. "Really."

"Okay," Billy said. "Gimme a call soon, okay?"

"Count on it."

It wasn't long before Gianni Saroni's houseguest repaid his longtime partner for his hospitality by saving the life of the man's toddler daughter, Laura.

In 1963, while in hiding out in Providence, Rhode Island, Rocco had rushed to the rescue of a helpless girl who was under attack by a pair of drunken sailors apparently intent on raping her. In 1967, while incarcerated, he'd come to the aid of a MCI-Walpole corrections officer who was trapped and facing certain death during a prison uprising. And in 1980, while on the lam in San Francisco, an unselfish Rocco Balliro once again prevented a funeral.

It was a splendid day for a July 4th celebration and there was not a better venue to hold such an event than historic San Francisco Harbor. Street actors of every type performed for captivated onlookers, both young and old. Purveyors of all types of delicious cooked foods contributed to the blend of enticing smells saturating the festive, sun-splashed air. And assorted vendors sold their wares, including small toys and little American flags, their colors flapping in a steady breeze lifted by the churning azure waters of the Bay.

It was in the midst of this joyous, carnival-like atmosphere that two-year-old Laura slipped away from the grasp of her parents, Gianni Saroni and Fran Oliver, and stumbled headlong off a pier into the chilly waters of San Francisco Bay.

"Somehow, my daughter wandered to the boat dock," later wrote Fran Oliver in a letter describing the alarming moment. "We heard a scream as she fell into the Bay."

While a guest in the Saroni home, Rocco was affectionately referred to as "Uncle Nick" by Laura. He played toys with her and read to her. Rocco even spent a memorable day at Disneyland, riding the rides with Laura and her parents.

"Imagine," he later said with a chuckle, "a fugitive from justice whoopin' it up on a roller coaster in a crowded amusement park."

He'd grown quite fond of Laura. There were countless photographs depicting the special bond behind them. It stands to reason that when Laura stumbled and fell into the waters of the Bay, Rocco would be the first to react.

"It was Mr. Tzannos," wrote Fran, "who ran to the dock, dove in, and pulled Laura out. He saved my baby's life."

The restaurant owner and a number of customers patronizing Sam's Anchor Café witnessed the unfolding drama and suggested that the newspapers be contacted. Such heroism, they insisted, shouldn't go unrecognized. Rocco abstained, however. The last thing he needed was for his photograph to appear in a newspaper.

Rocco Balliro soon met Barbara George, thirty-one, at a nondescript barroom in the Marina District on Lombard Street. She was attractive, a former model, who turned a lot of heads when she walked into the smoke-filled lounge. She walked over to his table and sat down. They immediately struck up a conversation. It reminded Rocco of the first time he met Toby.

Barbara, who originally hailed from Texas, later described the first time she met the man who called himself Louis Monteforte and confided in her that he wanted to be a writer.

"I was living in Larkspur and had dropped by to have drinks with friends in the city," she told *San Francisco Examiner* staff writer Jim Wood. "When I first saw him, it was like there was no one else there. He had this light all around his head. We talk about auras. Well, he had one."

A relationship blossomed out of that first meeting and soon, the pair was inseparable. Barbara had a thing for dogs, specifically greyhounds. Her new boyfriend hadn't had much exposure to pets growing up in cramped quarters with a large family, but Rocco quickly adapted to her docile animals.

He'd since moved from Saroni's home to a place of his own. Barbara helped decorate his little hotel room which she described as a "crackerbox." Little did she know that his room was twice the size of that where he'd spent the last seventeen years.

Rocco and Barbara soon took an apartment in Pacific Heights. Through friends, she helped him nail down a decent job as a car salesman. Rocco specialized in the high end market, selling luxury cars such as Rolls Royces and Mercedes. On good weeks, he made as much as a grand, which was more than enough to live on.

He'd decided to ask Barbara for her hand in marriage. Life was finally looking up for him again and getting better as each day passed.

CHAPTER 47

"It looks like Alcatraz has got me licked." – Al Capone

Slicing through the cobalt waters of San Francisco Bay, the bow of the passenger ferry churned a fine mist and gently sprayed the exposed faces of the couple standing on deck. The sensation against their skin wasn't at all unpleasant. It had been an unseasonably warm day in the Northern California coastal city where prevailing temperatures seldom climbed above seventy degrees, even in the midst of summer. Late in the afternoon, the air was still relatively balmy and the cooling moisture was soothing.

Standing near the bow, Rocco Anthony Balliro leaned against the waist-high metal railing, gripping it for balance. The ferry pitched over the rolling swells of the waters. He stared into the depths as the boat whisked its passengers across the Bay. In deep thought, Rocco was startled by a musical voice behind him. His girlfriend Barbara had returned from the ferry's stern where she'd been taking photographs of the San Francisco skyline behind them.

Circling, she joined him alongside the railing, and asked with an expression of concern, "Something on your mind, honey?"

Rocco shifted his gaze away from the frothing water and looked at her. Standing to his right, she tightly held the safety railing as the ferry bobbed in the moderate chop. She was smiling ear-to-ear like a child cherishing a carnival thrill ride for the first time. Her shoulder-length auburn hair, feathered like fine silk, tossed against a stiff breeze. Her face, like his, was tinged reddish with windburn and she squinted against the sea spray. Her tiny, petite figure swayed with the rocking motion of the craft. In Rocco's eyes, his girlfriend was nothing less than exquisite.

Releasing her grip on the railing, Barbara wiped the moisture from her cheeks with the back of her hand. Rocco produced a fresh handkerchief from his pocket and held it out to her.

"Oh, thank you, honey," she said, gently dabbed her face.

"You're welcome."

"So what were you thinking about?" she repeated.

"Huh?"

"You looked depressed, like something was bothering you."

Obviously, she'd noticed him brooding as she drew near. "Oh, nothing much, just thinking 'bout my family, that's all."

"Miss them?"

Rocco nodded. "Uh huh."

"I'd love to hear more about them," she urged.

"Soon," he assured her as his arm encircled her slender waist.

Through the hazy glare of the afternoon sun, Rocco glanced ahead to see their destination looming on the distant horizon. Rising from the depths of San Francisco Bay, murky and foreboding, was the legendary Alcatraz Island and the infamous prison which was perched on the rocky outcropping.

"Impressive," he murmured aloud, scrutinizing the Rock, as it was better known to many of its illustrious former residents, including James "Whitey" Bulger, George "Machine Gun" Kelly, and of course, Al Capone.

Barbara silently agreed, nodding.

Reaching the island, which was mostly made up of ominous, rocky outcroppings, the ferry operator maneuvered the boat alongside the dock with the dexterity of a skilled surgeon. It was obvious he'd done so countless times before. As Rocco, his girlfriend Barbara, and about two dozen tourists disembarked, a California park ranger met them at the end of the pier.

"Afternoon, folks," greeted the uniformed guide with a well-rehearsed tip of his wide-brimmed hat. "Follow me, please."

Rocco and Barbara brought up the rear of the little procession as their guide led them through an immense steel door and into the dank, musty lower tier of Alcatraz. His oft-repeated oration, as they meandered, held most of the group spellbound.

"And in the cell just above our heads," he droned, "was where famous gangster Al Capone slept each night for a number of years."

Rocco was barely paying attention. He reached out and grasped Barbara's hand. She turned and smiled, squeezing his hand. He was definitely smitten with her but couldn't avoid thinking about dear Toby. Each time he encountered something new and interesting in San Francisco, Rocco would think to himself, *Toby would've liked this*. Alcatraz was certainly no exception. She would have found the prison interesting and enjoyed the tour as much as Barbara seemed to be appreciating it now.

"Alcatraz opened in 1934 and ceased operating as a prison in 1963," the informative park ranger said.

That coincidental fact caught Rocco's attention. *So, this place closed the same year I ended up back in Walpole*, he thought as the group progressed deeper into the tier. *Interesting*.

Their tour guide was now babbling on about some of the noteworthy escape attempts from the remote island penitentiary. Barbara, he noted with mild amusement, seemed enthralled with the monologue.

"Thirty-six inmates *tried* to escape from Alcatraz between 1936 and 1962," the ranger said, adding a well-practiced inflection when he spoke the word *tried*. "According to records, none of them succeeded."

"Hmmmph!" spat Rocco, loud enough to be detected by several of the tourists near the rear of the throng. They turned and glared disapprovingly.

Barbara frowned and looked at him quizzically. "What is it, Louis?"

Louis. Sometimes, even he forgot that was the alias he'd assumed when he arrived in California. Rocco felt a pang of guilt every time she addressed him by the false name, Louis Monteforte. Soon, however, he would reveal his true identity to her. How she would react, he couldn't begin to predict.

"Sorry," he replied. "Look, Barb, there's something I've been meaning to tell you."

"Oh?"

"Yeah. Come with me." He firmly grasped her wrist and began to lead her away from the tour group.

"Where are you taking me?" Barbara asked, alarmed.

Rocco shepherded his disconcerted girlfriend along a narrow corridor that emptied into a disintegrating tier. After a brief walk, they arrived in an isolated wing of Alcatraz that clearly was not part of the packaged tour.

Rocco stopped abruptly and faced Barbara, gripping her bare upper arms. He drew her closer and looked into her green eyes. His heart was slamming against his inner chest in anticipation of what he was about to say.

"Louis, what's going on?" she asked. "Why are you acting like this? You're scaring me."

"My name isn't Louis," he blurted without hesitation. There, he'd said it. After months of dating Barbara and misleading her about who he really was, Rocco had opened the door to truth. He understood a confession of this nature might undo their relationship but it was better she found out from him rather than by some other means.

"What do you mean?" she asked, pulling away from him. Her pretty face was suddenly drawn and pale. "If you're not Lou—"

"My name," he began, pausing to draw a breath, "is Rocco Balliro."

"I don't understand." Tears were now welling up in Barbara's fearful, confused eyes. "What are you saying?"

Rocco was consumed with guilt for misleading her but pressed on. For a second, he regretted his decision to divulge his secret. But there was no stopping now.

"I'm not sure how to say this, honey, so I'll come right out with it," he said. "I'm on the run from the cops. Boston police. The FBI too."

Raising her voice in response, Barbara asked, "On the run! For what?"

"Shhh," Rocco urged, placing the tip of his index finger against her tender lips. The Alcatraz tour guide hadn't yet noticed that two members of his group had gone missing. Rocco wanted to keep it that way, at least until he had a chance to finish his disclosure.

"Louis … Rocco, or whatever your name is ... I don't understand."

"Barbara, please listen carefully," he urged. "I was in prison in Massachusetts for seventeen years until I walked away in June."

She tried to pull away from him but he tightened his grip.

"I ended up here in San Francisco."

"Why were you in prison?" she asked. Tears were now streaming down her face. She looked petrified.

Rocco released her and stepped back. He gave her a channel to leave; to end the painful discussion and return to the tour group. She remained planted.

"Why were you in prison?" she asked again with a faint tinge of anger.

He shrugged and bluntly replied, "Murder."

"Oh God."

"I didn't kill no one."

"No?"

Rocco shook his head.

"Then why were you in prison?" she asked again.

Rocco spent the next ten minutes chronicling the entire wretched story. He launched into an oft-repeated explanation starting with the whirlwind seven-month relationship with Toby Wagner up to her husband Barney Wagner's release from jail to the altercation with Clifford to the shootout with the Boston police. He also made mention of the two jail breaks. At times, during his animated narration, Rocco saw Barbara's eyes grow large. On several occasions, when he shared a particularly stunning fact, she shook her head in disbelief.

"So the police shot them?" Barbara inquired. "Is that what happened?"

Rocco nodded. "That's what a lot of people think. It wasn't me, that's for damn sure."

"And you went to jail, for life, because you had a lousy lawyer?"

"Pretty much, yeah," he declared. "I would've done time for going into that apartment but not as much as they gave me."

"Rocco, is it?"

"Yeah."

There was a prolonged pause. He really wasn't sure what to expect. Barbara could turn and walk away, board the ferry back to San Francisco, and disappear from his life forever. Or she could–

"Well, Rocco, it's very nice to meet you," she said, interrupting his musings with a grin.

He was ecstatic. Relief washed over him. Barbara didn't seem to care whatsoever that the man in her life for the past several months had misled her, with a fake name and what he made seem like an empty past. In fact, he noticed in her pretty eyes, she actually seemed to be quite enthralled with her *new* boyfriend.

"There's something I need to ask you, honey?" he said.

Rocco abruptly dropped to one knee and took her hand in his. "Will you marry me?"

Without hesitation, she nodded.

He stood up and embraced his newly-minted fiancée. Feeling her warmth against him, Rocco realized he hadn't felt this close to a woman since, well, Toby, seventeen years earlier. Not even his other wife, Ellen, ever made him feel this content.

"We better get back," he said, grasping her hand again and leading her toward the Alcatraz tour, which was winding down.

Weeks later, forty-four-year-old Rocco Anthony Balliro and Barbara George, ten years his junior, were joined in marriage in the Frank Lloyd Wright-designed San Francisco City Hall.

"Mr. Monteforte," said the justice of the peace as he examined Rocco's carefully-crafted false credentials, "who will be a witness to these marriage vows?"

"Damn!" Rocco uttered under his breath.

"No witness?" asked the justice, tilting his head in frustration.

"Wait right here," the groom-to-be said as he excused himself and dashed toward the building's lobby. Once there, he spotted a solitary man sitting on a bench reading a newspaper.

"Hey, buddy?" Rocco called out to the stranger.

"Who, me?" said the man with a heavy Middle Eastern accent as he lowered the paper, looked nervously around, and then pointed at himself. He donned a fearful expression.

"Yeah, you. What's your name?"

"Umm, I am Yabut," was the reluctant response. Rocco noticed him glancing toward the exit as if he was about to make a run for it.

"Relax, Yabut. I just need a quick favor, that's all."

"Favor?"

"Yeah, come with me," Rocco said, urging his new friend to join him with a gesturing wave. "C'mon, I'll explain."

Once he learned what the persistent man wanted from him, Yabut was more than happy to oblige. And he would have no part of the rolled up wad of cash Rocco offered for his services. "I'm happy to do this for my friend, Louis Montecarlo," Yabut enthusiastically proclaimed with a vigorous handshake.

"Monteforte," the groom corrected with a chuckle. He knowingly winked at his new bride who smiled warmly in return.

Not once did the groom mention to anyone, with good reason, that he already had a wife back in the Boston area. To Rocco's chagrin, he and Ellen remained legally married. There was simply nothing he could do about it as long he was on the run. And despite the recent disclosure to Barbara about his true identity, there were certain things better left unsaid.

Rocco wondered, as he strolled out of the San Francisco City Hall and into the afternoon sunshine, his new bride clinging to his arm, how many years the courts back in Boston would tack on for a bigamy charge.

It was by a simple twist of fate, and a bit of embarrassment, that Rocco Anthony Balliro ended up in the hands of the San Francisco police and subsequently, the FBI.

Rocco and Barbara, according to an article published in the *San Francisco Examiner*, were in the midst of rather robust lovemaking session when neighbors, mistaking the noise for an argument, summoned the cops.

"We were fooling around," Rocco's newlywed wife Barbara divulged to the reporter. "The police asked if there was a problem and we told them no."

But the authorities persisted and according to Barbara, conducted an illegal search and seizure of the premises and Rocco.

"They went through my husband's pockets and found six grams of cocaine."

It was a relatively small amount, enough for personal use but a sufficient weight to justify his arrest during the intolerant eighties. The era marked the early days of the War on Drugs.

Rocco was arrested for possession of a controlled substance and carted off to a nearby San Francisco precinct house where he was booked and jailed under his alias Louis Monteforte. The cops were oblivious to who was in their midst but as he rolled his fingertips in an inkpad and pressed them into individual blocks on a rectangular card, Rocco knew it was only a matter of time. His fate was inevitable.

Posting a $2,200 bond the next morning, he was released to Barbara. The couple collected his belongings, hastily exited the police station into the mild morning, and drove over to the Embarcadero, which was a waterfront neighborhood on the east side of San Francisco. He was famished after a night in the lock up and they settled into a booth at a cozy breakfast nook.

Across the street stood California State Route 480, which was constructed in the late fifties as part of President Dwight D. Eisenhower's interstate highway plan. Upon completion, the elevated three-lane roadway proved to be an eyesore and separated the city from the waterfront.

It was later demolished after the 1989 Loma Prieta earthquake severely damaged the structure.

The highway reminded Rocco of the Central Artery back home in Boston, which was yet another poorly-planned highway project that cut his beloved North End off from the rest of the city. It, too, was later deconstructed for aesthetic reasons.

"I'm screwed," he said to Barbara. He shoveled a forkful of scrambled eggs into his mouth and shook his head dejectedly.

"Why?"

"The cops fingerprinted me."

"But they let you go," she said, her face contorted in confusion.

Buttering a piece of toast, he said "Not for long."

Rocco knew the system, knew it probably better than the authorities themselves. He'd been at liberty for months, living a legitimate life in San Francisco. But the wheels of justice had inexorably begun to turn. He knew his fingerprints would make their way cross-country to FBI headquarters in Washington, DC, where a technician would process them through a criminal database. A match would be found and Louis Monteforte, a married, law-abiding San Francisco car salesman, would once again become Rocco Anthony Balliro, accused killer and three-time prison escapee.

In the months to follow, Rocco showed up in court as ordered to answer for the drug charges. "Having dedicated his unauthorized absence from Massachusetts to 'proving' that he could lead a responsible life," later wrote California defense attorney Michael Metzger, "Balliro continued to make all court appearances."

On November 7, 1980, however, the FBI was waiting for him in the courthouse and immediately took the fugitive into custody. He was later processed for extradition to Massachusetts.

"Can't we take the train?" a trembling Rocco Balliro asked as they neared the San Francisco airport.

One of the two FBI agents sitting in the front seat of the government-issued sedan turned and said, "Are you kidding me?"

"Flying scares the daylights out of me."

"Sorry, Balliro, a train would take too long."

He recalled his captors were somewhat accommodating on the plane and allowed him to fly sans handcuffs, to ease his anxiety and minimize embarrassment from the prying eyes of other passengers.

Barbara George, meanwhile, packed a few things and caught a flight to Boston hours after Rocco left with the feds. While her husband was ferried to maximum security MCI-Walpole and a likely return to solitary confinement, Barbara settled in with his sister Rosalie, who took in her sister-in-law and gave the girl work as a waitress at Jenny's restaurant in the North End.

Before long, Barbara paid Rocco a visit at the prison.

"How're they treating you?" she asked, speaking into a phone receiver to her husband, who sat on the other side of the visitor's partition.

"Caviar and champagne every night," he quipped.

"I miss you so much, honey."

"I miss you too," he said. "But look, I'm not getting outta here anytime soon, if ever."

"Don't say that," Barbara insisted. "We'll get the best lawyers. We'll–"

"Listen," he began. "You need to get on with your life. You're young. Go back to California. Or Texas, with your family."

"I'm staying."

"Barbara, I want you to go," he pleaded. "It would be torture for me to see you and not be able to touch you. I couldn't take it."

Rocco's thoughts fleetingly trekked back to 1962 when Toby would visit him at the New Bedford House of Corrections and later help him escape. He would be making no such request of Barbara. MCI-Walpole was airtight. At forty-three and rapidly aging, he was resigned to the fact that he would die in this wretched place, or somewhere similar.

"I love you," Barbara said, as the visit ran out of time.

Rocco signed annulment papers, effectively ending his marriage to Barbara George. Soon after, she left for Dallas to reunite with family members. He thought about her frequently over the next twenty years, as he had Toby the previous seventeen. There wasn't much else to do in prison but think about the past and count days toward an all but certain future.

CHAPTER 48

"Justice delayed is justice denied." – William E. Gladstone

While a despondent Rocco Anthony Balliro stewed in his cell at MCI-Gardner in early 2002, Cape Cod-based attorney Russell J. Redgate brought the lifer's thirty-nine year old murder case before a panel of judges representing the Massachusetts Supreme Judicial Court. The hearing marked a last-ditch effort on the part of Rocco to overturn his conviction and gain freedom. He was refused permission to attend the hearing, however.

Similar to previous attempts over the decades, Redgate sought a new trial based almost entirely on a stunning admission by cousin and prominent defense attorney Joseph Balliro that he'd dispensed substandard pre-trial advice on August 18, 1965.

Redgate reintroduced an affidavit in which attorney Balliro stated that he had indeed attempted to coerce his cousin into accepting a guilty plea to first-degree murder in exchange for lenient sentences for Rocco's fraternal twin Salvatore and the third accused, Al Ciocco.

"I judged this proposal to be in the best interest of my client, Salvatore Balliro," the accomplished attorney wrote in a document drafted in 1999. "I realized that my client's interests did not coincide with Rocco Balliro's interests; in fact, I realized that there was some conflict. I realized that by urging Rocco to accept this proposal, I was not actually promoting his best interest."

Rocco Balliro's lawyer at the time of the trial, Neil Colicchio, filed a similar affidavit but went further to state the obvious reasons for his failure to represent his client effectively. That certainly wasn't the case in the first trial in 1963, when he obliterated the allegedly tainted testimony of Mary Adams, the chief witness for the prosecution.

"My position at the time was awkward and difficult for many reasons," Colicchio conceded. "When I was newly admitted to the bar, I was interviewed by attorney Joseph Balliro for a position with the public defender's program. The outcome of the interview was favorable. Subsequently, attorney Balliro was a mentor to me. I did feel indebted to him."

Despite the staggering admission from his cousin, who risked blemishing his unrivaled reputation as a defense attorney in doing so, Rocco Balliro would be denied a new trial. Redgate failed to convince the court that this now sixty-five year-old client was deserving of a chance to spend his final years as a free man.

"The court was very aggressive, constantly questioning me, never letting me make the argument I would have liked to have made," Redgate wrote in a letter to Rocco soon after the mid-2002 hearing.

It wasn't Redgate's courtroom presentation that cost his client, but rather the prestige of Rocco's highly-regarded cousin Joe Balliro in the eyes of the ignorant justices, who wore blinders in this instance.

"After all these years, he's still the Dean A – a gifted trial lawyer jurors instantly love," later wrote Elaine McArdle in a *Boston Magazine* article. "In June, Balliro tried to take the fall for his cousin Rocco Balliro, in prison since pleading guilty in 1965 to killing his girlfriend and her child. But the Supreme Judicial Court apparently didn't buy attorney Balliro's claim that he was capable of anything less than a superb defense."

Redgate brought forth case law in an attempt to dispel the notion that any attorneys, no matter how successful or influential, were infallible. Attorney Balliro, like other excellent lawyers of his ilk, could still render poor decisions and dispense substandard advice.

In 1993, for instance, prominent Boston attorney Henry F. Owen III used what was described by a *Globe* reporter as a "foolhardy" approach in the defense of Abigail Gilliard, who was accused in the stabbing death of seventeen-year-old Yolanda Carter during a street fight in Roxbury. Instead of allowing Gilliard's fate to be decided by a jury, which because of a lack of evidence linking her to the murder, would likely have convicted her of a lesser charge of assault and battery, Owen rolled the proverbial dice and went with an "all or nothing" approach, seeking a full acquittal. But the tactic backfired, resulting in life imprisonment for his client when she would have faced a maximum two-to-three-year sentence.

Gilliard later earned a new trial based solely on an admission by Owen that he failed to effectively represent his client. "In the highest tradition of the law, he admitted that he was wrong," said Gilliard's new attorney John H. Cunha Jr. of Owens in a 1993 *Boston Globe* article. "He didn't try to hide behind his reputation, which is justifiably that of one of the best lawyers in town. I would say Henry acted with the greatest honor."

There were other examples cited, all pointing to the simple fact that lawyers are prone to making mistakes like any other human being. Attorney Joseph J. Balliro, like Henry F. Owen, was not an exception and admitted as much. Coercing Rocco Balliro to accept a guilty plea in 1965 effectively slammed the door on the case and future appeals. His cousin Rocco would likely never see the light of day, at least not outside of prison walls, partly because of him.

Attorney Balliro later tried to explain the logic behind his failed strategy. It wasn't simply trading one Balliro for the other, Salvatore for Rocco, as it seemed to observers.

"At the time I persuaded Rocco to plead guilty to first-degree murder I did not think he would have been convicted of murder, in either the first or the second degree, at a jury trial," attorney Balliro wrote. "Although he had been convicted at his first trial, the Supreme Judicial Court had ruled that he ought not to have been convicted, and could not be convicted again, unless it was proven beyond reasonable doubt that police had not fired the fatal bullets. In fact, I believe the physical evidence tended more to support the theory that police did fire the fatal bullets, rather than any contrary theory."

Rocco Balliro was understandably disappointed in the decision of the Massachusetts SJC. He was convinced that had he been there, at Redgate's side in the courtroom, he could have offered testimony and pled for the court's mercy.

"I dunno," he said, lowering his head dejectedly, "but maybe the justices would have looked at me, an old man in his sixties, and figured I'd done enough time."

Rocco's face grows clouded, almost angry, when he brings up the subject of his cousin's coercion in 1965.

"I wish I had it to do over again," he lamented. "I would never have taken the hit. I didn't kill Toby and Mark and I think there was plenty of evidence to prove that. We could have won a new trial. Instead, I let them talk me into that guilty plea."

Rocco feels his fraternal twin brother Salvatore let him down by not taking full advantage of the sacrifice he made in that dreary courtroom lockup so many years before.

"Yeah, Rudy got out of the can after just ten years but went right back to the life, partying and drinking, and it killed him in 1999," he recalled. "Diabetes, I think it was."

Al Ciocco also died of natural causes in 1980, several years after his early release from MCI-Plymouth.

In a later appeal attempt, Rocco Anthony Balliro earned support from an unlikely source. Perhaps the most damning affidavit of police misconduct came from Matthew F. King, former Boston Police detective sergeant and the man tasked with an internal investigation in the aftermath of the 1963 shootings.

"In my capacity as officer in charge," King wrote in a 1985 affidavit, "I must acknowledge that these unfortunate deaths came about as the result of improper police action and malfeasance."

"Failure to follow appropriate police procedures and to secure the safety of civilians during a stakeout operation, resulted in an unnecessary exchange of gunfire and tragic consequences. The evidence, upon my review at the time and to this date, was inconclusive as to which bullets from whose guns caused the deaths of Toby and Mark Wagner. We never determined who fired the fatal shots. Evidence indicated that Rocco Balliro never got beyond the entrance of the apartment.

"I believe that Rocco Balliro has served enough time in prison for an unintended result which was as much the fault of police ineptitude as his actions, if any."

CHAPTER 49

"Ain't gonna face no defeat, I just gotta get out of
this prison cell, someday I'm gonna be free, Lord." –
Freddie Mercury

"Morally, I'm guilty," said Rocco Anthony Balliro between bites of a sausage and pepper submarine sandwich during a May 2011 discussion in the MCI-Norfolk visiting center. "But that's because of the people we were mixed up with and the lifestyle we lived."

Gaunt in the face and pale from a chronic lack of the outdoors and sunlight, Rocco took another bite of the sandwich, dabbed the corners of his mouth with a napkin, and then downed several swigs from a bottle of Fanta orange soda.

"But criminally, I'm innocent," he continued, smoothing back a full head of salt-and-pepper hair after wiping his hands clean with a fresh napkin. He is eating his vending machine meal in a tidy, orderly fashion. His attention to personal hygiene and appearance borders on obsessive. Rocco Balliro is always impeccably groomed, clean cut, and wears only neatly-pressed clothing. He once got upset when an unannounced visit didn't allow time for a shower and shave.

The visiting center is bustling with activity on this mild spring evening. Most of the blue, hard plastic chairs, arranged in opposite facing semicircles, are occupied by MCI-Norfolk inmates and their parents, spouses, girlfriends, and children. The room is abuzz with conversation. At the far side of the circular space, adjacent to the exit leading back to the yard and the stacks of prison tiers, is a platform fronted by a chest-high counter. From this vantage point, several navy blue uniformed corrections officers oversee the throng like hawks on a perch.

Most of the men, like Rocco Balliro, are consuming food and snacks purchased by loved ones and dispensed from a half-dozen vending machines lined in rows in a narrow alcove. The packaged food, by most standards, is awful. But to these men, who regularly consume inedible meals, the plastic-encased fare is gourmet.

The inmates cannot purchase their own food. A red line of demarcation painted on the floor in front of the vending machine alcove is a stark reminder that this is, in fact, a prison. Only visitors may cross that line to make purchases; the area is designated off-limits to inmates.

"I've led a broken, antisocial life," Rocco remarked with humility. It's a comment he's made a number of times before. He was, if nothing else, brutally forthright in his self-description. "I often think of my behavior in my young adult and adult life and how by this behavior I really built my own 'jail' and put myself in it for most of my existence."

If given half a chance, any one of the fifteen hundred prisoners currently confined behind the imposing, razor-topped nineteen-foot walls surrounding this state penitentiary, would profess innocence to their crimes, complete with the inevitable corroborating legalese and much-practiced jargon. More often than not, these claims are little more than the often-repeated rants of men seeking a seam in the fabric of the justice system that might reduce their sentence or set them free.

Few, however, would have a more compelling case than Rocco Anthony Balliro. To serve time for invading the apartment at 107 Centre Street, Roxbury in 1963 was a given. But how much time is sufficient? What punishment would have fit the crime? Certainly, there were unintentional results of his actions but to spend his life in prison? To die in prison?

"I've never denied that we went to that apartment and got in a shootout with the cops, after we learned they was cops,"

Rocco said. "But I didn't kill her. I didn't kill Toby. I loved that girl."

"That girl," Toby Wagner, would have turned seventy a month earlier, on April 8th, had she survived that tragic night in 1963. Her son, little Mark, would have celebrated a milestone fiftieth birthday in March.

"I never had a chance to visit Mark's gravesite, ya know, like I did with Toby," said Rocco, shaking his head.

Mark Wagner, forever a toddler, was laid to rest several miles from the place where he succumbed. In the well-heeled Boston community known as West Roxbury sits an expansive cemetery that abuts LaGrange Street and wends southward toward the Charles River basin. There are stunning rolling green vistas and the landscape is calm and serene.

In the administrative office, a solitary visitor entered and silently waits for assistance.

"I'm sorry, but we're closing," said a harried clerk behind the counter, as she pointed at the clock hanging above a fireplace in the administrative office of the St. Joseph's Cemetery.

It read five minutes before noon.

It is the week before Memorial Day 2010, and from the looks of the stacks of paperwork scattered across the top of the counter and on several desktops behind her, it has surely been a hectic day. Adjacent to the counter is a large metal decanter, containing small, neatly-banded American flags. A handwritten sign is taped to the front of the container which reads, **Take one for your veteran**.

The clerk's denial to render aid earned a look of frustration from the visitor, prompting a change of heart on her part.

"Okay, okay." She sighed, brushing back a wisp of hair from her weary face while positioning herself in front of a nearby computer. "One more – last name?"

"Wagner. *W. A. G. N ...*"

"First," she interrupted, having already typed in the name before it was completely spelled out for her.

"Mark. Mark Wagner."

She watched the small screen, waiting for results and then uttered, "Hmmm."

"Yes?"

"Baby?" she asked, her voice softer now, not as gruff as it was at the outset of the exchange.

"Yes"

"The gravesite might be a little difficult to find," she admitted. "But I'll give you a map."

She produced a long sheet of white paper depicting a diagram of the large complex. Circling a site, she slid the map across the counter.

Five minutes had elapsed. It is now noon.

"Good luck," the clerk said.

Entering from Baker Street through a granite-framed, wrought iron gateway, the yard is located to the immediate left. Bordered on two sides by crumbling stone walls and huge shade trees, perhaps an acre in size, there are no gravestones to speak of.

A gravedigger dismounts from a backhoe and approaches. "Help you find someone?" he asked.

"Please," said the visitor, handing over the paper map and pointing out the red-circled gravesite.

The man gestured with a wave of his arm. "This way." He began to walk in short, choppy steps across the tract of grass. A weather-battered bucket of plastic flowers and a small white cross are the only indications this is a graveyard.

"Here it is, number 615," pointed out the helpful gravedigger.

"Thank you."

"Don't mention it," he said. "Sad place, this part of the cemetery. They call it a pauper's field. Mostly kids here; poor children whose parents couldn't afford to bury them properly. Really sad stuff, if you ask me."

Nearly five decades into a life sentence and approaching his seventy-fifth birthday, Rocco Balliro's curiosity hadn't dampened. He still yearned to learn more about those in his distant past, particularly those with ties to Toby and Mark.

"Do you know what happened to Toby's daughter?" he queried. "Bernice?"

Bernice Wagner, he was told, was eventually adopted and raised by a loving family in Canton, Massachusetts. Her biological father Barney, who later moved to Arizona, changed his name and remarried, was accurate in his assumption that neither pair of natural grandparents had an interest in taking in the child.

Barney Wagner's parents, living in Brookline at the time, barely tolerated their daughter-in-law Toby when she was alive. In death, their hostile opinion of her had changed little and they held a similar opinion for her surviving daughter.

Herman and Hilda Zimmerman were aging and financially strapped. Nine-year-old David was burden enough for a declining Hilda, whose depression understandably intensified following the death of her only daughter. Theirs was not a home for a one-year-old baby.

Bernice Wagner's name was changed soon after she was adopted. In a terrible twist of fate, her adoptive mother was killed in a dreadful accident when Bernice was in her teens. The woman was asphyxiated, along with her aunt, while stranded in a snow bank near the Norwood airport during the historic blizzard of 1978. As the storm raged around them, the two women kept the car running for warmth and were soon overcome by carbon monoxide when clumping snow obstructed the tailpipe.

"That's awful," Rocco said upon learning that the infant he helped care for had suffered the tragic loss of not one but two mothers. He brightened, though, upon learning that Bernice went on to earn a degree as an RN and later opened a successful Cape Cod business.

"Bernice's fate was in God's hands it seems," he announced with the confidence of a true believer.

At the outset of his fifth decade of imprisonment, Rocco Balliro claims to have found salvation with the Dominican Order, which traces its foundation in Catholicism to early thirteenth-century France. While incarcerated at MCI-Norfolk, Rocco fully immersed himself in the intense philosophical and intellectual ideals of the Order and at the time, often studied and prayed to near exhaustion. Through religious pursuits, Rocco said he discovered the path to righteousness and saw the error of his regrettable ways.

Under the guidance of highly-regarded Sister Ruth Raichle, the former MCI-Norfolk chaplain, and Dr. Leo Fahey, retired clergyman and psychotherapist, Rocco climbed to the level of Order of Preachers, or OP.

Understandably well-versed in Biblical history as a result of his readings, the significance wasn't lost on Rocco that it required exactly forty days for him to cut through the wrought iron bars of his jail cell at the New Bedford House of Corrections many years earlier.

"Forty days and forty nights," he emphasized with great fervor and enthusiasm when pointing out the symbolism. "That was the same amount of time that rains fell during the Great Flood."

Not once had Rocco Balliro denied his criminal past. Ask about some of his burglary exploits and he'll share with uncanny recall, down to minute details, including the prevailing weather conditions.

"I've done almost fifty years," insisted a steadfast Rocco Balliro. "That's enough. The bill is paid."

CHAPTER 50

"Just because you make horrendous and destructive choices does not mean you deserve less respect for what you inherently are – the pinnacle of my creation and the center of my affection" – William P. Young, The Shack

As the small contingent of Massachusetts state senators and representatives was ushered into the Health Services Unit of MCI-Shirley by prison officials on October 17, 2011, they were greeted by a gaunt, fragile man dressed in drab hospital garb. Despite the pajama-like clothing, the man exuded pride and dignity.

Clearly suffering from a debilitating illness, he somehow overcame underlying weakness, mustering newfound strength and sense of purpose upon hearing the objective of the group's visit.

"I'm Rocco Balliro," he announced in a raspy voice, beaming buoyantly for the audience now gathered around him in a semi-circle.

The spokesperson for the delegation of lawmakers, State Senator Patricia Jehlen, gripped his hand in both of hers and responded, "It's a pleasure to meet you, Mr. Balliro."

"Call me Rocco," he insisted with a friendly smile.

A far cry from the able-bodied, rugged man of five decades before, capable of outrunning police officers and scaling prison walls like some misguided comic book superhero, Rocco Balliro now resembled, in his own words, "a survivor of a Nazi concentration camp." He'd lost a third of his body weight in a matter of two months.

The cancer which now wracked his body and promised to soon end his life began in mid-September as a dull stomach ache. He tried to quell the pain by chewing antacids, Tums or Maalox, dispensed by the clinic staff at MCI-Norfolk. It quickly progressed to a persistent pain spreading throughout his entire abdomen. When he began to vomit blood, prison medical officials rushed Rocco via ambulance to Tufts Medical Center in Boston, a hospital ironically located directly adjacent to his former stomping grounds of the Combat Zone.

It was here, in the Tufts emergency room and later, the hospital oncology department, that Rocco learned that his life expectancy would now be measured in months, perhaps weeks.

"I'm not afraid to die," he said during one of the final visits at MCI-Norfolk. Rocco gestured with a wide sweep of a pale, sinewy arm. "But I don't want to die in this awful place."

"I used to work in the morgue here," he continued, "and I'll tell you, it's a dirty, disgusting place. I don't want them to put my body there. Not even for a minute."

Rocco Balliro earned his wish with a transfer to MCI-Shirley where he would be admitted to the HSU and cared for by a dedicated, skilled medical staff. He'd decided, literally hours after he was diagnosed, not to seek treatment for the treacherous, incurable disease rapidly spreading through his body. Well-studied, Rocco was aware that several of the side effects of therapeutic cancer treatments were, at times, worse than the illness itself. He chose, instead, to let nature take its course and accept only medication upon reaching a point where the pain could no longer be tolerated.

"I hope I'm able to die with some dignity," he stressed, seeking acknowledgement that he wasn't out of bounds asking for leniency after nearly fifty years behind bars. No, it wasn't too much to ask, he was told.

He also hoped to die in freedom, outside the prison walls. Thus, it was with great anticipation and high hopes that Rocco Balliro greeted the Massachusetts state senators and representatives, headed by Spokesperson Jehlen, as they arrived at MCI-Shirley on a fact-finding mission.

"Can you believe it?" he stated excitedly during a phone conversation just hours after speaking with the state lawmakers. "Someone is finally listening to us! Someone is finally helping us!"

While his criminal case was certainly compelling, Senator Jehlen didn't want to hear how Rocco Balliro landed in prison. Crime and punishment were not the issue at hand. The Massachusetts legislative quartet of Jehlen, Senator James Eldridge, Representative Kay Kahn, and Representative Jennifer Benson were gaining a better understanding of the plight of men who would benefit from the passage of Senate Bill No. 1213, which sought "medical release of seriously ill prisoners who no longer pose a threat to society."

Who better to plead their case than the terminally ill inmates themselves?

It was a straightforward premise, really. One that was already firmly in place in many states, both liberal and conservative, across the nation. Simply, what was so wrong with allowing these men a chance, no matter how brief, to spend time with family and friends before falling victim to the ravages of terminal disease? Passage of the bill should have been a cinch.

It was a campaign fought on two distinct fronts. From the statehouse, Jehlen and her elected colleagues drafted a bill and sought the votes to see it passed into law. And from within the confines of prison walls, a solitary but eloquent voice added his perspective.

Timothy J. Muise, a MCI-Norfolk inmate and outspoken member of the Lifers' Group Inc, was a well-written advocate for the passage of such legislation. In a letter published in the spring 2010 newsletter, *Criminal Justice Policy Coalition*, Muise stated, "Massachusetts is in need of compassionate release legislation in order to relieve itself of the cost of medically ailing inmates and allow for the peaceful end to their lives outside the walls of prison."

Muise cited stunning economic facts to back up his case including the claim that medical expenses for the incarcerated infirm often reached more than one hundred thousand dollars annually, twice the cost of that for a healthy inmate.

A study published in *USA Today* revealed that only fourteen states currently lack a medical release program, including Massachusetts. New England neighbors Vermont, New Hampshire, Connecticut, and Rhode Island, on the other hand, have joined the majority in the United States.

Opponents of compassionate release in Massachusetts don't have a leg to stand on, so to speak. While forty percent of able-bodied inmates perpetrate crimes soon after discharge, merely three percent of the terminally ill re-offend in the states that offer some form of medical release. The benefits for the taxpayers far outweigh the negligible risks.

There were pitfalls, however. Who would provide medical care for the newly-released convict during convalescence? External resources would have to be established. Would the family have the means to render care, both physically and financially, in a potentially months-long arrangement?

In the case of Rocco Anthony Balliro, yes, there was sufficient support in place. The Balliro family was large, indeed, and stood ready to pitch in with his medical care and expense. Lucy, his dear sister, had set aside a room in her lakeside home in Manomet, which is a village of Plymouth, Massachusetts. With stunning water views, she was sure that Anthony (her preferred name for her younger brother) could enjoy his remaining days in peace and solitude, reading a good book if that's what he chose to do. Or he could rest his weary frame in a comfortable lakefront chair and greet scores of nieces and nephews, many who'd never had the privilege to meet him in person. If his waning strength allowed, perhaps Rocco could launch a canoe and coast over the gently-rippling waters of the expansive Great Herring Pond.

Who, in their right mind, could deny such a simple request?

The Commonwealth of Massachusetts, as it turned out.

"Right now, in spite of the of the fact that recidivism drop precipitously with age, the sick and dying are not getting out early on medical exceptions," wrote journalist Jean Trounstine for the *Boston Daily* "Since Governor Deval Patrick took office, at least 280 pardon and 220 commutation petitions have been filed in Massachusetts, according to WBUR. Just one petition made it to Patrick's desk. It was denied. It is unknown how many of those were filed by the gravely ill, but it is clear that those who do apply and don't get out ultimately die in prison."

Time inexorably slipped away for Rocco Balliro. In early January 2012, he was made aware that the efforts of Jehlen, Muise, and the others would fall short. Senate Bill No. 1213 would ultimately fail in the state house. So, too, would a commutation try by friends and family.

Too weak to correspond himself, Rocco enlisted the help of MCI-Shirley inmate Ken Seguin, who was serving a life sentence for the brutal 1992 slaughter of his wife and two young children.

"We had also spoken much over the months of the great effort put toward the possibility of a commutation for him to be paroled to his sister's home, or a medical release when the severity of his stomach cancer became known," Seguin wrote. "At this point, it would be fruitless to pursue any of this because he is quite sure that he hasn't much time left on this earth."

Prescient words indeed.

"How the hell did that thing get in here?" breathlessly shouted a pillow case-wielding corrections officer as he chased an elusive sparrow from one corner of the elevator vestibule to the other.

"Shit!" shouted his colleague as he ducked to avoid the frantic flying creature. "Damned if I know. The windows are all sealed!"

"We gotta find a key. If we open one of the windows, maybe it'll fly out!"

One of the two elevators soon arrived and a pair of visitors, a man and a woman, who'd been observing the correction officers pursuit of the trapped bird, rushed through the opening doors. They hoped the sparrow didn't follow. Shouts of the harried guards could be heard as the doors closed and the elevator began a descent from the eighth floor to the lobby below.

Most of the residents of Lemuel Shattuck Hospital were indoors, hanging out in the lobby and foyer. Several hardy souls braved the prevailing bone-chilling cold but only long enough to smoke a quick cigarette before retreating inside.

The Shattuck, a brick high-rise located at 170 Morton Street, Jamaica Plain, Massachusetts, is a publicly run facility which offers both inpatient and outpatient medical services for the Commonwealth's downtrodden. There is also a secure hospital unit on the eighth floor, complete with steel doors and bars in the windows, managed by the Department of Corrections which houses both chronically and terminally-ill prison inmates.

It was here that Rocco Anthony Balliro spent his final days, in a single hospital room overlooking the rolling greens of the Franklin Park golf course and the adjacent wooded sprawl.

Earlier, he was granted permission to receive visitors and spent an hour in a small reading room with his sister Lucy and at a later time, brother Billy. Prior to that, Rocco had declined visitors for a number of weeks. The Shattuck medical staff had somehow misplaced his dentures and he didn't want anyone, not even family and close personal friends, to see him without them. As infirm as he was, Rocco's appearance remained foremost.

Eventually, however, a replacement set of teeth arrived and Rocco immediately resumed greeting visitors.

He'd grown a goatee and was told he looked like a ship's captain, which drew laughter that soon triggered a coughing fit.

"I'm finally at peace," he said with a strained, raspy voice that was barely distinguishable. It was days after Christmas and he was in remarkably good spirits. "I'm looking forward to meeting *Him*."

On the night of Wednesday, January 18, 2012, a pair of visitors sat in silent vigil at Rocco Balliro's bedside. Behind them, positioned in the doorway of the tiny hospital room, was a female corrections officer. She was there by regulation, overseeing the visit, but maintained a respectful silence throughout.

Earlier in the evening, Rocco had slipped into a coma and was barely clinging to life. After an hour, his companions said an emotional farewell and reluctantly took their leave.

Once processing out and passing through the thick steel door of the hospital-jail, the two encountered the corrections officers attempting to corral a distressed sparrow.

Reaching the Shattuck lobby moments later, the couple realized they'd inadvertently left their driver's licenses, required for entry, at the security desk. Returning to the eighth floor, the duo braced for a renewed ambush by the wayward sparrow but as the elevator doors parted, they saw that the bird had gained its freedom. Frigid air rushed through an open window. The corrections officers had obviously found the means to unlock it. The clock mounted over the security window, as the pair retrieved their licenses and departed for a second time, read 8:15.

Later, the telephone rang shrilly at the home of the couple. It was moments after they'd settled in for the night.

"Hello?"

"Yes, good evening, sir. This is the attending physician at Lemuel Shattuck."

"Yes?"

"I regret to inform you that Anthony Balliro has passed away."

"We were just there, at the Shattuck."

"I know," the doctor said. "The officers mentioned that."

"What time did he die, if you don't mind me asking?"

There a sound of shuffling papers. "Hmmm, let's see ... ah, here it is," he said, clearing his throat. "I have it recorded as 8:15."

"Thank you for calling."

Rocco Anthony Balliro was cremated and laid to rest alongside his parents, his departed brothers and sisters, and other family members in a large, flower-covered burial plot in the sprawling Woodlawn Cemetery in Everett, Massachusetts.

As little as a couple hundred yards distant, across a gently sloping meadow, in the peaceful, tree-shaded Beth Israel Graveyard, rests his beloved Toby.

They were, once again, united.

Their fifty year wait had come to an end.

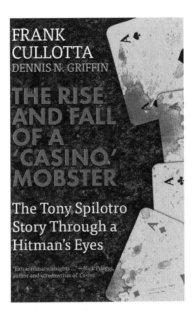
1

A Rocky Start

I'll never forget the first time I met Tony Spilotro. I was just a kid, twelve or thirteen, and I hated school. I was always in trouble with the teachers, and my mother had her hands full trying to get me into a school that could handle me. I loved to fight, too, which caused her even more grief.

Anyway, to hustle up some pocket money I started shining shoes up and down Grand Avenue. One day I noticed a kid about my age shining shoes on the opposite side of the street. He saw me at the same time, and we glared at each other for several seconds.

The other kid hollered to me, "What the fuck are you lookin' at?"

"I'm looking at you. What about it?"

We started walking toward each other, met in the middle of the street, and put down our shine boxes.

He said, "This is my fuckin' territory, and I don't want you on this street. Understand?"

He was short but looked pretty solid, and I figured he could probably take care of himself. That didn't bother me, though, because, like I said, I was a scrapper myself. "I don't see your name on any street signs, and I'm not leaving."

We shoved each other a little bit, but no punches were thrown. Then he said, "I'm coming back here tomorrow, and if I see you, we'll have to fight."

"Then that's what we'll have to do."

I went to that location the next day, but the other kid wasn't there. In fact, it was about a week later when we met again on the street. This time his attitude was different—he wasn't combative. He said, "I've been asking around about you. What's your last name?"

"Cullotta."

"Was your father Joe Cullotta?"

"Yeah. So what?"

"Your father and my father were friends. Your old man helped my old man out of a bad spot one time." He told me his name was Tony Spilotro and his father ran a well-known Italian restaurant on the east side called Patsy's.

I remembered hearing about the incident Tony was talking about. My father (who had been a gangster) liked Patsy and was a regular customer at the restaurant. Back then there was a gang called the Black Hand. It consisted of Sicilian and

Italian gangsters who extorted money from their own kind, and my father hated them with a passion. Their method was to shake down business owners by demanding money in return for letting the business stay open. They were making Patsy pay dues every week. When my father heard about it, he and his crew hid in the back room of the restaurant until the Black Handers came in for their payoff. Then they burst out and killed them. After that Patsy wasn't bothered anymore.

From that day Tony and I became friends and started hanging around together. I found out he was a few months older than me, and we had some other things in common besides age and being short. We both hated school and would fight at the drop of a hat.

On weekends I'd see Tony at Riis Park, where he hung out. The first time I went there this guy, who was probably in his twenties, dressed in a shirt and tie and looking like a wiseguy, walked up to me and said, "I'll give you five dollars if you fight my brother."

"Who's your brother?"

He pointed to Tony. "Tony, he's right there."

I laughed. "No, I already had a beef with him. We're friends now."

"Oh, you must be Cullotta. Tony told me about you. I'm Vic Spilotro."

I went over with Tony. A little later Vic came over and said he'd found a kid for Tony to fight. Tony beat the hell out of the kid, and then Vic paid him the five bucks. Tony said, "Hey, what about me? I did all the work. Don't I get anything?"

Vic laughed. "Not you, you're not getting shit. I'm doing this to toughen you up, not so you can make money."

We messed around for a while longer, and then Tony said, "Come with me, and I'll show you where I live. It's right off Grand Avenue."

On the way to his house Tony told me he had five brothers. Vince was the oldest, followed by Vic and Patrick.

And then came Tony and his two younger brothers, Johnny and Michael.

Tony showed me through the house. All the boys slept in one bedroom with three sets of bunk beds. While we were in the bedroom Tony's mother walked in. She was a very tiny lady, and I had the impression she wasn't very happy about me being there. She asked who I was, and I told her. If she knew about my father and the Black Hand thing, it didn't seem to make any difference. I still sensed she didn't like me. She said to Tony, "Hurry up and get out of here, the both of you."

After she left I said to Tony, "I don't think your mother likes me and probably doesn't want me around."

He laughed. "Don't worry about it. She doesn't like any of my friends. If she had her way I'd only hang around with altar boys."

As we walked out of the house Tony's mother and father were in the kitchen. Tony said something to them, but neither of them spoke to me. My name wasn't mentioned, and I don't think the father even looked at me as I passed by. Over time I got to know Tony's parents better. They were hard working, nice people. I never knew either of them to be involved in anything illegal.

After that initial meeting I didn't see much of Tony during the week because of school. But on weekends I'd catch up with him at Riis Park. I saw Vic quite a bit, too, at Riis or on the streets. I became convinced he was a gangster because of the way he dressed and that he always had a big wad of money with him. At the time I didn't really understand what it meant to be a bookie, but I'd see Vic getting slips of paper and money from people. I found out later that he was taking sports bets and his operation was backed by the Outfit. He used to run crap (dice) games, too, in the alleys behind the houses in the neighborhood. Although Tony and I were just kids, sometimes Vic let us in the games. Even then, it was obvious to me that Tony was in his element when he could bet on something.

Another guy I met hanging around with Tony was Joey Hansen. Next to me, he probably came to know Tony as well as anybody. He was jealous of my relationship with Tony, and we had a couple of fights over it. I mention him here because he played a role in some of the incidents I'll tell you about later.

Did I know then what the future held for Tony? No, I didn't. But looking back, it's my opinion that Vic Spilotro was the person most instrumental in Tony taking to the criminal life and becoming an Outfit guy. Tony idolized Vic and his lifestyle. Vic introduced Tony to a lot of his associates as he was growing up—more guys with nice clothes, women, and money. And what may have been even more important: power.

* * *

About a year after first meeting Tony we started spending more time together. The reason for that was we both got placed in the same facility—Montefiore School. It was a place that provided educational services for troublemakers— kids who couldn't get along anywhere else. I was sent there first, and Tony showed up about a week later. I don't think he was into criminal stuff then. But like me, he was a kid that most teachers couldn't control.

The student body of Montefiore was primarily black. (We called them "colored" at that time.) Tony and I were two of the half-dozen or so white kids in the place and were constantly in physical confrontations with the blacks. Another thing we didn't like was having to use public transportation to get to and from the school. We couldn't do much about the blacks, but I figured out how to take care of the other.

I'd already learned how to hotwire my mother's car. I started using that knowledge to steal cars from around my neighborhood. I drove the hot car to school and parked it a couple of blocks away. After school I'd drop Tony off at his father's restaurant, where he worked every day, and then I'd drive it back to my neighborhood. Having our own transportation was nice, but it didn't stop the fighting inside the school.

One day when I came out of wood shop I found Tony in the hallway surrounded by four or five blacks. One of them wanted to fight him alone. "Come on, white boy," he said, "just you and me."

Tony agreed. The black kid picked him up and flung him over his head to the floor. Tony got up and put a beating on the guy. Then one of the other blacks said, "Let's kill that white motherfucker," and they started to attack.

I grabbed one of the long poles with a hook on the end that was used to open and close the upper windows. I swung it at the blacks and caught a couple of them in the head, and then Tony and I ran out of the building.

When Tony told Vic what was going on with the blacks, Vic said it was time we taught them a lesson by going after their leader—a kid named Jackson—and he'd go with us.

A few days later Tony and I didn't go to classes, and Vic drove us to the school in his four-door Mercury. We got there at lunch time when we knew all the students would be in the cafeteria. Vic brought along a .45-caliber pistol.

Vic crashed the car through the gates of the fenced-in playground and parked it near the cafeteria. Tony took the gun, and he and I ran inside and grabbed Jackson out of his seat at the lunch table. As we dragged him outside to the car he was scared to death, crying, and screaming. The other blacks were shocked. They followed us outside but didn't do anything. We drove away, pistol-whipped Jackson, and then drove back to the school and dumped him off.

Tony said he wasn't going to go back to school. His father didn't want him to and said he needed him at the restaurant. I did go in the next day, and the juvenile officers were waiting for me—they wanted to throw me in jail for the Jackson thing. They wrote me up and told me I couldn't come back to

Montefiore. And then they contacted my mother and said we had to appear before a juvenile court judge.

Tony got charged, too, but his lawyer told the judge that Tony worked at his father's restaurant and any action against him would cause a hardship on his family. It worked, and Tony was released to work at the restaurant. I wasn't as lucky and got placed in a reformatory for six months.

After I got out, I got into more trouble and drew nine months in another reformatory called St. Charles. So I didn't see much of Tony again until we were seventeen or so. We would run into one another from time to time and catch up on the latest happenings in the neighborhood. By that time he was making quite a name for himself as a tough guy and a thief. People already respected and feared him.

Just before Tony turned eighteen we talked about the Outfit. I'll never forget his words to me at that time: "Frankie, I'm going to become one of them. Someday I'm going to be a boss, and I'll take you with me."

At that time I didn't want anyone to run my life for me. I said, "I'm not interested in becoming a gangster."

After that we kind of went our separate ways. I was content with being a thief and running my own crew. Tony was pursuing his ambitions of becoming a member of the Outfit, and I heard he was hooked up with some big time gangsters out of Cicero.

And then one day, about a year and a half later, Tony stopped in to see me. He said he and some other guys had a big job coming up with a lot of money to be made. They were short a man, and he offered me the spot. I immediately said I was in. It was then I learned we were going to take down a bank.

http://wbp.bz/mobstera

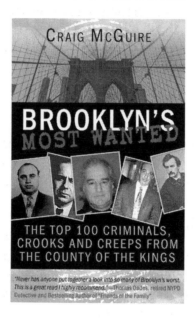
Introduction

If Times Square is the crossroads of the world, then across the East River you'll find the crossroads of the underworld.

Welcome to Gangland, U.S.A. – A.K.A. the bloody, brutal killing grounds of Brooklyn, New York.

From crime bosses to career criminals to corrupt politicians, pedophile priests to Ponzi scammers to psychotic serial killers, this is not your usual crime chronicle.

Walk with me as I rip open the underbelly of Brooklyn, the broken land, to see what spills out on a tour that takes us from the South Brooklyn Boys to the Soviet thugs of Brighton Beach's "Little Odessa."

Want to know what Billy the Kid, John Wilkes Booth and the Son of Sam all have in common?

Brooklyn.

Anthony "Gaspipe" Casso, Al Capone, Frankie Yale, Paul Vario, Roy DeMeo and so many more mischievous malcontents and maniacs stalk these pages, as I rank a rogues' gallery of the best of the worst from Brooklyn's crime-ridden past and present.

Much more than Murder, Incorporated, "Brooklyn's Most Wanted" chronicles kingpins and lone wolves alike, including modern multi-ethnic mobs mimicking the original La Cosa Nostra – the Russian Mafia, the Albanian Mafia, the Polish Mafia, the Greek Mafia, in fact more Mafias than you can shake a bloody blackjack at.

You want labor racketeering, hijacking, murder, loan sharking, arson, illegal gambling, money laundering?

Fugetaboutit!

We've ranked them all, barreling through a guided tour of the New York City's most notorious criminal stomping grounds, where you'll learn that when they say "In Brooklyn They Don't Play" they really mean it. Seriously!

Welcome to the County of the Kings!

Now watch your back.

100

Julius Bernstein – The Last Jewish Mobster

The media is always looking for latest Last Mohican.

In 2012, the *New York Daily News* heralded the end of an era when it christened Julius Bernstein "The Last Jewish Mobster," lowering the curtain on a storied chapter in Brooklyn crime lore.

Born in 1922, Bernstein was raised during the Great Depression in impoverished East New York, Brooklyn. This was the heyday of the Jewish Gangster, when Murder, Incorporated rose to prominence as the Italian Mafia's personal hit squad. (Dubbed "Murder, Incorporated" by the media, the organized crime group comprised mainly of Jewish and Italian-American gangsters from the Brooklyn neighborhoods of Brownsville, East New York, and Ocean Hill and terrorized the city in the 1930s and 1940s.)

Serving in the United States Army during World War II as an infantryman, Bernstein charged the beaches in Normandy as part of the D-Day invasion, before returning to Brooklyn for a long career as a low-level gangster.

While "Spike" Bernstein never earned the notoriety of such Jewish underworld luminaries as a Meyer Lansky or a Benjamin "Bugsy" Siegel, he was a solid earner for the Italian mob as an associate of the Genovese Crime Family. Forbidden from becoming a "Made" member of the Mafia, as he was not of Italian heritage, Bernstein formed a close relationship with Matthew "Matty the Horse" Ianniello, who reached the rung of acting boss of the Genovese clan in 1995 when Vincent Gigante was packed off to prison. Ianniello went on to serve more than just jail time, standing in as Spike's best man at his wedding.

Back in Brooklyn, fresh off the beaches of northern France, Bernstein became what was known as a bagman, collecting extortion payments for more than four decades, including a bus union, the Sbarro Italian restaurant chain and other Brooklyn businesses bent backwards for shakedowns.

According to FBI records, by 1971 Bernstein was bumped up in the Brooklyn underworld, placed by the Genovese family in a leadership position in Amalgamated Transit Union Local 1181, a union for New York City school bus drivers and matrons. But Bernstein was no bus driver. His sole role was managing the Genovese family's shakedown for Ianniello. He held the post for 35 years, siphoning off thousands of dollars in hard-earned union dues and channeling it to the mob. Bernstein also ran a successful gambling book under the watch of notorious Brooklyn Genovese crime boss Frank "Funzi" Tieri.

Most notable of Bernstein's criminal exploits was his role in the extortion of the popular Sbarro restaurant chain. Gennaro Sbarro opened his first *salumeria* on the corner of 65th Street and 17th Avenue in Bensonhurst, Brooklyn, in 1956. Sbarro opened his first mall location in 1970 in the Kings Plaza Shopping Center on Flatbush Avenue in Marine Park, Brooklyn, and grew the business to become the fifth-largest pizza chain in America.

Taking a slice of the American Dream, Sbarro debuted its Initial Public Offering in 1977, and by the early 1990s was launching up to 100 stores per year. The company was brought private by the family in 1999 and sold for $450 million in 2006, though it has struggled in recent years, declaring bankruptcy in 2011 and again in 2014.

Based on Bernstein's testimony, the FBI learned that the mob's extortion of Sbarro began as far back as the 1960s. By 2004 the Genovese family was being passed $20,000 annually under the table. Bernstein personally collected the twice-annual $10,000 payments.

At the age of 82, Bernstein was caught up in an FBI probe of Sbarro and arrested in July 2005. Facing a lengthy prison term, Spike spilled the family secrets. Pleading guilty on multiple extortion counts, Bernstein began cooperating with the government in 2006.

Yet even after flipping for the feds, the wily Bernstein accepted a $20k payoff from a bus company owner inside a bathroom at the Staten Island Hilton, according to the *New York Daily News*.

Bernstein died on October 21, 2007. Though he provided damning evidence about his criminal career that implicated his cohorts, his death spared him the awkward humiliation of standing witness against them in open court.

When Bernstein's FBI papers became available in 2012 through a Freedom of Information Act request filed by *The New York Daily News*, in a subsequent article he earned that final distinction, dubbed the Last Jewish Gangster.

Yet in truth, that era had long since passed.

99

John Wilkes Booth – Lincoln Assassin

Was John Wilkes Booth, dastardly assassin of U.S. President Abraham Lincoln, gunned down by a Union soldier?

Or did he escape to Europe via the Brooklyn waterfront? Oh, you never heard that one?

That little-known conspiracy theory lands Booth the rank of No. 99 on the "Brooklyn's Most Wanted" list.

Long before "The Grassy Knoll" entered our lexicon, multiple conspiracy theories shrouded the assassination of U.S. President Abraham Lincoln.

In fact, the Lincoln assassination's own version of the Zapruder film — missing pages torn from the diary of the villainous John Wilkes Booth — may be hidden in a 19th century subway tunnel located beneath the bustling streets of Downtown Brooklyn.

We know Booth murdered Lincoln in dramatic fashion, shooting the president in the head during a performance of the play "Our American Cousin" at Ford's Theater on the evening of April 14, 1865.

What we don't know is the full extent of the plot and its many tentacles. That's because after 12 days on the run, Booth was shot dead by Union Sergeant Boston Corbett.

In the aftermath of the killing of Booth, rumors of a cover-up bubbled up, speculating that Booth did not die on a farm in Virginia surrounded and gunned down by enraged Union forces, but rather he escaped to Europe through the Brooklyn docks.

A famous actor, Booth never served in the Confederate Army, yet was a staunch Southern sympathizer who interacted with members of the Confederacy's secret service. The theory follows that Booth was not a lone wolf, but a Confederate spy using his cover as a travelling thespian to journey throughout the Northern United States gathering and passing intelligence during and after the war. His role in the assassination was part of a larger conspiracy, or so the speculation goes.

Supposedly, Booth wrote down details of this nefarious plot in his diary, on pages now missing from the original manuscript, and possibly hidden in a locked box sealed in a bricked-up tunnel under Atlantic Avenue.

Records show Booth did perform on October 24th through October 26th in 1863 at the original site of the Brooklyn Academy of Music on Montague Street, between Court and Clinton streets. That puts him in close proximity to the tunnel.

At the time, there was a strong contingent of Southern sympathizers in New York, known as the Copperheads. The Copperheads, also known as Peace Democrats, lobbied for an end to the bloodshed and urged for negotiation with the South to end the conflict. The mayor of New York City at the time, Fernando Wood, suggested to the City Council that New York secede from the Union, to preserve its lucrative cotton trade with the South.

Did Booth slip out of New York through the bustling piers in Brooklyn, to live out his life in obscurity in some far-flung hamlet in rural Europe or remote Asia? The mystery may lie in the tunnel under Atlantic Avenue, a quest that captured the imagination of historian Bob Diamond.

The Atlantic Avenue tunnel itself is steeped in Brooklyn lore, as the oldest subway tunnel ever constructed in America, created as the final leg of an extension to connect the above-ground Long Island Railroad to Manhattan and then on to Boston. Beset by corruption and mismanagement, the project foundered and the tunnel was sealed at both ends.

Diamond accessed the tunnel in the 1980s, removing the first of two concrete walls to lead guided underground tunnel tours.

However, beyond the second, still-sealed concrete wall lays a train platform, and supposedly a vintage locomotive with a box containing Booth's long-lost diary pages. Diamond waged a campaign to unseal the tunnel. The National Geographic Channel was even involved for a time, investing in pre-production that included high-tech scan tests that identified an object about the size of a locomotive.

The story was featured in a *Newsweek* article and in an episode of the popular "Cities of the Underworld" series on The History Channel that delved into the tunnel's connection to the Freemasons (members helped finance the tunnel), its use as a hideout for bootleggers, and as a gangster graveyard where crime syndicate Murder, Inc. stashed the dead bodies of some of its victims.

Yet it was the Booth connection that draws the most sensational speculation. While there is no actual evidence supporting the theory, there is the nagging historical footnote that Booth's diary, recovered after the assassination, *is* missing 18 pages.

Was Booth a Southern spy?

Did he escape to Europe through Brooklyn?

Was the Lincoln assassination part of a larger conspiracy?

Are those lost diary pages in that Brooklyn tunnel, and if so, what do they contain?

Well, we likely will not know if that tunnel can answer these questions anytime soon. Diamond's tours have since been shut down, prompting him to bring a suit against New York City in federal court.

The New York City Department of Transportation has cited expense and safety concerns and declines further comment on the matter.

http://wbp.bz/brooklynsmostwanteda

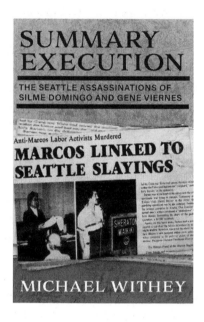
INTRODUCTION:

THE MURDERS

June 1, 1981
Local 37 Union Hall, Seattle

On the eastern edge of the Pioneer Square district in Seattle stood an historic but nondescript two-story terra-cotta building, crowned by a large, weatherworn sign that read "Cannery Workers ILWU Local 37" in blue and white paint peeling from the soft but incessant Seattle rain.

The union hall's entrance opened to a corridor that led to the dispatch hall. This was where seasonal laborers – predominantly Filipino – received assignments each summer for back-breaking jobs on the slime lines of the seafood canneries that hugged the shores of Alaska.

To get to the dispatch hall, the corridor first paralleled two offices on its left; the first office led into the second, an interior space used by the president of Local 37, Constantine "Tony" Baruso. Over Baruso's desk was a prominent picture of himself shaking hands with the president of the Philippines, Ferdinand Marcos.

The outer office was the domain of Local 37's Secretary-Treasurer Silme Domingo and Dispatcher Gene Viernes. Both men had been recently elected as union officers, but they did not share Baruso's politics. In fact, that afternoon they were waiting for their friend and fellow activist, David Della, to arrive for a meeting about their anti-Marcos efforts.

Dave was running late. While they waited, both men worked diligently in the stale air of the windowless office. Silme sat hunched over his desk, piles of yellowed papers at his right elbow. Gene stood at the filing cabinet, searching for information on a Local 37 member, Ben Guloy, who had called to find out if he could qualify for the next dispatch of cannery workers.

It was a question many of the union members had been asking recently. At the union's first dispatch of the season a few days before, to the Peter Pan Cannery in Dillingham, there had been trouble. On May 26, Gene had gathered the members in the dispatch hall and announced a controversial new procedure, which assigned jobs at the canneries based solely on union member seniority and past work history in the industry. This replaced the prior arrangement, where individual cannery foremen worked with Baruso to create lists of workers based on their personal preferences – as well as who paid them the most money under the table – to dispatch to each cannery. Both Gene and Silme explained to the members that they wanted to end the system where members felt they needed to bribe their own union in order to get work.

Gene's announcement was interrupted by a union member who was also the head of the local Filipino Tulisan gang. Tony Dictado rose from his metal chair so fast it collapsed backwards onto the concrete floor with a thwack. "My boys need to get dispatched now," he'd said in no uncertain terms. He demanded that Gene change the list to include Tulisan gang members who worked in the canneries and also ran gambling operations in the bunkhouses. When Gene refused, explaining that there were no exceptions to the new procedures, Dictado exploded, swearing in Ilocano before storming out.

Dictado was used to getting his way. So was Baruso. In addition to the bribes he received in exchange for priority in dispatch, it was common knowledge that Baruso was getting a percentage of the gambling proceeds from the foremen. But the two new officers were idealists, elected on a platform to reform the union and bring about a fair dispatch and stronger negotiations with the industry. Before their election, they had founded a Rank and File Committee (RFC) of union activists, and the independent Alaska Cannery Workers Association (ACWA). Both groups had bravely and aggressively confronted the Alaska seafood industry about the blatant race discrimination that existed in the canneries. Without Baruso or Local 37's support, they had been vigorously filing race discrimination lawsuits and challenging powerful industries in court.

Those were big accomplishments for two men who were not yet thirty years old, and their successes were largely a credit to how well they worked together.

Silme Domingo was born in Seattle in 1952 to a large Filipino family. His father, Nemesio Sr., was the vice president of Local 37. Silme often told me he admired how hard his father worked in the canneries, for his family, and for the union, but they often disagreed on how to oppose the dictatorial Marcos regime, which had ruled the Philippines with an iron hand since declaring martial law in 1972. Silme and his brother, Nemesio Jr., liked confrontation. Nemesio Sr. did not. He and Silme's mother, Ade, had expressed concern about Silme and Gene's recent efforts to present and push through a resolution at the International Longshore and Warehouse Union (ILWU) Convention, demanding an investigation into the plight of workers in the Philippines. "Don't make waves" was always Ade's advice. At twenty-nine, in his youthful exuberance, he didn't always follow her advice.

Gene Viernes was also twenty-nine years old that June, but beyond that, he and Silme seemed as different as night and day. Born in Wapato, a small town in eastern Washington, to a Filipino father and Caucasian mother, and family of ten, Gene grew up doing farm work and seasonal labor, including summer seasons in the Alaska canneries. He was the first in his family to go to college, attending Central Washington State College on a wrestling scholarship.

Gene was a born organizer who had great rapport with work crews. He had an avid interest in both the history of the "Alaskeros," the migrant Filipino workforce who traveled to the Arctic each year to work long hours in the canneries, and the history of the Philippines itself. Just a few weeks before, he'd returned from his trip to his father's homeland, where he'd met both his family and major organizations of the opposition to Phillipine dictator Ferdinand Marcos.

Gene and Silme worked well together: Silme was the sophisticated strategist who wore fancy clothes and drove a large purple Monte Carlo. Gene was a country boy who almost always wore blue denim overalls and a stained white beret. When I picture them, I always remember a typical day when the anti-Marcos activists were planting a community garden in the International District. Silme stood on a boulder and gave orders while Gene steered the wheelbarrow around the grounds and got his hands dirty.

Despite their differences, the two were close friends and comrades in the Union of Democratic Filipinos or KDP, an anti-Marcos organization they were leaders of. As Bob Santos, the unofficial mayor of Seattle's International District (ID), once said, "They were quite a pair. Inseparable."

At 4:20 p.m. on that sunny Seattle day, Ben Guloy entered the union hall with Jimmy Ramil, another member of the Tulisan gang. They stopped in the office doorway and Ramil pulled a .45-caliber MAC-10 , with a suppressor attached, out of a brown paper bag, pointed it at Gene, and fired.

Gene dove for the floor too late and landed with a dull thud, probably already dead. Blood seeped from two wounds in his chest, oozing across the tiles and dyeing his white shirt scarlet.

Ramil then swung his firearm to his right, firing at Silme. The force of the bullets spun Silme halfway around in his swivel chair and punched four gaping holes in his chest.

Not waiting to check the bodies, Ramil tucked his weapon back into the bag and, together with Guloy, left through the front door of the union hall, turning south and escaping down the adjoining alley. On the steps they passed a third Filipino, Teodorico Domingues, also known as Boy Pilay, who had been standing lookout at the entrance. When they were gone, Pilay limped across the street to a black Trans-Am with a large golden eagle on its hood. He slipped into the front passenger seat and the car sped off, a death wagon bursting through the bright day.

The driver beside him was none other than Tony Dictado.

Back in the Local 37 office, Silme gasped for air. He could see Gene bleeding out onto the scuffed white tiles of the office's floor. He gripped the edges of the desk and managed to stagger onto his feet. Clutching his chest, he moved from the office to the corridor, losing hot blood with every step. The door of the union hall rushed up to meet him, and he lunged through it, dragging his body down the steps before collapsing onto the sidewalk and calling for help.

Seattle firefighter James Huckins was working at Fire Station 10 on the corner of Main Street and 2nd Avenue, a block from Local 37, when a young girl ran in. She shouted that there was a man lying face down on Main Street. He looked injured and was crying for help. James immediately radioed for the aid car, grabbed a portable medic cart, and rushed out of the fire station toward the union hall.

Fellow first-responder Frank Urpman, upstairs at Fire Station 10, heard shouts for help outside. When he looked out the second-story window, he saw Silme lying on the sidewalk, blood staining the concrete beneath him. Frank ran downstairs and out into the street, reaching Silme at almost the same time James did.

"Were you robbed?" Frank said, his voice calm.

"N-no ... shot," Silme gasped, face twitching in pain as James and Frank ripped open packets of gauze and applied them to the gaping gunshot wounds.

"Do you know who shot you?" James asked.

Silme groaned, eyelids fluttering. "Yes ... I do. They ... might still be in the building."

"Who are they?"

"Ramil and Guloy," Silme said, his voice pained but otherwise clear.

Frank took out a piece of paper and a pen, wrote the names down, and showed them to Silme.

"It's Ramil, with an *L*," Silme corrected him. Frank crossed out the last letters, and wrote "Ramil" instead of "Rammo."

Silme was pale. His blood had fully soaked through his shirt, and he was breathing heavily. James continued to ask Silme questions to keep him alert – what day it was, where he was, and the names of the hitmen again. Finally, the aid car arrived, and Frank and Jim loaded Silme into the ambulance.

"Am I going to die?" Silme said, his voice a whisper.

Frank cradled Silme's head in his hands and spoke gently but honestly. "It looks bad." The ambulance roared off to Harborview Medical Center, sirens blaring.

Across the street from the union hall, a middle-aged man in a grey suit and dark glasses emerged from a telephone booth, looked at the scene in front of the union, and slipped into his car. As he pulled away from the curb, heading south on 2nd Avenue, he lifted a CB radio to his lips and started to speak.

Beacon Hill, Seattle

Terri Mast first met Silme in 1977 at a meeting of the Anti-Martial Law Coalition, a national organization that opposed the repressive regime of Ferdinand Marcos. She, Silme, and Gene were also deeply involved in the Union of Democratic Filipinos, or KDP, a US-based democratic socialist organization that supported leftist opposition parties in the Philippines and advocated for Filipino rights in the US.

Patient, organized, and level-headed, Terri met her love match in the passionate Silme, who soon became her common-law husband. They shared major responsibilities for implementing reforms within Local 37, organizing in the Filipino community, and attending rallies and demonstrations as part of the anti-Marcos movement in Seattle. They also parented two young daughters, three-year-old Ligaya, and Kalayaan, a baby a few weeks shy of her first birthday. The girls were the joys of their lives.

Terri was at home in their Beacon Hill apartment, watching Ligaya play with trucks, when her friends and fellow KDP activists Elaine Ko, John Foz, and Shari Woo showed up unexpectedly.

"Terri, get your overnight stuff; we have to go to the hospital. Gene and Silme have been shot ..." Elaine's voice broke. Terri could see unshed tears in her eyes.

It took her words too long to form. "How ... Are they ...?"

"Gene is ... Gene didn't make it. Silme is going to go into surgery now. Shari will watch the girls."

Terri fell back onto the sofa when she attempted to stand, whispering, "No ... no ..." She felt shell-shocked. They all were.

Shari sat down beside her as tears poured down Terri's cheeks. "Silme was just talking last night about what would happen to us if something were to happen to him. What's ... what's his condition?"

"He was shot in the stomach," Shari admitted, "so not good. They need you and his folks down at Harborview as soon as possible." She forced herself to look into Terri's eyes. "Dave Della had a meeting with Gene this afternoon and showed up late ... When he got there, he found Gene dead on the floor of his office. By then, Silme was already on his way to the hospital. Dave called Glenn Suson at the headquarters, and Glenn called us."

Elaine held out her hand. "Come on. We have to go. For Silme. We have to go."

Terri wiped the tears from her cheeks. "You're right." She nodded once and rose to her feet, Shari helping her as she walked out the door.

Shari watched them go down the steps. The moment she closed the door, she took Ligaya and Kalayaan into her arms and gently cradled them, worrying.

Oakland, California

Cindy Domingo was at her apartment in Oakland when she received a visit from Dale Borgeson, a national leader of the KDP who also lived in Oakland. Motioning to Cindy's roommates that he needed to talk to Cindy alone, Dale spoke slowly as Cindy looked out the window at a peach-colored sky.

"I have some ... some terrible news."

"What is it? What happened?"

"Your brother ... Silme ... he was ..." He paused. To Cindy, those seconds of strained silence lasted for eternities, and when it ended and Dale told her what happened, she felt decades older than she had been.

The peach sky turned dark grey, suddenly ominous.

Cindy had earned a Master's Degree in Philippine History from Goddard College in Boston, Massachusetts, and worked at the KDP National Secretariat headquarters in Oakland in its National Education Department. The National Secretariat was the organizational center for the KDP's anti-Marcos movement, responsible for publishing its newspaper, *Ang Katipunan*, conducting educationals and scheduling membership and chapter activities. Cindy had recently been approved for a transfer back to Seattle to be closer to her family.

"It can't be," Cindy said, her voice louder than she'd meant for it to be.

"I'm so sorry," Dale repeated. "Cindy, can you fly up to Seattle with me tonight? We can go to Harborview where everyone is on vigil."

"Silme ..." She noticed that sometime in the past few moments she'd sat at her kitchen table. Now she stood. "Okay, let's go to the airport. Has someone ... has someone called my parents? I need to talk to them."

"Elaine is taking Terri to Harborview, and your folks are on their way there right now."

Harborview Medical Center, Seattle

Ade Domingo, the matriarch of the Domingo family, clung to Terri in a long hug when the two women met in the Harborview ER lobby. While Ade had taught and encouraged her children to take a stand for people who were less fortunate than they were, she always worried about their work. This was her worst nightmare.

"Silme's in surgery," Ade told her daughter-in-law. "He is fighting for his life, shot in the stomach four times ... Oh my son, my son...." She stopped, her voice catching on a sob.

"Can we see him? Is he conscious?"

"The surgeon said we need to wait until he is out of surgery. The staff will let us know." Ade clutched the rosary with enough force to turn her knuckles white.

Faced with a long wait, Terri's community organizing instincts kicked in. "We need to get everyone we know to the blood bank on Madison," she said, turning to the friends and family who already filled the small room. "He will need all the blood he can get with stomach wounds. After that, they can come here for a vigil."

She looked around the room. Nemesio Sr. sat on a couch beside his oldest son, Silme's brother Nemesio Jr., and his son's wife Curn. Nemesio Jr. had worked closely with his brother, and had founded the ACWA with Gene and Silme to investigate and file lawsuits against the industry for race discrimination.

Their sister Evangeline, or Vangie, lived with her family in Arizona. The youngest Domingo sibling, Lynn, sobbed quietly on one of the waiting room chairs. Kids were sitting nervously on the couches. Friends and family filled the foyer to offer their hope and condolences.

http://wbp.bz/sea

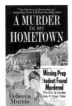

Made in the USA
Columbia, SC
08 September 2019